365

DAYS

— *of* —

CATHOLIC

WISDOM

A Treasury of
Truth, Beauty, and Goodness

Deal W. Hudson

TAN Books
Gastonia, North Carolina

Unless otherwise noted, Scripture quotations are from the Revised Standard Version of the Bible—Second Catholic Edition (Ignatius Edition), copyright © 2006 National Council of the Churches of Christ in the United States of America. Used by permission. All rights reserved.

Cover design by Caroline K. Green

ISBN: 978-1-5051-1714-1

Published in the United States by
TAN Books
PO Box 269
Gastonia, NC 28053
www.TANBooks.com

Printed in the United States of America

To Monsignor Richard Lopez

If you would tell me the heart of a man,
tell me not what he reads, but what he rereads.

—François Mauriac

I consider as lovers of books not those who keep their books hidden
in their store chests and never handle them, but those who, by nightly
as well as daily use thumb them, batter them, wear them out, who fill
out all the margins with annotations of many kinds, and who prefer the
marks of a fault they have erased to a neat copy full of faults.

—Erasmus of Rotterdam

The only real sadness, the only real failure,
the only great tragedy in life, is not to become a saint.

—Léon Bloy

At the end of life, we will not be judged by how many diplomas we have received, how much money we have made, how many great things we have done. We will be judged by "I was hungry, and you gave me something to eat, I was naked and you clothed me. I was homeless, and you took me in."

—St. Teresa of Calcutta

Everything now depends on whether the Christians of the new age are equal to their mission—whether they are able to communicate their hope to the world in which man finds himself alone and helpless before the monstrous forces which have been created by man to serve his own ends but which now have escaped from his control and threaten to destroy him.

—Christopher Dawson

God wants you to be in the world, but so different from the world that you will change it. Get cracking.

—Mother Angelica

FOREWORD

Those familiar with Deal Hudson's erudition, as exemplified in his discussions with guests on Ave Maria Radio's *Church and Culture*, will have little doubt that he is uniquely qualified to select the 365 gems of wisdom which adorn these pages. Thinking with the mind of the Church, Mr. Hudson has mined the riches of faith and reason with which the Church has blessed civilization and with which She has shone forth the splendor of truth across two millennia.

It was G. K. Chesterton who quipped that the Church is the one continual institution to have been thinking about thinking for two thousand years, and it is for this reason, as Chesterton also quipped, that She saves us from the ignominy of ignorance which makes us children of our own time and slaves of the Zeitgeist. It is She who enables us to think outside the temporal box so that we can perceive the time.

Mr. Hudson is additionally well-qualified to make this selection because he understands the triune splendor of the true, the good, and the beautiful. He knows that the Church thinks with the mind of the theologian and philosopher but also with the heart of the saint and with the eye of the poet. He also knows that God shows us Himself most powerfully through the art of narrative, through

storytelling and parable, and through that primary story which is history itself. Knowing this, he has filled these pages with the wisdom of the ages as perceived by a diverse range of sages, including theologians, philosophers, saints, mystics, poets, novelists, and historians. Thus, for instance, we find the Little Flower (St. Thérèse of Lisieux) appearing demurely between a contemporary American philosopher (J. Budziszewski) and a contemporary British historian (Paul Johnson), a rose between thorns!

Such unlikely juxtapositions proliferate throughout these pages. St. Louis de Montfort finds himself sandwiched between Frank Sheed and Malcolm Muggeridge; St. Albert the Great is squeezed between Marshall McLuhan and Charles de Foucauld; Russell Kirk is flanked by Fulton Sheen and Joseph Pieper; Chesterton finds Léon Bloy to his left and Flannery O'Connor to his right; Alice Thomas Ellis makes way for Dietrich von Hildebrand who presents us, in turn, with Blaise Pascal; Romano Guardini proceeds from Paul Claudel and precedes Evelyn Waugh; Fr. Benedict Groeschel forms an unlikely trio with Bernard Nathanson and Monsignor Ronald Knox.

As if these quirky triumvirates are not enough to keep us intrigued and intellectually alert, there are some equally surprising couplings. Jim Caviezel rubs shoulders with Montaigne, Graham Greene with St. Anselm, Boethius with Henri de Lubac, Joris-Karl Huysmans with St. Francis de Sales, Georges Bernanos with Thomas Aquinas, and Thomas Merton with Orestes Brownson.

One thing that is evident from this array of Catholics of all stripes is the breadth as well as the depth of Mr. Hudson's selection. It is not merely the profundity of the wisdom that commands our

respect but the omnivorous array of centuries and cultures that are represented. Mr. Hudson is as comfortable with the Fathers of the Church as he is with his twenty-first-century contemporaries, and he is equally at home in the Catholic cultures of France, Spain, Germany, Italy, England, and the United States. This astonishing diversity enables the reader to both deepen and broaden his own understanding of the Catholic heritage with which the Church has blessed him.

Yet another strength of Mr. Hudson's selection is its unpredictability. Alongside those Catholic sages whom we'd expect to see, such as Augustine, Aquinas and Newman, and Dante and Shakespeare, we are also introduced to important and yet tragically neglected figures. We discover forgotten poets, such as Roy Campbell, David Jones, Lionel Johnson, and Elizabeth Jennings, and are reminded of apologists whose influence, great in their own time, has waned with the passage of time—Christopher Derrick, for instance, and Arnold Lunn.

In this selection which provides a plenitude of surprises, there were nonetheless some surprises that are especially welcome, at least to this particular reader. I was surprised and delighted in equal measure to see the inclusion of great but neglected poetic pearls, such as Ernest Dowson's "Extreme Unction", as well as extracts from letters, such as Maurice Baring's letter to G. K. Chesterton upon the latter's reception into the Church, and J. R. R. Tolkien's letter to his son on the beauty and majesty of the Blessed Sacrament, "the one great thing to love on earth."

It is truly an honour and a privilege to raise the curtain on the treasure trove of penetrating wisdom that fills these pages. Having

done so, and with a nod of deferential respect and reverence to Mr. Hudson for this admirable selection, I will let the sages of the ages speak for themselves with those words of wisdom they've learned from Holy Mother Church.

—JOSEPH PEARCE

ACKNOWLEDGMENTS

I'd like to thank Claire Smith and Lisa Waddell who helped me at every stage of this project. I'm grateful to Stephanie Mann and Stephen Phelan who answered the call for editing help as the finish line approached.

Some friends offered me good advice at crucial moments in my writing: Father Simeon, Dana Gioia, Frank Buckley, Robert Reilly, Sam Gregg, Scott Bloch, Jeffrey D. Wallin, Marjorie Dannenfelser, and Joseph Pearce who also graciously agreed to write the foreword.

Editor John Moorehouse has turned out, once again, to be a delightful editor to work with, honest and flexible. Copyeditor Nick Vari and designer Caroline Green have again produced a beautiful book, as is the norm with TAN titles.

My wife, Theresa, reassured me about the worthiness of the book as I wrote and did her share of editing.

My son Cyprian made some excellent suggestions, and my daughter Hannah encouraged me from afar.

This book could not have been written without the friendship of Allan and Alyssa Carson, David Hanna, and Frank Hanna III.

INTRODUCTION

L et's avoid all the technical definitions of wisdom. Such flights into abstraction can distance the interested reader from what can and should be an enjoyable topic of thought and conversation.

In assembling this book, I have read about poets, mystics, historians, philosophers, theologians, apologists, psychologists, saints, theologians, priests, professors, converts, and a film director and an actor.

Being a convert myself, who read himself into the Church, and a former philosophy professor, I had a sense of where to start looking for words that I thought were worth sharing. I made my choices based upon a single criterion: words that would stand the test of time and deepen the faith of believers.

Some of my selections, such as those from the Church Fathers and Doctors of the Church, have stood the test of time. Others, like the much-loved apologists—Dawson, Belloc, Chesterton, Sheen, and Sheed—are very likely to be read a century from now. A few others, less known or unknown, I have put forward as purveyors of wisdom, but, once again, it is time that will tell.

"Time will tell" . . . just saying that should give us hope: the passing of time, it appears, filters out and rejects the nonsense of passing fads and outright intellectual error. History is on our side

and on the side of wisdom.

In preparing this book, I was reminded of how often wisdom is found in laughter and poetic utterance. There may be no discernible principle being expressed, but the gut, so to speak, gets the message.

I've decided not to include much from the popes and bishops, only because many of them deserve books of their own. The presence of their papal authority might sway the reader to take them more seriously than the rest.

The reader especially will wonder why some highly-regarded figures, such as Benedict XVI and Saint John Paul the Great, are not included. The reasons are simple: first, their writings are available and already widely-read, and second, if I started choosing quotations from their writings, they could fill a book of their own.

Yes, there are familiar names to be found, and with all of them, I had to remind myself to limit my choices, for the richness found in each is astonishing.

This collection gathers the familiar with the unfamiliar, the philosopher with the poet, the historian with the mystic, the sinner with the saint.

Herein you will find that some selections are short and easily digested while others are longer and require a slower pace of reading. I trust the reader to make those adjustments and experience the joy of recognizing a truth when it is told.

—DEAL W. HUDSON,
EASTERTIDE, 2020

365
DAYS
— of —
CATHOLIC
WISDOM

DAY 1

JACQUES MARITAIN (1882–1973)

Forgetting wisdom—

"A time will come, when people will give up in practice those values about which they no longer have any intellectual conviction. . . . These remarks apply to democracy in a particularly cogent way, for the foundations of a society of free men are essentially moral. There are a certain number of moral tenets—about the dignity of the human person, human rights, human equality, freedom, law, mutual respect and tolerance, the unity of mankind and the ideal of peace among men—on which democracy presupposes a common consent; without a general, firm, and reasoned-out conviction concerning such tenets, democracy cannot survive."[1]

On the Use of Philosophy: Three Essays, 1961

Jacques Maritain was a French philosopher who championed the relevance of St. Thomas Aquinas in the twentieth century. As a neo-Thomist, Maritain addressed nearly every field of intellectual endeavor—science, politics, aesthetics, metaphysics, epistemology, ethics, history—and had a level of public

---

1 Jacques Maritain, *On the Use of Philosophy: Three Essays* (Princeton: Princeton University Press, 1961), 12.

influence that has not been seen in a Catholic intellectual since. After his conversion and that of his wife, Raïssa, they hosted regular meetings at their home in Meudon, which resulted in numerous conversions. Knowing the Nazis would imprison him for his criticism of the Vichy government, Maritain and his wife moved to New York, where he continued to write and teach. From 1945 to 1948, he served as the French ambassador to the Holy See; afterward, he returned to the United States to teach at Princeton University.

DAY 2

JEAN-PIERRE DE CAUSSADE (1675–1751)

Nothing will harm you—

"The soul that does not attach itself solely to the will of God will find neither satisfaction nor sanctification in any other means however excellent by which it may attempt to gain them. If that which God Himself chooses for you does not content you, from whom do you expect to obtain what you desire? If you are disgusted with the meat prepared for you by the divine will itself, what food would not be insipid to so depraved a taste? No soul can be really nourished, fortified, purified, enriched, and sanctified except in fulfilling the duties of the present moment. What more would you have? As in this you can find all good,

why seek it elsewhere? Do you know better than God? As he ordains it thus why do you desire it differently? Can His wisdom and goodness be deceived? When you find something to be in accordance with this divine wisdom and goodness ought you not to conclude that it must needs be excellent? Do you imagine you will find peace in resisting the Almighty? Is it not, on the contrary, this resistance which we too often continue without owning it even to ourselves which is the cause of all our troubles? It is only just, therefore, that the soul that is dissatisfied with the divine action for each present moment should be punished by being unable to find happiness in anything else."[2]

Abandonment to Divine Providence, c. 1733–1740

Jean-Pierre de Caussade entered the Jesuit novitiate in Toulouse at the age of eighteen and was ordained a priest in 1705. For six years, he taught in the Jesuit college in Toulouse and then became an itinerant missionary and preacher. It was the nuns of the Order of Visitation in Nancy who preserved the notes of his conferences he gave them while he was running the Jesuit Retreat House there. After years of hard work, his eyes gave out. His blindness allowed him to live even more intensely his principle of "self-abandonment to the will of God." He died at the age of seventy-six.

---

2 Jean-Pierre de Caussade, *Abandonment to Divine Providence* (digitreads.com Publishing, 2009), loc. 313 of 2465, Kindle Edition.

DAY 3

HANS URS VON BALTHASAR (1905–1988)

Beauty and prayer—

"Our situation today shows that beauty demands for itself at least as much courage and goodness and decision as do truth and goodness, and she will not allow herself to be separated and banned from her two sisters without taking them along with herself in an act of mysterious vengeance. We can be sure that whoever sneers at her name [Beauty] as if she was the ornament of a bourgeoise past—whether he admits it or not—*can no longer* pray and soon will be no longer able to love."[3] (Emphasis added)

The Glory of the Lord: A Theological Aesthetics, 1961–1969

Hans Urs von Balthasar was the greatest Catholic theologian of the twentieth century. As Pope Benedict XVI commented, "Never again have I found anyone with such a comprehensive theological and humanistic education as Balthasar." Like St. Thomas Aquinas, Balthasar composed a vast systematic theology, a fifteen-volume trilogy written over twenty-four years. The first part is a *Theological Aesthetics*; part two, a *Theo-Drama,*

---

3 Hans Urs von Balthasar, *Glory of the Lord: A Theological Aesthetics,* vol. 1, *Seeing the Form,* trans. Erasmo Leiva-Merikakis, eds. Joseph Fessio, S.J. and John Riches (San Francisco: Ignatius Press), 18.

and the third part, a *Theo-Logic*. But this systematic work forms only a portion of von Balthasar's published works, much of which is available in English and most of which has been published by Ignatius Press.

DAY 4

CHRISTOPHER DAWSON (1889–1970)

Christian vocation—

"Every Christian mind is a seed of change so long as it is a living mind, not enervated by custom or ossified by prejudice. A Christian has only to *be* in order to change the world, for in that act of being there is contained all the mystery of the supernatural life. It is the function of the Church to sow this divine seed, to produce not merely good men, but spiritual men—that is to say, supermen. In so far as the Church fulfills this function it transmits to the world a continuous stream of spiritual energy. If the salt itself loses its savor, then indeed the world sinks back into disorder and death, for a despiritualized Christianity is powerless to change anything; it is the most abject of failures, since it serves neither the natural nor the spiritual order. But the life of the Church never fails, since it has an infinite capacity for regeneration. It is the eternal organ through which the Spirit enters the social process and builds up

a new humanity—*populus qui nascetur queen fecit Dominus.* The spirit breathes and they are created and the earth is renewed."[4]

Christianity and the New Age, 1931

Christopher Dawson was the preeminent Catholic historian of Great Britain in the twentieth century. After graduating from Trinity College, Oxford, Dawson converted to Catholicism in 1913 after reading the great Protestant theologian Adolf von Harnack's history of Christian doctrine. Dawson was disturbed by Harnack's lavish praise for Luther's reforming zeal. For Dawson, the historical record could not be so easily dismissed. After teaching nearly thirty years at colleges in the UK, Dawson was named Chauncey Stillman Professor of Roman Catholic Studies at Harvard University (1958–62). A central thesis of his twenty-six books is that Christianity is the foundation of Western culture and civilization. Aidan Nichols, OP, describes Dawson's work as a "latter-day *City of God*" for its insistence on seeing history as an ongoing clash between revelation and the contingencies of societies, nations, and their leaders.

---

4 Christopher Dawson, *Christianity and the New Age* (Manchester: Sophia Institute Press, 1985), 103.

DAY 5

ST. BERNARD OF CLAIRVAUX (1090–1153)

No greater love—

"You wish me to tell you why and how God should be loved. My answer is that God himself is the reason why he is to be loved. As for how he is to be loved, there is to be no limit to that love. Is this sufficient answer? Perhaps, but only for a wise man . . . . Hence I insist that there are two reasons why God should be loved for his own sake: no one can be loved more righteously and no one can be loved with greater benefit."[5]

On Loving God, 1129

St. Bernard of Clairvaux was one of the most influential churchmen in the history of the faith. At age twenty-two, Bernard joined the new Cistercian Order, which was to revitalize monastic life throughout Europe. The combination of his charismatic presence and oratory won him a large following throughout his life. When the First Crusade ended in disaster, it was St. Bernard's preaching that ignited enthusiasm, when there was none, for the Second Crusade (1146–49). His many

---

5 St. Bernard of Clairvaux, *On Loving God, Treatises II: The Steps of Humanity and Pride and On Loving God,* trans. Robert Watson OSB (Kalamazoo: Cistercian Publications, 1973), 93.

treatises, sermons, and letters set the standard for the austere Cistercian spirituality that remains in force.

DAY 6

ST. AUGUSTINE (354–430)

On regret and gratitude—

"Too late have I loved you. O Beauty so ancient and so new, too late I have loved you! Behold, you were within me, while I was outside: it was there that I sought you, and, a deformed creature, rushed headlong upon these things of beauty which you had made. You were with me, but I was not with you. They kept me far from you, those fair things which, if they were not in you, would not exist at all. You have called me to you, and have cried out, and have shattered my deafness. You have blazed forth with light, and have shone upon me, and you have put my blindness to flight! You have sent forth fragrance, and I have drawn in my breath, and I pant after you. I have tasted you, and I hunger and thirst after you. You have touched me, and I have burned for your peace."[6]

Confessions, 397

---

6 St. Augustine, *Confessions,* 10.27, trans. and introduction by John K. Ryan (Garden City: Doubleday and Company, Inc.,1960), 254-55.

St. Augustine's journey into the Church is told in his *Confessions,* one of the most remarkable books ever written. Nothing like this book—part memoir, part-prayer and praise, part-theological and philosophical—had been published in the ancient world. The *Confessions* combines aesthetic diversion and accounts of sexual temptations with philosophical and theological reflections. The final books offer an *account of time,* which remains the touchstone of all subsequent explorations. In this passage, St. Augustine expresses regret for having "rushed headlong" to embrace the beauty of the creation rather than the Creator Himself.

DAY 7

ST. FRANCIS DE SALES (1567–1622)

Fake humility—

"We are very apt to speak of ourselves as nought, as weakness itself, as the offscouring of the earth; but we should be very much vexed to be taken at our word and generally considered what we call ourselves. On the contrary, we often make-believe to run away and hide ourselves, merely to be followed and sought out; we pretend to take the lowest place, with the full intention of being honorably called to come up higher. But true humility does not affect to be humble, and is not given

to make a display in lowly words. It seeks not only to conceal other virtues, but above all it seeks and desires to conceal itself; and if it were lawful to tell lies, or feign or give scandal, humility would perhaps sometimes affect a cloak of pride in order to hide itself utterly. Take my advice, my daughter, and either use no professions of humility, or else use them with a real mind corresponding to your outward expressions; never cast down your eyes without humbling your heart; and do not pretend to wish to be last and least, unless you really and sincerely mean it. ...A really humble man would rather that some one else called him worthless and good-for-nothing, than say so of himself; at all events, if such things are said, he does not contradict them, but acquiesces contentedly, for it is his own opinion."[7]

Introduction to the Devout Life, 1609

St. Francis de Sales was a great churchman of the Counter-Reformation. His classic book, *Introduction to a Devout Life* (1609), argued that spiritual perfection is possible in the active life, for people involved in the affairs of the world, and not limited to contemplatives. He became the bishop of Geneva, where he continued to proclaim the spiritual and theological problems with Calvinism.

---

7 St. Francis de Sales, *Introduction to the Devout Life*; read here: https://www.catholicspiritualdirection.org/devoutlife.pdf.

DAY 8

ST. BERNADINE OF SIENA (1380–1444)

Listen twice as much as you speak—

"God has given us only one tongue, even though that's not the case with other members of the body, nor even with the other senses. God has given us two eyes, he's given us two hands, he's given us two feet, he's given us two nostrils to smell with. What does it mean that he hasn't given us more than one tongue? Why, I ask you? It must be for some quite excellent reason. Do you know why? So that you'll have only one tongue to speak with. He hasn't done that with the other senses. No — he's given you two ears and one tongue, so you can hear more than you speak. In the same way, he's given you two eyes so you can see more than you speak. He's given you two hands so you can touch more than you speak. And even with regard to the sense of smell, he's given you two openings in your nose so you can smell more than you speak. In short, God wants you to do more smelling than speaking, more touching than speaking, more hearing than speaking, and more seeing than speaking. He wants you to do less with your tongue than with all the other senses. So listen up, you chatterbox! A wise person once

gave this advice to the human race: If you speak, say little and speak low; don't shout. Truly, this is a most useful saying!"[8]

Sermons

The Franciscan priest St. Bernadine of Siena was one of the greatest preachers of his era. He lived in one of the storm-filled periods of the Church, especially in Italy, with the rise of the Borgias in Rome and the Medici family in Florence. The various Italian city-states were constantly at war with each other. All of this strife was complicated by regular outbursts of the plague. Yet he preached throughout Italy, often to crowds of over 30,000. We get a good idea above of why so many flocked to hear him preach: St. Bernadine derives a moral lesson out of the fact of our possessing only one tongue. The listener is bound to remember, and perhaps emit a chuckle when thinking of it, for a very long time.

8 Paul Thigpen, *A Year With the Saints: Daily Meditations With the Holy Ones of God* (Charlotte: Saint Benedict Press, 2013), 245.

DAY 9

ST. GREGORY THE GREAT (540–604)

St. Gregory explains how a "ruler ought to be careful to understand how commonly vices pass themselves off as virtues"—

"The ruler also ought to understand how commonly vices pass themselves off as virtues. For often niggardliness palliates itself under the name of frugality, and on the other hand prodigality hides itself under the appellation of liberality. Often inordinate laxity is believed to be loving-kindness, and unbridled wrath is accounted the virtue of spiritual zeal. Often precipitate action is taken for the efficacy of promptness, and tardiness for the deliberation of seriousness. Whence it is necessary for the ruler of souls to distinguish with vigilant care between virtues and vices, lest either niggardliness get possession of his heart while he exults in seeming frugal in expenditure; or, while anything is prodigally wasted, he glory in being as it were compassionately liberal; or in remitting what he ought to have smitten he draws on those that are under him to eternal punishment; or in mercilessly smiting an offense he himself offends more grievously; or by immaturely anticipating what might have been done properly and gravely; or by putting off the merit of a good action change it to something worse."[9]

On the Life of the Pastor, c. 590

9 Saint Gregory the Great, *Saint Gregory the Great Collection* (Aeterna Press,

Born in Rome, St. Gregory the Great, like his father, chose to pursue a political career, becoming the prefect of Rome in 540. Having reached this goal, Gregory gave all his money to the poor and entered a monastery. Following God's calling, he became abbot and one of Rome's seven deacons. Gregory spent five years as a papal legate in Constantinople. In 590, he became the first monk ever to become pope. As pope, Gregory had the existing liturgical plainsong organized, which is why it's often called "Gregorian chant." Only three other people in the Church have been called "'the Great." His writing was mostly pastoral, though Gregory was a successful political leader in negotiating a treaty with the invading Lombards.

DAY 10

YVES CONGAR, OP (1904–1995)

Remembering the angels—

"Why is it that the holy angels play so small a part in our spiritual life? One reason, among many others, would seem to be that Christians in general hardly ever read the Scriptures. They feed their devotion with the reading of good books, devotional books, which give them, often at second or third hand, the teaching of scholastic writers of the sixteenth and seventeenth

2016), loc. 6949 of 9739, Kindle Edition.

centuries. In literature of this kind the most living truths of Christianity, even when not expressed sentimentally and as a mere matter of words, are made to appear theoretical and artificial. As a result, the ensuing conviction is equally theoretical, sentimental, and verbal, and lacks that intimate, warm, and strengthening persuasion which the Holy Spirit intrinsically promotes. There is another more general reason for our indifference to angels: this is the individualism and the moralism of our piety. It is true, of course, that a guardian angel is personally given to each of us, but the very fact that we have guardian angels is the result of a social plan, of salvation thought of in terms of the Church, of a corporate body, a plan and point of view which has largely been lost from sight in the individualistic and moralistic mentality that has developed since the sixteenth century."[10]

Faith and the Spiritual Life, 1962

A French Dominican priest, ordained in 1930, Yves Congar was a significant influence at the Second Vatican Council (1962–65). It was Congar's work in ecclesiology, the theology of the Church, and the theology of the Holy Spirit that was most admired. All of his scholarship made use of Scripture, Patristics, and Scholastic thought. In using these sources, especially that of St. Thomas Aquinas, Congar made a special effort

---

10 Yves Congar, *Essential Writings*, selected with an introduction by Paul Lakeland (Maryknoll: Orbis Books, 2010), 125.

to read them in their historical context rather than merely as the origin of dogmatic pronouncements. During WWII, the Germans held him captive for five years, during which time he made many attempts to escape. After the war, some of Congar's writing was censored, and he was not allowed to publish new books due to an article written in support of a worker-priest movement. Nevertheless, Congar served on the preparatory theological commission of the Second Vatican Council. He was appointed to the College of Cardinals in 1994 by Pope John Paul II.

DAY 11

ST. JOHN HENRY NEWMAN (1801–1890)

The cause of truth—

"For it is our plain duty to preach and defend the truth in a straightforward way. Those who are to stumble must stumble, rather than the heirs of grace should not hear. While we offend and alienate one man, we secure another; if we drive one man further the wrong way, we drive another further the right way. The cause of truth, the heavenly company of saints, gains on the whole more in one way than in the other. A wavering or shallow mind does perhaps as much harm to others as a mind

that is consistent in error, nay, is in no very much better state itself."[11]

Tracts for the Times no. 85, 1838

The 1845 conversion of St. John Henry Newman from Anglicanism to Catholicism rocked the ecclesial, intellectual, and academic establishment of Victorian England. The anti-Catholic sentiment of the English Reformation was still deeply felt. As an Anglican scholar teaching at Oxford, Newman was the leader of an evangelical wing of his church called the "Oxford movement," which was moving towards a "high church" version of Anglicanism more closely resembling Catholicism. Once his break came and Newman was ordained a Catholic priest, he became to the modern era what St. Augustine and St. Thomas Aquinas had been to their ages: St. John Henry Newman intellectually engaged all the disbelief of his age, taking on the claims of secularism, atheism, and historicism which had coalesced with full force against the Church. His major writings include *The Grammar of Assent* (1870), *Apologia Pro Vita Sua* (1866), and *An Essay on the Development of Doctrine* (1845). His canonization in 2019 recognized the depth and influence of his extraordinary spiritual example which, among other things, led to countless conversions to the Catholic faith from Anglicanism.

---

11 Dave Armstrong, ed., *The Quotable Newman: A Definitive Guide to John Henry Newman's Central Thoughts and Ideas,* foreword by Joseph Pearce (Manchester: Sophia Institute Press, 2010), loc. 24. Kindle Edition.

DAY 12

FLANNERY O'CONNOR (1925–1964)

The reader's expectation—

"I have observed that most of the best religious fiction of our time is most shocking, precisely to those readers who claim to have an intense interest in finding more 'spiritual purpose'—as they like to put it—in modern novels than they can at present detect in them. Today's reader, if he believes in grace at all, sees it as something which can be separated from nature and served to him raw as Instant Uplift. This reader's favorite word is compassion. I don't wish to defame the word. There is a better sense in travail with and for creation than in its subjection to vanity. This is a sense which implies a recognition of sin; this is suffering-with, but which blunts no edges and makes no excuses. When infused into novels, it is often forbidding. Our age doesn't go for it."[12]

"Novelist and Believer," 1963

Flannery O'Connor was a Southern Catholic writer whose two novels, thirty-six short stories, many essays and letters place her among the most important Catholic artists in Church history. Her famous short story "A Good Man Is Hard to Find"

---

12 Flannery O'Connor, *Mystery and Manners: Occasional Prose*, eds. Sally and Robert Fitzgerald (New York: Farrar, Straus and Giroux, 1975), 165-66.

has become to the present generation what, say, Hemingway's *Old Man and the Sea* was to the previous. Her 1962 novel *Wise Blood* was made into an exceptional film by director John Huston in 1979. Unlike some notable Catholic writers, O'Connor's work is held in the highest regard by critics who share nothing of her Catholic worldview; they regard her as one of the major writers in modern American literature. Her achievement is made all the more remarkable by the fact that she lived only thirty-six years, a life cut short by lupus. When her literary executor, Sally Fitzgerald, published a collection of her letters, *The Habit of Being* (1979), it became a best seller and served to give its readers insight into O'Connor's personal life and spirituality. In the quote above, O'Connor chastises readers, especially Catholics, who only want to read books that make them feel good and offer "Instant Uplift."

DAY 13

ST. THOMAS AQUINAS (1225–1274)

The limits of reason—

St. Thomas asks whether, besides philosophy, any further doctrine is required—

"I answer that, it was necessary for man's salvation that there should be a knowledge revealed by God besides philosophical science built up by human reason. Firstly, indeed, because man is directed to God, as to an end that surpasses the grasp of his reason: 'The eye hath not seen, O God, besides Thee, what things Thou hast prepared for them that wait for Thee' (Is. 66:4). *But the end must first be known by men who are to direct their thoughts and actions to the end.* Hence it was necessary for the salvation of man that certain truths which exceed human reason should be made known to him by divine revelation. Even as regards those truths about God which human reason could have discovered, it was necessary that man should be taught by a divine revelation; because the truth about God such as reason could discover, would only be known by a few, and that after a long time, and with the admixture of many errors. Whereas man's whole salvation, which is in God, depends upon the knowledge of this truth. Therefore, in order that the salvation of men might be brought about more fitly and more surely, it was necessary that they should be taught divine truths by divine revelation. It was therefore necessary that besides philosophical

science built up by reason, there should be a sacred science learned through revelation."[13] (Emphasis added.)

Summa Theologica, 1265–1273

St. Thomas Aquinas has had as much influence on the teaching of the Church as any one individual since the finalization of the canon of Holy Scriptures in the early fourth century. His *Summa Theologica* and *Summa Contra Gentiles* formed the core of philosophical and theological seminary instruction employed well into the twentieth century. Most American seminaries continue to teach St. Thomas but not exclusively as in the past. His work synthesized what he considered the soundest philosophy of the ancient world—primarily Aristotle, but also Plato, the Neo-Platonists, and some Islamic thinkers— with Scripture and tradition. St. Thomas took great care in distinguishing the philosophical from theology and the revelation of Scripture, as can be seen in the quotation above.

---

13 Thomas Aquinas, *Summa Theologica,* trans. Dominican Fathers, loc. 371–402 of 117511, Kindle Edition.

DAY 14

GERARD MANLEY HOPKINS, SJ (1844–1889)

God's Grandeur

The world is charged with the grandeur of God.
 It will flame out, like the shining from shook foil;
 It gathers to a greatness, like the ooze of oil
Crushed. Why do men then now not reck his rod?
Generations have trod, have trod, have trod;
 And all is seared with trade; bleared, smeared with toil;
 And wears man's smudge and shares man's smell: the soil
Is bare now, nor can foot feel, being shod.

And for all this, nature is never spent;
 There lives the dearest freshness deep down things;
And though the last lights off the black West went
 Oh, morning, at the brown brink eastward, springs —
Because the Holy Ghost over the bent
 World broods with warm breast and with ah! bright
 wings.[14]

      1877, published posthumously in 1918

---

14 Gerald Manley Hopkins, *A Hopkins Reader,* revised and enlarged edition,
 ed. and introduction John Pick (New York: Doubleday and Company, Inc.,
 1966), 47.

As an act of humility, Gerard Manley Hopkins decided never to publish any of his poems while he lived. The poet Robert Bridges began publishing Hopkins's poetry in 1918, and by 1930, the Jesuit's work had been recognized as among the most innovative and powerful of the previous century. As religiously infused verse, his poetic achievement ranks with Dante, though smaller in scope and cut short by the poet's death at age forty-four. With daring and startling images such as "shining from shook foil" and irresistible rhythmic lines such as "And all is seared with trade; bleared, smeared with toil," Hopkins's verse makes both an immediate impression and leaves a lasting memory.

DAY 15

BOETHIUS (477–524)

Embracing suffering—

"A wise man ought not to regret his struggles with fortune any more than a brave soldier should be intimidated by the noise of battle; for difficulty is the natural lot of each. For the soldier it is the source of increasing glory; for the wise man it is the means of confirming his wisdom. Indeed, virtue gets its name from that virile strength which is not overcome by adversity. And you, who are advancing in virtue, should not expect to be

weakened by ease or softened by pleasure. You fight manfully against any fortune, neither despairing in the face of misfortune nor becoming corrupt in the enjoyment of prosperity. Hold fast to the middle ground with courage. . . . *You can make of your fortune what you will; for any fortune which seems difficult either tests virtue or corrects and punishes vice.*[15] (Emphasis added.)

The Consolation of Philosophy, 524

Boethius wrote his *Consolation* while in jail awaiting his execution. Born a Roman aristocrat, Boethius had a distinguished career as a teacher, translator, writer of both philosophy and theology, and mediator of disputes between the Latin and Greek churches. Emperor Theodoric rewarded Boethius by appointing him a senior official, "Master of Offices," but his defense of the Trinity led to his falling out of favor in court, being imprisoned for treason and sentenced to death. Emperor Theodoric was an Arian who believed Jesus a created human being. The *Consolation* is constructed as an imaginary dialogue between Lady Philosophy and the prisoner. The book became so influential that C. S. Lewis could write, "Until about two hundred years ago it would, I think, have been hard to find an educated man in any European country who did not love it." Boethius was killed by a rope wound around his head and tightened until it crushed his skull.

---

15 Boethius, *The Consolation of Philosophy*, trans. Richard Green (Bloomington: The Bobbs-Merrill Company, Inc., 1962), 99.

DAY 16

G. K. CHESTERTON (1874–1936)

The instant matters most—

"All Christianity concentrates on the man at the cross-roads. The vast and shallow philosophies, the huge syntheses of humbug, all talk about ages and evolution and ultimate developments. The true philosophy is concerned with the instant. Will a man take this road or that? —that is the only thing to think about, if you enjoy thinking. The aeons are easy enough to think about, if you enjoy thinking. The instant is really awful: and it is because our religion has intensely felt the instant, that it has in literature dealt much with battle and in theology dealt much with hell. It is full of *danger*, like a boy's book: it is in immortal crisis."[16]

Orthodoxy, 1908

G. K. Chesterton was attending a London art school when he realized he wanted to be a journalist—he was twenty years old. His column in the *Illustrated London News* and the *Daily News* made him a public figure by the time he turned thirty. His first novel, *The Napoleon of Notting Hill* (1904), is thought by critic Adam Gopnic as his real masterpiece, rather than his better-known *The Man Who Was Thursday* (1908). It was as a High

---

16 G. K. Chesterton, *Orthodoxy* (San Francisco: Ignatius Press, 1995), 143.

Church Anglican that Chesterton published *Heretics* (1905) and *Orthodoxy* (1908). Chesterton did not convert to Catholicism until 1922. Three of his best books were published after that decisive event: *Saint Francis of Assisi* (1923), *The Everlasting Man* (1925), and *Saint Thomas Aquinas* (1933). Chesterton was a man who, one might say, "cut a figure" walking London's streets wearing a cape, a well-worn hat, tiny glasses, and tapping the pavement with a swordstick. By the time he died in 1936, he had written approximately eighty books, four thousand essays, hundreds of poems, and several plays.

DAY 17

ST. JUSTIN MARTYR (100–165)

The nihilism of suicide—

"Why Christians do not kill themselves: But lest some one say to us, 'Go then all of you and kill yourselves, and pass even now to God, and do not trouble us,' I will tell you why we do not so, but why, when examined, we fearlessly confess. We have been taught that God did not make the world aimlessly, but for the sake of the human race; and we have before stated that He takes pleasure in those who imitate His properties, and is displeased with those that embrace what is worthless either in word or deed. *If, then, we all kill ourselves, we shall become the*

cause, as far as in us lies, why no one should be born, or instructed in the divine doctrines, or even why the human race should not exist; and we shall, if we so act, be ourselves acting in opposition to the will of God. But when we are examined, we make no denial, because we are not conscious of any evil, but count it impious not to speak the truth in all things, which also we know is pleasing to God, and because we are also now very desirous to deliver you from an unjust prejudice."[17] (Emphasis added.)

Second Apology, 150

St. Justin Martyr was born in Palestine in the city now called Nablus. His family was well-to-do and gave Justin the opportunity to travel and receive the best education available in places like Alexandria and Ephesus. He was fully versed in the latest Greek and Roman philosophy when he converted to Catholicism in about 130. Anticipating St. Augustine, he viewed Christianity as the fulfillment not only of Old Testament prophecy but pagan philosophy. It is important to view Justin's legacy as beginning the Catholic tradition of wedding theology and philosophy where possible. Justin Martyr got his head chopped off in Rome after beating a popular philosopher in a debate (yes, it reminds us of Socrates) which caused the prefect to find him guilty of teaching an illegal religion.

17 http://www.earlychristianwritings.com/text/justinmartyr-secondapology. html.

DAY 18

DOM JEAN LECLERCQ, OSB (1911–1993)

A hollow Christianity—

"The humanist movement took shape in Italy as early as the fourteenth century. It flowered in the course of the fifteenth, but it was only in the second half of that century and especially in the sixteenth that it extended to the whole of Europe. . . . It began in a society which was still wholly permeated with the Christian way of life and with Christian dogma: in going back to pagan antiquity, it ended, if not in questioning the truth of Christianity itself—for that, men waited till the modern world—at least in ignoring all that was essential in its doctrine. In the fifteenth century and at the beginning of the sixteenth, the inhabitants of a certain world of letters were living a hollow Christianity, from which the core had been removed. They fed upon the illusion that pagan wisdom in its highest forms—and it had assumed sublime forms—is one with Christian wisdom, provided that the latter silences the demands of dogma and of the Gospel. Ultimately, such a wisdom has no use for God or for Christ. Only man remains. . . . It was a new conception of the world and of man. And man, as

a result of a sort of Copernican revolution, now tended to take the place of God."[18]

"From Gregory to St. Bernard," 1968.

Dom Jean Leclercq, OSB, was a French Benedictine monk best known for his book *The Love of Learning and the Desire for God: A Study of Monastic Culture* (1957). Other books by Leclercq in English include *Alone With God* (1955), *Monks and Love in Twelfth-century France: Psycho-Historical Essays* (1979), *Survival or Prophecy?: The Letters of Thomas Merton and Jean LeClercq* (2002). His work in ecclesiastical history and medieval studies remains respected worldwide.

DAY 19

ROMANO GUARDINI (1885–1968)

Our uniqueness—

"First, what irrevocably is a man? A man is a person called by God. As that man he is capable of answering for his own action and of participating in reality through an inner and

---

18 Dom Jean Leclercq, "Part One: From St. Gregory to St. Bernard—From the Sixth to the Twelfth Century," *A History of Christian Spirituality II: The Spirituality of the Middle Ages* (New York: The Seabury Press, 1968), 507-8.

innate source which is one with himself. This capacity makes each man unique. A man is not unique because of his peculiar talents; a man is unique in the clear and absolute sense that, as is each of his fellows, he is a being himself, indispensable, irreplaceable, inviolate."[19]

The End of the Modern World, 1956

Romano Guardini was German not Italian as his name would suggest. Romano and his family moved to Germany a year after he was born in Verona. A few years after completing his dissertation on St. Bonaventure, Guardini was appointed to a chair at the University of Berlin in the philosophy of religion. The rise of the Nazi movement moved Guardini to publicly excoriate their anti-semitism in a 1935 essay. By 1939, he had been forced to resign and spent the war years as a parish priest. After WWII, he taught at the universities of Tübingen and Munich before retiring in 1962. His most popular books in English include *The Lord*, *The Spirit of the Liturgy*, and *The Death of Socrates*. Guardini turned down Pope Paul VI's offer to become a cardinal, but Pope Francis quoted *The End of the Modern World* eight times in his encyclical *Laudato si'*. Pope Francis never completed the doctoral dissertation he started to write on Guardini as a younger man.

---

19 Romano Guardini, *The End of the Modern World*, trans. Joseph Theman and Herbert Burke (Chicago: Henry Regnery Company, Chicago,1961), 81–82.

DAY 20

JOSEF PIEPER (1904–1997)

The age of sloth—

"We have said that slothful sadness (*acedia*) is one of the determining characteristics of the hidden profile of our age, of an age that has proclaimed the stand of a 'world of total work.' This sloth, as the visible mark of secularization, determines the face of every age in which the call to tasks that are genuinely Christian begins to lose its official power to bind. Acedia is the signature of every age that seeks, in its despair, to shake off the obligations of that nobility of being that is conferred by Christianity and so, in its despair, to deny its true self."[20]

On Hope, 1986

The philosopher Josef Pieper was Germany's leading exponent of the legacy of St. Thomas Aquinas in the twentieth century. As a young scholar and teacher, Pieper's work did not please the Nazis who confiscated some of his early works. After the war, however, he taught at the University of Munster from 1950 to 1996. Pieper's work became known in the United Kingdom and the United States following the 1952 publication in English of *Leisure, The Basis of Culture* with a foreword by T. S. Eliot.

---

20 Josef Pieper, *On Hope*, trans. Sister Mary Frances McCarthy, S.N.D. (San Francisco, Ignatius Press, 1986), 59.

Other translations quickly followed: *The End of Time,* 1954; *The Silence of St. Thomas,* 1957; *Happiness and Contemplation,* 1958; *The Four Cardinal Virtues.* 1959; *Scholasticism,* 1960; and *Guide to St. Thomas;* 1962, to name a few. (Most of Pieper's work is available from Ignatius Press and St. Augustine's Press.) Pieper's explanation of the virtues has been very influential in part because of his ability to communicate the teaching of St. Thomas Aquinas to the ordinary reader. He could make difficult thought understandable but without sacrificing any probity or accuracy. His work *About Love* is a masterpiece (available from Ignatius Press in *Hope, Love, and Faith,* 2000).

DAY 21

JOHN EMERICH EDWARD DALBERG-ACTON, 1ST BARON ACTON (1834–1902)

Great men are bad men—

"I cannot accept your canon that we are to judge Pope and King unlike other men, with a favourable presumption that they did no wrong. If there is any presumption it is the other way against holders of power, increasing as the power increases. Historic responsibility has to make up for the want of legal responsibility. Power tends to corrupt and absolute power corrupts absolutely. Great men are almost always bad men, even

when they exercise influence and not authority: still more when you superadd the tendency or the certainty of corruption by authority. There is no worse heresy than that the office sanctifies the holder of it. . . . The inflexible integrity of the moral code is, to me, the secret of the authority, the dignity, the utility of history."[21]

Letter to Bishop Mandell Creighton, April 5, 1887

John Emerich Edward Dalberg Acton—First Baron Acton of Aldenham—was born in Naples. Because Lord Acton was Catholic, he was not allowed to attend Cambridge. At the University of Munich, he studied under Ignaz von Döllinger, a church historian of great repute. As a historian, Acton entered politics and was named a Lord by Prime Minister William Gladstone in recognition of his support of liberal causes. A consultant at the First Vatican Council, his reputation as a Catholic apologist grew, and in 1895 he was appointed Regius Professor of Modern History at Cambridge. By the time of his death in 1902, Lord Acton was widely regarded as a true sage, a man whose depth and breadth of knowledge was unmatched for his age.

---

21 John Emerich Edward Dalberg-Acton, 1st Baron Acton, *The Collected Works of Lord Acton*, ed. John Neville Figgis and Reginald Verve Laurence (1907), loc. 8951 of 35935, Kindle Edition.

DAY 22

DIETRICH VON HILDEBRAND (1889–1977)

The discretion of Christian living—

"True freedom means that we see nothing with either the eyes of the world or with the eyes of our nature, but in the light of Christ, and with the eyes of the Faith. He who is truly free is not, then, simply unaware of the effect his behavior may produce on others, but essentially independent of it and superior to the plane of considerations to which it belongs. His conduct will be decided by Christ and His holy word, and not determined, for instance, by an inordinate zeal which, spurning the virtue of discretion, gives vent indiscriminately to one's natural enthusiasm rather than translate into action a true and unreserved surrender to Christ."[22]

Transformation In Christ, 1948

Dietrich von Hildebrand converted to Catholicism in 1914 at age twenty-five. At the Universities of Munich and Göttingen, the young philosopher was a student of Edmund Husserl and Max Scheler whose phenomenology and personalism helped form a unique kind of Christian philosophy, the Theology of the Body. His teaching career began, after his service in

---

22 Dietrich von Hildebrand, *Transformation In Christ* (Chicago: Franciscan Herald Press, 1948), 215.

WWI, at the University of Munich in 1924. His public opposition to Hitler's Nazism led to him leaving Germany first for Austria, where he published an anti-Nazi newspaper. After the Anschluss, he had to leave Austria for Toulouse, where he taught until France was invaded in 1940. Von Hildebrand then went to Portugal whence he sailed to New York City, where he taught at Fordham University until 1960. After retirement, he continued to write in both German and English. His major works are now being published in English by the Hildebrand Project. Von Hildebrand regarded the affective life of persons as a necessary part of his philosophical anthropology, ethics, and aesthetics. As a result, his works often possess a spirituality missing from other twentieth-century Catholic philosophers.

DAY 23

FRIEDRICH HEER (1916–1983)

The Bard and modern man—

"In a thousand forms, Shakespeare unveiled the first, comprehensive presentation of modern man. A new anthropology was outlined for the first time. Man was a being of many contradictions, which are reciprocally awakened and nourished. In these fields of tension, the whole man comes to self-realization. . . . In Shakespeare's figures, Heaven and Hell, submerged

and revealed, clash with the individual spirit. Vice and talents, gifts and lusts, temptations from below and above interplay in such a manner that a vice (pride, ambition, love of power, envy) can turn dialectically in to a virtue, say the lofty aspiration of a noble spirit, if the conditions are right. . . . Man as the world riddle, as cosmos and chaos, was for the first time seen as a world of inner dimensions in Shakespeare. He transferred the journeys to Hell of Ulysses and Dante into the inner dimensions of man."[23]

An Intellectual History of Europe, 1964

Born in Vienna in 1916, Frederick Heer earned his doctorate in history from the University of Vienna in 1938. Heer immediately came into conflict with the proponents of anti-Semitic National Socialism. In March 1938, he was arrested by Nazis. Once free, he founded a Catholic resistance group hoping to combine it with other resistance factions. He later served as a soldier in WWII. After the war, Heer edited *Der Furch* [*The Burrow*], was appointed chief of literacy at the Vienna Burgtheater, and taught at the University of Vienna. For his work about the Jews, *God's First Love*, Heer was awarded the first Martin Buber-Franz Rosenzweig Medal. Books in English translation include *The Holy Roman Empire, Charlemagne and His World*, and *Medieval World 1100-1350*. His biographer

---

23 Friedrich Heer, *An Intellectual History of Europe*, trans. Jonathan Steinberg (New York: World Publishing Company, 1953), 356-557.

describes Heer's life as full controversies, the making of enemies, and public attacks, while Heer himself always showed
respect for his adversaries. He died in 1983.

DAY 24

ST. TERESA BENEDICTA OF THE CROSS
(1891–1942)

The model from Avila—

"They agree on the article of faith, which was familiar to John,
the theologian, while Teresa had to discover it at first: God the
Creator is present in each thing and sustains it in existence. He
has foreseen each, and knows it through and through with all
its changes and destinies. By the might of his omnipotence he
can do with each, at every moment, whatever he pleases. He
can leave it to its own laws and the normal flow of events. He
can also intervene with extraordinary measures. God dwells
in this manner in every human soul, also. He knows each one
from all eternity, with all the mysteries of her being and every
wave that breaks over her life. She is in his power. It is up to
him whether he leaves her to herself and the course of worldly
events or whether, with his strong hand, he will interfere in her

destiny. Such a marvel of his power is every rebirth of a soul through sanctifying grace."[24]

The Science of the Cross, 1950

St. Teresa Benedicta of the Cross, first known as Edith Stein, was born to a Jewish family in Breslau; she was quite brilliant with a radical atheistic and unruly bent. When she went to college, she studied with one of the most important philosophers of her time—Edmund Husserl, who is the father of phenomenology. When Stein became Husserl's assistant, she began being exposed to Christian thinkers and, out of curiosity, began to read the autobiography of St. Teresa of Avila. After reading the book, she declared, "This is the truth." She was thirty years old. After being baptized in 1922, though she wanted to become a Carmelite, Stein started teaching at a Dominican college for women teachers. There she began reading St. Thomas Aquinas and started lecturing to women's groups about the role of Catholic women. Since she was of Jewish origin, the Nazis demanded she leave the college, and she decided to enter the Carmelites as Sister Teresa Benedicta of the Cross. Even there, she was forced to wear the yellow Star of David. Knowing she was in danger, she joined a Carmel in Holland, but when the Dutch bishops denounced Hitler, all the Jewish converts to Catholicism were put into boxcars and sent to Auschwitz,

---

24 Edith Stein, *The Science of the Cross, The Collected Works of Edith Stein, Vol. 6* (Washington, D.C.: ICS Publications, 2002), loc. 3581 of 7396, Kindle Edition.

where Sister Teresa Benedicta of the Cross died on August 9, 1942.

DAY 25

CZESLAW MILOSZ (1911–2004)

In the eyes of another—

"Yes, for me the Fall and original Sin are the key mysteries. And I think I've always written too little about them. To study and analyze original sin is extraordinary, absorbing. In the Book of Genesis, Adam and Eve make themselves clothing from animal skin. They have lost their innocence. God asks them, 'And who told you you were naked?' This is what it means to exist in the eyes of another person. The problem of nakedness did not exist before. Now Adam is conscious that he is not Eve, and Eve is conscious that she is not Adam. Eyes that look and see. . . . What matters here is the consciousness, the realization of duality."[25]

Conversations with Czeslaw Milosz, 1987

---

25 Ewa Czamecka and Aleksander Flut, eds., *Conversations with Czeslaw Milosz* (New York: Harcourt, 1987), 296.

Czeslaw Milosz was awarded the Nobel Prize in 1980. His youth was spent in Czarist Russia where his father worked, but after WWI, the family returned to Poland where Milosz attended Catholic schools. He worked with underground resistance groups when Germany and the USSR invaded Poland. After the war, Milosz was appointed to diplomatic service and sent to Paris as cultural attache: he defected to the West in 1951. He left his native Poland because he clashed with the Communist regime and lived in the United States from 1960 until his death in 2004. All his published works—novels, poetry, essays—are written in Polish, with many being available in excellent English translations. Having lived under two totalitarian regimes, Milosz found his faith being tested, but he never abandoned it. Terrence Des Pres, writing in the *Nation,* stated that "political catastrophe has defined the nature of our [age], and the result—the collision of personal and public realms—has produced a new kind of writer. Czeslaw Milosz is the perfect example. In exile from a world which no longer exists, a witness to the Nazi devastation of Poland and the Soviet takeover of Eastern Europe, Milosz deals in his poetry with the central issues of our time: the impact of history upon moral being, the search for ways to survive spiritual ruin in a ruined world."

DAY 26

LOUIS BOUYER, CONG, ORAT. (1913–2004)

The Church and Scripture—

"It is utterly inconceivable how many Protestants could persist in viewing Catholic asceticism as 'magic,' and Catholic mysticism as 'idolatry.' If this error receives frequent support from the infidelities, the inconsequence, the clumsiness, of Catholics, it still remains so gross that its root, too, must lie in a misunderstanding for which Protestantism is itself responsible. . . . It is better to show how an unbiased acquaintance with the mystical teaching most characteristic of Catholicism, and most closely and explicitly bound up with its ascetical doctrine, annihilates these accusations of magic and idolatry. If the Catholic Church, at the very period when Protestantism came into conflict with it, acknowledged the teaching of one writer in particular as the purest account of her spiritual doctrine, it is the teaching of St. John of the Cross, proclaimed by the Popes the doctor *par excellence* of ascetical and mystical theology. Now the most striking thing about St. John of the Cross is that he draws his teaching from exactly the same Biblical sources as Calvin."[26]

The Spirit and Forms of Protestantism, 1954

---

26 Louis Bouyer, *The Spirit and Forms of Protestantism*, trans. A.V. Littledale (New York: The World Publishing Company 1956, 92-93.

Louis Bouyer was a French Lutheran minister who converted to Catholicism in 1939. In fact, when Bouyer started writing *The Spirit and Forms of Protestantism,* he was still a Lutheran. By the end, he once told me, he was a Catholic. Bouyer joined the French Oratory and became a professor at the Institute Catholique in Paris. He served as a consultant at the Second Vatican Council on liturgy and Christian unity. In 1963, Father Bouyer started teaching at different venues around the world, including in the United States. Much of his scholarship has been translated into English and published by Ignatius Press, works such as *Women in the Church* (1979), *The Word, Church and Sacraments* (2004), *The Church of God* (2011), and *The Memoirs of Louis Bouyer* (2015). Along with Cardinal Ratzinger, he founded the journal *Communio* and was chosen by Pope Pius VI as a founding member of the International Theological Commission in 1969.

DAY 27

MATTHIAS JOSEPH SCHEEBEN (1835–1888)

Hypostatic union—

"By the hypostatic union Christ's own humanity was invested with the divine dignity of the Son of God, who assumed it to Himself; and to such an extent, indeed, that even in His human

nature the God-man had to be adored by all creatures, and loved by His Father with the same infinite love with which He is loved in His divinity. In consequence of this dignity, that human nature had to be endowed with the sanctity and splendor of the divine nature, so that it might possess an equipment comfortable to its infinite dignity. If, then, the human race, in analogous fashion, likewise becomes the body of Christ, and its members become the members of God's son, if the divine person of the Son of God bears them in Himself as His own, then, with due proportion, must not the divine dignity of the Son of God flow over to men, since they are His members? Must not God the Father extend to these members the same love which He bears for His natural Son?"[27]

Mysteries of Christianity, 1886

Matthias Scheeben—whose book *The Mysteries of Christianity* influenced subsequent figures such as Reginald Garrigou-Lagrange, Hans Urs von Balthasar, and Pope Benedict XVI—was a giant among mid-nineteenth century theologians. Ordained in 1858, Father Scheeben, who was himself a mystic, taught at the diocesan seminary in Cologne from 1860 to 1875. As a theologian, he wrote, his purpose had been "to make the Christian feel happy about his faith. Because the beauty and eminence of our faith consist in this: that through

---

27 Matthias Joseph Scheeben, *Mysteries of Christianity*, trans. Cyril Vollert (St. Louis: B. Herder Book Co, 1951), 377.

the mysteries of grace it raises our nature to an immeasurably high plane and presents to us an inexpressibly intimate union with God." Those works include *Nature and Grace, The Glories of Divine Grace*, and a two-volume *Mariology*, all available in English translation. Pope Pius XI said of Scheeben, "He was a model of theology, and a model of spirited defense of the Church, the Holy See and the Pope. Above all, he was a model of saintly Christian life" (*L'Osservatore Romano,* March 11-12, 1935).

DAY 28

THOMAS MERTON (1915–1968)

Here Merton describes a visit to St. Francis in Havana and is struck by the moment of Consecration—

"There formed in my mind an awareness, an understanding, a realization of what had just taken place on the altar, at the Consecration: a realization of God made present by the words of Consecration in a way that made Him belong to me. But what a thing it was, this awareness: it was so intangible, and yet it struck me like a thunderclap. It was a light that was so bright that it had no relation to any visible light and so profound and so intimate that it seemed like a neutralization of every lesser experience. And yet the thing that struck me most of all this

night was in a certain sense 'ordinary'—it was a light (and this most of all was what took my breath away) that was offered to all, to everybody, and there was nothing fancy or strange about it. It was the light of faith deepened and reduced to an extreme and sudden obviousness. It was as if I had been suddenly illuminated by being blinded by the manifestation of God's presence."[28]

Seven Storey Mountain, 1948

Thomas Merton wrote more than fifty books in a period of twenty-seven years, mostly on spirituality, social justice, and pacifism, as well as a score of essays and reviews. Merton's bestselling autobiography, *The Seven Storey Mountain* (1948), influenced many to try out the monastic life. Merton was born in France, the son of a New Zealand-born father and an American-born mother who were both artists. During WWI, the Merton family moved to the United States. After his mother died, he attended boarding schools in England and France, then spent a year at Cambridge before attending Columbia University, graduating in 1939. Merton converted in 1941. He taught for a few years at two Catholic colleges and Columbia before entering the Trappist Abbey of Gethsemani near Louisville, Kentucky. Merton was the most influential religious in the United States since Bishop Fulton Sheen.

---

28 Thomas Merton, *Seven Storey Mountain* (Orlando: Harcourt Brace & Company, 1976), 284.

DAY 29

BLAISE PASCAL (1623–1662)

The wager—

"Yes, but you must wager. There is no choice, you are already committed. Which will you choose then? Let us see: since a choice must be made, let us see which offers you the least interest. You have two things to lose: the true and the good; and two things to stake; your reason and your will, your knowledge and your happiness; and your nature has two things to avoid: error and wretchedness. Since you must necessarily choose, your reason is not more affronted by choosing one rather than the other. That is one point cleared up. But your happiness? Let us weigh up the gain and the loss involved in calling heads that God exists. Let us assess the two cases: if you win you win everything, if you lose you lose nothing. Do not hesitate then; wager that he does exist."[29]

Pensées, 1670

Blaise Pascal lived only to the age of thirty-nine. Yet, during his life, Pascal revolutionized the study of mathematics and physics and left a spiritual testament, *Pensées,* that rivals St. Augustine's *Confessions* for his self-scrutiny and its spiritual heft. The *Pensées*

---

29 Blaise Pascal, *Pensées,* trans. A. J. Krailsheimer (New York: Penguin Books, 1984), 150–51.

are often viewed as a precursor of Existentialism, but I know of no Existentialists who wore a cincture of nails to mortify a body already plagued with chronic pain and illness. According to his sister, after the age of eighteen, he never passed a single day without pain. After a mystical experience on November 23, 1654, Pascal's interest in science and math diminished, and he devoted himself to the defense of the Catholic faith, though somewhat tainted by the Jansenism of his age. Jansenists espoused some of the Reformer's themes—original sin, justification by faith, and human depravity. Pascal defended his Jansenism in *The Provincial Letters* (1556–57) aimed at the Jesuits. His early death was caused by a malignant stomach tumor that metastasized in his brain.

DAY 30

JOHN HOWARD GRIFFIN (1929–1980)

Feeling the hatred—

"Once again a 'hate stare' drew my attention like a magnet. It came from a middle-aged, heavyset, well-dressed white man. He sat a few yards away, fixing his eyes on me. Nothing can describe the withering horror of this. You feel lost, sick at heart before such unmasked hatred, not so much because it threatens you as because it shows humans in such an inhuman light. You

see a kind of insanity, something so obscene the very obscenity
of it (rather than its threat) terrifies you. It was so new I could
not take my eyes from the man's face. I felt like saying: 'What
in God's name are you doing to yourself?'"[30]

Black Like Me, 1961

Born in 1920, John Howard Griffin is best known for his book
Black Like Me (1961), an account of his travels in the South
after using a chemical to turn his skin black. Griffin was a
Texan, born in Dallas but raised in Ft. Worth. His mother was a
classical pianist, his father an Irish tenor, both were local celebrities. Griffin left high school at fifteen to study in France,
first studying literature at the University of Poitiers followed
by medicine at the École de Médecine. Under the tutelage
of Nadia Boulanger, he received certificates of musical study
from the Conservatoire de Fontainebleau. Griffin specialized
in Gregorian chant, aided by his study with the Benedictines at
the Abbey of Solesmes. Griffin worked in the French Resistance
as a medic helping to evacuate Austrian Jews to safety from the
Nazis. He served in the United States Army Air Corps in the
South Seas. During WWII, he was decorated for bravery but
lost his sight from 1946 until 1957. During his twelve years of
blindness, he wrote novels. Griffin's books include *The Devil
Rides Outside* (1952), *Nuni* (1956), and *A Time to be Human*

---

30 John Howard Griffin, *Black Like Me: The Definitive Griffin Estate Edition*
(Wings Press), loc. pp. 47-48, Kindle.

(1977). The blind, he wrote, "can only see the heart and intelligence of a man, and nothing in these things indicates in the slightest whether a man is white or black." He was a close friend of Thomas Merton and published several books about him with his own photographs.

DAY 31

DOROTHY DAY (1897–1980)

The duty of justice—

"I felt that the Church was the Church of the poor, . . . but at the same time, I felt that it did not set its face against a social order which made so much charity in the present sense of the word necessary. I felt that charity was a word to choke over. Who wanted charity? And it was not just human pride but a strong sense of man's dignity and worth, and what was due to him in justice, that made me resent, rather than feel proud of so mighty a sum total of Catholic institutions. Besides, more and more they had to render to the state."[31]

The Long Loneliness, 1952

---

31 Dorothy Day, *The Long Loneliness: The Autobiography of the Legendary Catholic Social Activist* (New York: Harper One, 1952) loc. 193-195 of 288, Kindle.

Dorothy Day was one of the most remarkable Catholic laywomen of the last century. Her family moved from Brooklyn, where she was born, to San Francisco and Chicago, where Dorothy was baptized in an Episcopal Church. She left the University of Illinois at Urbana and moved to New York City, where she became involved in social causes to help the workers and the poor. She worked as a journalist, protested, befriended famous artists and writers, and had a disastrous personal life; an abortion, and a failed marriage led to a suicide attempt. When her daughter Tamar was born in 1926, Day decided to join the Catholic Church and baptize her child. With her friend Peter Maurin, they started the *Catholic Worker* newspaper, which grew nationally, and created farming communes and houses of hospitality. Her conversion story is told in her *From Union Square to Rome* (1938) and her autobiography, *The Long Loneliness* (1952). Pope Benedict XVI cited her story as an example of a "journey towards faith . . . in a secularized environment." The Holy See has accepted the cause for Dorothy Day's possible canonization.

DAY 32

PETER ABELARD (1079–1142)

Not offending God—

"For the more we cleave to him [God] by love, the more carefully we ought to guard against what offends him more and what he himself condemns more. For he who truly loves someone has enough to do to beware less of injuring himself than of hurting or showing contempt for a friend; according to the Apostle, 'Charity seeketh not her own' and again: 'Let no man seek his, but that which is another's.' So if we should guard against sins less for the sake of avoiding injury to ourselves than for the sake of avoiding to hurt God, surely what should be more guarded against are those in which more hurt is given."[32]

Ethics, 1138

Peter Abelard was the leading philosopher and theologian of the twelfth century. Abelard, though also being a poet and a musician, championed the use of reason in theology and treated doctrines with a systematic approach that presaged St. Thomas Aquinas. Abelard's renown as a teacher and scholar began to grow when he taught at the Cathedral School of

---

32 Peter Abelard, *Ethics*, trans. D. E. Luscombe (Oxford: Oxford University Press, 1979), 73.

Notre Dame where he quarreled with his former teacher William of Champeaux. William forced him out of the Cathedral School, so Abelard set up his own schools where his faithful students followed him before returning to Notre Dame as Master and canon of Sens, the archdiocese of Paris. At the height of his fame, thousands of students moved to Paris to attend his lectures. Abelard's star soon fell when his love affair with a private student, Héloïse, was exposed. Her uncle sent men to Abelard's room at night where they succeeded in castrating him. She became a nun and he a monk, and until his death, they exchanged a famous group of letters which once collected and published have remained in print ever since, *The Letters of Abelard and Heloise.*

DAY 33

THOMAS E. WOODS (1971–) AND ST. CYPRIAN OF CARTHAGE

The Church and acts of charity—

"One could go on at great length citing the good works of the early Church, carried out by both the lowly and the rich. Even the Church fathers, who bequeathed to Western civilization an enormous corpus of literary and scholarly work, found time to devote themselves to the service of their fellow men. Saint

Augustine established a hospice for pilgrims, ransomed slaves, and gave away clothing to the poor.... Saint John Chrysostom founded a series of hospitals in Constantinople. Saint Cyprian and Saint Ephrem organized relief efforts during times of plague and famine. The early Church also institutionalized the care of widows and orphans and saw after the needs of the sick, especially during epidemics. During the pestilences that struck Carthage and Alexandria, the Christians earned respect and admiration for the bravery with which they consoled the dying and buried the dead, at a time when the pagans abandoned even their friends to their terrible fate. In the North African city of Carthage, the third-century bishop and Church father Saint Cyprian rebuked the pagan population for not helping victims of the plague, preferring instead to plunder them: 'No compassion is shown by you to the sick, only covetousness and plunder open their jaws over the dead; they who are too fearful for the work of mercy, are bold for guilty profits. They who shun to bury the dead, are greedy for what they have left behind them.' Saint Cyprian summoned followers of Christ to action, calling on them to nurse the sick and bury the dead. Recall that this was still the age of intermittent persecution of Christians, so the great bishop was asking his followers to help the very people who had at times persecuted them. But, he said, 'If we only do good to those who do good to us, what do we more than the heathens and publicans? If we are the children of God, who makes His sun to shine upon good and bad, and sends rain on the just and the unjust, let us prove

it by our acts, by blessing those who curse us, and doing good
to those who persecute us.'"[33]

How the Catholic Church Built Western Civilization, 2005

Thomas E. Woods, Jr., is a senior fellow of the Ludwig von
Mises Institute in Auburn, AL. He has authored twelve books,
including the best-selling *The Politically Incorrect Guide to
American History* (2004). Woods is a Catholic convert from
Lutheranism. For eleven years, he was the associate editor of
The Latin Mass Magazine.

DAY 34

ST. AMBROSE (340–397)

You sow and you reap—

"Mercy, also, is a good thing, for it makes men perfect, in that it
imitates the perfect Father. Nothing graces the Christian soul
so much as mercy; mercy as shown chiefly towards the poor,
that thou mayest treat them as sharers in common with thee
in the produce of nature, which brings forth the fruits of the

---

33 Thomas E. Woods, Jr., *How the Catholic Church Built Western Civilization*
(Washington, DC: Regnery Publishing Company, 2013), loc. 184 of 285,
Kindle Edition.

earth for use to all. Thus, thou mayest freely give to a poor man what thou hast, and in this way help him who is thy brother and companion. Thou bestowest silver; he receives life. Thou givest money; he considers it his fortune. Thy coin makes up all his property. Further, he bestows more on thee than thou on him, since he is thy debtor in regard to thy salvation. If thou clothe the naked, thou clothest thyself with righteousness; if thou bring the stranger under thy roof, if thou support the needy, he procures for thee the friendship of the saints and eternal habitations. That is no small recompense. Thou sowest earthly things and receivest heavenly. Dost thou wonder at the judgment of God in the case of holy Job? Wonder rather at his virtue, in that he could say: 'I was an eye to the blind, and a foot to the lame. I was a father to the poor. Their shoulders were made warm with the skins of my lambs. The stranger dwelt not at my gates, but my door was open to every one that came.' Clearly blessed is he from whose house a poor man has never gone with empty hand. Nor again is any one more blessed than he who is sensible of the needs of the poor, and the hardships of the weak and helpless. In the day of judgment he will receive salvation from the Lord, Whom he will have as his debtor for the mercy he has shown."[34]

On the Duties of the Clergy, 391

---

34 St. Ambrose, *On the Duties of the Clergy, St. Ambrose Collection* (Aeterna Press, 2016), loc. 7875 of 22406, Kindle Edition.

St. Ambrose was bishop of Milan and is a Doctor of the Church. He foresaw the Church rising to greater authority over the pagan remnants of the Roman Empire. Ambrose was also an innovator of the composition of hymns—writing them in four stanzas of eight syllables. He is remembered for his strong opposition to the Arian heresy, his promotion of the *Theotokos* doctrine, and his defense of the *Filioque* clause, the procession of the Holy Spirt from the Father *and* the Son. Those who denied the *Filioque* asserted the Holy Spirit proceeded only from the Father, which has serious theological consequences. However, it's probably true to say that in spite of all his accomplishments, St. Ambrose is best known for his decisive role in the conversion of St. Augustine.

DAY 35

FRANÇOIS MAURIAC (1885–1970)

"To me, the priest goes on being what he was at the dawn of my life, but first and above all, he is the one who binds and releases, the one who, when he raises his hand to absolve us, can no longer be distinguished from the Son of Man to Whom was given the power to grant the remission of sins here on earth. This is a power which perhaps dazzles us the most when we have no grave sin to confess, because it is then that the Grace attached to the Sacrament of Penance acts in its pure

state, if I may dare say so, and that we feel it right down to our very flesh."[35]

Letters on Art and Literature, 1953

François Mauriac won the Nobel Prize in Literature 1952 "for the deep spiritual insight and the artistic intensity with which he has in his novels penetrated the drama of human life." Mauriac lost his father when he was only eighteen months old and was raised by his mother along with four siblings. After his education with the Marianites, he attended university in both Bordeaux and Paris, but he soon decided to leave and become an independent writer. With his novel *A Kiss for the Leper* (1922), Mauriac become a public figure. His highly regarded novels *Thérèse Desqueyroux* (1927) and *The Vipers' Tangle* (1932) soon followed. In 1933, he was elected to the Académie française and was the only member to publish a resistance text during the German occupation. Mauriac wrote twenty-three novels, all of which are told in a world where individuals wrestle with sin and its consequences, damnation or redemption.

---

35 François Mauriac, *Letters on Art and Literature* (New York: Philosophical Library, Inc., 1953), loc. 151 of 848, Kindle Edition.

DAY 36

HILAIRE BELLOC (1870–1953)

Thanks to the "Dark Ages"—

"There is no parallel to this survival in all the history of mankind. Every other great civilization has, after many centuries of development, either fallen into a fixed and sterile sameness or died and disappeared. There is nothing left of Egypt, there is nothing left of Assyria. The Eastern civilizations remain, but remain immovable; or if they change can only vulgarly copy external models. But the civilization of Europe—the civilization, that is, of Rome and of the Empire—had a third fortune differing both from death and from sterility: it survived to a resurrection. Its essential seeds were preserved for a Second Spring. For five or six hundred years men carved less well, wrote verse less well, let roads fall slowly into ruin, lost or rather coarsened the machinery of government, forgot or neglected much in letters and in the arts and in the sciences. But there was preserved, right through that long period, not only so much of letters and of the arts as would suffice to bridge the great gulf between the fifth century and the eleventh, but also so much of what was really vital in the mind of Europe as would permit that mind to blossom again after its

repose. And the agency, I repeat, which effected this conservation of seeds was the Catholic Church."[36]

Europe and the Faith, 1920

Hilaire Belloc was a pessimist about European civilization. When he wrote this in 1920, there was good reason to doubt the future: the First World War had just ended, a war that accomplished nothing except the postponement of the war to come in 1939. But during the period between 1914 and 1918, the largest and bloodiest war in European history had mobilized over seventy million soldiers who faced each other in trenches stretching from the coast of the English Channel to the Swiss Alps. The soldiers on both sides entered the war believing in God and Country. By the middle of the war, the same soldiers were questioning the reality and validity of both. The Church, he affirms, had sowed the seeds that brought Europe out of its "dark ages" and flourished once again in the Renaissance. Western history since 1920, it appears, confirms that those seeds continue to bear fruit. This can be said, however, only if one keeps in mind what Jacques Maritain said about history: it contains the progress of both good and evil.

---

36 Hilaire Belloc, *Europe and the Faith* (Serapis Classics), loc. 31 of 141, Kindle Edition.

DAY 37

ST. THOMAS MORE (1478–1535)

St. Thomas More describes, for his daughter, his answer to the Master Secretary in his second interrogation. The Master Secretary had accused him of influencing other men's opinions by his example.

"Whereto I answered, that I give no man occasion to hold any point one or other, nor never give any advice or counsel therein one way or other. And for conclusion I could no further go, whatsoever pain should come thereof. I am quoth I, the King's true faithful subject and daily bedesman [one who prays for another] and pray for his Highness and all his and all the realm. *I do nobody harm, I say none harm, I think none harm, but wish everybody good. And if this be not enough to keep a man alive, in good faith, I long not to live.*"[37] (Emphasis added.)

A letter to his daughter Margaret Roper, May 2 or 3, 1535

St. Thomas More is best known for the martyrdom he suffered as a result of his refusal to sign Henry VIII's Oath of Supremacy, recognizing him as head of the Church in England. Before his conflict with the king, More's career had taken off as soon as he was elected to Parliament in 1504. More had chosen a career in public life after spending two years

---

37 St. Thomas More, *St. Thomas More: Selected Letters*, ed. Elizabeth Frances Rogers (New Haven: Yale University Press, 1961), 247-48.

participating in the spiritual exercises of Carthusian monks. His first wife, Jane Colt, died in 1511 after bearing three children. He then remarried Alice Middleton, rather too quickly for some of his friends, but their marriage flourished though they had no children of their own. After becoming Master of Requests and a Privy Counsellor, More was knighted and entered Henry VIII's inner circle, serving as liaison between the king and Cardinal Wolsey. More succeeded Wolsey as Lord Chancellor in 1529 and, like Wolsey, did what he could to oppose Protestant reformers and the Tyndale translation of the Scriptures. Apart from politics, More published books such as *Utopia* (1516) and his *Apology* (1533). *A Dialogue of Comfort Against Tribulation* was published shortly after his death.

DAY 38

MSGR. RONALD KNOX (1888–1957)

An appropriate shyness—

"And you ought to be keeping step with the priest in this first movement, as it were, of the religious dance. The priest is standing there with his arms in front of him staring up at the crucifix over the altar; an attitude of appeal. And that ought to be the attitude of your mind to start with; you oughtn't ever to go to Mass, and still more obviously you oughtn't ever to

go to Communion, without some of this shyness, the sense of butting in somewhere where you aren't wanted. We're terribly in danger all the time of taking God's goodness too much for granted; of bouncing up to Communion as if it were the most natural thing in the world, instead of being a supernatural thing belonging to another world."[38]

The Mass in Slow Motion, 1948

Msgr. Ronald Knox was baptized into the Church of England; both of his grandfathers and his father were Anglican bishops. His education was the best England had to offer: he read Virgil in Latin at the age of six, attended Eton, and won a scholarship to Balliol College, Oxford. When he was seventeen, Knox decided to remain celibate. Ordained an Anglican priest in 1912, Knox first served as chaplain to Trinity College, and when WWI came, he served in military intelligence. In spite of his father's strenuous objections, Knox was received into the Church on September 22, 1917. The next year he published his *Spiritual Aeneid* (1918) about his conversion. His father removed Ronald from his will. He taught over seven years at a college seminary before being ordained in 1919. He was Catholic chaplain at Oxford from 1926 to 1939, the year he became a monsignor. He was extremely prolific. In addition to his regular broadcasting on BBC Radio about Christianity

---

38 Ronald Knox, *The Mass In Slow Motion* (New York: Sheed & Ward, 1948), 7-8.

and his works of apologetics, satires, and translations, Knox wrote detective stories and novels. His favorite, and possibly his most influential book, was *Enthusiasm: A Chapter in the History of Religion with Special Reference to the XVII and XVIII Centuries* (1950) about Christians whose "enthusiasm" was claiming the direct guidance of the Holy Spirit.

DAY 39

CLARE BOOTH LUCE (1903–1987)

An age of unbelief—

"The climax of Catholic Instruction concerns the Doctrine of the Divinity of Jesus Christ. The historical and intellectual proofs of that Doctrine are many, and curiously compelling. They are so compelling indeed that for 1900 years even those who refused to believe them were at all times under the fiercest of inner compulsions to rationalize their disbeliefs. Never have so many men, and men often with superior minds, spent so much time and effort to disprove an 'error.' That circumstance alone is suspicious. Errors have an extraordinarily simple way of disproving themselves. Today, freedom from worship prevails everywhere. There is no condign punishment and no social ostracism attached to atheism and often much prestige. And still one can seldom find a book by a well-known scientist,

philosopher, sociologist, historian or psychoanalyst which does not devote pages to lengthy explanations of why the author cannot accept the Divinity of Jesus. Paradoxically enough, in most books by Western authors we are cautioned to hold on to Christian 'virtues' and 'principles,' but to do away with the belief in the Christ. This is much as though the authors should advocate that we keep our streets and houses well lighted, but do away with power plants."[39]

"The 'Real' Reason," 1947

Born in New York City, Clare Boothe Luce grew to be a dazzling beauty with a keen intellect; she used both attributes to excel in the world of publishing, theatre, film, and politics. Her father left her family when she was eight, and her first marriage at twenty was over in six years. But her second marriage to the co-founder and editor of Time, Inc., Henry R. Luce, placed her at the center of East Coast society. After a stint at *Vanity Fair*, Luce left to write for the theatre; her play, *The Women* (1936), about wealthy New York City women was a hit and was made into an equally successful film in 1939. When her nineteen-year-old child died, she went to Bishop Fulton Sheen and, as a consequence, entered the Church in 1946.

---

39 Clare Boothe Luce, "The 'Real' Reason," *Crisis*, December 1, 1987. Read at https://www.crisismagazine.com/1987/the-real-reason.

DAY 40

ROBERT R. REILLY (1946–)

God prefers the tonic—

"However, the hieratic role of music was lost for most of the 20th century before the belief on which it was based was lost. Philosophical propositions have a very direct and profound impact on composers and the kind of music they produce. John Adams, one of the most popular American composers today, said that he had 'learned in college that tonality died somewhere around the time that Nietzsche's God died, and I believed it.' The connection between the two is quite compelling. At the same time God disappears, so does the intelligible order in creation. A world without God is literally unnatural. If there is no God, there is no Nature, that is, the normal and ideal character of reality. Stripped of its normative power, reality no longer serves as a reflection of its Creator."[40]

Robert E. Reilly, "Is Music Sacred," 2016

Robert R. Reilly, born in 1946, is Director of the Westminster Institute. In his twenty-five years of government service, he has taught at National Defense University and served in the office of the secretary of defense, where he was senior advisor for

---

40 Robert R. Reilly and Jens F. Laurson, *Surprised by Beauty: A Listener's Guide to the Recovery of Modern Music* (San Francisco, Ignatius Press, 2016), 21.

information strategy (2002–2006). He was appointed director of the Voice of America, where he had worked the prior decade. Mr. Reilly served in the White House as a special assistant to the president (1983–1985) and in the US Information Agency, both in DC. He has published widely on foreign policy, the "war of ideas", and classical music. His books include *America on Trial: A Defense of the Founding* (2020) and *The Closing of the Muslim Mind: How Intellectual Suicide Created the Modern Islamist Crisis* (2010).

DAY 41

CORNELIO FABRO (1911–1995)

The metaphysical problem—

"The problem of atheism, of the loss of God, provides the key to the burning problems of our day: the loss of man, the radical desperation, the profound despair that is presently throttling all the peoples of the world, and the very mastery of the most hidden forces of nature. The difficulty does indeed lie at a deeper level and would appear from a purely structural analysis of the opposite teaching: the riddle of man is not simply phenomenological; it is strictly metaphysical. The uneasiness gnawing at modern man is not to be eliminated by a simple formal recourse to the Absolute. Indeed, this improperly assimilated

Absolute solves nothing and even represents a new danger, only increasing the uneasiness and confusion of mind.... Only a natural religion lived in its fullness or a total commitment to Christianity can cope with the task of an effective cleansing of existence and provide the real foundation of freedom."[41]

God in Exile, 1964

Cornelio Fabro was an Italian priest, a member of the Stigmatine Order, who played a major role in the Thomistic revival of the twentieth century. Fabro earned his doctorate from the Lateran University at the age of twenty. His philosophical work emphasized the role of "participation" in Thomistic metaphysics and the influence of St. Augustine and Neo-Platonic thinkers on St. Thomas Aquinas. He taught at a variety of universities in Urbino, Naples, Padua, Rome, Milan, and Perugia. A multi-volume selected works of Fabro in English is presently underway by the Cornelio Fabro Cultural Project. Fabro's *God in Exile* is a magisterial account of modern philosophy and critique of modern atheism beginning with Descartes.

---

41 Cornelio Fabro, *God in Exile: modern atheism;: A study of the internal dynamic of modern atheism, from its roots in the Cartesian cogito to the present day*, trans. Arthur Gibson, foreword by John Macquarrie (New York: Newman Press, 1968), 2.

DAY 42

RICHARD CRASHAW (1613–1649)

Satan

Below the bottom of the great Abyss,
There where one centre reconciles all things,
The world's profound heart pants; there placed is
Mischief's old Master! close about him clings
A curled knot of embracing snakes, that kiss
His correspondent cheeks: these loathsome strings
Hold the perverse prince in eternal ties,
Fast bound since first he forfeited the skies.

Heaven's golden-winged herald late he saw
To a poor Galilean virgin sent;
How long the bright youth bowed, and with what awe
Immortal flowers to her fair hand present:
He saw the old Hebrew's womb neglect the law
Of age and barrenness; and her Babe prevent
His birth by his devotion, who began
Betimes to be a saint before a man!

Yet, on the other side, fain would he start
Above his fears, and think it cannot be:
He studies Scripture, strives to sound the heart
And feel the pulse of every prophecy,

He knows, but knows not how, or by what art
The heaven-expecting ages hope to see
A mighty Babe, whose pure, unspotted birth
From a chaste virgin womb should bless the earth!

But these vast mysteries his senses smother,
And reason, — for what's faith to him! — devour,
How she that is a maid should prove a mother,
Yet keep inviolate her virgin flower:
How God's eternal Son should be man's brother,
Poseth his proudest intellectual power;
How a pure spirit should incarnate be,
And life itself wear death's frail livery.

That the great angel-blinding light should shrink
His blaze, to shine in a poor shepherd's eye;
That the unmeasured God so low should sink
As prisoner in a few poor rags to lie; milk should drink,
Who feeds with nectar Heaven's fair family;
That a vile manger his low bed should prove
Who in a throne of stars thunders above.

That He whom the sun serves, should faintly peep
Through clouds of infant flesh: that He the old
Eternal Word would be a child, and weep;
That He who made the fire should feel the cold;
That Heaven's high Majesty his court should keep
In a clay-cottage, by each blast controlled:

That Glory's self should serve our griefs and fears:
And free Eternity submit to years.[42]

Richard Crashaw describes the fallen angel Satan entrapped by his obsessive devotion to reason. Satan cannot grasp, for example, "How a pure spirit should incarnate be," the Incarnation itself. Crashaw describes what Satan cannot comprehend in even greater detail: "That a vile manger his low bed should prove / Who in a throne of stars thunders above." Satan is mocked as "The world's profound heart" surrounded by a" curled knot of embracing snakes." The poet never mentions pride explicitly, but pride's rage seethes just below the surface of every line, the final blow being that God would send himself to "serve our griefs and fears: / And free Eternity submit to years." Richard Crashaw himself was an Anglican priest who converted to Catholicism after leaving England to avoid imprisonment by Oliver Cromwell, whose Puritan forces had taken over the government. Crashaw eventually settled in Rome, where after a time of political struggle, he taught at the Venerable English College and served at the cathedral in Loreto.

---

42 Richard Crashaw, "Satan," PoemHunter.com, https://www.poemhunter.com/poem/satan-12/.

DAY 43

CARDINAL AVERY DULLES, SJ (1918–2008)

Some initial fear—

"Having become a Catholic, I was surprised to discover that my conversion had scarcely begun. I had previously imagined that I would instantly embark upon a heroic course of action. I had imagined that I would not share the weakness and timidity which made the Catholic men and women of my acquaintance act so much like their non-Catholic neighbors. In this I was wrong, totally wrong. One's human nature remains, and with it all the tendencies of pride and selfishness which faith condemns. I find myself, as a Catholic, incapable of living without compromise according to my beliefs. Indeed, my faith, strong as it is, has penetrated only a small portion of my mind. . . . When it comes to the most elemental acts of public devotion, I am so embarrassed to appear different from others that it is a painful effort even to bless myself at meals."[43]

A Testimonial to Grace, 1946

Cardinal Avery Dulles, SJ, lived long enough to witness some of the reforms he had urged as a young theologian turned into something he didn't have in mind at all (based upon several

---

43 Avery Dulles, *A Testimonial to Grace* (New York: Sheed and Ward, 1946), 117–18.

personal conversations). The book he had in mind was the hugely influential *Models of the Church* (1974). He was born into a prominent Protestant family, but by the time he matriculated to Harvard University, he was doubting Presbyterianism, and in 1940, he converted to Catholicism. Though he publicly opposed the war, Dulles served as a Navy officer in WWII, and for his liaison work with the French Navy, Dulles was awarded the French *Croix de guerre*. After the war, Dulles entered the Jesuits in 1946 and was ordained in 1956. He taught at Fordham and the Catholic University of America, publishing twenty-three books and over seven hundred book reviews and articles. Dulles was created a cardinal on February 21, 2001 by Pope John Paul II.

DAY 44

ALEXIS DE TOCQUEVILLE (1805–1859)

Freedom and faith—

"There are others, however, who see the republic as a permanent and tranquil state, a necessary goal towards which ideas and mores are steadily sweeping modern societies, and who would sincerely like to prepare men to be free. When people such as these attack religious beliefs, they obey their passions rather than their interests. Despotism can do without faith,

but freedom cannot. Religion is much more necessary in the republic they advocate than in the monarchy they attack, and most necessary of all in a democratic republic. How can society fail to perish if all political bonds are loosened, and more moral bonds are not tightened? And what is to be done with a people that is its own master, if not obedient to God?[44]

Democracy in America, 1835–1840

Alexis de Tocqueville supported the July Revolution of 1830 and supported the liberal constitutional government of Louis Phillipe that succeeded. He and a friend, Gustave de Beaumont, visited America in 1831 to study its prison system, and travelled throughout the country as it was then demarcated. His two-volume account of his travels, *Democracy in America* (1835 and 1840) found much wanting in the culture and individualism of the young democracy. But aside from his inclination to find fault, Tocqueville admired the sheer will, liberty, and ingenuity of the citizenry. He warned above all against the decline of religion which he, as a Catholic, believed leavened society with a necessary humility before traditional moral principles. After his trip to America, he became a member of the Chamber of Deputies. Poor health led to his death in 1859.

---

44 Alexis de Tocqueville, *Democracy in America*, trans. George Lawrence, ed. J.P. Mayer (New York: Harper Perennial Modern Classics, New York, NY, 2006), 340.

DAY 45

CHRISTOPHER DERRICK (1921–2007)

All the false smiles—

"The fear of Venus, the flight from sexual reality, is a conspic-
uous thing indeed. The case against Playboy and everything
similar is that one's attention is thereby fixed, not upon sex,
but upon sexual unreality. So far as the observer is concerned,
those are not real girls. They are never going to sulk, or answer
back rudely, or turn awkwardly recalcitrant in this way or that,
and they are not going to make tearful accusations of preg-
nancy. Their welcoming smiles are fixed forever and are forever
false: they are not even shaped like most real girls, since only an
exceptionally well-formed few get accepted for this well-paid
work of the model, as corresponding to the ideal currently
cherished by male fantasy. They are further removed from reality by the fact that the camera (which always lies, since it abol-
ishes time) isolates them from growth and change: they will
never grow older, each of them will remain fixed eternally at
the precise moment of transition from schoolgirl to whore."[45]

Sex and Sacredness, 1982

---

45 Christopher Derrick, *Sex and Sacredness* (San Francisco: Ignatius Press,
   1982), 167.

After attending Oxford and serving in WWII, Christopher Derrick married Helen Sharratt and had nine children. Derrick was printing officer of the University of London, as well as working as a reader for Macmillan from 1953 to 1965 before beginning his career as an independent writer. Derrick's tutor at Oxford was C. S. Lewis; he was asked so many times why Lewis never became a Catholic that he wrote *C. S. Lewis and the Church of Rome* (1981). His list of apologetic works is long and all are noted for an ease and beauty of style found in his tutor's work. *Escape from Skepticism* (1977) was a tribute to the Great Books program at Thomas Aquinas College in California. Other books include *The Delicate Creation: Towards a Theology of the Environment* (1972), *Joy Without a Cause: Selected Essays of Christopher Derrick* (1979), *The Rule of Peace: St. Benedict and the European Future* (1980), and *Church Authority and Intellectual Freedom* (1981).

DAY 46

ARNOLD LUNN (1888–1974)

Self-contradictions—

"The principle characteristic of modern philosophy is an implicit premise which, in effect, denies the validity of all philosophy. If Marx and Freud are to be believed, neither Freud

nor Marx should be believed. Marx maintained that the religion, philosophy and art of a given period are the by-products
of its economic processes. [Therefore] Scholastic theology is
nothing more than the mirror of the feudal system of land tenure. But, if this be true, Marxist Communism is nothing more
than the mirror of the laissez-faire liberalism and industrialism
of Victorian England. It has no objective validity. Freud maintained that the reasons with which a man justifies his beliefs are
nothing more than the rationalizations invented, post hoc, to
justify beliefs imposed on him by his environmental and sexual
complexes. We can safely ignore the reasoned arguments with
which a man defends his belief by psychoanalyzing the man in
question. If this be true, we shall learn all that is worth knowing about Freudianism by psycho-analyzing the Freudian. The
modern thinkers are busily engaged in sawing away the branch
on which they are sitting."[46]

Come What May, 1940

Before Arnold Lunn converted to Catholicism at the age of
forty-five, he had been a lay Methodist minister and a cham-
pion skier and mountaineer. Lunn invented slalom skiing, got
it established as part of the Olympic Games, and received a
knighthood for his contribution to British-Swiss relations. In
1924, he published a book, *Roman Converts*, highly critical of

---

46 Arnold Lunn, *Come What May: An Autobiography* (London: Eyre and Spottiswoode, 1940), 202-3.

Newman, Chesterton, and Knox, among others, but it was a year-long exchange of letters with Msgr. Ronald Knox that led to his conversion in 1933. His list of apologetic works include *A Saint in the Slave Trade* (1939), *The Third Day* (1941), *Revolt Against Reason* (1951), and two books of correspondence with nonbelievers, *Science and the Supernatural: A Correspondence Between Arnold Lunn and J. B. S. Haldane* (1935) and *Is Christianity True? A Correspondence Between Arnold Lunn and C. E. M. Joad* (1943).

DAY 47

ALLAN TATE (1899–1979)

The force of human nature—

"Man is a creature that in the long run has got to believe in order to know, and to know in order *to do*. For doing without knowing is machine behavior, illiberal and servile routine, the secularism with which man's specific destiny has no connection. I take it that we have sufficient evidence, generation after generation, that man will never be completely or permanently enslaved. He will rebel, as he is rebelling now, in a shocking variety of 'existential' disorders, all over the world. If his *human nature* as such cannot participate in the action of society, he will not capitulate to it, if that action is inhuman: he will turn

in upon himself, with the common gesture which throughout history has vindicated the rhetoric of liberty: 'Give me liberty or give me death.' Man may destroy himself but he will not at last tolerate anything less than his full human condition."[47]

"The Man of Letters in the Modern World," 1952

A native of Kentucky, Allan Tate entered Vanderbilt University in 1918 and joined a group of poets and writers who would have considerable importance in the decades after WWI. This group first called the Southern Agrarians consisted of twelve notable writers, including John Crowe Ransom, Donald Davidson, and Robert Penn Warren who espoused the ethos of the Deep South in poetry, essays, and novels. Tate moved to New York where he scraped out a living working for various literary magazines. His first book of poetry in 1928 contained his most famous poem, "Ode to the Confederate Dead." After meeting fellow writer Caroline Gordon, the two began living together, ending up living together in the home of the poet Hart Crane. Tate and Gordon married in 1925—it was to be a stormy marriage because of Tate's infidelities. After divorcing and remarrying, Tate and Gordon separated for good in 1959. Tate's conversion in 1950 at the age of fifty-one came after twenty years of intellectual flirtation with religious ideas. A book of essays published after the conversion, *The Forlorn*

---

47 Allan Tate, *Essays of Four Decades, The Man of Letters in the Modern World* (New York: William Morrow and Company, Inc., 1970), 7.

Demon (1953), expressed his new Catholic and Thomistic world view. He saw in the Church the answer to the problems of secular modernity.

DAY 48

BARTOLOMEO DE LAS CASAS, OP (1484–1566)

They are our brothers—

"Again, if we want to be sons of Christ and followers of the truth of the gospel, we should consider that, even though these people may be completely barbaric, they are nevertheless created in God's image. They are not so forsaken by divine providence that they are incapable of attaining Christ's kingdom. They are our brothers, redeemed by Christ's most precious blood, no less than the wisest and the most learned men in the whole world. Finally, we must consider it possible that some of them are predestined to become renowned and glorious in Christ's kingdom."[48]

In Defense of the Indians, 1550

---

48 Bartolomeo de las Casas, *In Defense of the Indians*, trans. Stafford Poole, C.M. (Dekalb: Northern Illinois University Press, 1992), 39.

Bartolomeo de las Casas, OP, was a Dominican friar who spent fifty years defending the human dignity of indigenous people and attacking the practice of slavery. His writing reflects the Christian foundation of the ideas of human rights and human dignity that would not be widely accepted until the late eighteenth century. He knew what he was talking about since de las Casas had himself been a slave owner and colonist on the island of Hispaniola near Cuba. In 1510, he became the first priest to be ordained in the New World. However, as a priest, he continued to serve as a chaplain in Spain's military colonization of more land. He was rewarded with more land and slaves. It was in 1514 while reading in the book of Sirach, chapter 34:18–22, he realized the treatment of indigenous tribes was morally wrong and illegal. Those lines read, "If one sacrifices from what has been wrongfully obtained, the offering is blemished; the gifts of the lawless are not acceptable. The Most High is not pleased with the offerings of the ungodly; and he is not propitiated for sins by a multitude of sacrifices. Like one who kills a son before his father's eyes is the man who offers a sacrifice from the property of the poor. The bread of the needy is the life of the poor; whoever deprives them of it is a man of blood. To take away a neighbor's living is to murder him; to deprive an employee of his wages is to shed blood."

DAY 49

JOHANNES JORGENSEN (1866–1956)

Saved from the abyss—

"And it seemed as if a ray of love passed through me. One little ray of compassionate love. Then it was as if my whole being melted. All the crushing self-contempt, all the hardened hopelessness, the feeling of baseness and impurity retreated and was swept away by an inrushing stream of cleansing, consuming light. I felt that it was the Lord of Life who was coming to my aid; He who had promised that not even a cup of cold water given to a disciple shall go unrewarded. That tiny, almost imperceptible movement of love has been like a hand stretched out to the Lord of Love. And He has seized it. . . . He had saved me on the brink of the abyss."[49]

An Autobiography, 1929

Johannes Jorgensen was a Danish writer who was nominated for the Nobel Prize for Literature five times but never won. As a young political radical in Copenhagen, Jorgensen flirted with nihilism and the rejection of Christianity until he met a Jewish convert to Catholicism, Mogens Ballin, and began exploring mysticism. With Ballin in 1894, Jorgensen visited the Basilica of

---

49 Johannes Jorgensen, *An Autobiography*, two volumes, trans. Ingeborg Lund (London: Longman, Green and Co., 1929), 125.

St. Francis, which led to his conversion in 1896. Because of his considerable stature as a poet and man of letters, his conversion caused a considerable public stir throughout Scandinavia. He published his biography of St. Francis in 1907 (English trans. 1912) and translated the *Fioretti* of St. Francis into Danish. His first novel about the German invasion of Belgium in 1914 elicited official German complaints to the Danish government as well as legal action. He moved to Assisi in 1915, where he lived into the war years of 1943–45. He published major biographies of St. Catherine of Siena (1915) and St. Bridget of Sweden. His autobiography was written between 1916 and 1927.

DAY 50

JACQUES MARITAIN (1882–1973)

Progress has two edges—

"But what I would like to emphasize particularly now is that the parable of the wheat and the cockle has a universal meaning and bearing which is valid for the world as well as for the kingdom of grace. And we must say, from the philosophical point of view, that the movement of progression of societies in time depends on this law of double movement—which might be called, in this instance, the law of degradation, on the one

hand, and the revitalization, on the other, of the energy of history, or the mass of human activity on which the movement of history depends. While the wear and tear of time and the passivity of matter naturally dissipate and degrade the things of this world and the energy of history, the creative forces which are proper to the spirit and to liberty and which are their proof, and which normally have their point of application in the effort of the few, constantly revitalize the quality of this energy. Thus the life of human societies advances and progresses at the cost of many losses."[50]

On the Philosophy of History, 1957

Jacques Maritain published this book based upon lectures he gave at the University of Notre Dame in 1955. He makes an important point about *progress* in history that seems to be unknown to modern historians—it is this: progress in morality and politics, the good, is accompanied by progress in evil. Over the past century, we have witnessed great advances in the recognition of human equality and human rights, while at the same time seeing a terrible increase in the number of abortions and a gradual forgetting of the natural law. Technology reached great heights with the discovery of nuclear energy, which, sadly, has made the extermination of all life on Earth a possibility.

---

50 Jacques Maritain, *On the Philosophy of History*, ed. Joseph W. Evans (New York: Scribner Publishing, 1957), 46–47.

DAY 51

FLANNERY O'CONNOR (1925–1964)

Beware of tenderness—

"In this popular pity, we mark our gain in sensibility and our loss in vision. If other ages felt less, they saw more, even though they saw with the blind, prophetical, unsentimental eye of acceptance, which is to say, faith. In the absence of this faith now, we govern by tenderness. It is a tenderness which, long since cut off from the person of Christ, is wrapped in theory. When tenderness is detached from the source of tenderness, its logical outcome is terror. It ends in forced-labor camps and in the fumes of the gas chamber."[51]

"Introduction," *Memoir of Mary Ann*, 1961

Flannery O'Connor wrote this introduction at the request of the Dominican Sisters of Hawthorne at Our Lady of Perpetual Help Cancer Home in Atlanta (established in 1939). Mary Ann Long lived at the home for twelve years—she was born in 1949 with an inoperable tumor on her face and was not expected to live. The next year her parents drove from Louisville and placed Mary Ann in the sisters' care. As she grew older, her personality and presence had a remarkably positive influence on both the

---

51 Flannery O'Connor, "Introduction,' *Memoir of Mary Ann By the Dominican Nuns Who Took Care of Her* (New York: Farrar, Straus and Giroux, 1961), 19.

sisters and the other children in the home. Mary Ann was baptized Catholic and died with a rosary in her hand at the age of twelve. The sisters approached O'Connor, who lived an hour away, to write about Mary Ann, but she convinced them that they needed to write it themselves. O'Connor edited the manuscript, added a luminous introduction, and it was published by a major New York publishing house.

DAY 52

BISHOP FULTON J. SHEEN (1895–1979)

The Devil's shortcuts—

"It is part of the discipline of God to make His loved ones perfect through trial and suffering. Only by carrying the Cross can one reach the Resurrection. It was precisely this part of Our Lord's Mission that the devil attacked. The temptations were meant to divert Our Lord from His task of salvation through sacrifice. Instead of the Cross as a means of winning the souls of men, Satan suggested three short cuts to popularity: an economic one, another based on marvels, and a third, which was political. Very few people believe in the devil these days, which suits the devil very well. He is always helping to circulate the news of his own death. The essence of God is existence, and He defines Himself as: "I am Who I am." The essence of the

devil is the lie, and he defines himself as: "I am who I am not." Satan has very little trouble with those who do not believe in him; they are already on his side."[52]

The Life of Christ, 1958

Bishop Fulton J. Sheen was an American bishop who had an unprecedented influence on our nation's culture. His NBC radio show, *The Catholic Hour,* was broadcast from 1930 to 1950 with a weekly audience of four million, and the TV programs in the '50s drew a larger viewership, thirty million, more than the hugely popular comedian Milton Berle. From the beginning of his career, as a priest in the Diocese of Peoria, Sheen's remarkable intellectual gifts were recognized. He taught philosophy at the Catholic University of America until 1951 when he was appointed auxiliary bishop of New York. He was made bishop of Rochester in 1966 but resigned in 1969. Sheen wrote seventy-three books, all remarkable for their combination of deep learning and readability. A cause of canonization began in 2002 and seemed headed toward finalization when the Vatican Congregation for the Causes of Saints postponed the beatification. However, the Venerable Fulton J. Sheen's legacy of radio, TV, lectures, and books remains an important and active part of the Church's evangelization.

---

52 Fulton J. Sheen, *Life of Christ* (General Press), loc. 67, Kindle Edition.

DAY 53

DANTE ALIGHIERI (1264–1327)

Dante enters the lowest circle of hell and sees Satan himself with three faces and "half his chest sticking out of the ice."

Under each face protruded two great wings,
Each as would seem right for a bird that size,
Broader than any sea-sails I ever saw.

They had no feathers, but their make-up was
More like a bat's: and he so fluttered them
That three several winds went out from him.

It was by them all Cocytus was frozen;
With six eyes he wept, and down three chins
Dripped tears and dribble, mixed with blood.

In each mouth he was chewing with his teeth
A sinner, as if pounding him with spikes,
So that he kept the three of them in torment.

For the one who was in front, the biting was nothing
Compared with the clawing, so that at times his spine
Was left stripped of every scrap of skin.

'The soul there, which has the worst punishment,

Is Judas Iscariot, my master said,
'With his head inside and kicking his legs.'[53]

Inferno, Canto XXXIV

Between 1308 and 1320, Dante Alighieri wrote *The Divine Comedy*, his poetic trilogy of a journey of a pilgrim from earth to hell, purgatory, and paradise. His 14,233 lines reflect the life of a man who was deeply versed in philosophy and theology along with a first-hand knowledge of secular and religious politics. Reading the *Commedia* is staggering and edifying like no other work of imagination.

DAY 54

ANDREW LYTLE (1902–1995)

On identity—

"Our trouble with identity depends upon the acceptance of the world as the end in itself, not the stage where the drama of the soul, salvation or damnation, is played. This is particularly western and Christian. I once in an essay spoke of the second fall of man, the fall into history: that is, man judging man as

---

53 Dante, *The Divine Comedy: a new verse translation by C.H. Sisson* (Carcanet New Press Limited, 1980), 148.

final truth. This was particularly relevant to the Nineteenth Century, where people asked the question, What will history think of this—not was the act a good act. History made no answer, but man made a-plenty."[54]

From Eden to Babylon, 1990

Andrew Lytle graduated from Vanderbilt University in 1925 and would achieve fame as part of "The Fugitives and Southern Agrarians" in the late '20 and '30s. These groups espoused a cultural and religious conservatism based on the values of Southern rural culture. Their manifesto, *I'll Take My Stand: The South and the Agrarian Tradition* (1930), contained essays by John Crowe Ransom, Donald Davidson, Allen Tate, Robert Penn Warren, and Lytle. They were incensed by the mocking of the South by H. L. Mencken's coverage of the famous Monkey Trial in Tennessee. Lytle taught at the Universities of Florida, Iowa, and Kentucky, Kenyon College, and the University of the South, where he edited the *Sewanee Review* from 1961 to 1973. He lived in a log cabin at the Monteagle Sunday School Assembly, grew his own crops, and lived without the aid of a telephone or television, to say nothing of a computer. Lytle wrote novels, short stories, essays, and a biography of his Civil War hero Nathan Bedford Forrest. *Velvet Horn* (1957) is considered his best novel. Late in life, Lytle published an exquisite

---

54 Andrew Lytle, *From Eden to Babylon: The Social and Political Essays of Andrew Nelson Lytle*, ed. with introduction by M.E. Bradford (Washington, DC: Regnery Gateway, 1990), 217.

reading of Sigrid Undset's trilogy *Kristin Lavransdatter* entitled *Kristin: A Reading* (1992). His Civil War novel, *The Long Night* (1936), had the misfortune of being published the same year as *Gone with the Wind*.

DAY 55

STANLEY L. JAKI (1924–2009)

God made the world knowable—

"To possess oneself is a fine thing, *but to find only one's sole self at the end of the quest* for the ultimate in intelligibility is in essence to lose hold of oneself. This at least seems to be one of the lessons science provides through its history. Science failed to become an open-ended avenue in the great ancient cultures as their quest for the ultimate in intelligibility, which is the quest for God, *failed to go convincingly beyond man's own self* and its cosmic extrapolation, an animated and self-contained nature. The ultimate in intelligibility was first placed firmly on a level transcending both man and nature during the Middle Ages and in a way that constituted a cultural matrix. It manifested a broadly shared conviction that a personal, rational, and provident Being, absolute and eternal, is the ultimate source of intelligibility insofar as he is the Creator of all things visible and invisible. Its most articulate spokesmen were mendicant

friars committed to an evangelical vision of man and world, a vision in which the order, beauty, and peace of nature were a shining reflection of the Creator and Father of all."⁵⁵ (Emphasis added.)

The Road of Science and the Ways to God, 1978

Stanley L. Jaki, born in Hungary, was a Benedictine priest who held doctorates in both theology and physics. His work in the philosophy of science established that Western science was built upon the foundation of the medieval worldview, one that deemed the entire cosmos intelligible, knowable to human reason because it was created through the Divine Word. Father Jaki served as a Distinguished University Professor at Seton Hall University from 1975 until his death.

DAY 56

EVELYN WAUGH (1903–1966)

Enough is enough—

"Just go on — alone. How can I tell what I shall do? You know the whole of me. You know I'm not one for a life of mourning.

---

55 Stanley L. Jaki, *The Road of Science and the Ways to God* (Chicago: The University of Chicago Press, 1978), 34.

I've always been bad. Probably I shall be bad again, punished again. But the worse I am, the more I need God. I can't shut myself out from His mercy. This is what it would mean; starting a new life with you, without Him. One can only hope to see one step ahead. But I saw to-day there was one thing unforgivable — like things in the schoolroom, so bad they are unpunishable, that only Mummy could deal with — the bad thing I was on the point of doing, that I'm not quite bad enough to do; to set up a rival good to God's."[56]

Brideshead Revisited, 1945

Evelyn Waugh converted to Catholicism in 1930. He had already published the highly successful novels *Decline and Fall* (1929) and *Vile Bodies* (1930). Being a public figure, Waugh published a short account of his conversion in the *Daily Express*, "Why It Happened to Me," on October 20, 1930. Waugh took an active part in the society of the aristocrats and Bohemians he satirized in his early work. He traveled widely as a newspaper correspondent in the '30s before joining the British army in WWII. His experiences as a soldier became central to many of his best-known novels—*Brideshead Revisited* (1945) and the *Sword of Honour* trilogy (1952–1961). *Brideshead* became familiar to the general public through the excellent 1981 TV series starring Jeremy Irons and Anthony Andrews.

---

56 Evelyn Waugh, *Brideshead Revisited: The Sacred and Profane Memories of Captain Charles Rider* (Boston: Little, Brown and Company, 1973), 356.

His Catholic faith, stalwartly anti-Vatican II, was expressed directly in *Edmund Campion, Jesuit and Martyr* (1947), *Helena. A Novel* (1950), and *Msgr. Ronald Knox* (1956). Oxford University Press is in the process of publishing the forty-three-volume complete works edited by his grandson Alexander Waugh.

DAY 57

ST. ATHANASIUS (296–373)

Choosing to die—

"The Word perceived that corruption could not be got rid of otherwise than through death; yet He Himself, as the Word, being immortal and the Father's Son, was such as could not die. For this reason, therefore, He assumed a body capable of death, in order that it, through belonging to the Word Who is above all, might become in dying a sufficient exchange for all, and, itself remaining incorruptible through His indwelling, might thereafter put an end to corruption for all others as well, by the grace of the resurrection. It was by surrendering to death the body which He had taken, as an offering and sacrifice free from every stain, that He forthwith abolished death for His human brethren by the offering of the equivalent. For naturally, since the Word of God was above all, when He offered His own temple and bodily instrument as a substitute for the

life of all, He fulfilled in death all that was required. Naturally also, through this union of the immortal Son of God with our human nature, all men were clothed with incorruption in the promise of the resurrection. For the solidarity of mankind is such that, by virtue of the Word's indwelling in a single human body, the corruption which goes with death has lost its power over all. You know how it is when some great king enters a large city and dwells in one of its houses; because of his dwelling in that single house, the whole city is honored, and enemies and robbers cease to molest it. Even so is it with the King of all; He has come into our country and dwelt in one body amidst the many, and in consequence the designs of the enemy against mankind have been foiled and the corruption of death, which formerly held them in its power, has simply ceased to be. For the human race would have perished utterly had not the Lord and Savior of all, the Son of God, come among us to put an end to death."[57]

On the Incarnation, 335

St. Athanasius was the bishop of Alexandria over a period of forty-five years which was interrupted by periods of exile totaling seventeen years ordered by various Roman emperors.

---

57 Athanasius of Alexandria, *On the Incarnation*, 2.9 (Blue Letter Bible), loc 7–8, Kindle Edition.

His famous treatise *On the Incarnation* demonstrates his theological and spiritual insight that helped to defeat the Arian heresy.

DAY 58

JOHN SENIOR (1923–1999)

Actions reap habits—

"We become the work we do. If farming reflects Divine attributes, farmers through their work become something like God. Appearances are not only signs of reality but in a sense are like sacraments; they effect what they signify. I mean that there is a cause-effect relation between the work we do, the clothes we wear or do not wear, the houses we live in, the walls or lack of walls, the landscape, the semiconscious sights, sounds, smells, tastes and touches of our ordinary lives—a close connection between these and the moral and spiritual development of souls. It is ridiculous but nonetheless true that a generation which has given up the distinction between fingers and forks will find it difficult to keep the distinction between

affection and sex or between a right to one's body and the murder of one's child."[58]

The Restoration of Christian Culture, 1983

Born in New York in 1923, John Senior studied at Columbia University under the legendary Mark Van Doren, went on to teach at Hofstra, Bard, Cornell, and the University of Wyoming, before taking a post in the Classics and English Departments of the University of Kansas where he met and teamed up with Professors Dennis Quinn and Frank Nelick to form the Integrated Humanities Program in 1970. His teaching and spirituality profoundly influenced several generations of students. As one student describes it, "He drew us, his students (his *discipuli*) towards the Truth, and then let us go, to tread the path on our own. When we stumbled, which was often enough, he was always there with a kind word, a nod to help us on our way again." The Integrated Humanities Program was shut down in 1979 because its growing reputation and the number of conversions threatened the secular standing of the University. His two books, *The Death of Christian Culture* and *The Restoration of Christian Culture,* attest to the legacy of a great Catholic teacher who did not compromise with the spirit of the age.

---

58 John Senior, *The Restoration of Christian Culture* (San Francisco, Ignatius Press, 1983), 222.

DAY 59

RENÉ GIRARD (1923–2015)

What Satan cannot see—

"The idea of Satan duped by the Cross is therefore not magical at all and in no way offends the dignity of God. The trick that traps Satan does not include the least bit of either violence or dishonesty on God's part. It is not really a ruse or trick; it is rather the inability of the prince of this world to understand the divine love. If Satan does not see God, it is because he is violent contagion itself. The devil is extremely clever concerning everything having to do with rivalistic conflicts, with scandals and their outcome in persecution, but he is blind to all reality other than that. Satan turns bad contagion into something I hope not to do myself, a totalitarian and infallible theory that makes the theoretician deaf and blind to the love of God for humankind and to the love that human beings share with God, however imperfectly."[59]

I See Satan Fall Like Lightning, 1999

René Girard is recognized worldwide for his theory of human behavior and human culture. Born in France, he attended a *grandes école* before moving to the United States, receiving his

---

59 René Girard, *I See Satan Fall Like Lightning*, trans. James G. Williams (Ossining: Orbis Books, 2012), loc. 152, Kindle Edition.

doctorate from Indiana University, then teaching at Duke, Bryn Mawr, and Johns Hopkins, where he published his first book, *Deceit, Desire and the Novel* (1966). Subsequent influential books led to Stanford University, where he taught until his retirement. In the course of his career, Girard developed a unique theory about how *mimesis* (imitation) operates in the violence of scapegoating. Girard saw in history how societies become unified by a collective focus on destroying a scapegoat who is blamed for the various wrongs being suffered in the community. His acknowledged contribution to the understanding of Scripture was in pointing out killing the scapegoat is unjust, and the crucifixion of Jesus reveals the truth about mob violence. In essence, the collective violence violates justice, and the self-described victims perpetrating the violence are always viewed as innocent.

DAY 60

HEINRICH BÖLL (1917–1985)

This short story begins after a wedding. The priest accompanies the wedding party to a breakfast nearby. The priest, who had been moved by the piety of the newly-married couple, inserts himself into the conversation after one of the wedding party proposes those present should create a "club."

"I'm convinced many club members who attend church regularly and are 'good' Christians would be far more upset,

perhaps even stirred to revolutionary action in spite of their normal apathy, if one of their club rules were broken—or club funds misused—far more upset than they would be if a sentence were to be struck from the Credo. That's only by way of example. Whether these things are called current fashion, sports, dance, exercise, or the cinema—or, as is most often the case, money—they are generally nothing more than well-laid, almost comfortably middle-class traps set by Satan. He consumes the still healthy core within them, using them—in nice, decent middle-class fashion (most people are too lazy, tired, and dull to sin wildly)—to divert people gradually from the truth—or better yet, from the tiny residue of truth that would have saved them. And when things take their natural course: Beauty is derided, the feeling for beauty is corroded, desire is whipped into a frenzy. It's easy to brew a vile broth from such swamps. So if someone truly wants to start a new club, it should be a 'Club for the Friends of the Absolute.' But that already exists. . . . It's called the Church."[60]

"Youth On Fire," 1935

The German writer Heinrich Böll won the Nobel Prize in 1972. A native of Cologne, he was raised in a liberal Catholic and pacifist family. After a youthful trial run as a bookseller, he was drafted into the national labor service in 1938 for six months. Afterward, Böll began his studies in Classical languages

---

60 Heinrich Böll, "Youth On Fire," *The Mad Dog Stories*, trans. Breon Mitchell (New York: St. Martin's Press, 1997), 42.

and Germanistics but was soon drafted once again, this time into the German army, where he served until the end of the war. He started writing in order to receive a food rationing card which required proof of an occupation. With his first novel, *The Train Was on Time* (1949), which recorded some of his experiences as a soldier, Böll became a leading voice in post-war German fiction. His best-known novels include *Billiards at Half-Past Nine* (1959), *The Clown* (1963), *Group Portrait with Lady* (1971), *The Lost Honor of Katharina Blum* (1974), and *The Safety Net* (1979).

DAY 61

HANS URS VON BALTHASAR (1905–1988)

A father's love—

"Man is led into the open realm in which he can love by the love he believes in because he has understood its sign. If the Prodigal Son had not already believed in his father's love, he would have never set out on his homeward journey—even though the love that received him back was beyond his dreams. The decisive thing is that the sinner has heard of a love that could be and actually is open to him: the initiative is not his; God has already seen in him the unloving sinner, the child he

loves as his son, and it is in the light of his own love that God considers him and confers his dignity upon him."[61]

Love Alone, 1963

One of the closest friends of Hans Urs von Balthasar was the greatest Protestant theologian of the twentieth century, Karl Barth (1886–1968). In spite of their deep theological differences, they had much in common: a love for Mozart, reproductions of the Grünewald crucifixion hanging over their desks, and each wrote multi-volume systematic theologies. Barth's *Church Dogmatics* (1932–1967) was left unfinished, with twelve part-volumes being published before his death. Their friendship included sharing vacations, seminars, and constant correspondence. Towards the end of his life, von Balthasar said of his multi-volume trilogy, "I wrote it all for Barth—to convert him." Von Balthasar also wrote one of the most perceptive studies of Barth's theology, *The Theology of Karl Barth* (1951). One of Barth's first books, *Anselm: Fides Quaerens Intellectum: Anselm's Proof of the Existence of God in the Context of His Theological Scheme* (1930), was a declaration of his fundamental differences with Catholic theology.

---

61 Hans Urs von Balthasar, *Love Alone: The Way of Revelation*, trans. and ed. Alexander Dru (London: Sheed and Ward, 1968), p. 84.

DAY 62

WALKER PERCY (1916–1990)

In The Thanatos Syndrome, *a priest pleads for life*—

"My brothers, let me tell you where tenderness leads."

A longer pause.

"To the gas chambers! On with the jets!

"Listen to me dear physicians, dear brothers, dear Qualitarians, abortionists, euthanasists! . . . Please do this one favor for me, dear doctors. If you have a patient, young or old, suffering, dying, afflicted, useless, born or unborn, whom you for the best of reasons wish to put out of his misery—I beg only one thing of you, dear doctors! Please send them to us. Don't kill them! We'll take them—all of them! Please send them to us! I swear to you you won't be sorry. We will all be happy about it! I promise you, and I know that you believe me, that we will take care of him, her—we will even call on you to help us take care of them!—and you will not have to make such a decision. God will bless you for it and you will offend no one except the Great Prince Satan, who rules the world. That is all."

Silence[62]

The Thanatos Syndrome, 1987

---

62 Walker Percy, *The Thanatos Syndrome* (New York: Farrar, Straus and Giroux, 1987), 361.

Walker Percy was one of the finest and most influential Catholic writers of the twentieth century. After his father's death, Percy moved to Mississippi to live with his uncle, William Alexander Percy. While in high school, Percy's mother drowned when her car plunged into a creek. He entered the University of North Carolina at Chapel Hill, and after graduating, he received his MD from the Columbia University medical school. While interning at Bellevue Hospital, Percy caught tuberculosis, which required complete bed rest for the next two years. During that time, he read voraciously in the existential philosophers and modern classics by Tolstoy and Dostoevsky. He moved to New Orleans knowing his medical career was over, got married, and decided to become a writer. Both Percy and his wife, Bunt, soon converted to Catholicism, which became an integral part of his fiction and non-fiction works. The Percy family, with an adopted daughter, moved to Covington, Louisiana, where he lived the rest of his life. When his first novel, *The Moviegoer* (1961), won the National Book Award, Percy's career was launched.

DAY 63

ALESSANDRO MANZONI (1785–1873)

The Betrothed tells the story of Renzo and Lucia whose marriage is thwarted by Don Rodrigo, the local feudal lord, who desires Lucia for

*himself. Both Renzo and Lucia escape from his scheme but are separated
by various tribulations. This scene comes towards the end of the novel:
Renzo has located where Lucia is staying in Milan in the midst of a
devastating plague. Father Cristoforo, an old friend, tells Renzo to look
in a certain chapel, and Renzo replied that if he cannot find her, he will
take revenge on Don Rodrigo.*

"'Miserable sinner!' cried Father Cristoforo, in a voice which
had recovered all its old full sonorous power. His head had
been bowed, but now it lifted itself proudly erect again; his
cheeks regained their old colour, and a strange and terrible
light came into his eyes. 'Look around you!' he went on. He
held Renzo fast, and shook his arm with one hand, while he
swept the other round in front of him to take in as much as
possible of that terrible scene. 'Look and see who it is that
chastiseth mankind, who it is that judgeth and is not judged,
who layeth on sore strokes and who granteth men his pardon! And you, worm that you are, crawling on the face of the
earth, you want to administer justice! You know what justice
is! Go, wretched sinner, leave my sight! And I hoped – yes, I
had hoped that before I died, God would have granted me
the happiness of knowing that my poor Lucia was still alive,
perhaps even of seeing her again, and of hearing her promise
to offer up a prayer over my grave. Go! for you have robbed
me of that hope. I know now that God has not left her in this
world for you. And you for your part cannot dare to hope, to
think yourself worthy that he should have any care for your
happiness. He will have taken thought for her, because she is

one of those souls that are destined to eternal felicity. Go! I have no more time to waste on listening to you!' He pushed Renzo's arm away from him, and walked off towards one of the huts where the sick lay. 'Ah, Father Cristoforo!' said Renzo beseechingly, following the friar. 'Are you really going to send me away like this?' 'What!' said the Capuchin, his voice no less severe than before. 'Do you dare to ask me to rob these poor people of the time I might give them, as they lie and wait for me to come and speak to them of the mercy of God, just so that I can listen to you, and your words of wrath, your plans for revenge? . . . 'I'll forgive him now! I really forgive him! I forgive him forever!' cried the young man. 'Renzo!' said the friar with calmer earnestness. 'Think for a moment; and then tell me how many times you have uttered those words before.' . . . You can hate your neighbour and lose your own soul."[63]

Those who like to argue about the "greatest Catholic novel" will often cite *The Betrothed* (1825–1827) by the Italian writer Alessandro Manzoni. While *The Betrothed* certainly belongs to the short list of great Catholic novels, no one disputes its status as a masterpiece, important both in the development of the novel form and the history of Italian literature. Manzoni chose to write his novel using a contemporary Florentine idiom to gather the largest possible readership. It worked—*The Betrothed*

---

63 Alessandro Manzoni, *The Betrothed*, trans. and introduction by Bruce Penman (London: Penguin Book Ltd, 1983), loc. 659-662, Kindle Edition.

became a great success immediately upon publication. For a novel so bursting with Catholic devotion, it's somewhat surprising to note that Manzoni abandoned his Catholic faith for Voltaire's skepticism as a young man in Paris. But after his Calvinist wife, Henriette Blondel, converted to Catholicism, he returned to the faith.

DAY 64

ST. THOMAS AQUINAS (1225–1274)

Sin leads to sin—

"We ourselves are weakened. Man believes that, once he has committed the sin, he will be able to keep from sin for the future. Experience shows that what really happens is quite otherwise. The effect of that first sin is to weaken the sinner and make him still more inclined to sin. Sin dominates man more and more, and man left to himself, whatever his powers, places himself in such a state that he cannot rise from it. Like a man who has thrown himself into a well, there he must lie, unless he is drawn up by some divine power. After the sin of Adam, then, our human nature was weaker, it had lost its perfection and men were more prone to sinning. . . . Man is so strengthened

by the Passion of Christ—and the effect of Adam's sin is so weakened—that he is no longer dominated by it."[64]

Meditations for Lent

It's sometimes forgotten that St. Thomas Aquinas was a Dominican preacher with the ability to speak effectively to anyone who would listen. His lively use of simile anticipates the master of simile himself, Dante: "Like a man who has thrown himself into a well, there he must lie, unless he is drawn up by some divine power." Also notable is his comment on how the human weakness caused by Original Sin is lessened by the passion of Christ. In other words, the human race was collectively lifted above the state they found themselves in after the Fall.

---

64 St. Thomas Aquinas, *Meditations for Lent*, trans. Father Philip Hughes (Fort Collins: Roman Catholic Books), 114; Father Hughes chose quotations from different places in the work of St. Thomas which is why no year is given for publication.

DAY 65

ELIZABETH FOX-GENOVESE (1941–2007)

Beyond the academy—

"The growing attention to euthanasia, assisted suicide, and partial-birth abortion steadily strengthened my conviction that individual human beings could not be entrusted with decisions about life and death and that a willingness to hold any life cheap or expendable corrupts those who claim the right to make those decisions. And the more I pondered, the more conscious I became of the hubris that pervades the secular academy and intelligentsia. Contemplating the pride of others made me only the more mindful of my own and of the danger lurking in our cavalier assumptions that our minds can encompass the consequences of our acts. Increasingly it seemed to me that the very material triumphs of modernity, including the dense interconnections of the far-flung parts of the globe—and increasingly, the universe—diminished our ability even to imagine the unforeseen consequences of our acts. Yet the escalating uncertainty and indeterminacy make the imperative of a moral and ontological center the more compelling. All around me, people seemed to be finding that center in the needs, wants, and feelings of the isolated self, but

for me such individualism or identity politics exacerbated the problem rather than eased it."[65]

"Caught in the Web of Grace," 1997

Elizabeth Fox-Genovese began her academic career as a political radical along with her husband, the respected historian Eugene Genovese. Together they founded the journal *Marxist Perspectives* in late 1970s. She founded the Institute for Women's Studies at Emory University in 1986 and served as its director until 1991. During those years, her thinking about abortion changed gradually until she became vocally pro-life and eventually entered the Catholic Church in 1995. Her husband, Eugene, later entered the Church himself, and they were married in the Church by a Catholic priest.

DAY 66

JAMES HITCHCOCK (1938–)

A Mystical Body—

"Thanks very much for your letter. I understand rather acutely, I think, the dilemma you find yourself in. I am sometimes

---

65 Elizabeth Fox Genovese, "Caught in the Web of Grace," *Crisis*, Nov. 1 1997, https://www.crisismagazine.com/1997/caught-in-the-web-of-grace.

embarrassed for my church in its present failings. I think my basic answer to your questions would be to say that when one becomes a Catholic one in effect enters into unity with the Church in its widest sense—not only the geographical breadth that exists at present but also all the ages which have gone before. . . . At the present time one would have to distinguish, I think, between the local church and the universal church. On the local level what one finds is often discouraging. . . . Again, with Roman Catholicism, it is legitimate to prescind from conditions at the local level in order to assert unity with the center. This is not an evasion or a rationalization—it is the reality of the Catholic concept of the Church. . . . On one level we may say the Church is concrete and visible. But on another level I seem to be proposing a kind of mystical unity that obliterates inconvenient specific realities. . . . We give our allegiance to a visible Church, but also know that ultimately our unity there is mystical."[66]

Letter to Deal W. Hudson, January 25, 1980

James Hitchcock is professor emeritus of history at St. Louis University, his alma mater, and holds degrees from Princeton University (MA, PhD). He is one of the foremost Catholic historians of the last forty years. Dr. Hitchcock writes and lectures frequently on Church issues as well as its history. His books

---

66 Deal W. Hudson, *An American Conversion: One Man's Discovery of Beauty and Truth in Times of Crisis,* James Hitchcock, Letter to Deal W. Hudson, January 25, 1980 (Chestnut Ridge: Crossroad, 2003), 95–97.

include, among others, *What is Secular Humanism?* (1982), *Years of Crisis: Collected Essays, 1970-1983* (1985), *Recovery of the Sacred; The Supreme Court and Religion in American Life* (2004), and *History of the Catholic Church* (2012). He is married to Helen Hull Hitchcock, editor of *Adoremus Bulletin* and president of Women for Faith & Family. The Hitchcocks live in St. Louis and are parents of four adult daughters.

DAY 67

ST. BONAVENTURE (1221–1274)

Be a person of prayer—

"If you would suffer patiently the adversities and miseries of this life, be a person of prayer. If you would gain power and strength to overcome the temptations of the enemy, be a person of prayer. If you would put to death the inordinate affections and lusts of your will, be a person of prayer. If you would understand the cunning devices of Satan and defend yourself against his deceits, be a person of prayer. If you would live joyfully, and with sweetness walk in the path of penitence and sorrow, be a person of prayer. If you would drive out the troublesome gnats of vain thoughts and cares from your soul, be a person of prayer. If you would sustain your soul with the richness of devotion and keep it ever full of good thoughts

and desires, be a person of prayer. If you would strengthen and confirm your heart in the pilgrimage with God, be a person of prayer. Finally, if you would root out from your soul all vices, and in their place plant the virtues, be a person of prayer. For in this way you obtain the anointing and grace of the Holy Spirit, who teaches all things."[67]

De Perfectione Vitae ad Sorores

This excellent translation of St. Bonaventure's Latin preserves its poetic power, a call to prayer that in itself is prayerful. The notion of driving out "troublesome gnats" is an unusual metaphor, but we all know exactly what he is talking about, don't we? Another striking phrase is his description of walking the penitential path "with sweetness." No doubt actually doing that is impossible without the grace that prayer can provide. No one naturally enjoys saying, "I'm sorry."

---

67 Paul Thigpen, *A Year With the Saints: Daily Meditations With the Holy Ones of God* (Charlotte: Saint Benedict Press, 2013), 312.

DAY 68

SIGRID UNDSET (1882–1949)

Bravery over fear—

"It is strange that we think [that] beneath the perspective of other Christians and non-Christians with their seeming reasonableness and connectedness lies a deep unreasonableness; they are simply far from life. Catholicism's unreasonableness, contradictions, and problems point to a fundamental, organic connection. The Church is built on a rock. Catholicism does not explain all the problems of existence, but it explains more and goes deeper than any other philosophy of life. If the world is a battleground where God and Satan fight and there is no hope that the battle shall finally be over before judgment day, not even on that day will it become more humane; on the contrary, it shall become more grim. As St. John prophesies, we should be prepared for the worst. The best soldier is not the one who hasn't the sense to be afraid, but the one who is braver than he is fearful. And each joy, each victory, each good thing becomes wonderful—a surprise, an experience and extra delicious—*A la guerre comme a la guerre*."[68]

"Catholic Propaganda," 1927

---

68 Sigrid Undset, "Catholic Propaganda," *Sigrid Undset On Saints and Sinners: New Translations and Studies*, trans. Rev. John E. Halborg, ed. Deal W. Hudson (San Francisco: Ignatius Press, 1993), 248.

The Danish writer Sigrid Undset received the Nobel Prize in Literature in 1928. Her parents were intellectual atheists, but they went along with the convention of having their daughter baptized in the Lutheran Church. Undset started her career, after vocational training, as a secretary but started writing at night. During her ten years as a secretary, she published her first two novels. Her talent was noticed, and she received a scholarship to visit Germany and Italy. In 1912, she married the Norwegian painter A. C. Svarstad and bore three children. When she entered the Church in 1924, her twelve-year old marriage was dissolved since her husband had been previously married. She was forty-two years old and chose to become a lay Dominican. Because of her public resistance to the Nazis, Undset and her children—a son had been killed in the war—traveled to the U.S. by train through the Soviet Union and across the ocean landing in San Francisco. Her trilogy, *Kristin Lavansdatter* (1920-1922), written before her conversion, is among the best Catholic novels ever written. However, the tetralogy, *The Master of Hestviken* (1925-1927), is just as good.

DAY 69

J. BUDZISZEWSKI (1952–)

How to unteach—

"How would a classical moral teacher go about teaching under such circumstances? As we have seen, his humble goal is to recalibrate the baloney-meter, not to replace but to refine the common sense of mankind. But one cannot recalibrate a baloney-meter that receives continuous interfering signals from another installed alongside it. It lights up and beeps at the very mention of an objective moral law. "Aren't we beyond all that now?" . . . In the classroom I answer such questions, "Tell this to the man who is trying to rape or murder you." . . . Today a classical teacher must be aggressive before he can exercise his humility. Before the students' original baloney-meters can be recalibrated, the ersatz baloney-meters that have been installed alongside them must be disconnected. So students must unlearn before they can learn. A classical teacher today is first, though not last, an unteacher."[69]

Written on the Heart, 1996

When J. Budziszewski converted to Catholicism in 2004, it surprised many Evangelicals who regarded him as one of their

---

69 J. Budziszewski, *Written on the Heart: The Case for Natural Law* (Downers Grove: InterVarsity Press, 1997), 174-75.

leading intellectual champions. Budziszewski received his PhD from Yale in 1981 and now teaches at the University of Texas, Austin in both the government and philosophy departments. His work on natural law theory became quite influential beyond the scholarly community because of his ability to discuss complex material in an accessible way. His books include *What We Can't Not Know: A Guide* (2003), *The Line Through the Heart: Natural Law as Fact, Theory, and Sign of Contradiction* (2009), *On the Meaning of Sex* (2014), and most recently, *Commentary on Thomas Aquinas's Treatise on Happiness and Ultimate Purpose* (2020).

DAY 70

ST. THÉRÈSE OF LISIEUX (1873–1897)

The Little Flower faces the Tempter—

"From the time of my childhood I felt that one day I should be set free from this land of darkness. I believed it, not only because I had been told so by others, but my heart's most secret and deepest longings assured me that there was in store for me another and more beautiful country—an abiding dwelling-place. I was like Christopher Columbus, whose genius anticipated the discovery of the New World. And suddenly the mists about me have penetrated my very soul and have enveloped me

so completely that I cannot even picture to myself this promised country . . . all has faded away. When my heart, weary of
the surrounding darkness, tries to find some rest in the thought
of a life to come, my anguish increases. It seems to me that out
of the darkness I hear the mocking voice of the unbeliever:
'You dream of a land of light and fragrance, you dream that
the Creator of these wonders will be yours for ever, you think
one day to escape from these mists where you now languish.
Nay, rejoice in death, which will give you, not what you hope
for, but a night darker still, the night of utter nothingness!'"[70]

The Story of a Soul, 1898

St. Thérèse of Lisieux had eight siblings and was the baby of
the family. The family moved to Lisieux after her mother died
of breast cancer. Four of her elder sisters became nuns when
Thérèse, at age fifteen, entered the Carmelite convent. She
had been rejected the previous year. That year, her father had
taken her on a diocesan pilgrimage to Rome. During a general
audience with Leo XIII, Thérèse approached the pope, knelt,
and asked him to allow her to enter Carmel at fifteen. Pope
Leo replied, "Well, my child, do what the superiors decide.
. . . You will enter if it is God's Will. After he blessed Thérèse,
she refused to leave his feet, and had to be carried out of the
room. Young Thérèse was deeply pious, but she struggled with

---

70 St. Thérèse de Lisieux, *Story of a Soul: The Autobiography of St. Thérèse of Lisieux* (1912 trans.), 110-111, Kindle Edition.

depression and scrupulosity. In spite of this, she exhibited a joyful countenance, always smiling and generous towards others. Tuberculosis killed her at the age of twenty-four. Her autobiography was finished in three stages, which were collected by the sisters as she was dying. Her burial site at Lisieux became a place of pilgrimage for thousands of Catholics who visit throughout the year.

DAY 71

PAUL JOHNSON (1928–)

God substitutes abound—

"Far more dangerous than the humanist impact have been the twentieth-century attempts to find substitutes for God—attempts both conscious and unconscious—which appeal not so much to the intellectual pretensions as to much deeper, darker and stronger instincts in mankind. The detonator of the modern tragedy of humankind was the First World War, which began in Europe in 1914 and which America joined three years later. Its destructive impact on established and improving notions of human behavior and international morality was immeasurable and we are still suffering from its consequences. This war was not merely without reason, it was plainly avoidable. What caused it? I suggest it was, above all, the worship

of money and still more power which already, by 1914, was becoming for many people a substitute for the worship of God. We have already noted that in Europe the percentage of the population attending church regularly began to decline, for the first time, from the end of the 1880s. Now church attendance is not a key, certainly not the key, to social and individual morality. But history suggests that the regular practice of a structured religion does impose restraints on human appetites, both individual and collective, which are difficult to achieve by any other means."[71]

The Quest for God, 1996

Paul Johnson was educated by the Jesuits at Stonyhurst College before entering Magdalen College, Oxford. He began his career as a journalist and then an editor at the New Statesman magazine. In the '50s, Johnson adhered to the left-wing of politics but gradually developed a staunchly conservative and Catholic outlook. He has been a prolific writer, with over fifty books thus far, and is probably best known for his *Modern Times: A History of the World from the Twenties to the Nineties* (1983), which contained a devastating account of the mass slaughters committed by Hitler, Stalin, and Mao making the twentieth century the most bloody in world history.

---

71 Paul Johnson, *The Quest for God* (HarperCollins e-books), loc. 23, Kindle Edition.

DAY 72

LESZEK KOLAKOWSKI (1927–2009)

Distinguishing the sacred and profane—

"The secularization of the Christian world does not necessarily take the form of a direct denial of the sacred; it came about indirectly, through a universalization of the sacred. This, by abolishing the distinction between the sacred and the secular, gives the same result. . . . It is the Church of *aggiornomento*, that peculiar term which manages to combine two ideas that are not only different but, in some interpretations, mutually contradictory. According to one, to be a Christian is to be not only outside the world but also in the world; according to the other to be a Christian is never to be against the world. . . . Christianity seems to be making frenzied efforts at mimicry in order to escape being devoured by its enemies—a reaction that seems defensive, but is in fact self-destructive. In the hope of saving itself, it seems to be assuming the colors of its environment, but the result is that it loses its identity, which depends on the just distinction between the sacred and the profane, and on the conflict that can and often must exist between them."[72]

Modernity On Endless Trial, 1990

---

72 Leszek Kolakowski, *Modernity on Endless Trial* (Chicago: The University of Chicago Press, 1990), 68-69.

Leszek Kolakowski was a Polish philosopher whose intellectual dissection of Marxism is still considered definitive. He had embraced Communism as a young man, but in his three-volume *Main Currents of Marxism: Its Rise, Growth and Dissolution* published in the 1970s, Kolakowski called Communism "the greatest fantasy of our century." His teaching and writing contributed to the rise of the Solidarity movement. He taught at Warsaw University until his writing led to his expulsion from both the Polish United Workers' Party and the University of Warsaw. He left Poland in 1969 and went to teach at several major universities in the United States.

DAY 73

ROY CAMPBELL (1901–1957)

Mass at Dawn

I dropped my sail and dried my dripping seines
Where the white quay is checkered by cool planes
In whose great branches, always out of sight,
The nightingales are singing day and night.
Though all was grey beneath the moon's grey beam.
My boat in her new paint shone like a bride,
And silver in my baskets shone the bream:
My arms were tired and I was heavy-eyed,

But when with food and drink, at morning-light,
The children met me at the water-side,
Never was wine so red or bread so white.[73]

A native of South Africa, Roy Campbell moved to England after finishing high school. The *Flaming Terrapin* (1924), his first book, was a great success. His third book, *The Georgiad* (1931), caused some consternation among London's literati due to its satirization of the celebrities in the Bloomsbury circle. This pleased the writer Wyndam Lewis, who had done the same a year before in *The Apes of God* where Campbell is found as a character. Campbell's life was something of an adventure. He first moved back to South Africa to edit a literary magazine, moved to Spain to fight in the Civil War, before serving as a soldier in WWII in North Africa. He spent his last years in Portugal where he died in a car accident. In 1935, Campbell, his wife, and two daughters converted to Catholicism in the midst of the Spanish Civil War, which often came to their very doorstep. Joseph Pearce, his biographer, calls Campbell one of the finest poets of the twentieth century.

---

73 Roy Campbell, "Mass at Dawn," https://allpoetry.com/Mass-at-Dawn.

DAY 74

XAVIER ZUBIRI (1898–1983)

Necessity of surrender—

"God happens in me, whether I know it or not, whether I wish it or not. In order for this to be my business something more is needed: it is necessary that I take it as mine. And this *making it my business* is the acceptance, the surrender. . . . The surrender consists in my incorporating formally and deeply into my happening, as something brought about by me, the happening through which God happens in me. That God occurs in me is a *function of God in life*. But the surrender to God is to make *life into a function of God*. . . . We can very well know by demonstration the existence of God and his grounding characteristics, and yet have an attitude other than surrender."[74]

Man and God, 1948

Xavier Zubiri was a leading philosopher in Spain from 1940 to 1980. He studied with the famous José Ortega y Gasset in Madrid before taking his doctorate at Louvain. While teaching in Madrid, Zubiri visited Freiburg to study under Edmund Husserl and Martin Heidegger. Moving to Berlin put Zubiri in

---

74 Xavier Zubiri, *Man and God*, trans. Joaquin Redondo, trans. critically revised by Thomas Fowler and Nelson Orringer (Lanham: University Press of America, 2009), 173.

contact with the classicist Werner Jaeger and the physicist Max
Planck. He moved to Paris in 1936 after the beginning of the
Spanish Civil War and returned to Spain in 1939 at the beginning of WWII. For several years he taught at the University of
Barcelona before leaving in 1943 to spend the rest of his career
as a private writer and teacher. Zubiri was fundamentally a
Neo-Thomist with, like St. Teresa Benedicta of the Cross, a
strong interest in phenomenology. The importance of his work
has only been recently recognized outside of Spain.

DAY 75

JOSEPH PEARCE (1961–)

Pearce describes his "cultural apologetics":

"Truth is trinitarian. It consists of the Interconnected and mys-
tically unified power of Reason, Love and Beauty. As with the
Trinity itself, the three, though truly distinct, are one. Reason,
properly understood, is Beauty; Beauty, properly understood, is
Reason; both are transcended by, and are expressions of, Love.
And, of course, Reason, Love and Beauty are enshrined in,
and are encapsulated by, the Godhead. Indeed, they have their
raison d'être and their consummation in the Godhead. Remove
Love and Reason from the sphere of aesthetics and you remove
Beauty also. You get ugliness instead. Even a cursory glance

at most modern 'art' will illustrate the negation of Beauty in most of today's 'culture.' Once this theological understanding of the trinitarian nature of Truth is perceived, it follows that the whole science of apologetics can be seen in this light. Most mainstream apologetics can be seen as apologetics of Reason: the defense of the Faith and the winning of converts through the means of dialogue with the 'rational' and its sundry manifestations. On the other hand, the lives of the saints, such as the witness of Mother Teresa, can be seen as the apologetics of Love: the defense of the Faith and the winning of converts through the living example of a life lived in Love. Finally, the defense of the Faith and the winning of converts through the power of the beautiful can be called cultural apologetics or the apologetics of Beauty."[75]

Catholic Literary Giants, 2005

Joseph Pearce is a well-known Catholic apologist, historian, and literary scholar. He's originally from London, where he was a skin-head agnostic who espoused racist views. It was the work of G. K. Chesterton that led him to the faith, and in 1989, he became a Catholic. Since then, his contribution to the Church has been remarkable—his biographies and literary histories are unique in this generation of Catholic scholarship. His biographies of Chesterton, Tolkien, Belloc, Roy Campbell, and

---

75 Joseph Pearce, *Catholic Literary Giants: A Field Guide to the Catholic Literary Landscape* (San Francisco: Ignatius Press, 2005), loc. 116 -136 of 6271, Kindle Edition.

Solzhenitsyn are exemplary. For the last, Pearce was invited by Solzhenitsyn to his home in Russia for days of discussion, and once the book was published, the famous writer announced he was very pleased. Other important books include *Literary Converts* (2000), *The Quest for Shakespeare* (2008), and *Heroes of the Catholic Reformation: Saints Who Renewed the Church* (2017).

DAY 76

ROBERT SPAEMANN (1927–2018)

Human dignity is the bottom line—

"Dignity is not a property among other empirical data. Nor should we say that it is a human right to have one's own dignity respected. Dignity is rather the transcendental ground for the fact that human beings have rights and duties. They have rights, because they have duties, i.e., because the normal, adult members of the human family are neither animals who are instinctively integrated into their communities, nor merely instinctively indeterminate subjects of drives, who in the interest of their communities need to be kept under social or police control. Human beings can act based on insight, rationality and ethics, and they have the duty to do so. Article 6 of the German constitution, for example, says, 'The care and education of children are the natural right of the parents and are incumbent on

this as their first and foremost duty.' That parental rights follow from the capacity of the parents to fulfill their parental duty can be seen from the fact that this right ceases to exist in case of severe neglect of this duty."[76]

Love and the Dignity of Human Life, 1939

Robert Spaemann studied at the University of Münster before teaching in Stuttgart, Heidelberg, and at the University of Munich, where he became a professor emeritus in 1992. His field was ethics with a particular concentration on the philosophy of natural law. His books translated in English include *Basic Moral Concepts* (1990), *Happiness and Benevolence* (2000), *Essays in Anthropology: Essays On a Theme* (2010), and *Persons: The Difference between 'Someone' and 'Something'* (2017). The engaging quality of Spaemann's work is similar to that of fellow German Catholic philosopher Josef Pieper.

---

76 Robert Spaemann, *Love and the Dignity of Human Life, On Nature and Natural Law*, foreword by David L. Schindler (Grand Rapids: W.B. Eerdmans Publishing Company, 2012), 27-28.

DAY 77

FRANK SHEED (1897–1981)

On why a theologian finds modern novels chaotic—

"To one who has grasped the shape of reality, the most solemn, sombre, closely observed modern novel seems as grotesque and fantastic as *Alice in Wonderland*. What makes that
masterpiece obviously fantastic is that the law of cause and
effect does not operate; but this lack of connection between
cause and effect is at the level of the most superficial of secondary causes. Consider what derangement must follow if the
first cause is utterly unknown. The grotesqueness is not less
because the cause ignored is more fundamental; it is only less
obvious because the mind has lost contact with its own depths.
But if the theologian dismisses the novelist's world as lacking
shape, the novelist dismisses the theologian's world as lacking
flesh and blood. This counter-charge is worth examination,
because it draws attention to a real danger that lies in wait for
the student of ultimate reality. There is a danger that in han-
dling elements so far beyond the reach of daily experience one
might come to treat them as abstractions; and in that event our
philosophizing would come to be an exercise in getting these
abstractions rightly related to one another, in getting the shape
of reality right. But the universe is not simply something that
has a shape. It is something. The trouble is that the student, in
his student days at least, must to a large extent be conditioned

by his examinations; and examinations are almost invariably about shape; it is difficult to devise examinations that can test how real reality is to a man. It is possible to have a less detailed knowledge of all the relations that exist between all the various elements of reality, yet know reality better; a man who has never heard of some of the subtler truths may have a far better hold upon reality."[77]

Theology and Sanity, 1946

Frank Sheed was born in Australia and, after graduating with a law degree from the University of Sydney, moved to London with his wife, Maisie Ward. There they founded Sheed & Ward, which became a Catholic publishing house of extraordinary repute. Sheed wrote a number of books about the Catholic faith, all of them exhibiting a lawyer's acuity and an editor's clarity of language and thought. Sheed also took the time to become a popular street-corner speaker in Hyde Park. He, together with his wife, Maisie, were central to the English Catholic revival that began in the 1920s.

---

77 F. J. Sheed, *Theology and Sanity* (Aeterna Press), loc. 263, Kindle Edition.

DAY 78

ST. LOUIS DE MONTFORT (1673–1716)

A beautiful star fell—

"Man enjoyed his state of innocence but, alas, the vessel of the Godhead was shattered into a thousand pieces. This beautiful star fell from the skies. This brilliant sun lost its light. Man sinned, and by his sin lost his wisdom, his innocence, his beauty, his immortality. In a word, he lost all the good things he was given and found himself burdened with a host of evils. His mind was darkened and impaired. His heart turned cold towards the God he no longer loved. His sin-stained soul resembled Satan himself. The passions were in disorder; he was no longer master of himself. His only companions are the devils who have made him their slave and their abode. Even creatures have risen up in warfare against him."[78]

The Love of Eternal Wisdom, c. 1703

Louis de Montfort began study at a Jesuit college in Rennes at the age of twelve. Within a few years, he felt a call to the priesthood and walked to Paris where he studied theology at the Sorbonne. Severe poverty followed when promised financial help did not pan out. He fell very ill but recovered and

---

78 Louis de Montfort, *The Love of Eternal Wisdom* (Aeterna Press), loc. 17–18 of 92, Kindle Edition.

entered St. Sulpice Seminary when financial help did arrive. Ordained to the priesthood, Montfort faced more difficulties: he was fired from a hotel chaplaincy and ended up living under a staircase in an old building. He prayed, studied, and gave conferences at the Holy Spirit Seminary, an experience that produced his classic book *The Love of Eternal Wisdom*. Meeting Pope Clement XI in Poitier, Montfort was appointed an "Apostolic Missionary" to France. He spent the next seventeen years trekking around France preaching and teaching. Worn out from his ceaseless work, Montfort died in 1759 at the age of forty-three.

DAY 79

MALCOLM MUGGERIDGE (1903–1990)

Muggeridge describes "the precise moment of illumination" leading to his conversion. Filming a documentary in Bethlehem, he and his crew had a difficult time getting past all the beggars and children selling souvenirs. Once in the Church of the Holy Nativity, he took a seat in the crypt:

"How ridiculous the so-called 'shrines' were!, I was thinking to myself. How squalid the commercialism which exploited them! . . . The Holy Land, it seemed to me, has been turned into a sort of JesusLand, on the lines of Disneyland. As these thoughts passed through my mind, I began to notice the demeanor of

the visitors coming into the crypt. Some crossed themselves; a few knelt down; most were obviously standard twentieth-pilgrims, pursuers of happiness for whom the Church of the Nativity was just an item in a sightseeing tour. . . . None the less, each face as they came into the view was in some degree transfigured by the experience of being in what purported to be the actual scene of Jesus's birth. This was where it happened, they all seemed to be saying, Here He came in the world! Here we shall find Him! The boredom, the idle curiosity, the vagrant thinking all disappeared."[79]

Confessions of a Twentieth-Century Pilgrim, 1998

Malcolm Muggeridge lived an extraordinarily colorful, productive, and influential life. After graduating from Cambridge, he went to teach in India, returning to England to marry in 1927, after which he began a teaching stint in Egypt. As a young British journalist and committed socialist, he traveled to the Soviet Union, a country he admired, in the 1930s, thinking he might live there but soon discovered the murderous reality behind the propagandistic veneer and reported it all for the *Guardian* in his vivid prose style. Returning to England, his career flourished as a top editor of the *Daily Telegraph* and editor of the humor magazine *Punch*. In WWII, he worked as a spy in Africa before landing in Paris in time for the liberation.

---

79 Malcolm Muggeridge, *Confessions of a Twentieth-Century Pilgrim* (San Francisco: Harper and & Row, Publishers, 1998), 129–30.

Eventually, Muggeridge made regular TV appearances on the BBC, which stoked public controversy from time to time due to his caustic and eviscerating wit. His conversion to Christianity in 1969 resulted in the book *Jesus Rediscovered*, but he and his wife did not enter the Catholic Church until 1982 as a result of encountering Mother Teresa.

DAY 80

ST. AUGUSTINE (354–430)

Hearing what you want—

St. Augustine wonders where and how it was that he found God. The answer is "Everywhere," potentially. Showing his brilliant rhetorical skills, he fashions a particularly powerful final line.

"Where then did I find you [God], so that I might learn to know you? You were not in my memory before I learned to know you. Where then have I found you, if not in yourself and above me? There is no place, both backward we go and forward, and there is no place. Everywhere, O Truth, you give hearing to all who consult you, and at one and the same time you make answer to them all, but all men do not hear you clearly. All men ask counsel about what they wish, but they do not all hear what they wish. *Your best servant is he who looks not*

so much to hear from you what he wants to hear but rather to want what he hears from you."[80] (Emphasis added.)

Confessions, 397

St. Augustine wonders how a man like himself, proud and self-indulgent, was able to "find God." He records his willingness to hear from God what others prefer *not* to hear. Augustine reiterates the Pauline teaching in Romans 2:15 that the law of God is written upon our hearts making the Truth available to "all who consult you." But the sin of pride gets in the way when we ask God for what we wish rather than asking for God to speak to us as He wishes.

DAY 81

G. K. CHESTERTON (1874–1936)

Virtue on the loose—

"The modern world is not evil; in some ways the modern world is far too good. It is full of wild and wasted virtues. When a religious scheme is shattered (as Christianity was shattered at the Reformation), it is not merely the vices that are let

---

80 Augustine, *Confessions,* 10.26, trans. and introduction by John K. Ryan (Garden City: Doubleday and Company, Inc., 1960), 254.

loose. The vices are, indeed, let loose, and they wander and do damage. But the virtues are let loose also; and the virtues wander more wildly, and the virtues do more terrible damage. The modern world is full of the old Christian virtues gone mad. The virtues have gone mad because they have been isolated from each other and are wandering alone."[81]

Orthodoxy, 1908

Many have asked why G. K. Chesterton did not enter the Catholic Church in 1922 after publishing a book so "Catholic" as *Orthodoxy* in 1908. *Orthodoxy* is not a fluke. In the same year, 1908, he published *The Man Who Was Thursday*, and, later, his Father Brown stories, about a Catholic priest with a knack for detection, which started to appear in 1910. Chesterton was a committed Christian during the period leading up to 1922, but the specifically Catholic character of his published work is unquestioned. Ironically, Chesterton's writing before his conversion was helpful in the conversion to Catholicism of others, such as the actor Alec Guinness. Guinness was playing the role of Father Brown in a film being shot in a French village. One evening as he walked back to his hotel, still in costume, a little boy, thinking he was a real priest, took his hand and walked with him down the street. The easy trust and affection that little boy displayed for some strange priest made a profound impression on him, and he began to think that his prejudices against Catholicism were, perhaps, misplaced.

---

81 G. K. Chesterton, *Orthodoxy* (San Francisco, Ignatius Press, 1995), 35.

DAY 82

MARSHALL MCLUHAN (1911–1980)

Asked by E. I. Watkins whether he felt comfortable or uncomfortable as a Catholic, McLuhan answers—

"I don't expect to be comfortable. The Church has never claimed to be a place of security in any ordinary psychological sense. Anyone who comes to the Church for that purpose is wrong: nothing of that sort is available in the Church. There never has been; it isn't that kind of institution. At the speed of light, there is nothing but violence possible, and the violence wipes out every boundary. Every territory is violated at the speed of light. . . . [The Church is called] the custodian of civilized values and so on — that phase of the Church is all over, I'd say. Now we're on a life raft — a sort of survival operation. At the speed of light, now the normal speed of life — information's speed — there is no peace. The potential for teaching and learning in the Church was never greater than in this electric world. The Chair of Peter can jet around the world: it doesn't have to stay in Rome."[82]

Interview with E. I. Watkins, 1999

---

82 Marshall McLuhan, "Our Only Hope is Apocalypse, *The Medium and the Light: Reflections on Religion*, eds. Eric McLuhan and Jacek Szklarek (Toronto: Stoddart Publishing Company, 1999), 64-65.

The Canadian Marshall McLuhan earned a BA and MA at the University of Manitoba before matriculating at Trinity College, Cambridge where he was forced to start over as a sophomore. But the opportunity to study under I. A. Richards and F. R. Leavis at the birth of what is called the New Criticism was very fortunate. While at Cambridge, McLuhan started reading Chesterton and began his journey into the Catholic Church, which culminated in 1937. He taught at St. Louis University for seven years before moving back to Canada, teaching first at Assumption College then St. Michael's College at the University of Toronto. In 1964, he published *Understanding Media*, which revolutionized the understanding of how the medium of technology shapes the meaning of the message received by its audience. The devoutly Catholic McLuhan became an admired public figure during the decade of the counterculture, sex, drugs, and flower power.

DAY 83

ST. ALBERT THE GREAT (1200–1280)

Translated into light—

"Now the more the mind is concerned about thinking and dealing with what is merely lower and human, the more it is separated from the experience in the intimacy of devotion

of what is higher and heavenly, while the more fervently the memory, desire and intellect is withdrawn from what is below to what is above, the more perfect will be our prayer, and the purer our contemplation, since the two directions of our interest cannot both be perfect at the same time, being as different as light and darkness. He who cleaves to God is indeed translated into the light, while he who clings to the world is in the dark. So the supreme perfection of man in this life is to be so united to God that all his soul with all its faculties and powers are so gathered into the Lord God that he becomes one spirit with him, and remembers nothing except God, is aware of and recognizes nothing but God, but with all his desires unified by the joy of love, he rests contentedly in the enjoyment of his Maker alone. Now the image of God as found in the soul consists of these three faculties, namely reason, memory and will, and so long as they are not completely stamped with God, the soul is not yet *deiform*[83] in accordance with the initial creation of the soul. For the true pattern of the soul is God, with whom it must be imprinted, like wax with a seal, and carry the mark of his impress."[84]

On Cleaving to God, c. 1260

St. Albert the Great extended medieval philosophy into the areas of logic, psychology, metaphysics, meteorology, mineralogy, and

83 *Deiform* refers to the full actuality of the image of God in man.

84 St. Albert the Great, *On Cleaving to God,* loc. 43-64 of 452, Kindle Edition.

zoological sciences. Albert applied Aristotelian principles more widely than anyone that came before him, a practice perfected by his famous student, St. Thomas Aquinas. But like Aquinas, Albert also made use of the Neo-Platonists and its stress on an ordered cosmos. He outlived his student and friend Thomas Aquinas, and near the end of his life in 1277, he returned to the University of Paris to defend Aquinas's teaching.

DAY 84

CHARLES DE FOUCAULD (1858–1916)

What remains at death—

"We should attach no importance either to the events of this life or to material things: they are dreams of a night spent at an inn, and will vanish as quickly as images seen in dreams, leaving no more traces than they do. What will remain at the hour of death, except our merits and sins? . . . Like faith itself, the habit of seeing things in the light of faith raises us above the mists and mud of this world. It puts us into a new atmosphere, in full sunshine, full daylight, in a serene calm and luminous

peace far above the region of clouds, winds and storms, beyond
the realm of twilight and night."[85]

Spiritual Autobiography, July 21, 1899

Born into an aristocratic French family, Charles de Foucauld
was not a believing Catholic as a young man when he joined
the French army. With the money from an inheritance, he
took his mistress, Mimi, with him when his regiment went to
Algeria. Booted out of the army because he would not give
up his mistress, de Foucauld did eventually leave her and reen-
listed. He left the service to disguise himself as a Jew and go
on a year-long exploration. Returning to France, de Foucauld
also returned to the Church and became a Trappist monk. He
was assigned to a Syrian monastery but left to do menial work
for the Poor Clares in Nazareth. In 1901, he was ordained a
priest in France and left for Morocco where he lived a solitary
life until a friend from his army days asked him to live with
the Tuareg people in Algeria. Charles learned their language
and translated the *Gospels* into Tuareg. De Foucauld died vio-
lently on December 1, 1916 at the hands of a band of Senussi
Bedouin who intended only to kidnap him.

---

85 Charles de Foucauld, *The Spiritual Autobiography of Charles de Foucauld*, trans.
J. Holland Smith, ed. and annotated by Jean-Francios Six (Ijamsville: The
World Among Us Press, 2003), 124.

DAY 85

HENRI NOUWEN (1932–1996)

Grace where there is pain—

"If mourning and dancing are part of the same movement of grace, we can be grateful for every moment we have lived. We can claim our unique journey as God's way to mold our hearts to greater conformity to Christ. The cross, the primary symbol of our faith, invites us to see grace where there is pain; to see resurrection where there is death. The call to be grateful is a call to trust that every moment can be claimed as the way of the cross that leads to new life. When Jesus spoke to his disciples before his death and offered them his body and blood as gifts of life, he shared with them everything he had lived—his joy as well as his pain, his suffering as well as his glory—and enabled them to move into their own mission in deep gratitude. Day by day we find new reasons to believe that nothing will separate us from the love of God in Christ. Of course, it is easy for me to push the bad memories under the rug of my consciousness and think only about the good things that please me. It seems to be the way to fulfillment. By doing so, however, I keep myself from discovering the joy beneath the sorrow, the meaning to be coaxed out of even painful memories. I miss finding the strength that becomes visible in my weakness, the grace God told Paul would be 'sufficient for you, for power is made perfect in weakness' (2 Cor. 12:9). Gratitude helps us in

this dance only if we cultivate it. For gratitude is not a simple emotion or an obvious attitude. Living gratefully requires practice. It takes sustained effort to reclaim my whole past as the concrete way God has led me to this moment. For in doing so I must face not only today's hurts, but the past's experiences of rejection or abandonment or failure or fear."[86]

Turn My Mourning Into Dancing, 2001

As a spiritual advisor, Father Henri Nouwen continually urged his readers and followers not to ignore their suffering for the sake of achieving a form of false happiness. He writes about reclaiming the "whole past," not just the parts of it that are pleasure or about which we are proud. Nouwen reminds us of what St. Paul so often said, "to see grace where there is pain."

DAY 86

G. E. M. ANSCOMBE (1919–2001)

Chastity never practiced—

"The trouble about the Christian standard of chastity is that it isn't and never has been generally lived by; not that it would be

---

86 Henri J.M. Nouwen, *Turn My Mourning Into Dancing: Finding Hope In Hard Times*, ed. Timothy Jones (Nashville: Thomas Nelson, 2001), 18–19.

profitless if it were. Quite the contrary: it would be colossally productive of earthly happiness. All the same it is a virtue, not like temperance in eating and drinking, not like honesty about property, for these have a purely utilitarian justification. But it, like the respect for life, is a supra-utilitarian value, connected with the substance of life, and this is what comes out in the perception that the life of lust is one in which we dishonor our bodies. Implicitly, lasciviousness is over and over again treated as hateful, even by those who would dislike such an explicit judgment on it. Just listen, witness the scurrility when it's hinted at; disgust when it's portrayed as the stuff of life; shame when it's exposed, the leer of complicity when it's approved. You don't get these attitudes with everybody all of the time; but you do get them with everybody."[87]

Contraception and Chastity, 1972

Gertrude Elizabeth Anscombe was born in Limerick. She attended Oxford where she met another philosophy student named Peter Geach while both were receiving instruction from a Dominican priest. They married in 1941 and had seven children. After attending Cambridge, she went back to Oxford in 1964 as a teaching fellow. Returning to Cambridge in 1970, she took the chair of philosophy that once belonged to Ludwig Wittgenstein. She had once studied with Wittgenstein, and

---

87 Elizabeth Anscombe, "Contraception and Chastity," OrthodoxyToday.org, https://www.orthodoxytoday.org/articles/AnscombeChastity.php.

they were good friends. At a time when orthodox Catholicism was becoming rare, especially in the academy, Anscombe and her husband, Peter, did not hide their faith in the least—they defended innocent life with all the sophistication of their considerable intellects. Philosopher John Haldane said of Anscombe, she "certainly has a good claim to be the greatest woman philosopher of whom we know."

DAY 87

RALPH MCINERNY (1929–2010)

McInerny regarded the reaction to the 1968 promulgation of Humane Vitae very unfortunate—

"In reacting as they did to *Humanae Vitae*, the dissenting theologians assumed a novel view of the teaching role of the Church: the function of the Pope is to promulgate and endorse the consensus of the believers. . . . As the story unfolded, what most were aware of was that the Pope has affirmed the Church's ban on birth control and that a growing number of Catholic theologians were contesting the right to do so. Niceties apart, these theologians claimed that one could be as Catholic as the Pope—indeed, they were saying one could be *more* Catholic than the Pope—in refusing to follow the Pope. They created the impression that a rejection of the supreme teaching

authority of the Roman Catholic Church does not logically entail one should leave the Church. Indeed, they attempted to redefine the nature of the Church in such a way that it was the Pope who was out of step."[88]

What Went Wrong with Vatican II, 1998

Ralph McInerny taught at the University of Notre Dame for over fifty years. During that time, McInerny taught generation after generation of students about the philosophy of St. Thomas Aquinas and other medieval thinkers. As great as his intellectual legacy is, he also was very successful, and probably better known, as a writer of fiction, including the highly-popular Father Dowling mystery series. McInerny thought of becoming a priest as a young man, but after graduating from college, he pursued graduates studies in philosophy, earning a PhD from Laval University in Quebec. As Director of the Jacques Maritain Center at Notre Dame, he did more than anyone else in the academy to foster and encourage the tradition of Neo-Thomism. There are many in the teaching profession today who can attest to the generosity of McInerny as a professor, writer, and friend.

---

88 Ralph McInerny, *What Went Wrong with Vatican II: The Catholic Crisis Explained* (Manchester: Sophia Institute Press, 1998), loc. 566 of 1506, Kindle Edition.

DAY 88

ST. IRENEAUS OF LYONS (130–203)

Error always hides—

"Error, indeed, is never set forth in its naked deformity, lest, being thus exposed, it should at once be detected. But it is craftily decked out in an attractive dress, so as, by its outward form, to make it appear to the inexperienced (ridiculous as the expression may seem) more true than the truth itself. One far superior to me [not cited] has well said, in reference to this point, A clever imitation in glass casts contempt, as it were, on that precious jewel the emerald (which is most highly esteemed by some), unless it come under the eye of one able to test and expose the counterfeit. Or, again, what inexperienced person can with ease detect the presence of brass when it has been mixed up with silver? Lest, therefore, through my neglect, some should be carried off, even as sheep are by wolves, while they perceive not the true character of these men,—because they outwardly are covered with sheep's clothing (against whom the Lord has enjoined [Matthew 7:15] us to be on our guard), and because their language resembles ours, while their sentiments are very different—I have deemed it my duty (after reading some of the Commentaries, as they call them, of the disciples of Valentinus, and after making myself acquainted with their tenets through personal intercourse with some of them) to unfold to you, my friend, these portentous

and profound mysteries, which do not fall within the range of every intellect, because all have not sufficiently purged their brains. I do this, in order that you, obtaining an acquaintance with these things, may in turn explain them to all those with whom you are connected, and exhort them to avoid such an abyss of madness and of blasphemy against Christ."[89]

Against Heresies, 180

Saint Irenaeus was bishop of Lyons in the second century. His greatest legacy is his setting the theological parameters between Catholic orthodoxy and heresies such as Gnosticism. Though born in Asia Minor, Irenaeus did his apostolic work in Lyon, France. On a mission to Rome to meet Pope Eleutherius, Irenaeus was fortunate to avoid the Christian persecution of Marcus Aurelius. His *Against the Heresies* was formative in the history of theology for establishing that orthodox teaching comes from the Apostles who themselves pass on the true understanding of Scripture.

---

89 St. Ireneaus of Lyons, *Against Heresies, The Complete Works of the Church Fathers* (Toronto, 2016), loc. 322456–322482 of 635625, Kindle Edition.

DAY 89

ADRIENNE VON SPEYR (1902–1967)

Straight to the Son—

> "When Joan of Arc answers her judges that if she is not in grace she hopes to attain it, then she is indeed standing at this gate. It is a place where no further statements concerning one's 'I' are possible, a place where only perseverance in love and discipleship remains. From the moment of consent and thereafter, every believer is in a position of following this example, without detours, straight to the Son. And all tasks imposed by the rule—those of self-perfection, of obedience, even of studies and of the liturgy—are tasks of love which even a whole lifetime cannot bring to conclusion."[90]

They Followed His Call, 1955

Adrienne von Speyr was a wife, medical doctor, spiritual writer, Catholic mystic, and spiritual muse to the theologian Hans Urs von Balthasar. Under the spiritual direction of von Balthasar, she converted to Catholicism from the Reformed Church on the Feast of All Saints, November 1, 1940. She once told von Balthasar that on Christmas Eve when she was six years old, she had a mystical encounter with St. Ignatius while walking

---

90 Adrienne von Speyr, *They Followed His Call*, trans. Dr. Erasmo Leiva (Staten Island: Alba House, 1979), 29.

up a steep street. During her lifetime, she dictated nearly seventy books to von Balthasar, many of which are available in English from Ignatius Press. Her four-volume commentary on the Gospel of John is particularly treasured by those familiar with her writings. Von Speyr had mystical experiences, including some with the Holy Trinity, until her death in 1967.

DAY 90

REV. JAMES V. SCHALL, SJ (1928–2019)

Our need for the Word—

"It is useful to man to have much information about matter of fact; but that is not wisdom. It is useful to have scientific knowledge, to know the immediate what and why of things; but that is not wisdom either. It is better to have philosophy, which is the knowledge of things, not in their immediate but in their ultimate, causes; that is wisdom, though it is not the highest form of wisdom. It is wisdom because it does reduce the manifold of life to the one, and therefore makes things intelligible as a unity; but you need, to make the dry bones live, the vision, the intuition or awareness, of things in all their concreteness, their goodness and beauty as well as their truth; above all, you need some degree, at least, of direct knowledge of the nature of the one and when you have that vision in its

plenitude—the plenitude which, knowing something of God in Himself, sees all things in Him and Him in all things—and at the same time the wisdom which judges all things in the light of the highest of all causes, the Cause of all being itself, then you have wisdom in the fullest and deepest sense; and seeing things as it were with the eyes of God, you share something of the peace of God."[91]

Roman Catholic Political Philosophy, 2004

In a book devoted to wisdom, Father Schall's explanation above of how wisdom differs from other forms of knowledge is wonderfully clear. Schall writes that wisdom "makes things intelligible as a unity." In other words, to look with wisdom upon the world is to remain aware of what always lies in the distance behind the appearances. We are reminded of what Flannery O'Connor said about the prophet being "the realist of distances." The novelist and the philosopher can achieve only so much of that vision because divine revelation provides the only pathway to the "Cause of all being itself." Notice wisdom is not found in any form of conceptualization but in the lived experience of vision, "seeing things as it were with the eyes of God."

---

91 James V. Schall, *Roman Catholic Political Philosophy* (Lanham: Lexington Books, 2006), 165-66.

DAY 91

MAX PICARD (1888–1965)

The flight to art—

"The man of Flight cannot bear the reality of the God who is wholly other, for in God's presence the link between one thing and another is severed and the only possible link is that between the thing and God; for everything comes to rest before him: the Flight is over. For this reason one does not desire God to be the wholly other, for God is a hindrance to the Flight. . . . Man needs something 'wholly other' which *helps* the Flight. This is Art. . . . Nearly everything in Art is other than it is in the Flight. Here nothing flees, nothing is in a hurry; everything is tranquil, defined, classified, summarized. In a picture a fragment of the world stands firm. It is not as in the Flight, where every moment is changing. The [picture] frame is there as a kind of guarantee that one may quietly turn from the picture and allow oneself to be swept away by the Flight, and that on one's return the picture will still be there in its frame just as it was before. There in the frame is a fragment of the world. It was possible, then, for a fragment of the world to stand still."[92]

The Flight from God, 1934

---

92 Max Picard, *The Flight from God*, trans. Marianne Kuschnitzey and J.M. Cameron (Chicago: Henry Regnery Company, 1951), 138-40.

Max Picard was a Swiss doctor and psychologist who converted to Catholicism from Judaism. A friend described Picard
as a modern St. John of Patmos, a seer of mysteries, a cosmic
human. His books, most of which were translated into English,
had great influence in Europe, the UK, and America: *The Last
Man* (1921), *The Human Face* (1930), *The Flight From God*
(1934), *Hitler in Our Selves* (1947), *The World of Silence* (1948),
and *The Atomization of Modern Arts* (1954).

DAY 92

ÉTIENNE GILSON (1884–1978)

Faith's red flag—

"To any sincere [Catholic] believer who is at the same time a
true philosopher, *the slightest opposition between his faith and his
reason is sure sign that something is the matter with his philosophy.*
For indeed faith is not a principle of philosophical knowledge,
but is a safe guide to rational truth and an infallible warning
against philosophical error. A man who does not like to believe
what he can know, and who never pretends to know what can
but be believed, and yet a man whose faith and knowledge
grow into an organic unity because they both spring from the
same divine source, such is, if not the portrait, at least a sketch

of the typical member of the Thomist family."[93] (Emphasis added.)

Reason and Revelation in the Middle Ages, 1938

Étienne Henri Gilson was born and educated in Paris at the prestigious Lycée Henri IV. In 1907, he graduated from the Sorbonne studying under Lucien Lévy Bruhl, Henri Bergson and Emile Durkheim. Gilson finished his dissertation on Descartes in 1913. His intellectual trajectory moved backwards historically into medieval philosophy. Gilson served in WWI as second lieutenant, was captured at the Battle of Verdun, and spent two years in a German prison. He was awarded the *Croix de guerre*. After the war, he taught at Lille and Strasbourg before his appointment in 1921 to teach the history of medieval philosophy at the Sorbonne. His 1931 and 1932 Gifford Lectures were published as *The Spirit of Medieval Philosophy*, the book that brought him to fame outside of France. In 1951 he started teaching at the Institute of Medieval Studies in Toronto where he taught until 1968.

---

93 Étienne Gilson, *Reason and Revelation in the Middle Ages* (New York: Charles Scribner's Sons, 1938), 84–85.

DAY 93

ST. TERESA OF ÁVILA (1515–1582)

The grace to see—

"We might compare the soul to a person who is with others in a very bright room; and then suppose that the shutters are closed so that the people are all in darkness. The light by which they can be seen has been taken away, and, until it comes back, we shall be unable to see them, yet we are none the less aware that they are there. It may be asked if, when the light returns, and this person looks for them again, she will be able to see them. To do this is not in her power; it depends on when Our Lord is pleased that the shutters of the understanding shall be opened. Great is the mercy which He grants the soul in never going away from her and in willing that she shall understand this so clearly."[94]

Interior Castle, 1577

Born into a noble family, Saint Teresa left home at nineteen to join the Carmelite Monastery of the Incarnation in Ávila. She thought the Carmelite order was too undisciplined and began a reform effort. St. Teresa founded a new convent, St. Joseph's, in Ávila where she continued to practice mystical

---

94 St. Teresa of Ávila, *Interior Castle*, 7th Mansion, Ch. 1; read at http://www. catholictreasury.info/books/interior_castle/ic27.php.

contemplation and asceticism. As a mystic, St. Teresa received visions and moments of mystical ecstasy. After five years, St. Teresa began to travel, establishing new Carmelite convents, sixteen in all, and reforming old ones. She met St. John of the Cross, who became her spiritual advisor, and they worked together in reforming and building the Carmelite order, male and female.

DAY 94

RAÏSSA MARITAIN (1883–1960)

He will do His work—

"Error is like the foam on the waves, it eludes our grasp and keeps reappearing. The soul must not exhaust itself fighting against the foam. Its zeal must be purified and calmed and, by union with the divine Will, it must gather strength from the depths. And Christ, with all his merits and the merits of all the saints, will do his work deep down below the surface of the waters. And everything that can be saved will be saved."[95]

---

95 Raïssa Maritain, *Raïssa's Journal*, presented by Jacques Maritain (Albany: Magi Books, 1974), 158.

Raïssa Maritain was a Russian born in Rostov-on-Don to a Jewish family. Until the age of ten, she lived as an observant Jew in the bosom of a pious, extended family. Her parents, wisely acknowledging the pogroms soon to come, moved the Oumansov family to Paris. An intellectually curious ten-year-old, Raïssa suddenly found herself in a city where religious skepticism and literary decadence was widely embraced in cafe society, and she soon was questioning her own belief in God. However, entering the Sorbonne in 1900 led her to a meeting that would change her life and enrich the spiritual lives of Catholics both in Europe and the United States. A year ahead of her, Jacques Maritain shared her struggle with unbelief and the hope that science would provide an answer to questions about truth. Scientists, they found, were materialists, but they found hope in the lectures of Henri Bergson and in a novel, *The Woman Who Was Poor*, written by a ferocious Catholic, Léon Bloy. These encounters saved them from carrying out a suicide pact they had made in case they never found any basis for true knowledge. In 1906, both Jacques and Raïssa entered the Catholic Church.

DAY 95

KARL STERN (1906–1975)

Starting with me—

"There is only one: Jesus Christ. If we are concerned with the suffering of those innocent ones, we have first to look at Him. If we are concerned with the Evil which has brought it about, we have first to look at ourselves. Everything else is deception. If I want to renew the world I have to begin right in the depths of my own soul. This is the only true and permanent revolution which I am able to achieve. Class warfare leads to another set of oppressors and oppressed; national revenge leads to another set of persecutors and persecuted; and the Board of Social Scientists for the Prevention of Intergroup Hostilities is the most dangerous mirage of all because it makes us believe even more that the decisive battle is fought far away from us, outside ourselves; it turns Good and Evil into two pale abstracts; it seeks to de-humanize the issue."[96]

The Pillar of Fire, 1951

Karl Stern was born Jewish in Germany. A medical doctor and psychologist, Stern left his homeland when Hitler rose to power and moved to London in 1935 and to Montreal, where

---

96 Karl Stern, *The Pillar of Fire* (New York: Harcourt, Brace and Company, 1951), 294.

he taught as the University of Ottawa and served as Chief of Psychiatry at St. Mary's Hospital. In 1940, both Stern and his wife, Liselotte, converted to Catholicism. The story of his conversion is compellingly told in *Pillar of Fire*, his autobiography published in 1951. A close friend was the philosopher Jacques Maritain, who recommended that Stern attend to the influences that came not from "below" but from "above" his conscious life. Stern published four more books before his death in 1975.

DAY 96

HENRI DE LUBAC, SJ (1896–1996)

Courage is the core—

"In the present state of the world, a virile, strong Christianity must become a heroic Christianity. . . . Above all, this heroism will certainly not consist in constantly talking about heroism and raving about the virtue of strength—which would perhaps prove that one is under the influence of someone stronger and that one has begun to give up. It will consist, *above all*, in resisting with courage, in the face of the world and perhaps against one's own self, the lures and seductions of a false ideal and proudly maintaining, in their paradoxical intransigence, the Christian values that are threatening and derided. . . .

Gentleness and goodness, considerateness towards the lowly, pity for those who suffer, rejection of perverse methods, protection of the oppressed, unostentatious self-sacrifice, resistance to lies, the courage to call evil by its proper name, love of justice, the spirit of peace and concord, open-heartedness, mindfulness of heaven; those are the things that Christian heroism will rescue."[97]

The Drama of Atheistic Humanism, 1944

Henri de Lubac, SJ, was one of the most influential Catholic theologians of the twentieth century. He became a Jesuit in 1913 and a priest in 1927. During that time, he served in WWI. As a professor of theology at the University of Lyon, de Lubac's students include Hans Urs von Balthasar and Jean Daniélou. De Lubac was part of the resistance and a highly vocal opponent of Nazism and anti-Semitism. Though de Lubac stirred controversy with his works on nature and grace, his writings were influential at the Second Vatican Council. He was made a cardinal in 1983 by Pope John Paul II. Some of his important books include *The Mystery of the Supernatural* (1965), *The Discovery of God* (1956), and his four-volume *Medieval Exegesis* (1959–1965).

---

97 Henri de Lubac, S.J., *The Drama of Atheist Humanism*, trans. Edith M. Riley, Anne England, and Mark Sebanc (San Francisco: Ignatius Press, 1995), 129.

DAY 97

ROBERT HUGH BENSON (1871–1914)

Gothic needs Romanesque—

"In Rome I learned one supremely large lesson, among a hundred others. It has been well said that Gothic architecture represents the soul aspiring to God, and that Renaissance or Romanesque architecture represents God tabernacling with men. Both sides are true, yet neither, in the religion of the Incarnation, is complete without the other. On the one side, it is true that the soul must always be seeking, always gazing up through the darkness to God. . . . Then, on the other side, God became — 'the Word was made flesh.' . . . It is not only we who stand and knock: it is God Who, thirsting for love, died on the cross that He might open the kingdom of heaven to all believers."[98]

Confessions of a Convert, 1913

Robert Hugh Benson was the youngest son of a prominent Anglican clergyman who in 1982 was appointed archbishop of Canterbury. Robert, however, was on his way into the Catholic Church and was received in 1903. His conversion stirred much controversy; not only was Benson's father the leading Anglican

---

98 Robert Hugh Benson, *Confessions of a Convert* (New York: Longmans, Green, and Co., 1913), 152-53.

bishop in England, but both his brothers were prominent intellectuals and writers. Nonetheless, Benson was ordained a priest in 1904 and became both a popular preacher and a successful writer of fiction. A collection of his sermons from 1913, published as *The Paradoxes of Catholicism*, demonstrate his facility. Benson wrote fifteen novels, including the well-known *Lord of the World* (1907), before his early death in 1914. Another novel of distinction is *Come Rack! Come Rope!* (1912), which depicts Catholic persecution during the English Reformation.

DAY 98

WALTER M. MILLER, JR. (1923–1996)

Something was missing—

"The closer men came to perfecting for themselves a paradise, the more impatient they became with it, and with themselves as well. They made a garden of pleasure, and became progressively more miserable with it as it grew in richness and power and beauty; for then, perhaps, it was easier to see something was missing in the garden, some tree or shrub that would not grow. When the world was in darkness and wretchedness, it could believe in perfection and yearn for it. But when the world became bright with reason and riches, it began to sense

the narrowness of the needle's eye, and that rankled for a world no longer willing to believe or yearn."[99]

A Canticle for Leibowitz, 1959

Walter Miller, Jr. grew up in Florida and was educated at the University of Tennessee and the University of Texas. He flew in B-52s in WWII and participated in the bombing of Monte Cassino, the ancient Dominican monastery north of Naples. The trauma he experienced from the bombing led to his conversion to Catholicism after the war. Miller started writing science fiction, and in 1959, he published *A Canticle for Leibowitz* which won the 1961 Hugo Award for best novel. Miller never published another novel and eventually he began to avoid contact with everyone—family, friends, and even his literary agent. He was working on a sequel to *Canticle* when he committed suicide in 1996. The sequel, which was six-hundred pages long, was completed by another science fiction writer chosen by Miller and was published in 1997 with the title *Saint Leibowitz and the Wild Horse Woman*.

---

99 Walter M. Miller Jr., *A Canticle for Leibowitz* (New York: Bantam Books, 2007), 287-88.

DAY 99

WILLIAM E. MAY (1928–2014)

Children are not a burden—

"There may be 'burdens' in having and raising a good number of children, but the burdens involved pale in comparison to the great blessing and gift of every child and the blessings of a large family. Children are in fact the 'crowning gift' of marriage. They come into being when a husband and wife, who have already given themselves irrevocably to one another in marriage, become literally 'one flesh;' when they give themselves to each other and receive each other lovingly in the marital act, the only bodily act capable of generating new human life. And it is good for them and their parents to be 'begotten' in an act of marital love. Sexual 'partners' can of course generate new human life, but the child thus generated, while a precious and a singularly unique person, is harmed because mere partners who sexually engage their bodies, though not unconditionally and in a life-long commitment of love and responsibility, are not disposed to give the child the home it needs to take root and learn how to love and serve others."[100]

"The Blessings of a Large Family," 2010

---

100 William E. May, 'The Blessings of a Large Family,' July 8, 2010; read at https://www.culture-of-life.org/2010/07/08/the-blessings-of-a-large-family/.

William E. May was a professor of moral theology at Catholic
University of America from 1971 until 1991. He then joined
the faculty of the Pontifical John Paul II Institute for Studies
on Marriage and the Family. As a doctoral student, May was
a dissenter from *Humanae vitae*, but when he changed his
mind, the Religion Department at the Catholic University of
America fired him. Seeking a new academic home, he was
awarded tenure by a single vote in the Catholic University
of America's Graduate School of Theology. His students agree
that May loved teaching most of all, but his books and articles
were and still are widely read. His 2010 book, *The Theology of
the Body in Context*, is an excellent summary of St. John Paul
II's teachings on marriage, family, and sexuality.

DAY 100

JOSEF PIEPER (1904–1997)

On festivity—

"From this it follows that the concept of festivity is inconceivable without an element of contemplation. This does not mean
exerting the argumentative intellect, but the 'simple intuition'
of reason; not the unrest of thought, but the mind's eye resting on whatever manifests itself. It means a relaxing of the
strenuous fixation of the eye on the given frame of reference,

without which no utilitarian act is accomplished. Instead, the field of vision widens, concern for success or failure of an act falls away, and the soul turns to its infinite object; it becomes aware of the illimitable horizon of reality as a whole."[101]

In Tune With the World, 1963

As Catholics, we hear about celebration, and we talk about celebration, but the celebration described here by Josef Pieper is rarely met. It's exempted by those who cannot get out of church fast enough after receiving the Eucharist. They've left no moment for contemplation or the relaxation of "the mind's eye." The only horizon being considered is the way out of the parking lot. True festivity is both joyous and meditative, creating a wider "field of vision," more than what must be marked off the day's checklist. Festivity knows rest as well as motion, but without rest, the motion remains ordinary, part of the day-to-dayness of life.

---

101 Josef Pieper, *In Tune With the World: A Theory of Festivity*, trans. Richard and Clara Winston (Chicago: Franciscan Herald Press, 1965), 13.

DAY 101

CAROLINE GORDON (1895–1981)

No floating ideas—

"The proper subject of a novel, then, is love, and it must be incarnated, as Christ was. Christ could not have accomplished the redemption of mankind if he had stayed in Heaven with His Father. He had to come to earth and take human shape. So does every idea in your head that goes into your novel. It cannot float in the ether, that is, you cannot have a scene that is not located in time and space. Your business as a novelist is to imitate Christ. He is about his Father's business every moment of His life. As a good novelist you must be about yours: Incarnation, making your word flesh and making it dwell among men."[102]

Letter to Walker Percy, 1951

Caroline Gordon grew up in the Deep South of Kentucky. She was a Southern belle with bohemian tendencies. She graduated Bethany College in 1916 and worked as a society reporter for the *Chattanooga Reporter*. Her reporting there consisted mainly of the society news. She left the newspaper in 1924,

---

102 Letter to Walker Percy (c. 1951), Southern Historical Collection, University of North Carolina, Chapel Hill; read at https://scholarworks.wm.edu/cgi/viewcontent.cgi?article=4799&context=etd.

soon met the poet Allan Tate, and they were married in 1925 at New York's City Hall. She was already five months pregnant. Because of her husband's temper and infidelities, the marriage was not a happy one. Husband and wife were both writers hoping for success. After much travel, they made a home in Clarksville, Tennessee that they called Benfolly. Gordon converted to Catholicism in 1947 after having divorced Tate two years earlier, but remarried and divorced him again in 1959. Gordon published ten novels, including *Aleck Maury, Sportsman* (1934), *None Shall Look Back* (1937), *The Women on the Porch* (1944), and *The Malefactors* (1956), which reflects her conversion. She was a lively correspondent, as this letter to Walker Percy attests.

DAY 102

JAMES V. SCHALL (1928–2019)

Protecting ourselves—

"Revelation does agitate reason, does make it look outside of itself, which is indeed the purpose of reality before reason as well as the purpose of revelation before reason. But the human being can and does at times will or will not to accept certain truths of what it is. It makes this choice not because there is not some guidance from revelation, but because there is. This

is to say, that most of our intellectual problems are moral problems. We do not want to know the truth because we see where it might lead us and what it might entail in our way of living. We 'protect' ourselves from truth by looking away from revelation and then from reason."[103]

Roman Catholic Political Philosophy, 2004

Rev. James Schall, SJ, was a widely-respected and much-beloved teacher and political philosopher who taught for thirty-five years at Georgetown University, where he earned his doctorate in 1960. Before Georgetown, he taught in Rome at the Pontifical Gregorian University and the University of San Francisco. An extremely prolific writer, Father Schall published thirty-five books and regularly wrote for Catholic magazines and journals. Schall is particularly admired for his explanation and defense of natural law.

---

103 James V. Schall, *Roman Catholic Political Philosophy* (Lanham: Lexington Books, 2004), 119–20.

DAY 103

DANA GIOIA (1950–)

A painful liturgy—

"Whenever the Church has abandoned the notion of beauty it has lost precisely the power that it hoped to cultivate—its ability to reach souls in the modern world. Is it any wonder that so many artists and intellectuals have fled the Church? Current Catholic worship often ignores the essential connection between truth and beauty, body and soul, at the center of the Catholic worldview. The Church requires that we be faithful, but must we also be deaf, dumb, and blind? I deserve to suffer for my sins, but must so much of the punishment take place in church?"[104]

The Catholic Writer Today, 2013

Dana Gioia is an American poet who embraced New Formalism, a movement which brought more traditional forms of poetry back into the mainstream. He's known among Catholics for unapologetically expressing his faith not only through his poetry but also as an essayist, teacher, and public figure. From 2003 to 2009, Gioia chaired the National Endowment for the Arts and later taught as a professor of poetry and public culture

---

104 Dana Gioia, *The Catholic Writer Today and Other Essays* (Belmont: Wiseblood Books, 2018), 38.

at the University of Southern California from 2011 to 2015. In 2018 Gioia was named state poet laureate of California. He was previously a vice-president at General Foods, but after leaving the company, he soon became one of this nation's leading poets. His poetry collections are *Daily Horoscope* (1986), *The Gods of Winter* (1991), *Interrogations at Noon* (2001), which won the American Book Award in 2002, *Pity the Beautiful* (2012), and *99 Poems* (2016). Gioia has also written three opera libretti, poetry for song cycles with major composers, volumes of literary criticism, and several dozen literary anthologies. Of particular interest to Catholics is *The Catholic Writer Today and Other Essays* (2018), in which he addresses the isolation of Catholic artists and writers.

DAY 104

ST. JOHN HENRY NEWMAN (1801–1890)

Hearts lead minds—

"When men change their religious opinions really and truly, it is not merely their opinions that they change, but their hearts; and this evidently is not done in a moment — it is a slow work; nevertheless, though gradual, the change is often not uniform, but proceeds, so to say, by fits and starts, being influenced by external events, and other circumstances. This we see in the

growth of plants, for instance; it is slow, gradual, continual; yet one day by chance they grow more than another, they make a shoot, or at least we are attracted to their growth on that day by some accidental circumstance, and it remains on our memory. So with our souls: we all, by nature, are far from God."[105]

Parochial and Plain Sermons, January 25, 1832

Although we often talk about a "moment" when a person "loses his faith," St. John Henry Newman regards that loss as happening over a period of time. The moment of self-conscious realization has been foreshadowed by any number of events in a person's life. Just as faith is a journey, so is the way of unbelief. It's similar to the growth of a person's life, though not as protracted. Every person passes through stages of growth, from childhood and adolescence to adulthood, middle-age, and beyond. But at some moment, who you are is confirmed—you have become the person you are going to be, the person who was in preparation all those years.

---

105 *The Quotable Newman: A Definitive Guide to John Henry Newman's Central Thoughts and Ideas,* ed. Dave Armstrong (Manchester: Sophia Institute Press, 2012), loc. 65-66, Kindle Edition.

DAY 105

HEINRICH A. ROMMEN (1897–1967)

Families first—

"The family is prior to the state. The state may never take over entirely the ends and functions of the family, even though it may have the duty, in virtue of its right to guardianship, to intervene in case this or that family is delinquent in its own duty. The essential structure of the family, which exists prior to the state, signifies also that the family is an autonomous sphere of right. Parents, especially the father, have natural rights that positive law does not confer upon them, but which, as already existent, it protects and guarantees. From the marriage contract spring the natural rights of the husband and wife to each other's persons, so that the breach of such rights (adultery) is accounted unjust in itself and there unjust independently of the positive law. . . . The fact of the matter is the end or meaning of marriage and the family is independent of the will of the state as well as the will of the parties to the marriage contract."[106]

The Natural Law, 1936

---

106 Heinrich A. Rommen, *The Natural Law: A Study in Legal and Social History and Philosophy,* trans. Thomas R. Hanley, O.S.B., introduction by Russell Hittinger (Indianapolis: Liberty Fund, 1998), 212.

Heinrich Rommen was a Catholic German lawyer who practiced during the Weimar Republic before fleeing to the United States in 1938. He taught in Germany and England before concluding his distinguished scholarly career at Georgetown University (1953–67). Rommen is known in the United States primarily as the author of two widely-read books on political philosophy, *The State in Catholic Thought: A Treatise in Political Philosophy* (1945) and *The Natural Law* (1947). Before fleeing the Third Reich for the United States, Rommen devoted considerable energies to Catholic social action during the dissolution of the Weimar Republic and the rise of the Nazi Party, for which he was imprisoned by the Nazis.

DAY 106

GEORGES BERNANOS (1888–1948)

A sickly young French priest deals with his parishioner's scorn, cynicism, and disbelief—

"There are some thoughts which I never dare confide, though they don't seem mad to me—far from it. I wonder what I should become if I resigned myself to the part which many Catholics would have me play—those that are so preoccupied with social preservation, which really means their own preservation. Oh, I don't accuse these people of hypocrisy, I believe

them to be sincere. So many of us, supposedly standing for law and order, are merely clinging on to old habits, sometimes to a mere parrot vocabulary, its formulae worn so smooth by constant use that they justify everything and question nothing. It is one of the most mysterious penalties of men that they should be forced to confide the most precious of their possessions to things so unstable and ever changing, alas, as words. It needs much courage to inspect the key each time and adapt it to one's own lock. It is far easier to force up the latch with the nearest and handiest—so long as the lock works somehow. I wonder at revolutionaries who strive so hard to blow up the walls with dynamite, when the average bunch of keys of law-abiding folk would have sufficed to let them in quietly."[107]

The Diary of a Country Priest, 1936

A classmate of Charles de Gaulle, George Bernanos was taught by the Jesuits at Vaugirard College in Paris. After receiving a degree in law from the Sorbonne, he served in WWI, where he was wounded and was awarded the *Croix de guerre*. His marriage in 1917 to Jeanne Talbert d'Arc, a collateral descendant of Joan of Arc, produced three daughters and three sons. He was forty when he published his first book, the novel *Under the Star of Satan* (1926), which brought him immediate fame. Several of his novels have been made into distinguished films,

---

107 Georges Bernanos, *The Diary of a Country Priest*, trans. Gerard Hopkins (Classica Libris, 2019), loc. 41, Kindle Edition.

particularly *The Diary of a Country Priest* (1951), directed by Robert Bresson. All of his novels share portrayals of evil that make some Catholic readers uncomfortable, which is precisely what the author had in mind.

DAY 107

GERMAIN GRISEZ (1929–2018)

Hysterical reasoning—

"The hysteria in favor of contraception does evidence the working of a spirit, but one may doubt that it is the Holy Spirit. The spirit seems more that of a mob, of mass movement. In our time we have seen public opinion too often stirred to a fever pitch to place much confidence in it. One example can illustrate the point. During World War II, the British and American air forces—at first in reaction to German excesses—adopted a policy of strategic, saturated bombing. Non-military objectives were obliterated along with military targets. Almost all the public in Britain and America knew of this policy and supported it without reservation. Nevertheless, a strategic bombing survey carried out after the war revealed that this policy, adopted on the grounds of 'military necessity,' was not even very effective from a strictly military standpoint. . . . Where were Catholics and other Christians while the innocent

were being obliterated uselessly? Where were the priests, moral theologians, and bishops? . . . They were cheerleading."[108]

"Contraception and Reality," 1967

Germain Grisez was a highly-esteemed theologian whose work on ethics had a direct impact on Pope John Paul II's 1993 encyclical *Veritatis Splendor*. His most important work is the three-volume, three-thousand page *The Way of the Lord Jesus* (1983–1997). His friend Russell Shaw, a noted historian and apologist, calls it "a virtual Summa of moral theology." A Cleveland native, Grisez studied at John Carroll University, the University of Chicago, and the Dominican House of Studies in River Forest, IL. He taught at Mount St. Mary's Seminary in Emmitsburg, MD for thirty years before his retirement. Shaw also reports that Grisez was asked by a cardinal to submit a critique of the draft of the *Catechism of the Catholic Church* and, as a result, it was "significantly stronger and clearer than it otherwise might have been."

---

108 Germain Grisez, "Contraception and Reality, Parts I, II, III," *The Best of Triumph* (Front Royal: Christendom Press, 2001), 187.

DAY 108

DONALD DEMARCO (1937–)

Compassion gone crazy—

"Whereas chastity is the contemporary world's most unpopular virtue, compassion is clearly its favorite. It has become a cultural imperative that we have compassion for others. Compassion's popularity, unfortunately, is so great that it tends to isolate this virtue from all those other factors it needs in order to remain truly a virtue. Consequently, compassion becomes an argument unto itself, so to speak, to justify abortion, sterilization, euthanasia, and sundry other actions that are aimed at reducing the amount of misery that currently afflicts mankind. Separated from love, light, generosity, hope, patience, courage, and determination, 'compassion' becomes nothing more than a code word whose real name is expediency."[109]

The Heart of Virtue, 1996

Donald DeMarco is one of the most notable pro-life voices among Catholic philosophers in the past four decades. He is the author of twenty-eight books, professor emeritus at St. Jerome's University in Waterloo, Ontario, and adjunct professor at Holy

---

109 Donald DeMarco, *The Heart of Virtue: Lessons from Life and Literature Illustrating the Beauty and Value of Moral Character* (San Francisco, Ignatius Press, 1996), 38.

Apostles College and Seminary in Cromwell, Connecticut. He is a regular columnist for *Crisis*, *Imaginative Conservative*, and the *National Catholic Register*. Like all successful apologists, DeMarco has a remarkable gift for explaining Catholic philosophy and theology, especially in its moral dimension, to the laity. Some of his recent books include *How to Flourish in a Fallen World* (2019), *Apostles of the Culture of Life* (2018), and *Ten Major Moral Mistakes* (2015).

DAY 109

HANS URS VON BALTHASAR (1905–1988)

He catches us all—

"For his [Christ's] weakness would already be the victory of his love for the Father, reconciliation in the eyes of the Father, and, as a deed of his supreme strength, this weakness would be so great that it would far surpass and sustain in itself the world's pitiful feebleness. He alone would henceforth be the measure and thus also the meaning of all impotence. *He wanted to sink so low that in the future all falling would be a falling into him, and every*

streamlet of bitterness and despair would henceforth run down into his lowermost abyss."[110] (Emphasis added.)

The Heart of the World, 1945

It's difficult to comment on a passage as extraordinary and memorable as this one by Hans Urs von Balthasar. No doubt a portion of its beauty comes from the hand of the translator, Erasmo S. Leiva. Consider, "He wanted to sink so low that in the future all falling would be a falling unto him." To read this for the first time is like first seeing a great painting—it sets off sparks of thought and imagination which settle into the heart with a kind of redemptive emotion. The second half of that sentence contains an image just as surprising and moving, "and every streamlet of bitterness and despair would henceforth run down to his lowermost abyss." There can be no greater assurance, hope, or offer of forgiveness.

---

110 Hans Urs von Balthasar, *The Heart of the World*, trans. Erasmo S. Leiva (San Francisco: Ignatius Press, 1979), 43.

DAY 110

ST. TERESA OF CALCUTTA (1910–1997)

The greatest suffering—

"There is much suffering in the world—physical, material, mental. The suffering of some can be blamed on the greed of others. The material and physical suffering is suffering from hunger, from homelessness, from all kinds of diseases. But the greatest suffering is being lonely, feeling unloved, having no one. I have come more and more to realize that it is being unwanted that is the worst disease any human being can ever experience."[111]

Born to ethnic Albanians in Macedonia, Teresa Bojaxhiu was only eighteen when she joined the Institute of the Blessed Virgin Mary in Ireland. A year later, in 1929, she traveled to Calcutta, India where she was assigned to teach at St. Mary's School for girls. In 1946, Mother Teresa, as she was then called, was riding a train when she felt inspired by Jesus to start a ministry to serve the poor. She founded the Missionaries of Charity in 1948 to serve the poorest of the poor. For forty-nine years she led her sisters, and during that time she became world-famous, winning the Noble Peace Prize in 1979. She was admired by

---

111 *Mother Teresa: Her Essential Wisdom,* ed. Carol Kelly-Gangi (New York: Barnes & Noble Publishing, Inc., 2006), 89.

Christians and non-Christians alike for her example in serving the poor in places where most people would never dare take a step. A fierce defender of innocent life, Mother Teresa was not one to mince her words, even speaking in front of President Bill Clinton and First Lady Hilary Clinton. The tiny woman who, along with her sisters, took in all the suffering brought to their doorstep, spoke with an unassailable power that could not be ignored. Pope Francis Canonized Mother Teresa of Calcutta as a saint in Rome on September 4, 2016.

DAY 111

BALTASAR GRACIAN (1601–1658)

Learning to say no—

"Know how to Refuse. One ought not to give way in everything nor to everybody. To know how to refuse is therefore as important as to know how to consent. This is especially the case with men of position. All depends on the *how*. Some men's No is thought more of than the Yes of others: for a gilded No is more satisfactory than a dry Yes. There are some who always have No on their lips, whereby they make everything distasteful. No always comes first with them, and when sometimes they give way after all, it does them no good on account of the unpleasing herald. Your refusal need not be point-blank: let the

disappointment come by degrees. Nor let the refusal be final; that would be to destroy dependence; let some spice of hope remain to soften the rejection. Let politeness compensate and fine words supply the place of deeds. Yes and No are soon said, but give much to think over."[112]

The Art of Worldly Wisdom, 1647

The Spanish-born Balthasar Gracian entered formation to become a Jesuit priest in 1619. After ordination in 1627, he taught widely, becoming a preacher of note in Madrid and teaching philosophy at the University of Gandia. Something of a provocateur, Gracian lost his tenure over his more radical writing. His *The Art of Worldly Wisdom* contains three-hundred maxims on a wide range of personal and public subjects, and his wisdom remains immediately relevant to our day and age. His wit and concision appealed to a variety of subsequent writers who also used maxims and aphorisms in their work, such as Nietzsche, La Rochefoucauld, Voltaire, and Schopenhauer.

---

112 Baltasar Gracian, *The Art of Worldly Wisdom*, trans. Joseph Jacobs, loc. 994 of 2292, Kindle Edition.

DAY 112

ROBERT BRESSON (1901–1999)

A film director favors indirection—

"Hide the ideas, but so that people can find them. The most important will be hidden."[113]

***

"Not to shoot a film in order to illustrate a thesis, or to display men and women confined to their external aspect, but to discover the matter they are made of. To attain that 'heart of the heart' which does not let itself be caught either by poetry, or by philosophy, or by drama."[114]

Notes on the Cinematograph, 2016

Robert Bresson is the greatest Catholic film director in the history of cinema. For depicting the spiritual on screen, his only peer is Ingmar Bergman (1918–2007), whose Christian vision was deeply Protestant. Both Bresson and Bergman practiced the maxims above: a film should not be made to "illustrate a thesis"—any message must be "hidden" so that the viewers can discover it for themselves. Born in the provinces,

---

113 Robert Bresson, *Notes on the Cinematograph*, trans. Jonathan Griffin (New York: New York Review Books Classics, 2016), 25.

114 Ibid., 27.

Bresson moved to Paris to become a painter. At the beginning of WWII, he became a soldier and was captured in 1940, serving at a labor camp for a year before his release. Shortly after, Bresson turned to filmmaking and released his first movie, *Angels of Sin* (1943). The Catholic faith is an integral part of Bresson's cinematic vision and is expressed in various ways in all thirteen of his films. After making *Les dames du Bois de Boulogne* (1945), he made what many consider his masterpiece, *Diary of a Country Priest* (1951) based upon the novel by Georges Bernanos, which was met with widespread acclaim. Some critics find masterpieces among his other films, such as *A Man Escaped* (1956), *Mouchette* (1967), *Pickpocket*, (1959), *The Trial of Joan of Arc* (1962), and *Au Hasard Balthazar* (1966).

DAY 113

PIERRE MANENT (1949–)

Church at the center—

"The Catholic Church will not rid itself of the imputation of intolerance that attached to it, whatever it may say or do. Though past history provides ample justification for this accusation, it must be admitted that today the Catholic Church is the least intolerant and the most open of the spiritual forces that concern us. In particular, being alone capable of nourishing a

meaningful and substantial relationship with all the other spiritual forces, it is the center or the pivot of a configuration in which we have to live and to think. It is thus the mediator *par excellence*, not in the theological sense that makes the Church. ...The Pope has put down his tiara, and the Church no longer claims to gather humanity under its rule. Still, given the spiritual fragmentation that affects the Western world, it is the fixed point that is concerned to relate itself intelligently to all the other points, and to which the other points can try to relate."[115]

Beyond Radical Secularism, 2016

Pierre Manent was born into a Communist household and educated in communist schools. While a student, however, Manent learned about Catholicism from a teacher who had rejected Communism for the Church. It was during the Paris riots of May 1968 that Manent recognized the hollowness of Communist pretensions. His contact with the renowned philosopher Raymond Aron at his seminars put Manent side-by-side with many of France's leading intellectuals. Aron encouraged Manent to study the political philosophy of Leo Strauss. As Aron's assistant at the Collège de France from 1974 to 1992, Manent became an anti-communist and joined a group led by Francois Furet that was opposing totalitarianism

---

115 Pierre Manent, *Beyond Radical Secularism: How France and the Christian West Should Respond to the Islamic Challenge*, trans. Ralph Hancock, introduction by Daniel J. Mahoney (South Bend: St. Augustine's Press, 2016), 105.

with a "liberal political science of democratic society." Manent
has published widely, and until 2014, he was the director of the
Raymond Aron Center for the Study of Sociology and Politics
at the School for Advanced Studies in the Social Sciences in
Paris.

DAY 114

JOHN COURTNEY MURRAY, SJ (1904–1967)

An order of beings—

"Reason does not create its own laws any more than man
creates himself. Man has the laws of his nature given to him, as
nature itself is given. By nature he is the image of God, eternal Reason; and so his reason reflects a higher reason: therein
consists its rightness and its power to oblige. Above the natural law immanent in man stands the eternal law immanent in
God transcendent; and the two laws are in intimate correspondence, as the image is to the exemplar. The eternal law is the
Uncreated Reason of God; it appoints an order of nature—an
order of beings, each of which carries in its very nature also its
end and purposes; and it commands that this order of nature
be preserved by the steady pursuit of their ends on the part of
all the natures within the order. Every created nature has this
eternal law, this transcendent order of reason, imprinted on

it by the very fact that it is a nature, a purposeful dynamism striving for the fullness of its own being."[116]

We Hold These Truths, 1960

John Courtney Murray, SJ, entered the New York province of the Society of Jesus in 1920 and was ordained a Catholic priest in 1933. He spent his career teaching and writing at Woodstock College in Maryland, from where he graduated in 1934. His early scholarly work centered on the doctrine of the Trinity, but he found himself drawn into public debates about the relation of Catholicism, and other faiths, to politics and culture. Murray took issue with the coercive habits the Catholic Church carried over from the European heritage of Church-controlled states. For example, Murray argued that central concepts like human dignity and religious freedom were known by theists and believers outside the Church. He went even further regarding the relationship between church and state when he argued greater truths about religious freedom had been developed outside the Church, which led to his censuring by Rome. In spite of this, Murray attended the second session of Vatican II and drafted the final version of *On the Dignity of the Human Person* (1965). His influential book *We Hold These Truths: Catholic Reflections on the American Proposition*

---

116 John Courtney Murray, S.J., *We Hold These Truths: Catholic Reflections on the American Proposition* (New York: Sheed and Ward, 1960), 330.

(1960) is a collection of thirteen essays written between 1950 and 1960.

DAY 115

RÉMI BRAGUE (1947–)

The necessity of the Incarnation—

"If God entered into history, it is necessary, first, that the Son be in some sense the same as the Father. Otherwise, the history of salvation would not personally engage God. He would remain, as it were, on the balcony, like the Homeric gods observing the battles of men. It would refer to someone who simply observed what happened, which concerned him not, except perhaps by means of an intermediary. The destiny of the incarnate Son, therefore, would not be the Father's own. To send the Son would be a way of putting himself at a distance. But, if there is to be an entrance of God in history, it is also necessary that the Father not be the Son, purely and simply. Otherwise, it would not be God who became incarnate. Becoming man, by that very token he would cease to be God. Or rather, he could not *become* man, but would be a human from eternity, by his very nature, instead of entering the human realm — with all it

entailed — by his free choice. And the history of Christ would not have its particular relevance."[117]

On the God of the Christians, 2013

Rémi Brague is a French historian of philosophy, specializing in the Arabic, Jewish, and Christian thought of the Middle Ages. He is a professor emeritus of Arabic and religious philosophy at the Sorbonne. At the Sorbonne, as a young man, he studied Greek Philosophy before learning Hebrew to read the Old Testament. To read Moses Maimonides' *Guide to the Perplexed*, Brague learned Arabic. He credits the philosopher Leo Strauss for inspiring him to read the original ancient texts: "you must be open to the possibility that it contains different layers of meaning. All philosophical books written before the Enlightenment aim at both a wider audience and a small elite, able to understand the deeper meaning of the texts." Brague is best known in the United States for his book *Eccentric Culture: A Theory of Western Civilization* (1992).

---

117 Rémi Brague, *On the God of the Christians (and on one or two others)*, trans. Paul Seaton (South Bend: St. Augustine's Press, 2013), 104.

DAY 116

THOMAS MOLNAR (1921–2010)

Empty signs—

"What we witness today is the transformation—the degradation of the symbol into the sign. That is, the instrument that
participates in the reality of being is ever more transformed
into a simple reference, a reminder, as the green and red traf-
fic lights remind motorists of their duties on the road. And
the process does not even stop there. The new interpretation
displaces the religious emphasis itself. Many modern religious
authors (even some priests) and various analysts of the religious situation speak of the sacred as located now in human
contingency, in human dignity, in cosmic symbolism—in other
words, in humanity's assessment of themselves as the only conscious reality in the world. Outside of humanity nothing really
is, nothing has being. Behind the sign there is nothing; they are
merely convenient guideposts for human communication. . . .
In Christianity, not only does the Incarnate Word assume the
central symbolization; it also mediates between the divine and
human orders."[118]

The Pagan Temptation, 1987

---

118 Thomas Molnar, *The Pagan Temptation* (Grand Rapids: William B. Eerdmans
Publishing Company, 1987), 192-94.

Thomas Steven Molnar was born in Budapest and completed his undergraduate studies in Belgium, where he was as a leader in the Catholic student movement. He was arrested, sent to Dachau, and released after the war. Molnar witnessed the Communist takeover of Hungary. Moving to America, he received his PhD in philosophy and history from Columbia University. Molnar taught religious philosophy at universities throughout the United States, Europe, South America, and South Africa. He wrote over forty books in English, French, Spanish, and Hungarian. Molnar wrote frequently for *National Review, Triumph,* and *Modern Age. The Decline of the Intellectual* (1961) is his best-known book. Molnar received the Sczechenyi Award, the nation's highest honor from the president of the Republic of Hungary.

DAY 117

ST. JOHN HENRY NEWMAN (1801–1890)

On faith and reason—

"This opposition between Faith and Reason takes place in two ways, when either of the two encroaches upon the province of the other. It would be an absurdity to attempt to find out mathematical truths by the purity and acuteness of the moral sense. It is a form of this mistake which has led men to

apply such Scripture communications as are intended for religious purposes to the determination of physical questions. This error is perfectly understood in these days by all thinking men. This was the usurpation of the schools of theology in former ages, to issue their decrees to the subjects of the Senses and the Intellect. No wonder Reason and Faith were at variance. The other cause of disagreement takes place when Reason is the aggressor, and encroaches on the province of Religion, attempting to judge of those truths which are subjected to another part of our nature, the moral sense."[119]

University Sermon, December 11, 1831

What St. John Henry Newman says here could be applied to the experience of Galileo and other Catholic scientists who were censured and punished by the Church for contradicting a doctrine that should have never been based upon Scripture in the first place. Here's clearly a case, as Newman puts it, of faith encroaching on an issue that belongs to reason: does the Sun revolve around the earth or the earth around the sun? Since the time of Galileo, however, the momentum has moved in the opposite direction—reason regularly encroaches on matters of faith, for example, by claiming there is no God or Divine Creation. There are "degrees of knowledge," to borrow the title of a book by Jacques Maritain. Newman, of course,

---

119 Dave Armstrong, ed., *The Quotable Newman: A Definitive Guide to John Henry Newman's Central Thoughts and Ideas* (Manchester: Sophia Institute Press, 2012), loc. 158, Kindle Edition.

is well aware of those degrees although he does not elaborate them in this sermon. St. Thomas said, we must "distinguish in order to unite," and that is what needs to be kept in mind if faith and reason are to work together.

DAY 118

THOMAS E. WOODS, JR. (1972–)

Birth of the university—

"Although many college students today couldn't locate the Middle Ages on a historical timeline, they are nevertheless sure that the period was one of ignorance, superstition, and intellectual repression. Nothing could be further from the truth—it is to the Middle Ages that we owe one of Western civilization's greatest—unique—intellectual contributions to the world: the university system. The university was an utterly new phenomenon in European history. Nothing like it had existed in ancient Greece or Rome. The institution that we recognize today, with its faculties, courses of study, examinations, and degrees, as well as the distinction between undergraduate and graduate study, comes to us directly from the medieval world. The Church developed the university system because, according to historian Lowrie Daly, it was 'the only institution in Europe that showed consistent interest in the preservation and cultivation

of knowledge.' We cannot give exact dates for the appearance
of universities at Paris and Bologna, Oxford and Cambridge,
since they evolved over a period of time—the former beginning as cathedral schools and the latter as informal gatherings
of masters and students. But we may safely say that they began
taking form during the latter half of the twelfth century. In
order to identify a particular medieval school as a university, we
look for certain characteristic features. A university possessed
a core of required texts, on which professors would lecture
while adding their own insights. A university was also characterized by well-defined academic programs lasting a more or
less fixed number of years, as well as by the granting of degrees.
The granting of a degree, since it entitled the recipient to be
called master, amounted to admitting new people to the teaching guild, just as a master craftsman was admitted to the guild
of his own profession."[120]

How the Catholic Church Built Western Civilization, 2005

Thomas E. Woods, Jr. reminds us that the tradition of education in the West began with a university system created by
the Catholic clergy and religious in Bologna (1088), Oxford
(1096), Salamanca (1134), Paris (1150), Cambridge (1209),
Padua (1222), Naples (1224), and Toulouse (1229). The traditional Western curriculums of the Trivium and Quadrivium

---

120 Thomas E. Woods, Jr., *How the Catholic Church Built Western Civilization*
(Regnery History, 2005), loc. 47-48, Kindle Edition.

emerged from these universities, and their vestiges can still be seen in many high-school and college curricula.

DAY 119

CHATEAUBRIAND (1768–1884)

Religion and society—

"But, in the present order of things, how could you restrain an immense multitude of free peasants, far removed from the vigilance of the magistrate? How could you prevent the crimes of an independent populace, congregated in the suburbs of an extensive capital, if they did not believe in a religion which enjoins the practice of duty and virtue upon all the conditions of life? *Destroy the influence of the gospel, and you must give to every village its police, its prisons, its executioners.* If, by an impossibility, the impure altars of paganism were ever re-established among modern nations,—if, in a society where slavery is abolished, the worship of Mercury the robber and Venus the prostitute were to be introduced,—there would soon be a total extinction of the human race."[121] (Emphasis added.)

The Genius of Christianity, 1802

---

121 François-René, Vicomte de Chateaubriand, *The Genius of Christianity; or, The Spirit and Beauty of the Christian Religion* (Baltimore: J. Murphy, 1802), loc. 12929, Kindle Edition.

One of his biographers comments that François-René Chateaubriand was the dominant literary figure in France during the first half of the nineteenth century. When you recall that the French Revolution of 1789 to 1799 had destroyed much of the Church in France, egged on by the leading political and intellectual figures, Chateaubriand's eloquent and panoramic defense of Christianity has an important place in the history of Catholic apologetics. The exoticism of his early novels written in the same period, *Atala* (1801) and *Rene* (1802), combined with *The Genius of Christianity* to establish their author as the leading figure in the burgeoning Romantic movement in France. In spite of his fame, he lived a politically stormy and widely-flung life, including a stint in America to escape the excesses of the French Revolution, which provided the settings for the novels already mentioned plus his novel about the Natchez Indians, *Les Natchez* (1825).

DAY 120

THOMAS DUBAY, SM (1921–2010)

The eyes to see—

"A work of art possesses convincing power only to the extent that one is personally mature enough to appreciate it, that is, has the eyes to see and ears to hear. . . . Seeing the Christ

form is dependent upon our capacity to see natural beauty. While the latter is not enough, it is part of the maturing process that grace then uses to sharpen a new vision of divine glory. 'The same Christian centuries which masterfully knew how to read the natural world's language of forms were the very same ones which possessed eyes trained, first, to perceive the formal quality of revelation and by the aid of grace and its illumination and, second (and only then!), to interpret revelation' [Hans Urs von Balthasar]. Even more, notes Balthasar, the Incarnation perfects our grasp of created beauty. . . . It is not Sacred Scripture, which is God's original language and self-expression, but rather Jesus Christ. As one and Unique, and yet as one who is to be understood only in the context of the whole created cosmos, Jesus is the Word, the Image, the Expression, and the Exegesis of God.'"[122]

The Evidential Power of Beauty, 1999

A Marist priest for sixty years, Rev. Thomas Edward Dubay, SM, wrote over twenty books on Catholic spirituality, emphasizing the importance of contemplative prayer and spiritual renewal. He taught at colleges and seminaries across the United States, and for ten years, he was in residence at the Little French Church of Saint Louis, King of France in Saint Paul, MN, a parish entrusted by Archbishop John Ireland to

---

122 Thomas Dubay, S.M., *The Evidential Power of Beauty: Science and Theology Meet* (San Francisco: Ignatius Press, 1999), 299-300.

the pastoral care of the Marist Fathers in 1886. Father Dubay appeared on a number of very popular TV series on EWTN. He traveled widely to assist religious communities to respond to teachings of the Second Vatican Council.

DAY 121

JULIEN GREEN (1900–1988)

Supernatural coincidence—

"One afternoon in the autumn of 1915 a curious incident occurred. I was writing when I suddenly felt that I was not alone: someone, at the same instant, seated herself next to me. I felt no fear. It was not an illusion, simply the supernatural presence of my mother. I recognized her immediately as one would recognize a voice, a look, and I waited because I understood that she wanted to draw my attention to something. Without a word she drew me toward a small antechamber near where my father always dressed himself in the morning. There on the open shelves where his shirts were arranged I discovered a book, *The Faith of Our Fathers* by Cardinal Gibbons. The book was an explanation of the Catholic Faith and I started reading it with a passionate eagerness. It taught me, in fact, an enormous number of things that my mother had never mentioned, but which I was willing to accept without doubt. Page after

page I believed everything I read as unvarnished truth. I spent the whole day there reading the book, but I said not a thing of my secret reading. When I came to the sacraments and to the real presence in the Eucharist, I thought about my mother and my emotions were very strong. The following day I completed my reading. And then, what? How could I deal with this that had changed everything? I wanted to become a Catholic. To whom could I confide such a secret, and toward whom to turn except to my father who I knew to be forbearing. He listened to me, nodded his head and said simply, 'I became a Catholic myself, several months ago, in England.'"[123]

"Et in Jesum Christum," 1995

Julien Green, whose father was French and whose American mother was from the Deep South of Georgia, was prolific: he wrote seventeen novels, a four-volume autobiography, and nineteen volumes of *Diary* stretching from 1919 to 1998. Some of his early novels—*Avarice House* (1926) and *The Closed Garden* (1927)—were popular in English translations. His best-known and widely-translated novel, *Moira* (1950), recounts his student days at the University of Virginia. Along with Georges Bernanos and François Mauriac, Green is considered one of the finest Catholic novelists of twentieth-century France.

---

123 Julian Green, "Et in Jesum Christum: A Memoir," *Crisis Magazine*, July 1, 1995; available online at https://www.crisismagazine.com/1995/et-in-je-sum-christum-a-memoir.

DAY 122

JAMES MCAULEY (1917–1976)

Literature and life—

> "Literature is not disconnected from life. It can influence feel-
> ings, beliefs and values—and it can do so for good, it can also
> do so for evil. To deny this is to reduce literature to triviality.
> One has to find a point of balance as best one can. Some
> works invite a more realistic moral response than others. . . . If
> twentieth-century poetry seems too far away to be really prob-
> lematical to us, try the same treatment on modern pop songs,
> which in a very much lower degree may be of interest and
> show talent: they are a kind of play; but they are also at times
> products of the drug-cult or the cult of dropping-out, hanging
> loose, freeing up, or otherwise disregarding real responsibilities
> in favour of simple pseudo-solutions."[124]

Selected Prose, 1975

Born in a small town outside of Sydney in 1917, James
McAuley was a prominent man of letters who wrote poetry,
journalism, and literary criticism. Brought up in the Anglican
faith, McAuley lost his religious faith early. He founded
the literary journal *Hermes* in 1937. McAuley served in the

---

124 James McAuley, *Selected Prose 1959-1974* (Melbourne: Oxford University
Press, 1975), 136-37.

Australian Army during WWII, spending much time as a lieutenant in New Guinea, a land he came to love. McAuley was little known until he and Harold Stewart perpetrated a hoax on a modernist poetry journal, *Angry Penguins*, in 1943. They wrote sixteen poems in the modernist style they detested and sent them to editor Max Harris under the pseudonym of Ern Malley. The next issue of *Angry Penguins* hailed the greatness of Ern Malley and published all the poems. Modernist poetry in Australia suffered a hit when the hoax was revealed, and *Angry Penguins* went out of business. McAuley converted to Catholicism in 1952, and his subsequent prose and poetry reflect the seriousness of his faith. He founded another journal, *Quadrant*, and taught at the University of Tasmania until his early death from cancer in 1976. His *Versification: A Short Introduction* is still highly regarded while his poetry is known only to specialists.

DAY 123

JOHN SAWARD (1947–)

Martyrdom turns beautiful—

"The martyrdom of the Carmelite Nuns of Compiègne during the French Revolution has inspired four great works of twentieth-century art—four works, four art forms: a novel, a

film, a play, an opera. First, Gertrud von Le Fort wrote a novel. Then George Bernanos prepares the screenplay for a movie based upon the novel. Albert Beguin produces it on the stage. Finally, Francis Poulenc takes up the screenplay as a libretto for his *Dialogues des Carmelites*, one of the greatest operas of the twentieth century. Bernanos plunges into the theological depths of the drama. As the clouds of death gather (Bernanos wrote it in 1948 when he himself was dying of cancer), many of the nuns are bravely ready, but Sister Blanche of the Agony of Christ cannot master her fear of death. Her sisters—out of love, by prayer—take that fear from her and upon themselves. The Old Prioress dies a strange and disturbing death, one that does not seem to fit her. The Sub-Prioress, Marie de l'Incarnation, urges the community to take an oath of martyrdom, yet she does not die with the others; her cross is to go on living. As for Blanche herself, in the end she dies for Christ without dread. These acts of 'substitution and exchange' are not performed by the sisters' unaided human powers, but only through, with, and in Christ, in whose 'adorable Heart' in Gethsemane 'all human anguish was divinized.'"[125]

The Beauty of Holiness and the Holiness of Beauty, 1977

John Saward became a Catholic priest after being ordained an Anglican priest, marrying, and having three daughters. Saward

---

125 John Saward, *The Beauty of Holiness and the Holiness of Beauty: Art, Sanctity & The Truth of Catholicism* (San Francisco: Ignatius Press, 1977), 171-72.

is the parish priest of SS. Gregory & Augustine's in Oxford. From 1992 to 1996, he was professor of systematic theology at St. Charles Borromeo Seminary in Philadelphia. His books often stress the role of beauty in theology and spirituality. They include *Redeemer in the Womb: Jesus Living in Mary* (1993), *The Way of the Lamb: The Spirit of Childhood and the End of Age* (1999), and *Sweet and Blessed Country: The Christian Hope for Heaven* (2005).

DAY 124

THOMAS F. MADDEN (1960–)

The Crusaders made a difference—

"From the safe distance of many centuries, it is easy enough to scowl in disgust at the Crusades. Religion, after all, is nothing to fight wars over. But we should be mindful that our medieval ancestors would have been equally disgusted by our infinitely more destructive wars fought in the name of political ideologies. And yet, both the medieval and the modern soldier fight ultimately for their own world and all that makes it up. Both are willing to suffer enormous sacrifice, provided that it is in the service of something they hold dear, something greater than themselves. Whether we admire the Crusaders or not, it is a fact that the world we know today would not exist without

their efforts. The ancient faith of Christianity, with its respect for women and antipathy toward slavery, not only survived but flourished. Without the Crusades, it might well have followed Zoroastrianism, another of Islam's rivals, into extinction."[126]

"The Real History of the Crusades," 2011

Thomas F. Madden is a professor of history and director of the Center for Medieval and Renaissance Studies at Saint Louis University. His books include *Venice: A New History* (2012), *The Concise History of the Crusades* (2013), *Empires of Trust: How Rome Built—and America Is Building—A New World* (2008), *Enrico Dandolo and the Rise of Venice* (2003), and *Istanbul: City of Majesty at the Crossroads of the World* (2017). Madden is often seen as a commentator on television news shows and in the editorial pages of major newspapers.

---

126 Thomas F. Madden, "The Real History of the Crusades," *Crisis Magazine,* March 19, 2011, https://www.crisismagazine.com/2011/the-real-history-of-the-crusades.

DAY 125

TERTULLIAN (155–220)

Ancient voice against abortion—

"But in regard to child murder, as it does not matter whether it is committed for a sacred object, or merely at one's own self-impulse—although there is a great difference, as we have said, between patricide and homicide—I shall turn to the people generally. How many, think you, of those crowding around and gaping for Christian blood—how many even of your rulers, notable for their justice to you and for their severe measures against us, may I charge in their own consciences with the sin of putting their offspring to death? As to any difference in the kind of murder, it is certainly the more cruel way to kill by drowning, or by exposure to cold and hunger and dogs. A maturer age has always preferred death by the sword. In our case, murder being once for all forbidden, we may not destroy even the fœtus in the womb, while as yet the human being derives blood from other parts of the body for its sustenance. To hinder a birth is merely a speedier man-killing; nor does it matter whether you take away a life that is born, or destroy one that is coming to the birth. That is a man which is going to be one; you have the fruit already in its seed. As to meals of blood and such tragic dishes, read—I am not sure where it is told (it is in Herodotus, I think)—how blood taken from the arms, and

tasted by both parties, has been the treaty bond among some nations."[127]

Apology, 197

The importance of Tertullian can be immediately recognized by the fact that he was the first Latin writer to use the word *trinitas*. He came from the part of northern Africa, Carthage, where St. Augustine studied centuries later. His writings were so vast, and theological acumen so brilliant, that he has been called the father of Latin Christianity. Thirty-one books have survived. According to the historian Eusebius, Tertullian was both a lawyer and a priest, though the latter claim has been questioned. He was a convert to Catholicism and was married to a Catholic wife. Tertullian's *Apology* is one of several treatises written as a defense of Christianity in the face of Roman persecution.

---

127 Tertullian, *Apology, The Complete Works of the Church Fathers,* ed. Phil Schaff (Toronto, 2016), loc. 538538-538547, Kindle Edition.

DAY 126

HILAIRE BELLOC (1870–1953)

Coming home—

"The Faith, the Catholic Church, is discovered, is recognized, triumphantly enters reality like a landfall at sea which first was thought a cloud. The nearer it is seen, the more it is real, the less imaginary: the more direct and external its voice, the more indubitable its representative character, its 'persona,' its voice. The metaphor is not that men fall in love with it: the metaphor is that they discover home. 'This was what I sought. This was my need.' It is the very mould of the mind, the matrix to which corresponds in every outline the outcast and unprotected contour of the soul. It is Verlaine's 'Oh! Rome—oh! Mere!' And that not only to those who had it in childhood and have returned, but much more—and what a proof!—to those who come upon it from the hills of life and say to themselves, 'Here is the town.'"[128]

Letter to Katherine Asquith, March 29, 1960

Hilaire Belloc remains one of the premier Catholic apologists of the modern era. Son of a French father and English mother,

---

128 Joseph Pearce, *Catholic Literary Giants: A Field Guide to the Catholic Literary Landscape* (San Francisco: Ignatius Press, 2005), loc. 1713 of 6271, Kindle Edition.

Belloc served for a short time in the French artillery before attending Balliol College in Oxford. He was born in Paris but raised in England. A prodigious walker in addition to a prolific writer, he walked from the Midwest to California in order to impress his future wife. After marrying Elodie Hogan and taking her back to England, they had five children before she died of pneumonia. It's hard to imagine a more active life than Belloc's: in addition to his trekking, he was a soldier, poet, satirist, yachtsman, Catholic apologist, political activist, and a public minister. His life story bursts at the seams with a continuous stream of publication, public speaking, political service, political activism, public feuds, defense of the faith, and robust family life. His best-known books include *The Path to Rome* (1902) which told the story of his walking pilgrimage from France over the Alps to Rome. In this book, Belloc reveals that he had lost his faith as a younger man and that an unexplained event precipitated his return. He wrote over 150 books, making him one of the four most eminent men of letters in Edwardian England along with H. G. Wells, George Bernard Shaw, and G. K. Chesterton.

DAY 127

RICHARD JOHN NEUHAUS (1936–2009)

An exercise of love—

"The deeper truth is that reform, if it is real reform, is an exercise of love. Prophecy, if it is real prophecy, is an exercise of love. Amos, Hosea, and Jeremiah employed such harsh language in criticizing the children of Israel precisely because they thought more of the people than the people thought of themselves. The prophets were in love with, were possessed by, a vision of the dignity and destiny of those they addressed. The outrageousness of sin and failure was in direct proportion to the greatness of God's intent for his people. Prophecy was always an exercise of love, never of contempt, for those to whom the prophet addressed his criticism."[129]

The Naked Public Square, 1984

Richard John Neuhaus was a Canadian who immigrated to the United States and became a Lutheran minister, serving a black church in Brooklyn, marching with Martin Luther King, opposing the Vietnam War, and supporting the progressive presidential candidate, Senator Eugene McCarthy. Neuhaus, like other prominent neoconservatives, was "mugged by

---

129 Richard John Neuhaus, *The Naked Public Square: Religion and Democracy in America* (Grand Rapids: Eerdmans, 1984), 70.

reality," and after years of struggle within the Lutheran Church, he converted to Catholicism in 1990 and was ordained a priest by Cardinal John O'Connor the following year. Six years earlier, he had published his best-known book, *The Naked Public Square*, in which he argued that the people of faith must engage in politics and public debates about morality and social issues. In 1990, Neuhaus founded the influential journal *First Things*, which was notable for providing an ecumenical platform for religious conservatives. In all, Father Neuhaus wrote or edited nearly thirty books, wrote numerous columns and articles, and was often seen in the media as a commentator on religious and social issues. In his last book, *As I Lay Dying: Meditations Upon Returning* (2002), he wrote about his near-death experience during an early bout with colon cancer.

DAY 128

ALASDAIR MACINTYRE (1929–)

The stories we tell—

"It is through hearing stories about wicked stepmothers, lost children, good but misguided kings, wolves that suckle twin boys, youngest sons who receive no inheritance but must make their own way in the world, and eldest sons who waste their inheritance on riotous living and go into exile to live with

the swine, that children learn or mislearn both what a child and what a parent is, what the cast of characters may be in the drama into which they have been born and what the ways of the world are."[130]

After Virtue, 1981

A native of Scotland, Alasdair MacIntyre is one of the most influential moral philosophers in the world. MacIntyre was a Marxist until converted to Catholicism while writing a sequel to *After Virtue*. *After Virtue* spearheaded a return to virtue ethics among many philosophers and intellectuals, which, in turn, spread widely into the literate culture. His subsequent books contain short explanations of his embrace of the Church: *Whose Justice? Which Rationality?* (1988); *Three Rival Versions of Moral Enquiry: Encyclopedia, Genealogy, and Tradition* (1990), *The Objectivity of Good* (1993), and *Dependent Rational Animals: Why Human Beings Need the Virtues* (1999). The influence of MacIntyre's courageous example in the midst of a hostile academy cannot be overstated.

---

130 Alasdair MacIntyre, *After Virtue: A Study in Moral Theory*, 2nd Edition (Notre Dame: University of Notre Dame Press, 1984), 250.

DAY 129

JIM CAVIEZEL (1968–)

The praise of men—

"Your name may not appear down here in the world's hall of fame. In fact, you might be so unknown that no one knows your name. The praise of men may not come your way, but don't forget God has rewards for you He will hand out one day. These crowds on Earth, they will soon forget. When you're there at the top they will cheer like mad until you fall and the praise will stop. Not God! He never forgets, and you're in his hall of fame. Just by believing in his Son, forever there's your name. I wouldn't trade my name, however small, its written beyond the stars in that celestial hall. For all the famous names here on Earth or the glory they share, I'd rather be an unknown here and have my name up there!"[131]

Jim Caviezel was an established actor in Hollywood when he was cast as Jesus Christ in Mel Gibson's magnificent film *The Passion of the Christ* (2004). Two years earlier, Caviezel made it known publicly he was a devout Catholic when he refused to do love scenes with Ashley Judd in *High Crimes* (2002). The phenomenal success of *The Passion of Christ* made him a

---

131 https://www.malditanglibrarian.com/2017/03/11-quotes-from-jim-caviezel-actor-who.html?m=1.

worldwide celebrity and, in the eyes of Catholics, a defender of the faith. Caviezel has never shrunk from the spotlight placed upon his faith by that role, which he believes has cost him some in Hollywood. Caviezel, as well as anyone, knows the temptations of wealth and fame.

DAY 130

MICHEL DE MONTAIGNE (1533–1592)

Only by their words—

"If we held to God by the mediation of a living faith; if we held to God through him and not through ourselves; if we had a divine foothold and foundation, human accidents would not have the power to shake us as they do. Our fort would not be prone to surrender to so weak a battery; the love of novelty, the constraint of princes, the good fortune of one party, a heedless and accidental change in our opinions, would have the power to shake and alter our belief; we would not allow it to be troubled by every new argument or by persuasion, not even by all the rhetoric there ever was; we should withstand those waves with inflexible and immobile firmness. . . . If this ray of divinity touched us at all, it would appear all over; not only our words, but also our works would bear its light and luster. Everything that came from us would be seen to be illuminated by the

noble brightness. We ought to be ashamed that in human sects there never was a partisan, whatever difficult and strange thing his doctrine maintained, who did not to some extent conform his conduct and his life to it; and so divine and celestial teaching as ours marks Christians only by their words."[132]

"Apology for Raymond Sebond," 1588

The essays of Michel de Montaigne represent a high-water mark in the French Renaissance. He was the first person to use the word *essay*, a new genre of literature that remains the primary form of intellectual engagement. His voluminous collection of essays, published in 1580, influenced all the major figures in the subsequent period called the early modern age, including Shakespeare and Descartes. Instructed in Latin as a boy, Montaigne eventually earned a law degree. He rose to prominence in the courts of King Charles IX of France. It was after his withdrawal from public life in 1571 that he began writing the bulk of his essays. Montaigne is often called the Father of Modern Skepticism, but that is sad over-implication. His essays have what could be called a pastoral reach into every aspect of life, using both classical texts and the Christian.

---

132 Michel de Montaigne, "Apology for Raymond Sebond," *The Complete Works: Essays, Travel Journal, Letters*, trans. Donald M. Frame, introduction by Stuart Hampshire (New York: Everyman's Library, 2003), 390.

DAY 131

HENRI DE LUBAC, SJ (1896–1996)

No divine spark—

"The fact that the nature of the spiritual, as it actually exists, is not conceived as an order destined to close in finally upon itself, but in a sense open to an inevitable supernatural end, does not mean that it already has in itself, or as part of its basis, the smallest positively supernatural element. It does not mean that this nature, 'as nature and by nature,' is elevated. 'Without the presence of a certain salt in the mouth, no one would want to drink;' Yet it is quite clear that the salt which makes us thirsty is not the water which quenches our thirst. Thus, this fact does not mean that God is in the smallest degree bound. Nor does it mean that nature does not have its own proper stability and its own definite structure. Nor does it involve any disregard, either from the metaphysical or moral point of view, of what St. Thomas called the *ordo naturalis* [order of nature]."[133]

The Mystery of the Supernatural, 1965

Yes, human beings have by nature a "spiritual' element, but as Henri de Lubac, SJ, explains, that element by itself does not "elevate" our human nature. The spiritual in us does two things:

---

133 Henri de Lubac, S.J., *The Mystery of the Supernatural*, trans. Rosemary Sheed (New York: Herder and Herder, 1967), 41.

it creates a hunger for God, our Final End, and, secondly, the spiritual allows that hunger to be satisfied by supernatural grace. Think of it this way: every human person possesses a nature that has whatever is required to live a temporal life, but each individual experience of each temporal life will be nagged by the feeling there is something missing, something more to be found; that nag arises from the spiritual within all of us.

DAY 132

WILLIAM SHAKESPEARE (1564–1616)

Portia—

The quality of mercy is not strained.
It droppeth as the gentle rain from heaven
Upon the place beneath. It is twice blest:
It blesseth him that gives and him that takes.
'Tis mightiest in the mightiest; it becomes
The thronèd monarch better than his crown.
His scepter shows the force of temporal power,
The attribute to awe and majesty
Wherein doth sit the dread and fear of kings;
But mercy is above this sceptered sway.
It is enthronèd in the hearts of kings;
It is an attribute to God Himself;

And earthly power doth then show likest God's
When mercy seasons justice. Therefore, Jew,
Though justice be thy plea, consider this:
That in the course of justice none of us
Should see salvation. We do pray for mercy,
And that same prayer doth teach us all to render
The deeds of mercy. I have spoke thus much
To mitigate the justice of thy plea,
Which, if thou follow, this strict court of Venice
Must needs give sentence 'gainst the merchant
there.[134]

The Merchant of Venice, Act 4, Scene 1, 190–212.

William Shakespeare is still considered the greatest writer in the English language. None of Shakespeare's original manuscripts are known to exist today; it was the actors from his company that collected them for publication after he died. William was raised in Stratford, and when he turned eighteen, he married the twenty-six-year-old Anne Hathaway. There's considerable evidence that Shakespeare was a Catholic, though he kept it secret to avoid imprisonment and torture. The best resource for this is Joseph Pearce, *Quest for Shakespeare: The Bard of Avon and the Church of Rome* (2008).

---

134 http://shakespeare.mit.edu/merchant/full.html.

DAY 133

ERIK VON KUEHNELT-LEDDIN (1909–1999)

Too little, too late—

"It goes without saying that it is never the task of the Church to 'catch up with the times,' to take seriously neurotic fears of 'missing the boat.' The task of the Church, with her faithful, is to fashion and form the times, to heed the age-old scriptural injunction: *instaurare amnia in Christo* ['Restore All Things in Christ' was the title of an encyclical by Pius X]. She has the basic truth and the promises of Christ, and while admittedly there are other truths to be found outside her realm, she is the Mother—and should be the Teacher-of-the-world. She only makes herself ridiculous when she rushes around frantically trying to minister to problems which she failed to become aware of or chose to ignore when they arose and which, in typical case, are no longer acute. The vernacular rite is that kind of case."[135]

"Radical Christianity," 1967

Called by William F. Buckley "the most fascinating man in the world," Erik von Kuehnelt-Leddihn was born into Austrian nobility, studied theology, law, and canon law at the University

---

135 Erik von Kuehnelt-Leddin, "Radical Christianity," *The Best of Triumph* (Front Royal: Christendom Press, 2001), 592.

of Vienna before receiving his doctorate in political science at the University of Budapest. During his lifetime, he learned to speak eight languages and read seventeen others. His knowledge was considered encyclopedic, but his intellectual mission was the defense of liberty against all the forms of totalitarianism spawned by the French Revolution. He had to leave Austria following the Nazi onslaught before settling in a small town in the Tyrol, outside of Innsbruck, where he lived the rest of his life. Kuehnelt-Leddihn remained a vigorous traveler and much in demand as a lecturer, teacher, and writer. He wrote four novels in addition to his non-fiction books and an unending list of columns and articles in conservative magazines like *National Review*.

DAY 134

OSCAR WILDE (1854–1900)

Repentance changes the past—

"The world had always loved the Saint as being the nearest possible approach to the perfection of God. Christ, through some divine instinct in him, seems to have always loved the sinner as being the nearest possible approach to the perfection of man. . . . Of course the sinner must repent. But why? Simply because otherwise he would be unable to realise what

he had done. The moment of repentance is the moment of initiation. More than that. It is the means by which one alters one's past. The Greeks thought that impossible. They often say in their gnomic aphorisms, "Even the Gods cannot alter the past." Christ showed that the commonest sinner could do it. That it was the one thing he could do. Christ, had he been asked, would have said—I feel quite certain about it—that the moment the prodigal son fell on his knees and wept he really made his having wasted his substance with harlots, and then kept swine and hungered for the husks they ate, beautiful and holy incidents in his life. It is difficult for most people to grasp the idea. I dare say one has to go to prison to understand it. If so, it may be worthwhile going to prison."[136]

De Profundis, 1905

Oscar Wilde's life is one of the most glittering and tragic of any major literary figure. He won a scholarship to attend Trinity College in Dublin. From there, he went to Magdalen College, Oxford, distinguishing himself as a poet, speaker, scholar, and campus dandy. He sailed to America to give 50 lectures on aesthetics, but ended up giving 140. He married Constance Lloyd in 1884. They had two sons. In 1890, Wilde published the novel *The Picture of Dorian Gray*, and in the next few years, he struck gold with his plays *Lady Windermere's Fan* (1892), *An Ideal Husband* (1895), and particularly, *The Importance of Being*

136 https://www.gutenberg.org/files/921/921-h/921-h.htm.

Earnest (1895). However, during the same period, he began a relationship with Lord Alfred "Bosie" Douglas, which outraged Bosie's father, leading to his eventual arrest. Wilde foolishly sued the father for libel, but after he withdrew the case, he was arrested, convicted of gross indecency, and spent two years at hard labor. While in prison, Wilde wrote this letter about his Catholic faith, *De Profundis* or *From the Depths.*

DAY 135

HENRI DANIEL-ROPS (1901–1965)

Calvary is here—

"The Mass is the projection in time of the eternal values of Calvary. Similarly, Calvary was only one small place on the earth at the crossroads of Jerusalem, Athens and Rome, but what took place there, the sacrifice of the Omnipotent, can affect man everywhere in all corners of the earth. The Mass plants the cross in a town, in a village, in a mission, in a great cathedral; it draws back the curtains on time and space and makes what happened on Calvary happen here. The cross affected all past history by anticipation; all the sacrifices of bullocks, and goats, and sheep, and particularly the sacrifice of the paschal lamb, found their completion in the cross. The cross affected also the future, by flowing out through all time, like

a mighty waterfall or cascade which makes channels through valleys and plains."[137]

This Is the Mass, 1958

Henri Daniel-Rops, whose real name was Henri Petiot, was brought up Catholic but became agnostic in his twenties. He taught history in Lycées at Chambéry, 1923–28, at Amiens, 1928–30, and at Neuilly sur Seine, 1930–44. He resigned to become editor-in-chief of the prestigious Fayard publishing house in Paris. His first novels reflect his spiritual doubt, but in 1939, he was invited to write a book about religious history. Daniel-Rops accepted, in part to write about the history of Israel—Hitler's anti-semitic campaign was well underway. The book was published in 1943, but when the Nazis arrived in Paris twenty days later, all the copies were confiscated and the plates destroyed. His next book about Jesus sold four hundred thousand copies in France, spurring him on to write the work for which he is best known, *L'Histoire de l'Eglise du Christ* (1948–1965), published in English as *History of the Church of Christ* in ten volumes by Image. He published over seventy books in all, and since many of them appeared in English translation, Daniel-Rops was a significant influence on the Church in post-war America.

---

137 Henri Daniel-Rops, *This Is the Mass*, trans. Alastair Guinan, introduction by Fulton J. Sheen (Garden City: Doubleday and Company, Inc., 1958), 30.

DAY 136

DESIDERIUS ERASMUS (1466–1536)

Erasmus responds to Martin Luther's deeply pessimistic interpretation of the freedom of the will in Scripture—

"Moreover, if we grant that he who has the Spirit is sure of the meaning of the Scriptures, how can I be certain of what he finds to be true for himself? What am I to do when many bring diverse interpretations, about which each swears he has the Holy Spirit? And since the Spirit does not furnish the whole truth to anyone, even he who has the Spirit may be mistaken or deceived in some single point. So much for those who so easily reject the interpretation of the Fathers in Holy Scripture and oppose their views to ours as if delivered by an oracle. Finally, even supposing that the Spirit of Christ could have allowed his people to err in trivial matters on which the salvation of men does not greatly depend, how can it be believed that for more than thirteen hundred years he would have concealed the error in his Church and not have found anybody among so many saintly men worthy to be inspired with the knowledge of what these people claim to be the chief doctrine of the whole gospel?"[138]

On the Freedom of the Will, 1524

---

138 Erasmus of Rotterdam, *On the Freedom of the Will: A Diatribe or Discourse by Desiderius Erasmus of Rotterdam*, trans. E. Gordon Rupp, http://www.sjsu. edu/people/james.lindahl/courses/Hum1B/s3/Erasmus-and-Luther-on-Free-Will-and-Salvation.pdf.

Desiderius Erasmus of Rotterdam was a Dutch humanist, the first editor of the New Testament, a Patristics and classical scholar, who publicly debated Martin Luther about the Catholic view of grace, nature, and the freedom of the will. But he was also a proponent of ecclesiastical reform within the Church, becoming a leader in the Counter-Reformation. His writings on education moved curricula towards Renaissance humanism. His intellectual independence often made him a target for Catholics as well as Protestants. In his arguments about the freedom of the will, for example, he went beyond the traditional Catholic teaching based upon Scripture and St. Augustine.

DAY 137

HILDEGARD VON BINGEN (1098–1179)

A medieval hymn to the Virgin—

> Hail, girl of a noble house,
> shimmering
> and unpolluted,
> you pupil in the eye of chastity,
> you essence of sanctity,
> which was passing to God.
>
> For the Heavenly potion

was poured into you,
in that the Heavenly word
received a raiment of flesh in you.

You are the lily that dazzles
whom God knew before all others.

O most beautiful
and delectable one:
how greatly God delighted in you!
in the clasp of His fire
He implanted in you so that
His son might be suckled by you.

Thus your womb
Held joy,
When the harmony of all Heaven
Chimed out from you.
Because, Virgin, you carried Christ
Whence your chastity blazed in God.

Your flesh has known delight,
Like the grassland touched by dew
And immersed in its freshness:
So it was with you,
A mother of all joy.

Now let the sunrise of joy be

Over all Ecclesia
And let it resound in music
For the sweetest Virgin.
Mary compelling all praise.
Mother of God. Amen.[139]

>   Ave, Generosa—Hymnus de Sancta Maria

Born to a noble family, St. Hildegard of Bingen was educated at the Benedictine cloister of Disibodenberg and began
wearing the Benedictine habit at age fifteen. She experienced
visions throughout her life, though it wasn't until the age of
forty-three that she was called in to meet with the archbishop
of Mainz to discuss them. The theologians assigned to interview her confirmed the authenticity of her visions, which
were written down by a monk assigned to record them. The
resulting book, *Scivias* (1141–1152), contained twenty-six of
her visions. Apart from her sanctity, Hildegard has a permanent
place in the history of music. As a composer, she set seventy-
seven of her poems to music that was highly innovative for its
time. She also wrote the lives of saints and treatises on medicine and natural history. A large volume of her extensive correspondence has survived. Pope Benedict XVI declared her a
Doctor of the Church in 2012.

---

139 *A feather on the breath of God: Sequences and hymns by Abbess Hildegard of Bingen*, trans. Christopher Page, performed by Gothic Voices with Emma Kirk-
by, directed by Christopher Page (London: Hyperion Records Ltd, 1982).

DAY 138

JOHN HALDANE (1954–)

More than intellectual—

"However the blessed may be related to one another in paradise, their primary orientation is towards God, on whom they actively gaze, seeing in the divine nature their own source and perfection of every positive quality. . . . In this the intellectual powers of the blessed are fully realized, but not in a purely speculative mode. Rather, in finding what they have always craved—absolute, unconditional, and everlasting love—their minds are themselves made loving, but now their darkness and disturbance issued as a consequence of willful disobedience has now been healed, and their lives transfigured."[140]

An Intelligent Person's Guide to Religion, 2003

John Haldane began his college education in art schools in Rochester, Kent, and Wimbledon in London. He then turned to philosophy, first getting a BA and PhD in philosophy from Birkbeck College of the University of London. Haldane is presently a professor of philosophy and director of the Centre for Ethics, Philosophy and Public Affairs at the University of St. Andrews in Scotland and has taught at other universities

---

140 John Haldane, *An Intelligent Person's Guide to Religion* (City: International Publishers Marketing, 2003), loc. 203-4, Kindle Edition.

in Great Britain and in the United States. Haldane has combined analytic philosophy with the philosophy of St. Thomas Aquinas, exploring epistemology, aesthetics, philosophy of mind, ethics, politics, and the history of philosophy. He is a consultor to the Pontifical Council for Culture and a member of the Pontifical Academy for Life and the Pontifical Academy for Thomas Aquinas. His books include *Faithful Reason* (2006), *Reasonable Faith* (2010), *Seeking Meaning and Making Sense* (2008), and *The Church and the World* (2008).

DAY 139

J. R. R. TOLKIEN (1892–1973)

The romance of the Eucharist—

"Out of the darkness of my life, so much frustrated, I put before you the one great thing to love on earth: the Blessed Sacrament. . . . There you will find romance, glory, honour, fidelity, and the true way of all your loves on earth, and more than that: Death: by the divine paradox, that which ends life, and demands the surrender of all, and yet by the taste (or foretaste) of which alone can [find] what you seek in your earthly relationships (love, faithfulness, joy) be maintained, or take on

that complexion of reality, of eternal endurance, which every man's heart desires."[141]

Letter to his son Michael Tolkien, March 6–8, 1941

J. R. R. Tolkien was born in South Africa in 1892. After his father's death, Tolkien's mother moved the family to England when he was four years old. After graduating from Exeter College, having specialized in classics, Anglo-Saxon, and Germanic languages, Tolkien served in the trenches of WWI. Returning from the war, he continued to study languages, teaching at Leeds before becoming a professor at Oxford. At Oxford, he started a writing group called the Inklings, which included C. S. Lewis, among other notables. In 1937, Tolkien published *The Hobbit* and started writing *The Lord of the Rings* (1954, 1955). Amazingly, he wrote such a massive work while he was fulfilling his duties as an Oxford professor of English Language and Literature. As close readers and scholars have shown, *The Hobbit* and *The Lord of the Rings* bear the mark of a writer who was a devout Catholic. Indeed, Tolkien's witness to the Inklings helped convert C. S. Lewis to Christianity from atheism. When Lewis chose the Church of England, it was a disappointment to Tolkien. But, had he lived, he would have seen the worldwide impact his imaginative, mythological fiction had on the religious sensibilities of millions.

---

141 http://glim.ru/personal/jrr_tolkien_42-45.html.

DAY 140

WALLACE FOWLIE (1908–1998)

The two gates—

"The word most closely related to the book's title [this book, *Sites*] is *doors*. I was at first puzzled by the choice of words designating the rock group of four fellow: Ray, the pianist-organist; John, the drummer; Robbie, the guitarist; Jim, the tenor-baritone singer and poet. Why *The Doors*? But I know now that the phrase comes from William Blake: 'If the doors of perception were cleaned everything would appear to men as it truly is, infinite.' And Jim Morrison named his band *The Doors, open and closed*. Aldous Huxley took it for the title of his book: *The Doors of Perception*. During this search for my own past, I have followed, often unconsciously, the example, of these two Dionysian spirits of France and America who dared not only to open doors but to close them. In order to enter the City of Dis (*Inferno*, Canto 9), Dante and Virgil needed the help of an angel who with the touch of his wand opens the gate. And Homer, centuries before Dante, speaks in the *Odyssey* (XIX, 560-65) of two gates, the ivory gate opening onto sites of fantasies and dreams of illusions, and the gate of horn, more

honest, more realistic in what it offers to mortals. Gates of risk and adventure, as well as gates of portentous truths."[142]

Sites—A Third Memoir, 1987

Wallace Fowlie was one of the most respected French literature scholars of the twentieth century. His translations, commentaries, and biographies set the standard for future scholars. As a child, Fowlie was inspired to take up French after hearing the opera star Mary Garden sing the role of Melisande in Debussy's opera *Pelléas and Melisande* (1902). At Harvard, he was taught by T. S. Eliot, with whom he often had tea. He wrote of his entry into the Catholic Church in his twenties, "joining a supernatural world that represented stability existing within the more familiar world of change and independence and hesitation." He made a ground-breaking translation of Rimbaud's poetry. He taught at Duke University from 1964 until the end of his career. In the last book he wrote, Fowlie was far from the tottering old college professor: its title was *Rimbaud and Jim Morrison: The Rebel As Poet*, published by Duke University

---

142 Wallace Fowlie, *Sites—A Third Memoir* (Durham: Duke University Press, 1987), 173.

Press. Jim Morrison once wrote a note of thanks to Fowlie for his Rimbaud translations.

DAY 141

CHARLES PÉGUY (1873–1914)

Nothing so beautiful in the world as a child going to sleep
    while he is
    saying his prayers, says God,
I tell you nothing is so beautiful in the world.—
And yet I have seen beautiful sights in the world.
And I know something about it. My creation is overflowing
    with beauty.
My creation overflows with marvels.

(As that little creature going to sleep in all confidence)
And getting his *Our Father* mixed up with his *Hail, Mary.*
Nothing is so beautiful and it is even one point
On which the Blessed Virgin agrees with me—[143]

God Speaks, 1916

---

143 Charles Péguy, *God Speaks: Religious Poetry*, trans. and introduction by Julian Green (New York: Pantheon Books, Inc., 1950), 39.

Born to a poor family, Charles Péguy entered the École Normale Supérieure in Paris, intending to teach philosophy. The next year, 1895, he became a socialist and stopped practicing his Catholic faith, though he continued to believe it and express it through his poems, essays, and philosophy. In 1897, he wrote his first version of the three-part play *Jeanne d'Arc* (1897). Péguy's later poem, *The Mystery of the Charity of Joan of Arc* (1910), became one of his best-known works. He was never a hard-core Marxist. Along with his friend Jacques Maritain, he attended the lectures of the famed Henri Bergson, who was battling scientific materialism. When the First World War started in 1914, Péguy, out of love of his country, joined the army as a lieutenant but was shot in the forehead on the day before the Battle of the Marne. He was forty-one. Péguy's last important work was the 7,644 lines long poem *Ève* (1913), a prayer-like vision of Christian history. The three volumes of translations by Ann and Julien Green have kept the name of Péguy known to English readers.

DAY 142

ELIZABETH JENNINGS (1926–2001)

Lazarus

It was an amazing white, it was the way he simply

Refused to answer our questions, it was the cold pale glance
Of death upon him, the smell of death that truly
Declared his rising to us. It was no chance
Happening, as a man may fill his silence
Between two heart-beats, seem to be dead and then
Astonish us with the closeness of his presence;
This man was dead, I say it again and again.
All of our sweating bodies moved towards him
And our minds moved too, hungry for finished faith.
He would not enter our world at once with words
That we might be tempted to twist or argue with:
Cold like a white root pressed in the bowels of earth
He looked, but also vulnerable—like birth.[144]

Born a Catholic, Elizabeth Jennings grew up in Oxford and
attended St. Anne's College before becoming a librarian at
the city library. Her first book of poetry in 1953 brought her
to the attention of publisher Robert Conquest, who anthol-
ogized her work. She left the library and began work at a
publishing house while regularly writing poems for the *Daily
Telegraph*. By the 1960s, she was one of the most popular poets
in England, and by the end of her life, had published nearly
thirty books. She never married but had many friends and
enthusiasms, including ice cream (Haagen-Dazs), Shakespeare

---

144 Elizabeth Jennings, *Selected Poems* (Manchester: Carcanet Press Limited,
1985), 72.

productions at Stratford-Upon-Avon, and movies. Her faith was "a real and important part of my life, and because it was important, it tended to give me a lot of worries," which appear frequently in her poetry. She said of her work, "Only one thing must be cast out, and that is the vague. Only true clarity reaches to the heights and the depths of human, and more than human, understanding."

DAY 143

ST. GREGORY OF NYSSA (335–394)

Envy cast us out—

"Moses Envied: No longer does any offense which comes about through evil withstand the one who in this manner follows God. After these things the envy of his brothers arose against him. Envy is the passion which causes evil, the father of death, the first entrance of sin, the root of wickedness, the birth of sorrow, the mother of misfortune, the basis of disobedience, the beginning of shame. Envy banished us from Paradise, having become a serpent to oppose Eve. Envy walled us off from

the tree of life, divested us of holy garments, and in shame led us away clothed with fig leaves."[145]

The Life of Moses, c. 390

St. Gregory of Nyssa was educated by his brother, St. Basil the Great, and their friend, St. Gregory of Nazianzus. He first was a professor of rhetoric before turning to the serious study of theology and the Church. He became a priest at a time when celibacy was not required, and he did marry. When he was elected bishop of Nyssa in 372, Gregory faced the controversy with the Arians over the divinity of Christ. Gregory's writings were very effective in publicly battling with the Arians, who disputed the divine nature of Christ, at the Council of Constantinople (381). Gregory's writing also contributed to the formulation of Church doctrine of the Trinity.

---

145 Gregory of Nyssa, *The Life of Moses*, trans., introduction, and notes by Abraham J. Malherbe and Everett Ferguson, preface by John Meyendorff (New York: Paulist Press, 1978), 120.

DAY 144

ST. JOHN THE DAMASCENE (626–749)

Against those who forbid images—

"These injunctions [against graven images] were given to the Jews on account of their proneness to idolatry. . . . Speaking theologically, it is given to us to avoid superstitious error, to be with God in the knowledge of the truth, to worship God alone, to enjoy the fulness of His knowledge. We have passed the stage of infancy, and reached the perfection of manhood. *We receive our habit of mind from God, and know what may be imaged and what may not.* The Scripture says, 'You have not seen the likeness of Him.' What wisdom in the law-giver. How depict the invisible? How picture the inconceivable? How give expression to the limitless, the immeasurable, the invisible? How give a form to immensity? How paint immortality? How localise mystery? It is clear that when you contemplate God, who is a pure spirit, becoming man for your sake, you will be able to clothe Him with the human form. When the Invisible One becomes visible to flesh, you may then draw a likeness of His form. When He who is a pure spirit, without form or limit, immeasurable in the boundlessness of His own nature, existing as God, takes upon Himself the form of a servant in substance and in stature, and a body of flesh, then you may draw His likeness, and show it to anyone willing to contemplate it. Depict His ineffable condescension, His virginal birth, His baptism

in the Jordan, His transfiguration on Thabor, His all-powerful sufferings, His death and miracles, the proofs of His Godhead, the deeds which He worked in the flesh through divine power, His saving Cross, His Sepulchre, and resurrection, and ascent into heaven. Give to it all the endurance of engraving and colour. Have no fear or anxiety; worship is not all of the same kind."[146] (Emphasis added.)

On Holy Images, c. 730

St. John the Damascene was an Eastern monk who publicly opposed the iconoclastic severity of his Byzantine emperor, who forbad even images of Jesus Christ. His defense of images was condemned at the Council of Hieria in 754, which was controlled by Emperor Constantine, but it was upheld at the second council of Nicaea (787). There's good reason St. John of Damascus is called the Doctor of Christian Art.

---

146 Saint John of Damascus, *Saint John of Damascus Collection* (Aeterna Press, 2016), loc. 7099 of 15151, Kindle Edition.

DAY 145

CARYLL HOUSELANDER (1901–1954)

Beyond any complaint—

"Sanctity is a genius for love. That is why the saint never complains of not being 'fulfilled.' No matter what the circumstances of his life are, the saint loves to his fullest human capacity, not only supernaturally, though this is what matters, but naturally, too; and it is on the degree of his capacity for objective love, and on nothing else, that the fullness of any man's life depends. It does not depend upon circumstances or chance, on whether he is gifted or not, on whether he has a happy or melancholy temperament, on whether he is rich or poor, married or single, on whether he has a magnificent vocation or a humdrum one, on whether he travels the world over or is restricted to the same few streets for the whole of his life, on whether he is good-looking or plain, on whether he is healthy or unhealthy; it depends upon one thing and one thing only—whether he has or has not got the capacity to love."[147]

Guilt, 1951

Caryll Houselander was born into an English Anglican family, but her mother, Gertrude, converted to Catholicism along with her two daughters when Caryll was six years old. While

---

147 Caryll Houselander, *Guilt* (New York: Sheed & Ward, 1951), 140.

attending a Catholic boarding school, Houselander had her
first mystical vision. But after leaving school due to poor health,
she fell away from the Church and looked for another spiritual
home. The Russian Orthodox Church appealed to her most,
and she experienced a mystical vision of the Romanov family
being executed. A few days later, the news of their deaths (July
16–17, 1918) was announced in the newspaper. She returned
to the Church at twenty-five and was advised by a priest who
edited Catholic magazines to start writing. She became famous
through her writing and had many admirers, including Msgr.
Ronald Knox, who remarked, "She seemed to see everything
for the first time, and the driest of doctrinal considerations
shone out like a restored picture when she had finished with
it." During WWII, she was asked by doctors to take care of
traumatized patients. One prominent psychologist described
her success: "she loved them back to life." She died of breast
cancer at fifty-three.

DAY 146

ERIC GILL (1882–1940)

Hell is a compliment—

"I say the doctrine of hell implies the most stupendous compliment to man humanly conceivable. That man can *merit* the

'Beatific Vision,' the 'incorporation,' so to speak, of his being in Being itself, that is an even more stupendous conception; but it is not, I think, *humanly* conceivable. It is not humanly conceivable that the kingdom of heaven can be 'taken by violence.' The idea is an inspiration from on high. . . . The point here is that they are ideas implying a conception of man altogether amazing. It is not possible to exaggerate their importance. If we surrender them, we surrender ourselves 'at one fell swoop' to a negligible and even ignominious condition. Man! There is nothing in him."[148]

The Necessity of Belief, 1936

Eric Gill was a gifted sculptor, draughtsman, letterer, typographer, printer, and Catholic apologist. The son of an Anglican clergyman, he was brought up with a deep appreciation of all the arts that went to the building of a cathedral. All his art going forward contained clear traces of the medieval past, a dramatic simplicity of line coupled with a surprising eroticism. He enjoyed his first success as a sculptor with 'Madonna and Child' in 1912. In 1913, Gill converted to Catholicism. In 1921, he started a community of Catholic artists and became a lay Dominican. Among the typefaces he created are Perpetua (1925), Gill Sans Serif (1927), and Joanna (1930).

---

148 Eric Gill, *The Necessity of Belief: an inquiry into the nature of human certainty, the causes of skepticism and the grounds of morality, and a justification that the end is the beginning* (London: Faber and Faber Limited, 1936), 135.

DAY 147

ST. ROBERT BELLARMINE (1542–1621)

Renouncing the devil—

"Again: all Christians are asked, either by themselves or by their sponsors, whether they renounce the devil, and all his works and pomps. And they answer: 'I do renounce them.' But how many renounce them in word, but not in reality! On the other hand, how few are there who do not love and follow the pomps and works of the devil! But God sees all things, and will not be mocked. He therefore that desires to live well and to die well, let him enter into the chamber of his heart, and not deceive himself; but seriously and attentively consider over and over again whether he is in love with the pomps of this world, or with sins, which are the works of the devil; and whether he gives them a place in his heart, and in his words and actions. And thus, either his good conscience will console him, or his evil conscience will lead him to penance."[149]

The Art of Dying Well, 1619

St. Robert Bellarmine was ordained in 1560, having grown up in the Tuscan town of Montepulciano. Educated by the newly-established Jesuits, he entered the novitiate in 1560 and

---

149 St. Robert Bellarmine, *The Art of Dying Well* (Patristic Publishing, 2020), loc. 47-48, Kindle Edition.

studied and taught in Rome before beginning intense preparation for refuting the Protestants. These arguments are found in his most famous work, the three-volume *Disputations on the Controversies of the Christian Faith*, which, among other things, found no basis for the divine right of kings. Bellarmine was named a cardinal in 1599 by Pope Clement VIII, who called him the most educated man in the Church. As cardinal archbishop of Capua, he instituted the reforms of the Council of Trent (1545–63). Late in life, Bellarmine was required by the Holy Office to deliver an admonishment to his friend, Galileo, who had defended the heliocentric view of Copernicus. Six years after Bellarmine died in 1621, his canonization process began, but nothing happened until 1930, when Pope Pius XI canonized him, and the next year declared him a doctor of the Church.

DAY 148

ERASMO LEIVA-MERIKAKIS (1946–)

Eros is more than sex—

"Most of us have probably never thought of the distinction in this way between erotic attraction and the sexual urge. But the distinction can be literally life-saving. For one thing, while eros very often does lead to sexual union, eros does not strictly

speaking require sexual union in order to be fulfilled, and I would imagine that this distinction is vital above all in a monastic context. While sexual union is limited severely because confined to particular physical acts within time and space, eros can lead to an abiding interior relationship of hearts and whole beings. Although it may blossom in the senses and be expressed sexually, eros has not only roots but also its branches and fruit in our souls. This is the specific quality of eros that makes it possible for it to be both the image of, and the training ground for, divine love, as we have insisted."[150]

Love's Sacred Order: Four Meditations, 2000

Erasmo Leiva-Merikakis received his PhD in comparative literature and theology from Emory University. After graduating, he moved to San Francisco to teach in the newly-founded St. Ignatius Institute at the University of San Francisco, where he taught for over twenty years. Leiva-Merikakis was at the forefront of bringing the work of Hans Urs von Balthasar to English readers. He has translated many books of von Balthasar, including the first volume of *The Glory of the Lord, A Theological Aesthetics* (1982). Leiva-Merikakis's multi-volume *Fire of Mercy, Heart of the World, Meditations on the Gospel of St. Matthew* (1996, 2004, 2013) is highly regarded by scholars and lay readers. In 2003, he joined the Trappist community at Spencer Abbey

---

150 Erasmo Leiva-Merikakis, *Love's Sacred Order: Four Meditations* (San Francisco: Ignatius Press, 2000), 109.

and was ordained a priest in 2013, becoming Father Simeon. He is currently serving as secretary to the abbot general in Rome and edits the Monastic Wisdom Series for Cistercian Publications.

DAY 149

ST. JOHN VIANNEY (1786–1859)

The evil of spreading gossip—

"A great many people slander others because of pride. They think that by depreciating others they will increase their own worth. They want to make the most of their own alleged good qualities. Everything they say and do will be good, and everything that others say and do will be wrong. But the great bulk of malicious talk is done by people who are simply irresponsible, who have an itch to chatter about others without feeling any need to discover whether what they are saying is true or false. They just have to talk. And even though these latter are less guilty than the others—that's to say, those who slander and backbite through hatred or envy or revenge—yet they aren't free from sin. Whatever the motive that prompts them, they shouldn't soil the reputation of their neighbor. It's my belief that the sin of spreading gossip involves all that's most evil and wicked. Yes, my dear brothers and sisters, this sin includes the

poison of all the vices: the meanness of vanity, the venom of jealousy, the bitterness of anger, the malice of hatred, and the flightiness and irresponsibility so unworthy of a Christian. In fact, isn't it the spreading of gossip that sows almost all discord and disunity? It breaks up friendships; hinders enemies from reconciling their quarrels; disturbs the peace of homes; turns brother against brother, husband against wife, daughter-in-law against mother-in-law, and son-in-law against father-in-law. How many harmonious households have been turned upside down by one evil tongue, so that their members couldn't bear to see or to speak to one another? And only one malicious tongue, belonging to a neighbor, man or woman, can be the cause of all this misery."[151]

Sermons

St. John Vianney, also known as the Curé d'Ars, is one of the most beloved priests in the history of the Church. He was born in France a few years before the anti-clerical attack on the Church beginning with the French Revolution (1789) and culminating with the Terror (1793-1794). His family sheltered priests from arrest and execution and travelled miles to attend clandestine Masses. Vianney was sixteen when Napoleon reestablished the Church. With an eye on the priesthood, he began his studies but was drafted to serve in the French army.

---

151 Paul Thigpen, *A Year With the Saints: Daily Meditations With the Holy Ones of God* (Charlotte: Saint Benedict Press, 2013), 248.

Suffering illness, Vianney joined a group of deserters and hid for fourteen months in a farmhouse. In 1810, an amnesty was announced, and he went home to complete his studies and was ordained a priest in 1815. After ten years in the small town of Ars, Vianney's reputation for holiness in the confessional started to attract pilgrims around the world—for, example, 20,000 came in 1855 alone. As a result, he spent most of the day in the confessional as a "reader" of souls.

DAY 150

MAURICE BARING (1874–1945)

A letter to G. K.—

"Nothing for years had given me so much joy. I have hardly ever entered a church without putting up a candle to Our Lady or to St. Joseph or St. Anthony for you. And both this year and last year in Lent I made a Novena for you. I know of many other people, better people far than I, who did the same. Many Masses were said for you and prayers all over England and Scotland in centers of Holiness. . . . Well, all I have to say, Gilbert, is what I have already said to you, and what I have said not long ago in a printed book. That I was received into the Church on the Eve of Candlemas 1909, and it is perhaps the only act in my life which I am quite certain I have never

regretted. Every day I live, the Church seems to me more and more wonderful; the Sacraments more and more solemn and sustaining; the voice of the Church, her liturgy, her rules, her discipline, her ritual, her decisions in matters of Faith and Morals more and more excellent and profoundly wise and true and right, and her children stamped with something that those outside Her are without."[152]

Letter to G. K. Chesterton, August 25, 1922

Maurice Baring was educated at Eton College and Cambridge but left before earning a degree. An exceptional linguist, he joined the diplomatic service in 1898 and served as attaché in Paris, Copenhagen, and Rome. He resigned in 1904 and joined the *Morning Post*, reporting on the Russo-Japanese War. After working in St. Petersburg and Constantinople, Baring moved to the *Times* and reported from the Balkans. In 1909, he converted to Catholicism. During WWI, Baring was in the Royal Flying Corps, rising to the rank of a staff officer. The deaths of so many friends led him to write the highly-regarded poem "In Memoriam." Baring rarely wrote about his Catholic faith, except through his poetry and the biography *Robert Peckham* (1930) about Mary Queen of Scots and *In My End is My Beginning* (1931). His novels such as *C* (1924), *Cat's Cradle* (1925), and *The Lonely Lady of Dulwich* (1934) remain

---

152 Joseph Pearce, *Literary Converts: Spiritual Inspiration in an Age of Unbelief* (San Francisco: Ignatius Press, 1999), loc. 1845 of of 9969, Kindle Edition.

highly regarded but largely unread. G. K. Chesterton was a close friend who possibly used Baring as the model for the main character in *The Man Who Was Thursday* (1922).

DAY 151

ST. PHILIP HOWARD (1557–1595)

The Lament for Walsingham

> Bitter, bitter oh to behold
> The grass to grow
> Where the walls of Walsingham
> So stately did show.
>
> Such were the worth of Walsingham
> While she did stand,
> Such are the wrackes as now do show
> Of that so holy land.
>
> Level, level with the ground
> The Towers do lie
> Which with their golden, glitt'ring tops
> Pierced out to the sky.
>
> Where were gates no gates are now,

The ways unknown,
Where the press of friars did pass
While far her fame was blown.

Owls do scrike where the sweetest hymns
Lately were sung,
Toads and serpents hold their dens
Where the palmers did throng.

Weep, weep, O Walsingham,
Whose days are nights,
Blessings turned to blasphemies,
Holy deeds to dispites.

Sin is where our Lady sat,
Heaven turned to hell;
Satan sits where our Lord did sway,
Walsingham, oh, farewell![153]

St. Philip Howard, the twentieth Earl of Arundel, was imprisoned in the Tower of London for ten years by Elizabeth I.
He had been caught trying to escape England to avoid being
arrested for aiding Jesuit priests in hiding. He and his wife,
Anne, hid them in Arundel Castle, and Anne continued to do

---

153 Joseph Pearce, compiler, *Poems Every Catholic Should Know* (Charlotte:
TAN Books, 2016), 49-50.

so after her husband's arrest. Scholar Stephanie Mann describes an engraving of Howard in the Tower with his dog looking up at him. As she explains, the dog was used each day as a messenger between Howard and Father Robert Southwell, SJ, who was also in solitary confinement at the time. His "Lament for Walsingham" refers to the destruction of the Walsingham Priory and the removal of the figure of Our Lady by order of Henry VIII. The priory dated from the thirteenth century and was an important Marian shrine for Catholics in England and abroad. Many of England's kings made pilgrimages to the site, but with the dissolution of the Church by Henry VIII, such a sacred place could not be left standing. What was left of the priory and its lands were sold for ninety pounds. It should be added that St. Philip Howard was not executed but died of dysentery. Elizabeth I had never signed his death warrant.

DAY 152

ST. EDMUND CAMPION, SJ (1540–1581)

A letter from death row to "Her Majesty's Privy Council" before the execution—

"I confess that I am a priest of the Catholic Church in the Society of Jesus.

My charge is, of free cost to preach the Gospel, to minister the Sacraments, to instruct the simple, to reform sinners, to confute errors — in brief, to cry alarm spiritual against foul vice and proud ignorance, wherewith many of my dear countrymen are abused. I would be loath to speak anything that might sound of any insolent brag or challenge, especially being now as a dead man to this world and willing to put my head under every man's foot, and to kiss the ground they tread upon. Yet I have such courage in avouching the majesty of Jesus my King. And you will see upon what substantial grounds our Catholic Faith is built, and hearken to those who would spend the best blood in their bodies for your salvation. Many innocent hands are lifted up to heaven for you daily by those English students, whose posterity shall never die, which beyond seas, gathering virtue and sufficient knowledge for the purpose, are determined never to give you over, but either to win you heaven, or to die upon your pikes. And touching our Society, be it known to you that we have made a league — all the Jesuits in the world, whose succession and multitude must

overreach all the practice of England — cheerfully to carry the cross you shall lay upon us, and never to despair your recovery, while we have a man left to enjoy your Tyburn [where executions were held], or to be racked with your torments, or consumed with your prisons. The expense is reckoned, the enterprise is begun; it is of God; it cannot be withstood. So the faith was planted: So it must be restored. I have no more to say but to recommend your case and mine to Almighty God, the Searcher of Hearts, who send us his grace, and see us at accord before the day of payment, to the end we may at last be friends in heaven, when all injuries shall be forgotten."[154]

St. Edmund Campion, SJ, was hanged, drawn, and quartered on December 1, 1581 at the order of Elizabeth I, who had once admired his oration while she visited Oxford. He entered the Catholic seminary in Douai, France and then in Rome, where he became a Jesuit. Campion secretly returned to England and challenged the Privy Council to debate theology. He was arrested the following year, 1581, and was tortured. Queen Elizabeth I herself visited him in prison, urging him to recant, but to no avail.

---

154 http://jesuitinstitute.org/Resources/Campion%20Bragge%20Short%20Version.pdf.

DAY 153

ERNST JÜNGER (1895–1998)

Salvation comes first—

"Man must never forget that the images which now terrify him are from his heart. The world aflame, the burnt-out horses, the ruined towns, the trails of destruction are like leprosy whose germs had long multiplied within before it broke out on the surface. Such have long been the images in the hearts and minds of men. It is the innermost stuff of man's being which is reflected in the world around us, just as inner composure is revealed by external calms. Therefore spiritual salvation must come first, and only that peace can bring a blessing which has been preceded by the taming of the passions in these hearts and minds of men."[155]

The Peace, 1948

Ernst Jünger achieved fame with the 1920 publication of *Storm of Steele*, a book about his experience as a German soldier in the trenches of WWI. He would go on to write over fifty books of fiction, essays, and memoirs. In spite of his anti-Nazi novella, *On the Marble Cliffs* (1939), he served as an officer

---

155 Ernst Jünger, *The Peace*, trans Stuart O. Hood, introduction by Louis Clair (Hinsdale: Henry Regnery Company, 1948), 52; read at https://archive.org/details/ThePeace/page/n49/mode/2up.

in the Second World War, spending much of the war years in occupied Paris socializing with French artists and painters. In 2019, an English translation of *A German Officer in Occupied Paris: The War Journals, 1941-1945* was published. Its entries reveal a classically trained mind with a voracious intellectual appetite who included Catholic writers such as Léon Bloy in his circle. Jünger was suspected of being part of the conspiracy led by Claus von Stauffenberg to assassinate Hitler in 1944. He avoided execution and went on to live a long and productive life. *The Peace* was actually written in 1943 while in Paris but was not published until five years later. Jünger had been raised in an atheist family and did not convert to Catholicism until a year before his death. He had been a practicing Christian for some years prior to entering the Church.

DAY 154

GERALD VANN, OP (1906–1963)

Wisdom, not facts—

"It is useful for man to have much information about matters of fact; but that is not wisdom. It is useful to have scientific knowledge, to know the immediate what and why of things; but that is not wisdom either. It is better to have philosophy, which is the knowledge of things, not in their immediate but

in their ultimate causes; that is wisdom, though it is not the highest form of wisdom. It is wisdom because it does reduce the manifold of life to the one, and therefore make things intelligible as a unity; but you need, to make the dry bones live, the vision, the intuition or awareness, of things in their concreteness, their goodness and beauty as well as their truth; above all, you need some degree, at least, of direct knowledge of the nature of the one; and when you have had that vision in its plentitude—the plenitude which, knowing something of God in Himself, sees all things in Him and Him in all things."[156]

The Divine Pity, 1945

Gerald Vann, OP, entered the Dominican Order in 1923 and was ordained a priest in 1929. After studying modern philosophy at Oxford, he was sent to be a teacher and headmaster at the Blackfriars School. While at Blackfriars, Vann organized the international Union of Prayer for Peace. Vann lectured in the United States, including a series at the Catholic University of America. All of his work was infused by his study of St. Thomas Aquinas, about whom he wrote a book in 1940. His other books include *The Heart of Man* (1944), *The Pain of Christ and the Sorrow of God* (1947), and *The Water and the Fire* (1953).

---

156 Gerald Vann, O.P., *The Divine Pity: A Study in the Social Implications of the Beatitudes* (Garden City: Doubleday & Company, Inc., 1961), 165-66.

DAY 155

ANTHONY ESOLEN (1959–)

"Does Western Civilization possess the resources for renewal? It possesses a greater wealth of them than any previous falling civilization could count on. We might listen to Aeschylus again and be warned that natural law must be the foundation of a democratic state. We might turn to Virgil and recall that the role of the true father, one of self-sacrifice in leadership, is indispensable. We might turn to the Rule of Benedict and recover a healthy appreciation for the dignity of hard labor, and the richness of silence. We might turn to Dante and attempt to see all love as the expression of the Love that truly is. We might turn to Shakespeare and learn anything about man there is to learn. We might turn to the sage and serious Doctor Johnson and imitate the solid common sense of a man who could not be moved by the wispy intellectual fad, but could be moved by penetrating argument, or by a beggar on the streets of London. We might return to Dickens and remember that if we lose the child, we lose everything. We might turn to the dour Jeremiah of the twentieth century, Alexander Solzhenitsyn, and learn that if the West's victory over communism means a victory for license and banality and a real servitude for the human soul, then we are the losers, too. We might drink from all these fountains, but it will all be in vain if we do not keep our culture grounded in the one foundation without which Western civilization is inconceivable, and must fall. It may not be so

in India or China, not yet, but for us, it is the Messiah—to come, or having come—or it is Nothing. Reason may tell us to refrain from harming our neighbors; it is only God who can command us to love our neighbors as ourselves. Reason may suggest that the Good is ever to be sought, regardless of the pain it might cause us, regardless even of death. But only the One who loves can give us the strength to seek it, because it is He. Reason may falter in justifying itself, but the One who made the world in measure, weight, and number, guarantees also that reason is good and worthy of honor. And He promises more.[157]

The Politically Incorrect Guide to Western Civilization, 2008

Anthony Esolen serves as a member of the faculty and writer-in-residence at Magdalen College in New Hampshire. Esolen is a renowned scholar with many books, translations, and countless magazine and journal articles to his credit. His translation of Dante's *Divine Comedy* published by Modern Library is considered one of the very best ever published.

---

157 Anthony Esolen, *The Politically Incorrect Guide to Western Civilization* (Washington, D.C.: Regnery Publishing, 2008), loc. 308–309, Kindle Edition.

DAY 156

ST. ANSELM (1034–1109)

A proof of God's existence—

"How indeed has he [the fool] 'said in his heart' what he could not think; or how could he not think what he 'said in his heart,' since to 'say in one's heart' and 'to think' are the same? But if he really (indeed, since he really) both thought because he said 'in his heart' and did not 'say in his heart' because he could not think, there is only one sense in which something is 'said in one's heart' or thought. For in one sense a thing is thought when the word signifying it is thought; in another sense when the very object which the thing is understood. In the first sense, God can be thought not to exist, but not at all in the second sense. No one, indeed, understanding what God is can think that God does not exist, even though he may say these words in his heart either without any [objective] signification or with some peculiar signification. For God is that-than-which-nothing-greater-can-be-thought. Whoever really understands this understands clearly that this same being so exists that not even in thought can it not exist. Thus, whoever understands God exists in such a way cannot think of Him as not existing."[158]

Proslogion, 1078

158 St. Anselm, *Proslogion,* Ch. 4, *Anselm of Canterbury: The Major Works,* ed with introduction by Brian Davies and G.R. Evans (Oxford: Oxford University Press, 2008), 88.

St. Anselm was educated by the Benedictines. After his mother died, he traveled around Europe, settling at St. Stephen at Caen in Normandy where he was made abbot in 1063. It was here that Anselm wrote his famous works, *Monologium* and *Proslogium*, putting into practice his definition of theology as "faith seeking understanding." In 1093, Anselm was sent to England to become the archbishop of Canterbury. His years as archbishop brought political conflict with King William II and King Henry I. The kings twice banished him; and twice he returned to Canterbury. In addition to his philosophical and theological treatises, he wrote prayers and meditations and a great deal of correspondence. Anselm was archbishop until his death in 1109. The argument above has been subjected to centuries of commentary. Despite many claims of refutation, his argument keeps returning, as in Edward Feser's *Five Proofs for the Existence of God* (2017).

DAY 157

REV. GEORGE RUTLER (1945–)

Getting up—

"Winston Churchill long struggled with his 'Black Dog' of depression. His advocacy of the disastrous Gallipoli campaign in the First World War seemed to put him on the shelf of

ruined men, and from then on he was often mocked, painting pictures to keep moral balance during his 'Wilderness Years.' Only because Lord Halifax demurred the premiership following Chamberlain's resignation did King George VI appoint Winston his second choice in 1940. Early war defeats seemed overwhelming. The military occupation of Norway was a demoralizing calamity. The point is that if one falls, one can get up again. Churchill said, 'Success is not final, failure is not fatal; it is the courage to continue that counts.' . . . It is rooted in genuine humility that is willing to be helped up by a conviction of Providence, rather than refusing to get up out of crippling pride."[159]

A Year with Father Rutler: Lent, Easter, Spring, 2019

Rev. George Rutler was ordained a priest by Cardinal Cooke in 1981. He has served at parishes in Bronxville, NY and in Manhattan, on Wall Street, in Midtown, and Hell's Kitchen. Rutler is an extremely prolific writer—his sixteen books and hundreds of magazine columns are among the most widely-read works by any Catholic priest in the United States. He has made documentary films and has had a weekly television program on EWTN since 1988. Rutler was an Episcopalian priest before converting to Catholicism in 1979. After attending the North American College in Rome, he pursued further

---

159 Rev. George Rutler, *A Year with Father Rutler: Lent, Easter, Spring,* Volume 2, ed. Duncan Maxwell Anderson (Manchester: Sophia Institute Press, 2019), loc. 63-63, Kindle edition.

studies at the Angelicum and Gregorian Universities, also in Rome, the Institute Catholique in Paris, and Oxford University.

DAY 158

JOHN ALLAN WYETH (1894–1981)

A view from the war—

The Village Road

Too dark and late for any bugle call . . .
A wakeful horse along the picket line
stamps obstinately in the squashy loam.
No voice in either orchard with its dim
array of tents. Near by, a cracked old wall
gives, as I pass, a tiny blinking sign—
Bob must be still at work, or writing home.
I break in just to say goodnight to him . . .
Then half-way to my billet, being all
alone I bare my head before the shrine
That hallows all this stretch of road for me.
The sky-line flares and thunders, where a foam
of rockets drifts along the low charred rim

of hills that close in that infernal sea.[160]

> *This Man's Army: A War in Fifty-Odd Sonnets*, 1928

John Allan Wyeth is the "forgotten" poet of the First World War. Born in New York City and educated at Princeton, he began writing at thirteen and was the son of an ex-confederate soldier. He served on the Western Front later with the Army of Occupation in Germany. The section above comes from Wyeth's only book, a sequence of sonnets that follows an American troop division from its trip over the ocean, landing in France, and through the battles across the Western Front. In this sonnet, the narrator on horseback comes to one of the ruined forts of Verdun, the site of the longest battle of the war, in which over three hundred thousand French and Germans were killed. The poem begins as reportage but ends in a momentary vision of resurrection as the fort itself cries out, "Let the dead rise."

---

160 John Allan Wyeth, *This Man's Army: A War in Fifty-Odd Sonnets*, introduction by Dana Gioia, annotations by B. J. Omanson (Greenville: The University of South Carolina Press, 2008), 23.

DAY 159

FLANNERY O'CONNOR (1925–1964)

O'Connor answers a letter asking why she entitled her second novel The
Violent Bear It Away *(1960)—*

"About Matthew 12:11. The King James Version has it '. . . the
violent take it by force,' but I thought 'bear it away' sounded
better. What they take by force or bear away is the kingdom of
heaven itself. The violent in this case are the people who are
willing to act upon their faith and act vigorously. St. Augustine
and St. Thomas say the violent here are the ascetics. Anyway
it is the kind of passion for the things of God which makes
asceticism possible, which puts nothing in the way and lets
nothing interfere with winning heaven. Old Tarwater [a character in the novel] is this kind of Christian. All the saints are. I
guess John Wesley was. Call it a single-minded assault upon the
kingdom of heaven, often accomplished in part by self-denial.
Doing the will of God."[161]

Letter to La Trelle, February 14, 1963

Flannery O'Connor's answer to La Trelle is revealing. Notice
she explains the word *violence* used in the Gospel of St. Matthew

---

161 Benjamin B. Alexander, ed., *Good Things Out of Nazareth: The Uncollected
Letters of Flannery O'Connor and Friends* (New York: Convergent Books,
2019). 255.

and in her book title as persons acting "vigorously" and with "passion." This distance between a world of violence and a world of passion is quite wide in the minds of most people, but not to O'Connor. She will have nothing to do with the sentimental passion of so many novels and short stories—O'Connor's passion, following passion of Christ, revealed something far deeper than intense romantic feelings. She unites passion with violence to stun the reader out of moral and spiritual complacency. That's why O'Connor not only puts *violence* on the cover but also depicts violence in its most heinous form; in the case of *The Violent Bear It Away*, the deliberate drowning of a young boy.

DAY 160

BENEDICT GROESCHEL, CFR (1933–2014)

When the Church fails—

"When we are thinking clearly, we see that if Church leaders fail us it is not the Mystical Body of Christ. It is not our Divine Savior who fails us. Keep this in mind, because otherwise you will get angry at God. 'I'm not going to Church anymore. God let me down.' God didn't let you down. Msgr. Stoopnagle, or Sister Mary Officious, or Brother Grinch let you down. That's who let you down. They let God down, too. The reason the

Church fails us is that it is made up of human beings. The Church is a collection of people with original sin. I'm not talking about the heavenly Church of the saints or even that part of the life of the Church where the sacraments remain untouched in their integrity because that's the way Christ instituted them. . . . A few years ago I celebrated my fiftieth anniversary as an altar boy. I got hurt when I was an altar boy: I was corrected when I didn't deserve it. I went to Catholic schools for about twenty-five years, and I was hurt by some of my teachers. But I was helped by many more than those who hurt me. The same thing is true of priests and bishops I have known. I have been hurt by a few and helped by many. I've been hurt by religious communities but greatly helped by them. The problem is that when these representatives of the Church hurt me, I had the same angry reaction as a person who feels that God has failed him. It happens to us all."[162]

Arise from Darkness, 1995

A priest for fifty years, Benedict Groeschel, CFR, was one of the founding members of the Franciscan Friars of the Renewal in 1987. He was a psychologist with a doctorate from Columbia University, an internationally known speaker, and a retreat master. His many books and EWTN appearances rightfully made him a much-beloved figure in the Church.

---

162 Benedict Groeschel, C.F.R., *Arise from Darkness: What to Do When Life Doesn't Make Sense* (San Francisco: Ignatius Press, 1995), loc. 66-67, Kindle Edition.

DAY 161

CHARLES TAYLOR (1931–)

"I wanna be me."—

"We need to explain what is peculiar to our time. It's not just that people sacrifice their love relationships, and the care of their children, to pursue their careers. The point is that today many people feel *called* to do this, feel they ought to do this, feel their lives would be somehow wasted or unfulfilled if they didn't do it. Thus what gets lost in this critique is the moral force of the ideal of authenticity. . . . That the espousal of authenticity takes the form of a kind of self-relativism means the vigorous defense of any moral idea is somehow off limits. For the implications . . . are that some forms of life are indeed higher than others, and the culture of tolerance for individual self-fulfillment shies away from this claim. This means, as has often been pointed out, that there is something contradictory and self-defeating in their position, since the relativism itself is powered (at least partly) by a moral ideal. But consistently or not, this is the position usually adopted. The ideal sinks to the level of an axiom, something one doesn't challenge but also never expounds."[163]

The Ethics of Authenticity, 1991

---

163 Charles Taylor, *The Ethics of Authenticity* (Cambridge: Harvard University Press, 1991), 17.

Charles Taylor is professor emeritus of political science and philosophy at McGill University. After graduating from McGill, Taylor, a Rhodes Scholar, studied at Oxford, where he earned three degrees. Taylor was first recognized as a Hegel scholar, but his later work was focused on the question of identity in a secular age. In 2019, he was awarded the Ratzinger Award by Pope Francis, who said, "He invites us to intuit and seek new ways to live and express the transcendent dimensions of the human soul, those spiritual dimensions in which the Spirit continues to work imperceptibly. This allows us to deal with Western secularization in a way that is neither superficial nor given to fatalistic discouragement." The book that brought him worldwide attention was *Sources of the Self: The Making of the Modern Identity* (1989).

DAY 162

STEPHEN BASKERVILLE (1957–)

The unintended consequences—

"'No-fault' divorce introduced radical new legal concepts—including, ironically, unproven guilt. . . . 'Many husbands and wives who did not seek or want a divorce [and who had committed no legally recognized infraction] were stunned to learn that they were equally "at fault" in the dissolution of their

marriages.' [Barbara Dafoe Whitehead, *The Divorce Culture* (1998)]. So the 'fault' that was ostensibly thrown out the front door of the divorce proceedings re-entered through the back, but with no precise definition. The judiciary expanded its traditional role of punishing crime or redressing tort to punishing personal faults and private differences: suddenly, one could be summoned to court without having committed any legal infraction; the verdict pre-determined without any evidence being examined; and one could be found culpable for things that were not illegal."[164]

The New Politics of Sex, 2017

Stephen Baskerville is a professor of government and director of the International Politics & Policy Program at Patrick Henry College. Recipient of a PhD from the London School of Economics, he has been a Fellow at the Howard Center for Family, Religion, and Society and senior lecturer of political science at Howard University. His published books to date are *Taken Into Custody: The War Against Fathers, Marriage, and the Family* (2007), *The New Politics of Sex* (2017), and *Not Peace But the Sword: The Political Theology of the English Revolution* (2018). Baskerville appears often on national radio and television programs, including *The O'Reilly Factor, Hardball with Chris Matthews, Court TV with Fred Graham and Katherine Crier*, and

---

164 Stephen Baskerville, *The New Politics of Sex: The Sexual Revolution, Civil Liberties, and the Growth of Governmental Power* (Kettering: Angelico Press, 2017), 70-71.

many others. *The New Politics of Sex* is one of the most important works of Christian apologetics in the past half-century.

DAY 163

ERNST DOWSON (1867–1900)

Extreme Unction

Upon the eyes, the lips, the feet,
    On all the passages of sense,
The atoning oil is spread with sweet
    Renewal of lost innocence.

The feet, that lately ran so fast
    To meet desire, are soothly sealed;
The eyes, that were so often cast
    On vanity, are touched and healed.

From troublous sights and sounds set free;
    In such a twilight hour of breath,
Shall one retrace his life, or see,
    Through shadows, the true face of death?

Vials of mercy! Sacring oils!
    I know not where nor when I come,

Nor through what wanderings and toils,
　To crave of you Viaticum.

Yet, when the walls of flesh grow weak,
　In such an hour, it well may be,
Through mist and darkness, light will break,
　And each anointed sense will see.[165]

Ernest Dowson lived in London and was a member of the Rhymers' Club with W. B. Yeats and Arthur Symons. Both of his parents committed suicide. Living mostly in France, he was received into the Church in 1892. Dowson's poems contain such well-known phrases as "gone with the wind" and "days of wine and roses." He lived a sad life, suffering unrequited love, and dying of tuberculosis at the age of only thirty-two.

---

165 Ernst Dowson, *The Poems and Prose of Ernest Dowson with a Memoir by Arthur Symons*, loc. 966-1005 of 5569, Kindle Edition.

DAY 164

THOMAS MERTON (1915–1968)

Love wills goodness—

"God knows us from within ourselves, not as objects, not as strangers, not as intimates, but as our own selves. His knowledge of us is the pure light of which our own self-knowledge is only a dim reflection. He knows us in Himself, not merely as images of something outside Him, but as 'selves' in which His own self is expressed. He finds Himself more perfectly in us than we find ourselves. He alone holds the secret of a charity by which we can love others not only as we love ourselves, but as He loves them. The beginning of this love is the will to let those we love be perfectly themselves, the resolution not to twist them to fit our own image. If in loving them we do not love what they are, but only their potential likeness to ourselves, then we do not love them: we only love the reflection of ourselves we find in them."[166]

No Man Is an Island, 1955

Thomas Merton reminds us that God knows us better than we know ourselves. No matter how deeply we look within, God sees more deeply because our self is enfolded with his Divine

166 Thomas Merton. *No Man Is an Island* (HMH Books, 1955), loc. 168-169, Kindle Edition.

Self. God knows when we objectify someone we profess to love. True love starts with the embracing of what a person *is*, not what they might become by conforming to the lover's demands. Integral to loving the reality of an individual person is love for the potential that lies within, a potential to grow towards God and His love.

DAY 165

ORESTES A. BROWNSON (1803–1876)

A secret thought—

"The benevolent heart weeps in sorrow over the follies, the aberrations and inconsistencies of the children of men; it deeply deplores their misery and wretchedness, the severity with which they oppress each other; anxious for their amelioration it raises its inquiries—'Indulgent God'! Is man eternally ordained to be the dupe and slave of man? Shall he never regain his independence, and be free to exert his mental powers in the acquisition of knowledge; be free to study the works of his Creator, and while his bosom glows with gratitude to his Heavenly Father, be free to repose with confidence on the paternal affection of the Sovereign of nature? . . . Nature gave to man the law of liberty, and entwined a desire for independence around every fiber of his being. Amid all the usurpations

of tyrants, under all the usurpations so liberally heaped upon him, some secret thought recurs to his native dignity; he rises enraged at the shackles of his slavery, indignant spurns the thought and demands his ranks in the scale of being. He may be misled, he may mistake the road to the land of Freedom, he may deceive himself in the choice of means, to promote his felicity, but he will never relinquish the attempt. His errors shall serve to correct him, and his follies shall teach him wisdom."[167]

"An Essay on the Progress of Truth," 1827–1828

Born in Vermont, Orestes A. Brownson was not committed to any particular faith as a young man and became a political radical. He tried to rally the Democratic Party to address the "wage slavery" suffered by the working poor. After the Democrats ignored him, Brownson turned towards conservatism. At Brook Farm, a Transcendentalist commune, he got to know Emerson and Thoreau. But in 1844, at age forty-one, he became a Catholic, arguing that Catholic doctrine was conservative but liberating. He began to edit, assuming editorship of the *Boston Quarterly Review* before changing its name to *Brownson's Quarterly Review*. Brownson is considered one of America's most voluminous writers: his *Review* surpassed 2,500,000 words. He was admired by John Henry Newman,

---

167 Orestes A. Brownson, *The American Republic: Works in Political Philosophy*, introduction by Peter Augustine Lawler (Wilmington: ISI Books, 2003), 16.

and the man who had received him into the Church, Cardinal John "The Dagger" Hughes of New York City, remarked that Brownson, as a catechumen, knew more about the Faith than himself.

DAY 166

FLANNERY O'CONNOR (1925–1964)

O'Connor reflects on the life of Mary Ann—

"Most of us have learned to be dispassionate about evil, to look it in the face and find, as often as not, our own grinning reflections with which we do not argue, but good is another matter. Few have stared at that long enough to accept the fact that its face too is grotesque, that in us the good is something under construction. The modes of good have to be satisfied with a cliché or a smoothing down that will soften their real look. When we look into the face of good, we are liable to see a face like Mary Ann's, full of promise."[168]

"Introduction," *Memoir of Mary Ann*, 1961

---

168 Flannery O'Connor, *Memoir of Mary Ann By the Dominican Nuns Who Took Care of Her* (New York: Farrar, Straus and Giroux, 1961), 17–18.

Flannery O'Connor could see past labels and the surface of things. The time she spent with the Dominican sisters working on their book about the remarkable but disfigured Mary Ann (Day 51) leads her to think that all faces of goodness look like hers, incomplete, or as she puts it, "under construction." When we imagine or present goodness, O'Connor says, we are likely to "soften their real look," by removing whatever is ugly or disfigured.

DAY 167

EDWARD LEEN (1885–1944)

From one happiness to another—

"God does not demand unhappiness as the price of happiness. He plans happiness here as a prelude and foretaste of happiness hereafter. Such a statement sounds paradoxical to the average person. This is not surprising, considering the manner in which Christianity is ordinarily presented. A little reflection should suffice to dispel the difficulties that the proposition just enunciated finds in minds fixed in the unreal, conventional attitude towards life's realities. It is not the way of God to give

things at a price. This would be inconsistent both with His infinite generosity and with his Fatherhood of men."[169]

Why the Cross?, 1938

Edward Leen studied philosophy at University College, Dublin, and afterward went to Rome in 1912, earning his doctorate in theology from the Gregorian University. After serving in Nigeria for two years as a missionary, he returned to Dublin, becoming dean and then president of Blackrock College. He moved to join the staff of the Spiritan Senior Seminary and became its president in 1939. Leen's books were successful and influential both in the United Kingdom and the United States. Like other great Christian apologists, he could communicate a deeply informed theology and spirituality to lay readers. His works include *Progress in Mental Prayer* (1935), *In the Likeness of Christ* (1936), *The Holy Ghost* (1937), *Why the Cross?* (1938), *The True Vine and Its Branches* (1938), and *The Church Before Pilate* (1939).

---

169 Edward Leen, *Why the Cross?* (Cleveland: Scepter Books, 2001), 29.

DAY 168

ADRIENNE VON SPEYR (1902–1967)

Pushing greatness aside—

"God opens the meaning of existence beyond finitude. Men shrink back before such a God. They long for a religion that does not call into question earthly values and proportions. Thus there arises a sort of contest between the voice of man, which grows louder and louder in order to drown out God, and the voice of God, which maintains its divine volume. The more man wants to decide for himself about his destiny, and thus also about his past and future, the more he falls prey to the limitations of life on earth, the more everything becomes smaller for him. He pushes greatness to the side as absurd. Man would prefer anything rather than to appear absurd. And if he himself has so little knowledge of God, those who come after will know even less."[170]

Man Before God, 1966

Adrienne von Speyr calls attention to the unforeseen consequences of persons who reject the will of God in order to direct their own lives—they make themselves small by comparison with lives growing in the fullness of faith. Such egoists

---

170 Adrienne von Speyr, *Man Before God*, trans. Nicholas J. Healy and D.C. Schindler (San Francisco: Ignatius Press, 2009), 86.

create a world in which true greatness will always be denied them because they have rejected the only available way to greatness, God's love. They have, in short, created the kind of absurd world that is described in detail by existentialists such as Jean Paul Sartre, Samuel Beckett, and Albert Camus.

DAY 169

MARTIN C. D'ARCY, SJ (1888–1976)

Under a living Providence—

"The difference caused by the absence of the supernatural is unmistakable, and can easily be seen, for example, in a comparison between Sigrid Undset's *Kristan Lavaransdatter* and Galsworthy's *Forsyte Saga*. In both, men and women toil and suffer, love and grow estranged, and evil seems to conquer, as the seasons come and go year after year; but in one the sin and suffering and death take place under a living Providence, and the ravages of time are redeemed in some mystery of love; whereas in the other there is no hope."[171]

The Mind and Heart of Love, 1956

---

171 M. C. D'Arcy, S.J., *The Mind and the Heart of Love: Lion and Unicorn, A Study in Eros and Agape* (New York: Henry Holt & Company, 1956), 81.

Martin C. D'Arcy, SJ, entered the Society of Jesus in 1907 and was ordained in 1921. He attended Stonyhurst College and the Gregorian University in Rome. He spent most of his career as Master of Campion Hall, Oxford, but traveled and lectured extensively. He enjoyed an amazing array of friendships and correspondents, including Evelyn Waugh, Dorothy Sayers, W. H. Auden, Edith Sitwell, Kenneth Clark, and Eric Gill. As an author, D'Arcy is known primarily for *The Mind and the Heart of Love* (1945), which remains a classic on that subject, but other books, such as *The Meaning and Matter of History* (1959) and *The Nature of Belief* (1976), should not be overlooked.

DAY 170

BISHOP FULTON SHEEN (1895–1979)

Herod was deaf—

"Herod began by asking Our Lord many questions, not questions of doctrine and discipline as Annas had done, but questions prompted by curiosity. Jaded souls present intellectual difficulties, never pleas for moral regeneration. Therefore, to all the questions Our Lord answered him nothing. He tried to save Judas and Pilate, but for Herod—not a word. Why did Our Lord refuse to speak to Herod? Can it be that He who came to save all men and Who loved them enough to die for

them, should still not *even try* to win calloused souls *like Herod*. . . . Why should He Who spoke to Judas the traitor, Magdalen the harlot, and the thief, now be silent before a king? *Because the conscience of Herod was dead.* He was too familiar with religion. He wanted miracles, yes, but not to surrender his will, but to satisfy his curiosity. His soul was already so blunted by appeals, including even the Baptist's, that another appeal would only have intensified his guilt. He was stone deaf on the side of God. He was one dead in body and soul, eaten by luxury and sin. Herod was not offering his soul for salvation, but only his nerves for titillation."[172]

Characters of the Passion, 1947

Bishop Fulton Sheen addresses a question that readers of the Passion narrative often raise. Sheen explains that Herod was a completely lost soul. In other words, Jesus did not want to "cast his pearls before swine" (see Mt 7:6) as he taught in the Sermon on the Mount. Pilate had kept an open mind; he had no burning desire to execute Jesus, which is why he passed him onto Herod for questioning. In this way, Sheen is underscoring the connection between gross immorality and the stubbornness of intellectual confusion. Herod could not hear because all he cared about was "titillation."

---

172 Fulton Sheen, *Characters of the Passion* (Kettering: Angelico Press, 2015), loc. 35, Kindle Edition.

DAY 171

RUSSELL KIRK (1918–1994)

Overthrowing authority—

"Human nature being flawed, so that all of us in some degree rebel against the people and the institution to which we owe most, there is in every man a certain impulse to make himself God; that is, to cast off all authority but his own lust and whim. From this vice, this hankering for abnormality, comes the corrupting influence of total power upon even the best of natures. The rebellion of Lucifer is the symbol of this ancient anarchic impulse—the passion for overthrowing the authority of God, that upon the vacant throne of authority the rebel may make himself absolute. Yet the doom of all such risings is as sure as Lucifer's. For a grown man to rebel against all authority is as ludicrous as for a three-year-old child to defy his parents; whether they are good parents or bad, he can live scarcely a day without them."[173]

Enemies of Permanent Things, 1969

A native of Michigan, Russell Kirk attended Michigan State and Duke University. During WWII, he served in the army

---

173 Russell Kirk, *Enemies of Permanent Things: Observations or Abnormity in Literature and Politics*, introduction by Benjamin G. Lockerd (Providence: Cluny Media, 2016), 35.

and returned to his great-grandfather's home, Piety Hill, where he lived the rest of his days. He earned his doctorate from the University of St. Andrews, and his thesis, *The Conservative Mind: from Burke to Santayana*, became a classic of conservative literature. Kirk was received in the Church in 1963. He edited the quarterly journal *The University Bookman* and was founder and first editor of the quarterly *Modern Age*. He contributed articles to numerous serious periodicals on both sides of the Atlantic. For twenty-five years, he wrote a column on education for *National Review*. In addition to books on literature, politics, economics, and philosophy, Kirk wrote three novels, twenty-two short stories, and several volumes of ghost tales.

DAY 172

JOSEF PIEPER (1904–1997)

Freedom to believe—

"No one who believes *must* believe; belief is by nature a free act. However convinced we are of the credibility of the witness, it is not enough to compel us to believe; and however incontrovertible the content of a truth may appear to the knower, it is *not* so to the believer. The believer, therefore, in that he believes, is always free. Because this is so, moreover, belief is a particularly opaque phenomenon. Not only religious belief

in revelation, but also the credence which men pay to one another, is by nature adjacent to and akin to myself, because it springs from freedom."[174]

Belief and Faith, 1963

Believing something is always made easier when we believe in the person who expresses the belief. But, as Josef Pieper points out, this does not necessitate our belief; neither does the veracity of the message. Just as we are free to reject the belief of a trusted messenger, so we remain free to reject that which strikes us as completely true. Pieper is pointing to a mystery—what happens in ourselves when we believe, when we make "the leap of faith," as the Danish philosopher Søren Kierkegaard called it. The freedom of the individual is never coerced into believing: there is an "opaque" moment between freedom and faith, and that moment represents the unique status of a human being before the Creator, the possibility of either redemption or damnation.

---

174 Josef Pieper, *Belief and Faith: A Philosophical Tract* (Westport: Greenwood Press, Publishers, 1974), 43.

DAY 173

AIDAN NICHOLS, OP (1948–)

Life-giving liturgy—

"The liturgy is a necessary environment for the theologian. If he (or she) is cut off from these life-giving texts, his (or her) mind will soon cease to be the mind of the Church. It may remain, formally speaking, an orthodox mind, but it will not be a mind possessing that entire complex of attitudes which together reflect the Church's basic response to God: love, humility, gratitude for the redemption, and the rest. The liturgy expresses what we might call the 'inside' of the act of faith: the interiority of the relationship with God which God's own plan, once entered into, set up. As the human expression of the covenant, the liturgy articulates the inside of the life of the household of faith, just as the conversation of husband and wife brings out what is implicit in their marital and family living. The theological student must learn how to interpret this language so as to find the voice of the Church, the Bride, calling on Christ, the Bridegroom."[175]

The Shape of Catholic Theology, 1991

---

175 Aidan Nichols, O.P., *The Shape of Catholic Theology: An Introduction to Its Sources, Principles, and History* (Collegeville: The Liturgical Press, 1991), 186–87.

Aidan Nichols, OP, entered the Dominican Order in 1970 and was ordained a priest in 1976. Considered one of the most eminent Catholic theologians of our era, he presently has the honorary status of affiliated lecturer in the University of Cambridge after previously teaching at the Pontifical University of St. Thomas, Rome; St. Mary's College, Oscott; and Blackfriars Hall, Oxford. Nichols has published some thirty books and over seventy articles, many on the work of Hans Urs von Balthasar, such as *A Key to Balthasar* (2011), and *Hans Urs von Balthasar on Beauty, Goodness, and Truth* (2011). Other books of note include *The Shape of Catholic Theology: An Introduction to Its Sources, Principles, and History* (1991), *Christendom Awake: On Re-Energizing the Church in Culture* (1999), *Looking at the Liturgy* (2011), and *Redeeming Beauty: Soundings in Sacral Aesthetics* (2017).

DAY 174

ST. AUGUSTINE (354–430)

One seeks glory—

"Of the nature of the two cities, the earthly and the heavenly. Accordingly, two cities have been formed by two loves: the earthly by the love of self, even to the contempt of God; the heavenly by the love of God, even to the contempt of self. The

former, in a word, glories in itself, the latter in the Lord. For the one seeks glory from men; but the greatest glory of the other is God, the witness of conscience. The one lifts up its head in its own glory; the other says to its God, 'Thou art my glory, and the lifter up of mine head.' In the one, the princes and the nations it subdues are ruled by the love of ruling; in the other, the princes and the subjects serve one another in love, the latter obeying, while the former take thought for all.'"[176]

The City of God, 426

Like his *Confessions*, St. Augustine's magisterial *On the City of God Against the Pagans* was unlike any previously known book. Composed of twenty-two sections, *The City of God* surveys all of pagan religion, literature, politics, history, and philosophy. Augustine's central idea was his distinction between the "two cities" that have formed since the coming of Jesus Christ and His institution of the Church: "For *the one* seeks glory from men; but the greatest glory of *the other* is God, the witness of conscience." (Emphasis added.)

---

176 St. Augustine, *On The City of God Against the Pagans*, 14.28, trans. Marcus Dodds, introduction by Thomas Merton (New York: The Modern Library, 1993), 477.

DAY 175

JACQUES MARITAIN (1882–1973)

The depths of the soul—

"Reason does not consist of its conscious logical tools and manifestations, nor does the will consist only in its deliberate conscious determinations. Far beneath the sunlit surface thronged with explicit concepts and judgments, words and expressed resolutions or movements of the will, are the sources of knowledge and creativity, of love and supra-sensuous desires, hidden in the primordial translucid night of the intimate vitality of the soul. Thus it is that we must recognize the existence of an unconscious or preconscious which pertains to the spiritual powers of the human soul and to the inner abyss of personal freedom, and of the personal thirst and striving for knowing and seeing, grasping and expressing."[177]

Creative Intuition in Art and Poetry, 1953

Jacques Maritain's *Creative Intuition in Art and Poetry* contains the first A. W. Mellon Lectures in the Fine Arts delivered in 1952 at the National Gallery in Washington, DC. Though Maritain was a renowned metaphysician and ethicist, he had been writing about the arts and beauty since he was a young scholar. His

---

177 Jacques Maritain, *Creative Intuition in Art and Poetry* (Princeton: Princeton University Press, 1977), 94.

Art and Scholasticism was published in 1920, *Response to Jean Cocteau* in 1926, and *The Frontiers of Poetry* in 1927. Maritain's friendships and relationship with writers, painters, sculptors, composers, and poets constituted a Who's Who of European and American artists. The quote above displays Maritain's unique voice as a Thomist, one who is as comfortable talking to artists as to fellow philosophers. Here he is offering a rich explanation of how an artist's mind comprehends reality.

DAY 176

ST. THÉRÈSE OF LISIEUX (1873–1897)

No more hiding—

"And so it gives me great joy, dear Mother, to come to you and sing His unspeakable mercies. It is for you alone that I write the story of the little flower gathered by Jesus. This thought will help me to speak freely, without troubling either about style or about the many directions that I shall make; for a Mother's heart always understands her child, even when it can only lisp, and so I am sure of being understood and my meaning appreciated. If a little flower could speak, it seems to me that it would tell us quite simply all that God has done for it, without hiding any of its gifts. It would not, under the pretext of humility, say that it was not pretty, or that it had not a sweet

scent, that the sun had withered its petals, or the storm bruised its stem, if it knew that such were not the case."[178]

The Story of a Soul, 1898

Any sentence in St. Thérèse of Lisieux's autobiography resists comment. The extraordinary combination of joy, imagination, and spiritual probity are jaw-dropping. In this case, the introduction of a "little flower" imagining how it would speak of its own beauty and scent, avoiding the false humility of pretending otherwise, could inspire a long commentary, but who would want to attempt it? Her thoughts have a kind of musical quality: they move the heart the moment they are read. Turning to a commentary would only take us away from hearing her voice, her song.

---

178 St. Thérèse de Lisieux, *Story of a Soul: The Autobiography of St. Thérèse of Lisieux* (1912 trans.), loc. 2 of 274, Kindle Edition.

DAY 177

ST. TERESA BENEDICTA OF THE CROSS
(1891–1942)

Love never ceases—

"For the Christian there is no 'strange human being.' He is in every instance the 'neighbor' whom we have with us and who is most in need of us. It makes no difference whether he is related or not, whether we 'like' him or not, whether he is 'morally worthy' of help or not. The love of Christ knows no bounds, it never ceases, it never withdraws in the face of hatred or foul play. He came for the sake of sinner and not for the righteous. If the love of Christ lives in us, then we do as he did and seek after the lost sheep. Natural love seeks to possess the beloved entirely and as far as possible not to share him. Christ came to win back lost mankind for the Father; whoever loves with his love will want people for God and not for himself. Of course, that is the surest way to possess them forever; for wherever we have entrusted a person to God, then we are one with him in God, whereas the craving to overpower sooner or later always leads to loss. It is true of the other's soul as for one's own and for every external possession. Whoever is evidently out to win and to possess loses; whoever hands over to God, wins."[179]

The Mystery of Christmas, 1931

---

179 Edith Stein, *Essential Writings,* selected with an introduction by John Sullivan, O.C.D. (Marynoll: Orbis Books 2002), 42.

These are inspiring lines written by Edith Stein, who upon becoming a religious sister took the name Teresa Benedicta of the Cross. How instinctively easy it is to return hatred for hatred or to plan revenge in response to being wronged. The more egregious the harm, the more the revenge instinct kicks in. Counting from one to ten is not bad advice because by the time we reach ten we may well have recalled Christ's command to "love thy enemy" (see Mt 5:44). We should love others for God, not for ourselves, St. Teresa reminds us. If we are loving others only for ourselves, then answering hatred with hatred fits comfortably with what we call "love." Love, she says, is not possession but placing someone in God's care.

DAY 178

PETER GEACH (1916–2013)

The miracle of reason—

"We are told of the great probability that there are many other planets inhabited by rational creatures. Life must originate, we are told, wherever the physical conditions for life are favorable: and here must be so many planets on which life has originated that on millions of them rational beings will have evolved by natural selection. But rational beings cannot so come to be: the coming to be of a rational creature is strictly miraculous

— it exceeds all the power of sub-rational nature. . . . But an everyday miracle is none the less a miracle: the number of Masses said each day does not diminish the wonder that Transubstantiation would have to be."[180]

The Virtues, 1977

Peter Geach was a British philosopher whose Catholic faith was integral to all his work. In Jane O'Grady's obituary for Geach in the *Guardian*, she wrote, "Faith neither conflicted with reason nor trumped it: rather, the two nicely dovetailed. He was never a unitary, system-building philosopher, but produced sharp gems of analytical argument that brilliantly lacerated orthodoxies current in philosophy, while often simultaneously bolstering those of Catholicism." Geach taught at Leeds University from 1966 to 1981and was awarded the papal medal *Pro Ecclesia et Pontifice* in 1999. His wife, Elizabeth Anscombe, was also deeply Catholic, and together they represented the intellectual legacy of Catholicism in the midst of academic cultures of disbelief. O'Grady tells the story that Geach once stood up during a sermon, shouting, "This is heresy," and marched his family out of the church.

---

180 Peter Geach, *The Virtues: The Stanton Lecture 1973-4* (Cambridge: Cambridge University Press, 1977), 52.

DAY 179

RAINER MARIA RILKE (1875–1926)

Autumn Day

> Lord: it is time. Bright summer fades away.
> Let sundials darken as your shadows grow.
> Set loose your winds across the open fields.
>
> Let the last fruit still ripen on the vine,
> And give the grapes a few more southern days
> To warm them to perfection, and then press
> Their earthy sweetness into heavy wine.
>
> Whoever has no house now never builds one.
> Whoever is alone now stays alone.
> Now he will wake and read, writing long letters,
> Aimlessly wandering the empty lanes,
> Restless as the leaves swirling round his feet.[181]

Translated by Dana Gioia

Rainer Maria Rilke is considered one of the most significant poets in the German language. At the age of twenty-four, Rilke traveled to Russia and there met the great writer Leo Tolstoy, whose work influenced him and his attitude towards

---

181 Published with the kind permission of the poet and translator Dana Gioia.

the Catholic faith in which he was raised. He's a poet, always reaching towards the angels that populate much of his writing, though he avoids any explicit professions of faith. His poetry is filled with Christian symbols and allusions. Writing in an age increasingly weighed down by loss of belief, Rilke's mystical vision was not deterred. His best-known works are the poetry collection *Duino Elegies* (1922), begun in 1912, the novel *The Notebooks of Malte Laurids Brigge* (1910), and the *Letters to a Young Poet* published in 1929.

DAY 180

HERMAN BROCH (1886–1951)

Music is a shimmer of God—

"Let us for now assume that this state of grace will not occur, even though one day it will. When, then? Have Logos and Spirit disappeared from the earth because they can no longer have a mode of expression in language? But they still do, and it is the most audible means of all, in this ever-more-silent world, and it is becoming more audible and richer all the time: It is music that, like a final sign of the Spirit and Logos, floats above the human world in universal validity. . . . For man has thrown himself, in a kind of frenzy, into the arms of music, insatiably and in the radical and uncompromising manner that is a basic

trait of this age, with a passion explainable only by mankind's current muteness and incomprehension, and by the deep suffering this causes. Humanity sees music as a fading shimmer of God's mercy, granted as a last hint of faith and knowledge transcending the visible, a triumph over silence that transcends the tragic insight of rational intellect. Even in the remotest reaches he rejoices in this gift, and in listening, he becomes again what he once was, human."[182]

Geist and Zeitgeist: The Spirit in an Unspiritual Age, 1934

When Herman Broch was received into the Church in 1909, he was inspired by the cult of the Virgin Mary and the Church's belief in absolute good and absolute evil. Broch is acknowledged as one of the major writers of the twentieth century on the basis of his *Sleepwalkers* trilogy (1930–32), *The Unknown Quality* (1933), and his masterpiece, *The Death of Virgil* (1945). He was imprisoned by the Nazis in 1938. When released, he moved to the United States and continued to write extensively about literature, modern art and architecture, mass psychology, politics, and the preservation of human rights and democracy. *The Spell,* an unfinished novel he began in 1934, was published posthumously in 1969.

---

182 Herman Broch, *Geist and Zeitgeist: The Spirit in an Unspiritual Age,* ed., trans. and introduction by John Hargreaves (New York: Counterpoint, 2002), 63.

DAY 181

HENRYK SIENKIEWICZ (1846–1916)

A city of pride—

"It seemed that out of every tear of a martyr new confessors were born, and that every groan on the arena found an echo in thousands of breasts. Caesar was swimming in blood, Rome and the whole pagan world was mad. But those who had had enough of transgression and madness, those who were trampled upon, those whose lives were misery and oppression, all the weighed down, all the sad, all the unfortunate, came to hear the wonderful tidings of God, who out of love for men had given Himself to be crucified and redeem their sins. When they found a God whom they could love, they had found that which the society of the time could not give any one,—'happiness and love.' And Peter understood that neither Caesar nor all his legions could overcome the living truth,—that they could not overwhelm it with tears or blood, and that now its victory was beginning. He understood with equal force why the Lord had turned him back on the road. That city of pride, crime, wickedness, and power was beginning to be His city, and the double capital, from which would flow out upon the world government of souls and bodies."[183]

Quo Vadis, 1895

---

183 Henryk Sienkiewicz, *Quo Vadis: A Narrative of the Time of Nero* (digireads. com, 2009), loc. 652-3, Kindle Edition.

The Polish writer Henryk Sienkiewicz won the Noble Prize
in 1905 after emerging as one of the most important and prolific Polish writers of the latter half of the nineteenth century.
Raised in a family of activists in the cause of Polish independence, he began writing as a student in Warsaw. He toured the
United States in 1876 and later published his impressions in a
Polish newspaper. Back in Poland, he plunged into the study
of Polish history that led to his famous trilogy about Poland in
the seventeenth century: *Fire and Sword, The Deluge,* and *Pan
Michael,* published between 1884 and 1888. His most famous
novel about Christian persecution under Nero, *Quo Vadis,* was
published in 1895 and was translated into forty languages with
the English version selling eight hundred thousand copies in
the United States alone. Sienkiewicz believed literature should
"uplift the human soul," a purpose it appears he served well.
His complete works have been published in sixty volumes.

DAY 182

GABRIEL MARCEL (1889–1973)

A passing reality—

"We ought to be able to see more clearly just for what reason
mass-man is so easily turned into a fanatic. What I seem to
myself to have grasped is this, that the individual, in order to

belong to the mass, to be a mass-man, has had, as a prelimi-
nary, though without having had the least awareness of it, to
divest himself of that substantial reality which was linked to his
initial individuality or rather to the fact of his belonging to a
small actual group. The incredibly sinister role of the press, the
cinema, the radio, has consisted in passing that original reality
through a pair of flattening rollers to substitute for it a super-
imposed pattern of ideas and images with no real roots in the
deep being of the subject of this experiment."[184]

Man Against Mass Society, 1952

Gabriel Marcel was born in Paris and attended the Sorbonne.
During WWI, his work with the Red Cross directed his philosophical reflection to what he called "concrete existence."
He wanted nothing to do with forms of speculation, such as
German Idealism, that treated the search for wisdom in a series
of abstractions. Though his thought showed little of the influence of Soren Kierkegaard, it was through reading the Danish
existentialist's works that he came to Catholicism. He joined
the Church in 1929, and thereafter was avidly read by the new
Catholic theologians as he became a central figure in the French
Catholic intellectual revival centered around Jacques Maritain.
He differed with Maritain and other neo-Thomists on their
emphasis on metaphysics and focused directly on human

---

184 Gabriel Marcel, *Man Against Mass Society*, trans. G.S. Fraser (Chicago: Henry Regnery Company, 1952), 140-41.

experience of anxiety, loss, and love. Some of his major works are *Metaphysical Journal* (1927), *Being and Having* (1933), *Homo Viator* (1935), and *Man Against Mass Society* (1952). Marcel was also a playwright, a composer, and pianist of distinction.

DAY 183

WALKER PERCY (1916–1990)

A saving remnant—

"The point is that the time may come that the Catholic Church and the Catholic people, both priests and laymen, will have become a remnant, a saving remnant, and that will be both bad news and good news. The bad news is that the familiar comfort of the parish in which the Church was taken to be more or less co-extensive with the society in which we lived is probably going or gone. The good news is that in becoming a minority in all countries, a remnant, the Church also becomes a world church in the true sense, bound to no culture, not even to the West of the old Christendom, by no means triumphant but rather a pilgrim church witnessing to a world in travail

and yet a world to which it will appear ever stranger and more outlandish."[185]

"A 'Cranky' Novelist Reflects on the Church," 1983

Walker Percy imagines a time when the Catholic Church will become a "saving remnant," a thought that has become more common in the more than three decades since he wrote it. St. John Paul the Great was then pope, and he was busy fighting the nonsense that had become standardized since the capture of Vatican II by the media and liberal theologians and bishops. Percy's most telling irony is heard here: "the familiar comfort of the parish in which the Church was taken to be more or less co-extensive with the society in which we lived . . ." Percy regrets that Catholics who enter the average parish have not entered a sacred space but one that has conformed itself to the society outside. By contrast, the new "pilgrim church" will view the world outside in need of evangelization rather than our conformity.

---

185 Walker Percy, *Signposts In a Strange Land*, ed. and introduction by Patrick Samway, S.J. (New York: Farrar, Straus and Giroux, 1991), 319.

DAY 184

HUGO RAHNER, SJ (1900–1968)

Playing before God—

"The man who truly plays is, therefore, first of all, a man in whom seriousness and gaiety are mingled; and, indeed, at the bottom of play there lies a tremendous secret. We had some intimation of it, surely, when we are considering the creative play of God. All play—just as much as every task which we set ourselves to master with real earnestness of purpose—is an attempt to approximate to the Creator, who performs his work with the divine seriousness which its meaning and purpose demand, and yet with the spontaneity and effortless skill of the great artist he is, creating because he wills to create and not because he must."[186]

Man at Play, 1949

Hugo Rahner, SJ, entered the Jesuit novitiate of the North German Jesuit Province in 1919. He received doctorates in philosophy and theology at the University of Innsbruck, Austria. Beginning in 1937, he taught in Innsbruck, specializing in patrology and history of Catholic dogma until the Nazis forced his resignation and exile in 1940. Rahner was named

---

186 Hugo Rahner, S.J., *Man at Play*, trans. Brian Battersaw and Edward Quinn, preface by Walter J. Ong (New York: Herder and Herder, 1972), 28.

dean and later president of the University of Innsbruck after the war. In his teaching, preaching, and writing, Rahner sought to revitalize both theology and enthusiasm for the Church. This is the reason behind *Man at Play* (1949) and *Our Lady and the Church* (1951). In *Greek Myths and Christian Mystery* (1951), Rahner confirmed the positive role of Greek and Roman traditions adopted by the early Church. He wrote books about St. Ignatius of Loyola, including an edited volume, *Letters to Women by Ignatius Loyola* (1965). His career was cut short by the onset of Parkinson's disease.

DAY 185

FREDERICK FABER (1814–1863)

Purgatory on this side—

"I suppose pain is always the precious gift of God, and the greatest assimilation to our dear and blessed Lord. Yet I find in my own case the melancholy truth of Thomas a Kempis, *'Pauci ex infuriate meliorantur'* ['Few are made better by illness']. Pain does not altogether dispense either from penance or from prayer; and yet is hard to do penance or pray in illness. Ejaculations about the Passion, and mental acts of conformity to God's will, do me most good, only one wants to be continuous, and one would like them to be *hot*; however this last

quality is not necessary to their acceptableness. One feels it is most compassionate of God to let us have our purgatory this side of the grave. . . . Increased sweetness to others, increased thoughtfulness and legislation for the tiny comforts of others, and a snubbing of the body's inventive appetite for lots of little things and little extras not absolutely wanted: these are what I have set before myself in illness, and then, seeing how little way I have the pluck to go, at least makes me a trifle more humble and self-hating and so there is some good done."[187]

Letter of October 10, 1862 to his brother

Frederick Faber was the son of an Anglican clergyman who graduated from Balliol College, Oxford and was ordained an Anglican priest in 1844. After three years, Faber converted to Catholicism as part of the "Oxford movement." John Henry Newman had converted two years earlier. Faber established a London Oratory but moved it to a larger space in Brompton on the outskirts of London. He wrote many hymns, including his best-known "Faith of Our Fathers." His other writing includes *Lives of Modern Saints* (1847), *The Foot of the Cross* (1858), and *Notes on Doctrinal Subjects* (2 vol., 1866).

---

187 Frederick Faber, *Faber: Poet and Priest—Selected Letters by Frederick William Faber from 1833-1863*, ed. Raleigh Addington (Cowbridge and Bridgend: D. Brown & Sons, LTD., 1974), 335.

DAY 186

BERNARD NATHANSON (1926–2011)

The miracle of dying—

"We *think* we can create life in the laboratory (actually all we do is bring component pieces into contact with each other and measure the miracle) and therefore we think we can *take* life on an equally rational and empirical basis. What dialectical ingenuity it requires to believe in such nonsense! Ironically, we are not beginning to understand that the end of life is a series of miracles as well: Accompanying the pain and seeping away of energy in the terminal phases of illness is the outpouring into the bloodstream of a class of chemicals called endorphins, a variety of opiates (morphine-like substances) that calm us, alleviate the pain, and even allow us to exult in the knowledge that we have been loaned the gift of life and now the loan is being called."[188]

The Hand of God, 1996

Bernard Nathanson, MD, had overseen seventy-five thousand abortions (five thousand of which he performed himself) before experiencing a change of mind and heart. Nathanson

---

188 Bernard Nathanson, *The Hand of God: A journey from death to life by an abortion doctor who changed his mind* (Washington, DC: Regnery Publishing, 1996), 150.

changed his views about abortion in 1973, when he watched ultrasound images of an abortion. Nathanson said he could see the unborn child trying to pull back from the abortionist's tools. He went on to narrate the film "Silent Scream" (1985), which graphically shows a pre-born child trying in vain to deflect the abortionist's scalpel. The film was shown in the White House while Ronald Reagan was president and was a watershed in the history of the pro-life movement. He was baptized and entered into the Catholic Church in 1996.

DAY 187

NICOLAS OF CUSA (1401–1464)

The sacred icon—

"This picture, brethren, ye shall set up in some place, let us say, on a north wall, and shall stand around it a little way off, and look upon it. And each of you shall find that, from whatsoever quarter he regardeth it, it looketh upon him as if it looked on none other. And it shall seem to a brother standing to eastward as if the face locket towards the east, while one to southward shall think it looketh toward the south, and one to westward, toward the west. First, then, you will marvel how it can be that the face should look on all and each at the same time. For the imagination of him standing to eastward cannot conceive the

gaze such as west or south. Then let the brother who stood to eastward place himself to westward and he will find its gaze fastened on him in the west just as it was afore in the east. And, as he knoweth the icon to be fixed and unmoved, he will marvel at the motion of its immoveable gaze."[189]

The Vision of God, 1453

Nicolas of Cusa pursued his university studies began at Heidelberg and earned his doctorate in canon law in Padua in 1423, before studying philosophy and theology at Cologne. At the Council of Basel (1431–1449), he advanced the cause of Church unity by submitting his political treatise, *De concordantia Catholica*, which recommended concilliarism. But when Nicholas became frustrated by the council's inaction, he switched positions and supported papal supremacy. He served as papal legate to various missions, including mediating conflict between the Eastern and the Roman Churches. His best-known work, *De docta ignorantia* (*Of Learned Ignorance*), stresses the limitations of human knowledge. After ten years in the service of Pope Eugene IV, Nicholas was made a cardinal by the dying pope, an appointment confirmed in 1448 by Pope Nicholas V.

---

189 Nicolas of Cusa, *The Vision of God*, trans. Emma Gurney Salter, introduction by Evelyn Underhill (New York: Frederick Ungar Publishing Co., 1928), 4.

DAY 188

SERVAIS PINCKAERS, OP (1925–2008)

More than ideas—

"A more difficult reflection. Rediscovering Spiritual nature: The key to renewal is to rediscover our spiritual nature in its spontaneous yearning for truth, goodness, and happiness, flowing from a single primal dynamism. We refer here to 'nature' in its spiritual meaning, being the image of God's own life. It is part of the very constitution of our personality, as a principle of universality. To renew freedom in its roots requires more of us than merely a discussion of ideas. It is only attainable through the experience of personal action that is true and good; through a humble and patient reflection on this action; as well as through the grace of a quiet light that one must learn to await. It is here, under this intimate flash where the good shines forth, that the desire for happiness is revealed in its best light."[190]

Morality: The Catholic View, 2003

Servais Pinckaers, OP, was a Dominican moral theologian who taught for twenty-five years at the Friebourg in Switzerland.

---

190 Servais Pinckaers, O.P., *Morality: The Catholic View*, trans. Michael Sherwin, O.P., preface by Alasdair MacIntyre (South Bend: St. Augustine's Press, 2003), 76.

He was a contributor to the *Catechism of the Catholic Church* and the landmark encyclical *Veritatis Splendor* by Pope John Paul II. He studied at the Angelicum in Rome under legendary professors such as Reginald Garrigou-Lagrange. His mission to renew moral theology began with a close study of and commentary on St. Thomas Aquinas on human action, the virtues, and happiness. His books in English are *The Pursuit of Happiness God's Way: Living the Beatitudes* (2011), *The Sources of Christian Ethics* (1995), *The Spirituality of Martyrdom: to the Limits of Love* (2016), and *Passion and Virtue* (2017). The collection of Pinckaers's writings in *The Pinckaers Reader: Renewing Thomistic Moral Theology* (2005) displays the breadth and depth of his achievement.

DAY 189

CARDINAL CLEMENS AUGUST VON GALEN (1878–1946)

No one is safe—

"If you establish and apply the principle that you can kill 'unproductive' fellow human beings, then woe betide us all when we become old and frail! If one is allowed to kill the unproductive people then woe betide the invalids who have used up, sacrificed and lost their health and strength in the

productive process. If one is allowed forcibly to remove one's unproductive fellow human beings then woe betide loyal soldiers who return to the homeland seriously disabled, as cripples, as invalids. If it is once accepted that people have the right to kill 'unproductive' fellow humans—and even if initially it only affects the poor defenseless mentally ill—then as a matter of principle murder is permitted for all unproductive people, in other words for the incurably sick, the people who have become invalids through labor and war, for us all when we become old, frail and therefore unproductive. . . . Then none of our lives will be safe anymore. Some commission can put us on the list of the 'unproductive,' who in their opinion have become worthless life. And no police force will protect us and no court will investigate our murder and give the murderer the punishment he deserves. Who will be able to trust his doctor anymore?"[191]

Homily, August 3, 1941

Cardinal Clemens August von Galen came from a deeply pious, aristocratic family. Ordained in 1904, von Galen served in Münster and Berlin during the First World War. He was named bishop of Münster in 1933, the year Adolph Hitler was made chancellor of Germany. Von Galen's first pastoral letter in 1934 criticized the Nazis. As a result, he was asked by Pope Pius XI to help draft the encyclical "With Burning Anxiety"

---

191 http://www.historyplace.com/speeches/galen.htm.

(1937) condemning the Nazi racial policy. Instead of assassinating von Galen, Hitler sent thirty-seven priests to concentration camps, only ten of whom survived. When he died in 1946, he had aptly become known as "Lion of Münster."

DAY 190

ST. JOHN EUDES (1601–1680)

Recognizing God's will—

"Continual submission to the holy will of God is the most universal of all virtues. Its practice should be most familiar to you, since at every moment there arise opportunities of renouncing your own will and submitting to the will of God. And his will is always easy to recognize. God has willed that all things that are extremely necessary to us should also be very easy to obtain. For instance, the sun, air, water, and other elements of nature are most necessary for our natural life. So these things are also common and freely available to everyone. In a similar way, God has placed you in this world only to do his holy will, and your salvation depends upon doing it. So it's extremely necessary that you should easily know God's will in all that you must do. For that reason, he's made it easily recognizable, revealing his holy will in five primary ways that are very certain and evident: by his commandments, which we

must obey; by his counsels, which urge us on to perfection; by the laws, rules, and obligations of our state in life; by the authority of those placed over us or directing us; and by events, since everything that happens is an infallible sign that God wills what has happened, either by his absolute will or by his permissive will. So, if you'll only open the eyes of faith even a little, you'll recognize God's most holy will easily, at all times, and in every situation. And this knowledge will lead you to love him and to submit yourself to him."[192]

The Life and the Kingdom of Jesus in the Soul

The French priest St. John Eudes founded two orders—the Order of Our Lady of Charity (1641) and the Congregation of Jesus and Mary, also known at the Eudists (1643). The first of these orders was established to minister to "fallen women," giving them a place to live and start a new life. He was also known throughout France as a powerful preacher and proponent of the Sacred Heart devotion. The passage above reflects his life-long willingness to follow wherever God called. Calling "submission to the holy will of God" the "most universal of virtues" comports entirely with the Catholic view of pride as being the worst of the Seven Deadly Sins. Pride is the opposite of submission, and in the case of Satan, and us, too, when we sin, especially mortally, a conscious refusal to obey God's will.

---

192 Paul Thigpen, *A Year With the Saints: Daily Meditations With the Holy Ones of God* (Charlotte: Saint Benedict Press, 2013), 267.

DAY 191

JOSÉ MARÍA GIRONELLA (1917–2003)

Background: The subject of this story is the Italian writer Giovanni Papini (1881–1956). He converted in 1921 and published The Story of Christ, *which was widely-read even in the United Kingdom and the United States. But in 1953, he published* The Devil, *arguing hell was not eternal and God would forgive Satan and all sinners. Gironella depicts Papini's death, after a long illness, in a wheelchair and his journey into heaven where he wishes to meet Jesus Christ.*

"Papini's wish was fulfilled: but there was neither glory nor majesty. God showed infinite imagination, annihilating Papini, filling him with shame: The Son of Man, Jesus, appeared, taking in fact a human form: that of Papini himself in the last years of his life. He whom he glorified, who was to be the Judge, was facing him, paralyzed, with the large ears, seated in a wheelchair. He had renounced even perfection. It was the greatest manifestation of humility since the beginning of history. Papini turned in a cry; he wept with gratitude, that on earth he would have received pardon for all sin. 'Lord,' he stammered."[193]

"The Death and Judgment of Giovani Papini," 1963

---

193 José María Gironella, *Phantoms and Fugitives: Journeys to the Improbable,* trans. Terry Broch Fontseré (New York: Sheed and Ward, 1964), 155.

José María Gironella was a major Spanish writer beginning with the first volume of a trilogy, *The Cypresses Believe in God* (1953), a novel about the Spanish civil war which does not take the side of the Republicans or the Nationalists. Gironella did, however, include historical accounts of priest and nuns being murdered by the anti-Catholic Republican army. The other books of the trilogy, like *Cypresses*, have been translated into English—*A Million Dead* (1961) and *Peace Has Broken Out* (1966). A devout Catholic, Gironella's faith is always infused throughout his writing, though the author's own struggle with depression is found there as well. In the '60s, he published a book of apologetics, *One Hundred Spaniards and God*.

DAY 192

D. C. SCHINDLER (1970–)

Beyond being in love:

"To be sure, those who interpret love especially as a particular emotion do not necessarily intend thereby to trivialize it. While there are certainly some who translate subjective experience into its physiological substrate and subsequently, in effect, 'explain love away' by describing its 'scientific' causes—its evolutionary benefits, for example—others continue to idealize love precisely as a subjective experience. Believing that it

is just our feelings that constitute the most personal aspect of our existence, some are inclined to think that to call love an emotion is to offer an excellent reason to pursue it, perhaps excessively, even to the point of great personal cost or in defiance of all social conventions. Insofar as it is an emotion, the specifically subjective quality of love—the 'lived experience' [*Erlebnis*]—apparently cannot be explained by anything else. Even the scientific account of what causes such feelings and what biological purpose they serve has nothing to do with the actual revolution in our interior life, the overwhelming feeling of 'being in love,' which thus becomes a kind of absolute in itself that does not fit with anything else. It is just this discontinuity with everything else that leads people to cherish it as supreme—even divine. There are several problems with this conception of love. . . . In this case, one would have to admit that a drug, electrical stimulation, or any other generator of virtual reality, would be capable of producing, not just a feeling that imitates the experience of being in love, but in fact love itself. If love is just a feeling, what is the difference between a feeling that is like love, and the reality it is meant to mimic? The fact that we all recognize a difference here, even just enough to make the question intelligible, suggests that love cannot be simply a psychological event."[194]

Love and the Postmodern Predicament, 2018

---

194 D.C. Schindler, *Love and the Postmodern Predicament: Rediscovering the Real in Beauty, Goodness, and Truth* (Eugene: Cascade Books, an Imprint of Wipf and Stock Publishers, 2018), loc. 85–87, Kindle Edition.

D. C. Schindler is professor of metaphysics and anthropology at the John Paul II Institute. He earned his doctorate from the Catholic University of America with a dissertation on Hans Urs von Balthasar. His other books include *The Perfection of Freedom: Schiller, Schelling, and Hegel between the Ancients and the Moderns* (2012) and *Freedom from Reality: The Diabolical Character of Modern Liberty* (2017).

DAY 193

DARIUS KARLOWICZ (1964–)

It needs to be saved—

"Satan has not stolen our world from under our noses. The world was not created by an evil demon. Even if it seems to be broken, *Genesis* demands we remember it was created 'good' by God. The Christians (unlike those who succumb to Manichean temptations) cannot simply wipe out the world, which obviously does not mean the world is perfect, because, after all, a disposition toward the good and its actualization are two different things. Even if the world contains so much luster, even if it promises a compromise, we should still not forget that we are in conflict with it. The conflict is one of life and death. We can admire the world, learn about it, we can use it,

but we should know its dangers, and that it needs to be saved. Above all: the world needs to be saved!"[195]

Socrates and Other Saints, 2005

Philosopher Darius Karlowicz works in the rich Catholic tradition that has been at the heart of Polish culture for centuries. He brings the ancient Greeks, the Church Fathers, and the Scholastics into conversation with modern and contemporary philosophy on the issues of the human condition and the role of belief in individual life and society. *Socrates and Others Saints* (2005) and *The Archparadox of Death: Martyrdom as a philosophical category* (2016) are his only books available to English readers. Karlowicz has a weekly television show in Poland and regularly publishes columns in one of Poland's largest magazines. He holds the position of lecturer in political philosophy at the War Studies University in Warsaw.

---

195 Darius Karlowicz, *Socrates and Other Saints: Early Christian Understanding of Reason and Philosophy*, trans. Artur Sebastian Rosman, foreword by Rémi Brague (Eugene: Cascade Books, 2017), loc. 83, Kindle Edition.

DAY 194

EDWARD FESER (1968–)

On Natural Law—

"When we turn to human beings we find that they too have a nature or essence, and the good for them, like the good for anything else, is defined in terms of this nature or essence. Unlike other animals, though, human beings have intellect and will, and this is where moral goodness enters the picture. Human beings can know what is good for them, and choose whether to pursue that good. And that is precisely the natural end or purpose of the faculties of intellect and will—for like our other faculties, they too have a final cause, namely to allow us to understand the truth about things, including what is good for us given our nature or essence, and to act in light of it. Just as a 'good squirrel' is one that successfully carries out the characteristic activities of a squirrel's life by gathering acorns, scampering up trees, etc., *so too a good human being is one who successfully carries out the characteristic activities of human life, as determined by the final causes or natural ends of the various faculties that are ours by virtue of our nature or essence.* . . . So, a good human being will be, among many other things, someone who pursues truth and avoids error. And this becomes moral goodness insofar as we can choose whether or not to fulfill our natures in this way. To choose in line with the final causes or purposes

that are ours by nature is morally good; to choose against them is morally bad."[196] (Emphasis added.)

The Last Superstition, 2008

Edward C. Feser is an associate professor of philosophy at Pasadena City College. As a graduate student at the University of California Santa Barbara, his study of Aristotle and St. Thomas Aquinas overcame his atheism and led him back to the Church. Feser has become one of the leading Catholic philosophers in the English-speaking world. He has taken on the so-called "New Atheists" and defended classical arguments for the existence of God. He has reinvigorated philosophy in the Aristotelian–Thomistic tradition with books such as *The Last Superstition: A Refutation of the New Atheism* (2008), *Aquinas: A Beginner's Guide* (2009), and *Scholastic Metaphysics: A Contemporary Introduction* (2014).

---

196 Edward Feser, *The Last Superstition: A Refutation of the New Atheism* (Notre Dame: St. Augustine's Press, 2005), loc. 2586–2599 of 5799, Kindle Edition.

DAY 195

MARTIN MOSEBACH (1951–)

He was sacrificing—

"Now, for the first time in so many years, I was watching a priest in the magnetic field of the altar. The things he said and sang slid past me: they were not so important. What was important was the impression that he was *doing something*. His standing and stretching out his arms and making the sign of the cross was an action, a doing. The priest up there was at his work. What he did with his hands was every bit as decisive as his words. And his actions were directed towards things: While white linen clothes, a golden chalice, a little golden plate, wax candles, little jugs of water and wine, the moonlight white Host, and the great leather-bound book. The altar boys served him ceremoniously, turned the pages for him, poured water over his fingertips, and held out a little towel to him. And after he raised the Host in the air, avoiding touching anything else with his thumb and first finger and kept them together—even when picking up the chalice or opening the golden tabernacle. . . . We shall leave aside, for the moment, the question of precisely *what* the priest was sacrificing on the altar. The main thing for me, at the time, was that he *was* sacrificing."[197]

The Heresy of Formlessness, 2003

197 Martin Mosebach, *The Heresy of Formlessness: The Roman Liturgy and Its Enemy*, trans. Graham Harrison (San Francisco: Ignatius Press, 2003), 21-22.

Martin Mosebach is a highly-esteemed German writer whose novels, short stories, poems, libretti, essays, and travel writing won him the prestigious Georg Büchner Prize in 2007. He writes about the Catholic faith in books such as *The Heresy of Formlessness* (2003), *Subversive Catholicism: Papacy, Liturgy, Church* (2019), and *The 21: A Journey into the Land of Coptic Martyrs* (2019), the latter based upon his visit to the families of twenty-one Coptic men murdered on a Libyan beach by ISIS terrorists in 2015. His only novel translated into English is *What Was Before* (Seagull Books, 2014).

DAY 196

PETER KREEFT (1937–)

Happiness comes to rest—

"Joy is neither homeostasis nor agitation. Its quiet is far more lively than agitation and far more peaceful than the deepest sleep, for it is not deep sleep but deep waking. Agitated waking spills out spiritual energy, wastes it into the future by refusing the present. . . . This state of mind is like light: traveling faster than matter, yet making no sound, no perturbation. Pleasure is the restless mind moving along a line, never reaching the end. Happiness is the mind resting at the end. Joy is the mind

eternally moving *at* the end, motion at a point: the cosmic dance."[198]

The Heart's Deepest Longing, 1989

A professor of philosophy at Boston College since 1965, Peter Kreeft has published ninety-five books in a career of that has had a profound influence on generations of students, readers, and the Church itself. Kreeft converted to Catholicism as an undergraduate student at Calvin College as a result of a professor asking him to investigate the claim that the Catholic Church had existed since the earliest years of Christianity. What he discovered about the Eucharist and the Real Presence, among other doctrines, combined with Gothic architecture, St. Thomas Aquinas, St. John of the Cross, and a visit to St. Patrick's Cathedral, convinced him he wanted to be a Catholic. Some of his major books include *Fundamentals of Faith* (1988), *The Summa of the Summa* (1998), *The Philosophy of Jesus* (2007), and *Forty Reasons I Am a Catholic* (2018).

---

198 Peter Kreeft, *Heaven: The Heart's Deepest Longing* (San Francisco: Ignatius Press, 1989), 143.

DAY 197

ST. JOHN HENRY NEWMAN (1801–1890)

Religion requires doctrines—

"Religion cannot but be dogmatic; it ever has been. All religions have had doctrines; all have professed to carry with them benefits which could be enjoyed only on condition of believing the word of a supernatural informant, that is, of embracing some doctrines or other. And it is a mere idle sophistical theory, to suppose it can be otherwise. Destroy religion, make men give it up, if you can; but while it exists, it will profess an insight into the next world, it will profess important information about the next world, it will have points of faith, it will have dogmatism, it will have anathemas. Christianity, therefore, ever will be looked on, by the multitude, what it really is, as a rule of faith as well as of conduct."[199]

Tracts for the Times, #85, Sep. 1838

St. John Henry Newman takes on the commonly-heard boast that a person can be "religious" and "spiritual" without believing in any dogmas or doctrines. As Newman explains, in the history of the world's religions, each has a set of core beliefs

---

199 Dave Armstrong, ed., *The Quotable Newman: A Definitive Guide to John Henry Newman's Central Thoughts and Ideas* (Manchester: Sophia Institute Press, 2012), loc. 137, Kindle Edition.

which their adherents profess. We can go further and ask, without affirming doctrine of any kind, what would the "religious" person belong to? The harder you press this person, the conclusion would be reached that his or her form of religion is a religion of the self—the subjective experience of whatever is identified as "religious." This is why when, say, a "New Age" religion forms, it quickly dies, only to be born again when some charismatic individual finds a platform to invite others to re-experience his or her subjective experience, now deemed "religious." As Newman concludes, as long as Christianity exists, the Church invites us all to embrace not only dogma and morality but also the attitude that some things deserve to be called "anathema."

DAY 198

REGINALD GARRIGOU-LAGRANGE (1877–1964)

The final cause—

"Finally, Thomism is a theocentric doctrine that affirms the primacy of God, pure Actuality, over all creation, because actuality is more perfect than potentiality. There is more in what *is* than in what *becomes*. God is, thus, not universal becoming, but externally subsistent Being itself, infinitely more perfect

in His fullness than all that participates in His perfections. It follows from this that nothing exists and nothing perseveres in existence if not by God, creator and conserver, and that no creature can act without His cooperation, not even the free creature. Indeed, no creature can pass from potentiality to actuality except under the influence of a superior cause in actuality and, in the final analysis, under the influence of the Supreme Agent, that alone is its activity, pure Actuality, that alone is Being itself, Good itself, and the supreme liberty of which ours is but a participation, certainly noble, but always limited. These three characteristics—realism, intellectualism, theocentrism—are the essence itself of Thomism."[200] (Emphasis added.)

The Essence & Topicality of Thomas, 1946

Rev. Reginald Garrigou-Lagrange was an outstanding scholar whose fifty-plus books and three hundred articles had huge influence on the direction of the Church and Catholic theology in the first half of the twentieth century. He served as theological advisor to four popes, including St. John XXIII, and also oversaw the doctoral work of Karol Wojtyla, the future St. John Paul II. Garrigou-Lagrange first studied medicine but felt himself converted after reading *Life, Science, and Art* by the writer Ernest Hello (1828–85). He joined the French

---

200 Reginald Garrigou-Lagrange, *The Essence & Topicality of Thomism*, trans. Alan Aversa (lulu.com, 2013), loc. 405 of 2450, Kindle Edition.

Dominicans, and studied and taught at Le Saulchoir before moving to Rome, where he lectured at the Angelicum from 1909 until his retirement in 1960. There he wrote his magnum opus, *The Three Ages of the Interior Life*, in 1938.

DAY 199

DENIS FLORENCE MACCARTHY (1817–1882)

The Fireside

I have tasted all life's pleasures, I have snatched at all its joys,
The dance's merry measures and the revel's festive noise;
Though wit flashed bright the live-long night, and flowed
    the ruby tide,
I sighed for thee, I sighed for thee, my own fireside!

In boyhood's dreams I wandered far across the ocean's breast,
In search of some bright earthly star, some happy isle of rest;
I little thought the bliss I sought in roaming far and wide
Was sweetly centred all in thee, my own fireside!

How sweet to turn at evening's close from all our cares away,
And end in calm, serene repose, the swiftly passing day!
The pleasant books, the smiling looks of sister or of bride,
All fairy ground doth make around one's own fireside!

"My Lord" would never condescend to honour my poor
  hearth;
"His Grace" would scorn a host or friend of mere plebeian
  birth;
And yet the lords of human kind, whom man has deified,
For ever meet in converse sweet around my fireside!

The poet sings his deathless songs, the sage his lore repeats,
The patriot tells his country's wrongs, the chief his warlike
  feats;
Though far away may be their clay, and gone their earthly
  pride,
Each god-like mind in books enshrined still haunts my fireside!

Oh, let me glance a moment through the coming crowd of
  years,
Their triumphs or their failures, their sunshine or their tears;
How poor or great may be my fate, I care not what betide,
So peace and love but hallow thee, my own fireside!

Still let me hold the vision close, and closer to my sight;
Still, still, in hopes elysian, let my spirit wing its flight;
Still let me dream, life's shadowy stream may yield from out
  its tide,
A mind at rest, a tranquil breast, a quiet fireside![201]

---

201 https://www.gutenberg.org/files/12622/12622-h/12622-h.htm#p026.

Denis Florence MacCarthy was an Irish writer of great repute who wrote poetry, biographies, and translations. His translations from the Spanish of Calderon's plays remain highly praised though published in the mid-nineteenth century. MacCarthy's poetry, published between 1846 and 1882 is suffused with a natural beauty that immediately delights the reader. MacCarthy was an Irish patriot and a devout Catholic, and both passionate beliefs are expressed throughout his writing.

DAY 200

FRANCIS O'GORMAN (1967–)

What catches on—

"'Modernity,' properly comprehended, is a state of mind that is expectant of, and values, change: here is the recategorization of 'alteration' as 'fashion.' *Kairos* ceases to be a category that refers to what of significance has happened and is, instead, a hope for what can be expected from the future. . . . This is modernity as experience; as a set of platoons and ways for feeling. . . . In this modernity, a notion dependent on discontinuities rather than continuations, men and women register the passage of days and hours as the bringer of difference—a kind of revolutionary experience of the dislocation of history apprehended as ordinary urban and suburban life. . . . Modernity privileges

what 'catches on' (a phrase first recorded in Great Britain and Ireland in 1884 as modernity is in full swing)."[202]

Forgetfulness, 2017

Francis O'Gorman is Saintsbury professor of English literature at the University of Edinburgh. He previously held a chair in Victorian literature at the University of Leeds. He was educated at Lady Margaret Hall, Oxford where he took a double first as an undergraduate before earning his doctorate. O'Gorman is also an organ scholar and player—he directed his college choir from the organ bench while he played. O'Gorman heads the John Ruskin Society about whom he is an internationally recognized expert. He has written or edited twenty-three books and is editing the complete Emily Brontë for the twenty-first century Oxford Authors series, due out in 2024. O'Gorman brings his Catholic faith to bear on all he writes whether about literature, music, or cultural change.

---

202 Francis O'Gorman, *Forgetfulness: Making the Modern Culture of Amnesia* (London: Bloomsbury Academic, 2017), 43–44.

DAY 201

FRANK H. BUCKLEY (1948–)

Anti-Catholicism at the Founding—

"Protestants might be content to coexist with other brands of Protestants in that way, but Catholics were another matter. Many Americans saw Catholicism not as a source of moral teaching but as a glaring example of man's natural depravity. . . . During the Revolutionary War, the sermons of New England Protestant divines explicitly identified the cause of liberty with the repudiation of what was routinely called the Whore of Babylon. What Catholicism had done, John Adams concluded, was to reduce its adherents 'to a state of Sordid ignorance and staring timidity . . . in a cruel, shameful and deplorable servitude [to the pope] and his subordinate tyrants.' Had Charles II gotten his way, he would have 'established the Romish religion and a despotism as wild as any in the world.' In that case, 'the light of science would have been extinguished, and mankind drawn back to a state of darkness and misery like that which prevailed from the fourth to the fourteenth century.' In Catholicism, Americans saw a fatal conjunction of corruption and tyranny of sly Jesuits and *éminence grises*, of Stuart pretenders and the Inquisition."[203]

The Republic of Virtue, 2017

203 F.H. Buckley, *The Republic of Virtue: How We Tried to Ban Corruption, Failed, and What We Can Do About It* (New York: Encounter Books, 2017), 68-69.

Frank H. Buckley is a foundation professor at George Mason University's Scalia School of Law. Buckley's work is seen often in the major media, newspapers, and magazines commenting on cultural, political, religious, and legal issues. His most recent books are *American Secession* (2020), *The Republican Workers Party* (2018), *The Republic of Virtue* (2017), *The Way Back: Restoring the Promise of America* (2016), and *The Once and Future King* (2015). He is a Senior Editor at the American Spectator, a contributing editor to the Dorchester Review and a columnist for the New York Post. He is a citizen of Canada and also became an American citizen on Tax Day, April 15, 2014. He lives in Alexandria, VA, with his wife, Esther.

DAY 202

LIONEL JOHNSON (1867–1902)

The Precept of Silence

I KNOW you: solitary griefs
Desolate passions, aching hours!
I know you: tremulous beliefs,
Agonized hopes, and ashen flowers!

The winds are sometimes sad to me,
The starry spaces, full of fear;

Mine is the sorrow on the sea,
And mine the sigh of places drear.

Some players upon plaintive strings
Publish their wistfulness abroad;
I have not spoken of these things,
Save to one man, and unto God.[204]

Lionel Johnson studied at Winchester and New College, Oxford before moving to London to be a writer, becoming a member of the Rhymers Club co-founded by W. B. Yeats. He converted to Catholicism from Anglicanism in 1891, and his subsequent poetry was deemed "Catholic puritanism" for its austerity and expressions of spiritual anguish. Johnson was a homosexual who struggled to follow the moral teachings of his Church. Johnson publicly denounced Oscar Wilde in the poem "The Destroyer of a Soul" (1892) after a scandal resulting from their affair. He was only thirty-five when he died, after cracking his skull falling in a street. His collected poetry was edited and published by Ezra Pound in 1915.

---

204 https://www.theotherpages.org/poems/johns01.html.

DAY 203

CHARLES BAUDELAIRE (1821–1867)

Convert my heart—

"What oddities one finds in big cities when one knows how to roam and how to look! Life swarms with innocent monsters. Lord, my God, You the Creator, you the Master; you who have made both Law and Liberty; you the sovereign who permits, you the judge of pardons; you who contain all motives and all causes, and who, perhaps, have put a taste for the horrible in my mind in order to convert my heart, like the cure at the point of the knife. Lord have pity on, have pity on mad men and mad women! O Creator! Can monsters exist in the eyes of the One who alone knows why they exist, who alone knows how they have been made and how they could not have been made?"[205]

Paris Spleen, 1869

T. S. Eliot called Charles Baudelaire "the greatest Christian poet since Dante." No doubt Baudelaire was celebrated in his time and held in the highest regard ever since by lovers of literature and poetry. But Dante continues to be read, translated, and studied, while Baudelaire's status as a Catholic writer is rarely

---

205 Charles Baudelaire, *Paris Spleen*, trans. Louise Varese (New York: New Directions Publishing Company, 1970), 98.

mentioned. He made some money by translating Edgar Allen Poe into French, which made the American writer popular in France. A tortured soul, Baudelaire remained and regarded himself a Catholic until he died in 1967.

DAY 204

JON HASSLER (1933–2008)

Grand Opening *takes place in a small Minnesota town as a Catholic family arrives and re-opens a dilapidated grocery store. The town, predominately Lutheran, does not make it easy on the newcomers. Their son Brendan and his family befriend the town outcast Dodger Hicks only to find most of the town disapproves. The tension comes to a head when Wallace Flint, who works at the store, out of jealousy towards Dodger sets fire to the store and flees. Dodger dies trying to put out the fire. The local priest refuses to do the funeral because the family is not "registered." The son of a local minister steps in to address the few who arrived at the funeral:*

> "Paul put down his Bible and stated, to the amazement of most of the mourners, that Dodger had been a lot like Jesus Christ, and with this he embarked on the daring sort of sermon he couldn't get away with in church, his father's parishioners being (in his view) too hidebound and smug to understand

Christianity's challenge to love one another. 'Dodger's ways were not our ways, and our ways were not Dodger's ways,' he said, his voice low and resonant, his eyes roving the faces before him. 'Like Christ, Dodger passed through the world wanting next to nothing for himself. All he asked was to be accepted.' (Here Brendan lowered his head, afraid that Paul's accusing eyes would fasten on him.) 'For all we know, God might have sent Dodger on the same a mission as His Son—to put us to the test, to bring us a message about loving one another to see how we reacted to it. True, Dodger was a thief, but he did not steal to accumulate the goods of the world. He stole in order to keep his body and soul together and he gave away the rest. His heart was larger than most, and he deserved better than he got from us. . . . Take at least one thing home from Dodger's funeral: my assurance that each time we fail to care for one another we carry out, one more time, the act of crucifixion.'"[206]

Grand Opening, 1996

Jon Hassler, a life-long resident of Minnesota, attended Saint John's University and the University of North Dakota. He taught English in a high school before joining the faculty at Bemidji State University. He began writing fiction in 1970, and in 1980 Hassler was named writer-in-residence at Saint John's where he taught until his retirement in 1997. When he

---

206 Jon Hassler, *Grand Opening: A Novel* (New York: Ballantine Books, 1996), 305.

died in 2008, America magazine called him the "Last Catholic Novelist." His legacy consists of twelve novels, two short story collections, some children's literature and non-fiction.

DAY 205

SCOTT HAHN (1957–)

United to Christ—

"As great as unfallen human nature could be, it could not compare to what God has given us in Christ. We might say that God let us break a bone so that He Himself could reset it, making it not just stronger but unbreakable. God has allowed us to lose not only divine grace, but also the standing we had as His servants, His obedient slaves. He foresaw that we would fall. He didn't cause it, but He did freely permit it. He did so in order to bring about a glorious new creation that exceeds every possibility belonging to human nature. So Christ took our fallen human nature, and didn't merely bring it back to life. He united it to Himself, so that the life He restored in us was divine life. The grace He gave us was His own sonship."[207]

Reasons to Believe, 2007

---

207 Scott Hahn, *Reasons to Believe* (New York: Doubleday, 2007), loc. 52, Kindle Edition.

Scott Hahn was a prominent evangelical biblical scholar when he became a Catholic in 1986. Since then, Hahn has become one of the leading Catholic apologists in the nation. Both his books and media appearances have made him into a widely recognized and respected figure. In 1979, he married his wife, Kimberly, a well-known apologist herself, and they have six children and eighteen grandchildren. His books and lectures have been effective in helping thousands of Protestants and fallen away Catholics to embrace the Catholic faith. Hahn has taught at the Franciscan University of Steubenville since 1990 and is founder and president of the Saint Paul Center for Biblical Theology. His many books include a series of Bible commentaries published under the title *Ignatius Catholic Study Bible, The Lamb's Supper* (1999), *Joy to World* (2014), and *The Creed: Professing the Faith Through the Ages* (2016).

DAY 206

JULIEN GREEN (1900–1988)

Challenge of standing alone—

"A man who lives by his faith is necessarily isolated. At every hour of the day, he is in acute disagreement with this century; at every hour of the day, he is alone and, in a certain fashion, appears to be mad. This is one of the most peculiar aspects of

the tragedy our conscience is going through in Europe. No matter how numerous Christians still are in this world, no matter how close their mystical union, they cannot help but have at some time or other a feeling of terrible solitude."[208]

Diary entry for July 11, 1947

Julian Green touches on an issue experienced by many Christians but rarely expressed aloud—the loneliness of being a Christian in a secular world. But it's not only the isolation of living in an age of scornful unbelief; there is also the factor of a Church divided against itself since the Reformation and the proliferation of denominations. A mystical union, as Green notes, does not translate necessarily into a felt communion among Christians. In fact, there are some post-Reformation denominations that do a far better job welcoming and befriending lost souls than the average Catholic parish. The Protestant denominations grew because they evangelized—they did not accept that it was enough that a person be born into a Christian family. There have been heroic eras of Catholic evangelization, especially in the Post-Reformation period, but our age, sadly, is not one of them.

---

208 Julian Green, *Julian Green: Diary 1928-1957,* trans. Anne Green, selected by Kurt Wolff (New York: Harcourt, Brace & World, Inc., 1964), 185.

DAY 207

SISTER PRUDENCE ALLEN, RSM (1940–)

The equal dignity of women—

"It has taken over two thousand years for the concept of woman to achieve a solid metaphysical foundation enabling an accurate rendering of how a woman is a human person in relation with other persons. The key to this accuracy is a neo-Thomist philosophical framework that integrates science and theology within a metaphysical *hylomorphism*, that is, with the human person understood as a *soul/body composite identity*. . . . Without a descriptive metaphysics to explain the living reality of the human person as a *soul/body composite identity*, either the principle of the equal dignity of woman and man slides into nondifferentiation, or the principle of the significant differentiation of women and men slides into a polarity in which either man is considered naturally superior to woman or woman is considered naturally superior to man. The structure of a renewed theistic *hylomorphism* is necessary to hold the tension of equal dignity and significant difference."[209]

The Concept of Woman, 2016

---

209 Sister Prudence Allen, R.S.M., *The Concept of Woman, Volume 3, The Search for Communion of Persons, 1500-2015* (Grand Rapids: William B. Eerdmans Publishing, 2016), 488.

Sister Prudence Allen, RSM, is an American Catholic philosopher and member of the Religious Sisters of Mercy of Alma, Michigan. She received her PhD in philosophy from Claremont Graduate School of California in 1967. She converted to Catholicism in 1964 and married in 1965, raising two sons and teaching philosophy. Her marriage was annulled in 1972 and she joined the US Mercy sisters in 1983. Her first major book, *The Concept of Woman: The Aristotelian Revolution (750 BC- 1250 AD)*, was published in 1985, with a new edition in 1997 with two subsequent volumes released in 2002 and 2012. She is one of five women named to the International Theological Commission that was set up in 1969 to advise the pope and Vatican on doctrinal issues.

DAY 208

KARL ADAM (1876-1966)

An organic identity—

"We Catholics acknowledge readily, without any shame, nay with pride, that Catholicism cannot be identified simply and wholly with primitive Christianity, nor even with the Gospel of Christ, in the same way that the great oak cannot be identified with the tiny acorn. There is no mechanical identity, but an organic identity. And we go further and say that thousands

of years hence Catholicism will probably be even richer, more luxuriant, more manifold in dogma, morals, law and worship than the Catholicism of the present day. A religious historian of the fifth millennium A.D. will without difficulty discover in Catholicism conceptions and forms and practices which derive from India, China and Japan, and he will have to recognize a far more obvious complex of opposites. It is quite true, Catholicism is a union of contraries. But contraries are not contradictories. Wherever there is life, there you must have conflict and contrariety. Even in purely biblical Christianity, and especially in Old Testament religion, these conflicts and contraries may be observed. For only so is there growth and the continual emergence of new forms. The Gospel of Christ would have been no living gospel, and the seed which He scattered no living seed, if it had remained ever the tiny seed of A.D. 33, and had not struck root, and had not assimilated foreign matter, and had not by the help of this foreign matter grown up into a tree, so that the birds of the air dwell in its branches."[210]

The Spirit of Catholicism, 1924

Karl Adam was ordained in 1900 and received his doctorate in theology from the University of Munich in 1904. Adam began his teaching career in Munich before moving to Strasbourg

---

210 Karl Adam, *The Spirit of Catholicism* (Newman ePress), loc. 4, Kindle Edition.

and the prestigious University of Tübingen in 1919 where he taught until retiring in 1949. *The Spirit of Catholicism* (1924) is his best-known work but also in English are *Roots of the Reformation* (1951), *One and Holy* (1948), *The Son of God* (1934), and *Christ and the Western Mind Love and Belief* (1928–1932). Unlike other Catholic leaders, Adam tried to bridge the gap between Catholicism and the Nazis. However, this political misjudgment, prompted in part by the Vatican Concordant with Hitler (1933), is not reflected in any of the works mentioned.

DAY 209

ST. BONAVENTURE (1221–1274)

To persevere to the end—

"It is not enough to be virtuous. To be firmly rooted in virtue, to possess virtuous habits, does not render us glorious in God's sight. Something else is still wanting. To be an object of glory to the eye of God we must possess the culminating virtue, the crown and consummation of all virtues: perseverance. No mortal being whatever, no matter how perfect he may seem, should be praised while he is still living. Let a man be praised not because he has begun a good work but because he has brought it to a good and happy completion. 'Perseverance is

the end, acme and crown of the virtues. It nurtures and fits one for merit; it leads to and culminates in reward' (S. Bern. Ep. cxxix, 2.) Hence St. Bernard says, 'Take away perseverance and nothing remains. For the fulfillment of duty, the performance of good deeds and the exercise of fortitude will not procure the grace sufficient to obtain eternal praise' (Ibid.) It will avail a man little to have been a religious, to have been patient and humble, devout and chaste, to have loved God and to have exercised himself in all the virtues, if he continues not to the end. He must persevere to win the crown. In the race of the spiritual life all the virtues run, but only perseverance 'receives the prize' (1 Cor. ix, 24.) It is not the beginner in virtue but 'he that shall persevere unto the end that shall be saved' (Matt. x, 22.) 'What is the use of seeds sprouting if afterwards they wither and die?' asks St. Chrysostom (Hom. xxxiii, 5.) None whatever! If then, dear spouse of Jesus Christ, your virtues are productive of good works—and I assume that this is so—be sure to continue in your good practices. Persevere in your virtuous habits. Make it a practice ever and constantly to increase in the performance of good works. Wage the war of Christ with all your might. Practice and increase in virtue up to the very moment of death. Then, when your last moment comes and your life is brought to a close, God will give you the crown of honour and glory as the prize and reward of your labour."[211]

Holiness of Life, c. 1260

---

211 Saint Bonaventure, *Saint Bonaventure Collection* (Aeterna Press, 2015), loc. 36-37, Kindle Edition.

St. Bonaventure wrote this instruction for St. Isabelle of France, the sister of King St. Louis IX of France while being assigned to her monastery of Poor Clares at Longchamps. Called the "Seraphic Doctor," Bonaventure was a Franciscan priest and theologian who taught in Paris with St. Thomas Aquinas, who became his good friend. St. Bonaventure had to leave his teaching post when the friars elected him their general minister. For seventeen years, he dealt with differing view of poverty with the Order, but he managed to resolve most of the disputes before his death in 1274.

DAY 210

ST. TERESA OF CALCUTTA (1910–1997)

Embracing the child—

"If a mother can kill her own child, how long will it be before we start to kill one another? We should not be surprised when we hear about murders, deaths, wars, and hate in the world today. Don't ever allow even one child, born or unborn, to be unwanted. Let us go with Our Lady to search out the child and take her home."[212]

---

212 Carol Kelly-Gangi, ed., *Mother Teresa: Her Essential Wisdom* (New York: Barnes & Noble Publishing, Inc., 2006), 84.

In his novel *The Brothers Karamozov* (1880), Fyodor Dostoevsky wrote, "If there is no God, everything is permitted," but St. Teresa of Calcutta does him one better—we are already killing children by the hundreds of thousands: how long will it be before we are killing each other? In other words, we already live in a world where "everything is permitted." Someone might object that "we do not see killing on the streets." True, but the law, both natural and civil, against the taking of innocent life is being broken every day, and less than a century ago innocent lives were taken by the millions. In other words, the moral door is ajar only waiting for the emboldened madmen to enter in. (The Dostoevsky quote is found in Part 4, Bk. 11, Ch. 4 of *The Brothers Karamazov*.)

DAY 211

ST. JOHN CHRYSOSTOM (347–407)

On rebuking the sinner—

"What then is one to do? For if you deal too gently with him who needs a severe application of the knife, and do not strike deep into one who requires such treatment, you remove one part of the sore but leave the other: and if on the other hand you make the requisite incision unsparingly, the patient, driven to desperation by his sufferings, will often fling everything

away at once, both the remedy and the bandage, and throw himself down headlong, 'breaking the yoke and bursting the band.' I could tell of many who have run into extreme evils because the due penalty of their sins was exacted. For we ought not, in applying punishment, merely to proportion it to the scale of the offense, but rather to keep in view the disposition of the sinner, lest while wishing to mend what is torn, you make the rent worse, and in your zealous endeavors to restore what is fallen, you make the ruin greater. For weak and careless characters, addicted for the most part to the pleasures of the world, and having occasion to be proud on account of birth and position, may yet, if gently and gradually brought to repent of their errors, be delivered, partially at least, if not perfectly, from the evils by which they are possessed: but if any one were to inflict the discipline all at once, he would deprive them of this slight chance of amendment. For when once the soul has been forced to put off shame it lapses into a callous condition, and neither yields to kindly words nor bends to threats, nor is susceptible of gratitude, but becomes far worse than that city which the prophet reproached, saying, 'you had the face of a harlot, refusing to be ashamed before all men.' (Jeremiah 3:3) Therefore the pastor has need of much discretion, and of a myriad of eyes to observe on every side the habit of the soul."[213]

On the Priesthood, c. 393

---

213 St. John Chrysostom, *On the Priesthood*, trans. W.R.W. Stephens (Veritatis Splendor Publications, 2012), loc. 34–37 of 194, Kindle Edition.

St. John Chrysostom was the archbishop of Constantinople. His eloquence earned him the nickname the "golden-tongued." As archbishop, he made enemies for speaking out against the accumulation of wealth, and was ultimately banished. Today he is a beloved and important saint in the Eastern Orthodox Church where the Liturgy of Saint John Chrysostom is often celebrated.

DAY 212

JOSEF M. SEIFERT (1945–)

Not a perfect world—

"To demand the 'greatest possible work' or 'the greatest possible gift' from God is not only wrong because of the impossibility of an absolute maximum of goodness in a finite world, but also inadmissible because it leaves no room for the superabundant and unforced gifts of God. . . . To demand, however, the best possible work, the greatest possible gift of God, consequent upon the possible-world-calculus and the necessity of creating the best one, would discard, or show disrespect for, the divine freedom of choice and the whole sphere of gratuitously given gifts. These seem to belong even far more to God than to human givers. For God does not owe us anything, wherefore all He gives has its root in gratuitously given gifts.

To create limited goods and to bestow freely chosen gratuitous gifts, even though He could create or give either nothing or even more than He gives and creates, does not contradict His infinite goodness; on the contrary, freely given gifts are an outgrowth of the essence of His infinite goodness."[214]

Where Was God in Auschwitz?, 2016

The Austrian professor Josef Seifert was born in 1945 in Seekirchen near Salzburg. He received his doctorate in philosophy from the University of Salzburg in 1969 under Professor Robert Spaemann. From his early youth (age twelve) on, Seifert admired the philosopher Dietrich von Hildebrand not only as a person and as a convert to Catholicism but also as a great philosopher. He received personal, philosophical, and religious formation through von Hildebrand, whom Seifert met many times in person in Austria and Italy during vacation periods. From 1973 to 1980 Seifert was professor and director of the doctoral program of philosophy at the University of Dallas where he was able to bring von Hildebrand as a visiting professor. In 1980, Seifert co-founded and became director of the International Academy of Philosophy (IAP) in Irving, Texas. A prolific author and widely respected scholar and translator, Seifert's academic career has taken him to numerous countries and various prestigious universities.

---

214 Josef Seifert, *Where Was God in Auschwitz?* (Irving: International Academy of Philosophy Press, 2016), loc. 1450 of 4680, Kindle Edition.

DAY 213

HILAIRE BELLOC (1870–1953)

Beware of what you wish for—

"Of all things desired Fame least fulfills the desire for it; for if Fame is to be very great a man must be dead before it is more than a shoot; he therefore has not the enjoyment of it (as it would seem). Again, Fame while a man lives is always tarnished by falsehood; for since few can observe him, and less know him, he must have Fame for work which he does not do and forego Fame for work which he knows deserves it. Fame has no proper ending to it, when it is first begun, as have things belonging to other appetites, nor is any man satiated with it at any time. Upon the contrary, the hunger after it will lead a man forward madly always to some sort of disaster, whether of disappointment in the soul, or of open dishonor. . . . [How] shall men treat Fame? How shall they seek it, or hope to use it if obtained? To these questions it is best answered that a man should have for Fame a natural appetite, not forced nor curiously entertained; it must be present in him if he would do noble things. Yet if he makes the Fame of those things, and not those things themselves his chief business, then not only will he pursue Fame to his hurt, but also Fame will miss him. . . . The judgment of Fame is this: That many men having done great things of a good sort have not Fame. And that many men have Fame who have done but little things and most of them

evil. The virtue of Fame is that it nourishes endeavour. The peril of Fame is that it leads men towards itself, and therefore into inanities and sheer loss."[215]

This and That and the Other, 1912

If anyone wants to learn the art of the essay, they could hardly do better than to read the book cited above. The subject of each essay, rarely more than four pages, varies widely, but they all have one thing in common: each begins with a paragraph that draws the reader in whether or not he or she is interested in the topic. Are you interested, for example, in an essay on "Inns"? Probably not, but here is Belloc's first graph: "Here am I sitting in an Inn, having gloomily believed not half an hour ago that Inns were doomed with all other good things, but now more hopeful and catching avenues of escape through the encircling decay." It's hard to resist finding out just where Belloc is going from here. For the Catholic writer, Belloc is a model of how to allow moral and spiritual reflection to enter. In the case of "Inns," he worries that the sin of gluttony will further their demise: "It is an abomination, and this abomination has the power to destroy a Christian Inn and to substitute for it, first a gin-palace, and then, in reaction against that, the very horrible house where they sell only tea and coffee and

---

215 Hilaire Belloc, *This and That and the Other* (1912), loc. 223-224 of 2513, Kindle Edition.

bubbly waters that bite and sting both in the mouth and in the stomach."

DAY 214

ST. ALPHONSUS LIGUORI (1696–1787)

Don't hold back—

"You ought therefore never to forget God's presence, as most men do. Speak to Him as often as you can, for it does not tire Him, nor does He hold it in contempt, as do great men of the world. If you love Him, you will always have something to say to Him. Tell Him whatever comes to your mind about yourself and your affairs, as you would tell an intimate friend. Do not look upon Him as a high and mighty lord who desires to speak only to great ones—and then, only of great things. Our God delights in stooping down to converse with us, and He rejoices when we make known to Him our most trivial everyday affairs. Such is His love and care for you that He seems to have no one else but you of whom to think. He is so concerned with your interests that He seems to have no providence except to preserve you, no almighty power except to help you, no mercy or kindness except to have compassion on you, to do you good and win you to His love and confidence by His kind attention. Then freely open your heart to Him and

ask Him to lead you to do His Divine Will in a perfect manner. Let all your designs and desires be directed only toward knowing His good pleasure and gratifying His Divine Heart. 'Bless God at all times, and desire of Him to direct thy ways, and that all thy counsels may abide in Him.' (Tob. 4:20). Do not say: 'But why should I make known to God all my needs, since He sees and knows them better than I?' Surely He does, but He acts as if He were not aware of the wants which you neglect to disclose to Him and for which you do not ask His divine help. Our Saviour knew very well that Lazarus was dead; yet He did not reveal the fact that He knew it until Magdalen told Him, and then He consoled her by raising her brother to life."[216]

How to Converse with God, c. 1780

St. Alphonsus Liguori was the founder of the Redemptorists whose mission was to foreign missions and local parishes. He first spent eight years as a lawyer before being ordained in 1726. He became bishop of St. Agatha in 1756, which he led until 1775. Pope Benedict XVI said, "St. Alphonsus Maria Liguori is an example of a zealous Pastor who conquered souls by preaching the Gospel and administering the sacraments combined with behavior impressed with gentle and merciful goodness that was born from his intense relationship with God."

---

216 St. Alphonsus Liguori, *How to Converse With God* (Charlotte: TAN Books, 2005), loc. 17 of 71, Kindle Edition.

DAY 215

REV. JAMES V. SCHALL (1928–2019)

How to receive—

"Yet revelation, it is to be noted, like being itself, is not the result of or subject to the choice of the human will or the power of the human intellect, except its power to accept or reject it. The 'receptivity' characteristic of philosophy is also characteristic of revelation. In fact, this similarity begins to make us wonder if the two are not somehow related. Both revelation and philosophy are free only insofar as they are open to *what is*. The character of the highest things is determined outside our human capacities. Nevertheless, the philosopher does have a proper mind that does enable him, and ought to enable him, to reject, firmly and legitimately, what is false and contradictory, even in presumed revelation. The 'receptivity' of being revelation was not designed to destroy the proper functioning of human powers, but rather to exult them."[217]

Another Sort of Learning, 1988

Rev. James V. Schall stresses the "receptivity" that believers have in common with philosophers because each is committed to know that which exists beyond their own minds. In other

---

217 James V. Schall, *Another Sort of Learning* (San Francisco: Ignatius Press, 1988), 259-60.

words, both the faith of the believer and the reason of the philosopher are not interested in constructing a version of reality;
rather, each begins with the assumption that the knowledge
of faith and reason is reality that exists beyond the minds and
hearts of each. To know, then, is to discover rather than create.

DAY 216

ÉTIENNE GILSON (1884–1978)

Knowing the why—

"When a man falls to wondering whether there is such a being
as God, he is not conscious of raising a scientific problem, or
hoping to give it a scientific solution. Scientific problems
are all related to the knowledge of *what* given things actually
are. An ideal scientific explanation of the world would be an
exhaustive rational explanation of what the world actually is;
but *why* nature exists is not a scientific problem, because its
answer is not susceptible to empirical verification. The notion
of God, on the contrary, always appears to us in history as an
answer to some existential problem, that is, as the *why* of a certain existence."[218]

God and Philosophy, 1941

---

218 Étienne Gilson, *God and Philosophy* (New Haven: Yale University Press,

Étienne Gilson asks the fundamental metaphysical question that has been raised since the Pre-Socratic philosophers: why is there anything at all? Scientific exploration, he explains, no matter how sophisticated, cannot go beyond secondary causes in the universe. No matter how far they look into the cosmos, scientists will always be confronted with a something, an existence of some sort, that raises the question: why does it exist at all?

DAY 217

LÉON BLOY (1846–1917)

Writing for non-believers—

"I have rarely obtained the approval of Catholics and still less of priests who choose to see in me a very dangerous spirit, because I think in the Absolute and because I call myself independent. They need followings and flocks: solitaries are to them suspect. There are two causes for the ostracism of my writings in the Catholic world: The astounding unintelligence of modern Christians and their deep aversion to the Beautiful. This last has something Satanic about it. As between a page written with splendor and another page expressing the same idea in the dullest terms, their choice is never in doubt: they

1941), 148.

instinctively turn towards the platitudinous. You have had a thousand opportunities to see this, and you will see it more and more, for the level falls lower every day. In consequence, I have long since chosen to write for non-believers, and not in vain, since I have had the joy of bringing several of them into the Church. The perfectly hideous injustice of those who ought to be my brothers I endure as well as I can, with the help of God, knowing His help to be invincible, but not without suffering and bitterness of heart. So when a Catholic, a priest, comes to me as you are doing, it seems to me that Our scourged Lord kisses me upon the lips and I feel a delicious consolation."[219]

Quatre ans de captivité, 1900–1904

Léon Bloy was the spiritual godfather to several generations of French Catholic writers and painters, in spite of having grown up as an agnostic and vehement critic of the Church. Bloy is all but forgotten now in spite of his prominence and influence. Imagine that at some time in the future C. S. Lewis is forgotten and you will grasp Bloy's importance to French-speaking Catholics of the first half of the last century. Surprisingly, Pope Francis, in his first papal homily, made reference to almost-forgotten Bloy.

---

219   Léon Bloy, *Pilgrim of the Absolute*, trans. John Coleman and Harry Lorin Binsse, ed. Raïssa Maritain, introduction by Jacques Maritain (London: Eyre & Spottiswoode, 1947), 217.

DAY 218

G. K. CHESTERTON (1874–1936)

A complex birth—

"Here it is the important point that the Magi, who stand for mysticism and philosophy, are truly conceived as seeking something new and even as finding something unexpected. That tense sense of crisis which still tingles in the Christmas story and even in every Christmas celebration, accentuates the idea of a search and a discovery. The discovery is, in this case, truly a scientific discovery. For the other mystical figures in the miracle play; for the angel and the mother, the shepherds and the soldiers of Herod, there may be aspects both simpler and more supernatural, more elemental or more emotional. But the Wise Men must be seeking wisdom; and for them there must be a light also in the intellect. And this is the light; that the Catholic creed is catholic and that nothing else is catholic. The philosophy of the Church is universal. The philosophy of the philosophers was not universal. Had Plato and Pythagoras and Aristotle stood for an instant in the light that came out of that little cave, they would have known that their own light was not universal. It is far from certain, indeed, that they did not know it already. Philosophy also, like mythology, had very much the air of a search. It is the realization of this truth that gives its traditional majesty and mystery to the figures of the Three Kings; the discovery that religion is broader than philosophy and that

this is the broadest of religions, contained within this narrow space. The Magicians were gazing at the strange pentacle with the human triangle reversed; and they have never come to the end of their calculations about it. For it is the paradox of that group in the cave, that while our emotions about it are of childish simplicity, our thoughts about it can branch with a never-ending complexity. And we can never reach the end even of our own ideas about the child who was a father and the mother who was a child."[220]

The Everlasting Man, 1925

G. K. Chesterton writes so beautifully about a distinction which if explained theoretically can make little impression. Put the great philosophers in front of the manger, he writes, and they would know who they truly are, not the Wise Men because the true Wise Men came from the East not from Athens. Seeing the "the child who was a father and the mother who was a child," the philosophers must stand in wonder with the realization that their "Good" lies before them.

---

220 G.K. Chesterton, *The Everlasting Man* (Tacoma: Angelico Press, 2013), loc. 352-353, Kindle Edition.

DAY 219

FLANNERY O'CONNOR (1925–1964)

The body matters—

"I am always astonished at the emphasis the Church puts on the body. It is not the soul she says will rise but the body, glorified. I have always thought that purity was the most mysterious of the virtues, but it occurs to me that it would never have entered the human consciousness to conceive of purity if we were not to look forward to a resurrection of the body, which will be flesh and spirit united in peace, in the way they were in Christ. The resurrection of Christ seems the high point in the law of nature."[221]

"Writing Short Stories"

I can imagine how Flannery O'Connor might have reacted if someone remarked that after death a Christian becomes an angel—a smile and a gentle correction. It's a common misunderstanding often the result of helping children to understand the meaning of death in a hopeful way. But such "childish things" (1 Cor 13:11) have to be put aside to understand how the resurrection of the "spiritual body" (1 Cor 15:42) makes

---

221 Flannery O'Connor, *Mystery and Manners: Occasional Prose*, selected and ed. by Sally and Robert Fitzgerald (New York, Farrar, Straus and Giroux, 1975), 100. The editors were unable to date this essay.

Christianity so distinctive. The need to inculcate the virtue of purity, explains O'Connor, becomes far more pressing when we realize the body and soul united will be received into paradise.

DAY 220

JEFF CAVINS (1957–)

Offer It Up—

"'Just offer it up.' Some of us grew up hearing this phrase from our Catholic parents. Even if we heard that phrase repeatedly, we most likely didn't understand fully what it meant. Certainly this is a foreign phrase to our Protestant brothers and sisters. It sounds strange—after all, what does God want with my broken arm or seven stitches in my knee? In the midst of our pain and suffering, we really have two choices. We can draw attention to ourselves, or we can exercise our will and our suffering to Christ to use for his purposes. Many times we end up focusing on ourselves in our weakness, hoping for sympathy, relief—anything to make us feel better. Doing this draws attention to us rather than the greater good of humanity and Christ's Kingdom. . . . If your suffering is all about you, then nothing beyond you is accomplished; lives aren't changed. . . . Remember that when you suffer you have the opportunity to

be perfected. Once again, this is the opposite of the way the world approaches pain. This world says pain is a setback—a hurdle that keeps you from becoming all you can be. But in the Kingdom of God, suffering is a catalyst to be and do all you were meant to."[222]

When You Suffer: Biblical Keys for Hope and Understanding, 2015

Jeff Cavins is best known for his Great Adventure Bible Timeline which has been studied by over two million people. Born a Catholic, Cavins became discouraged by the Church and became an evangelical minister for twelve years. He returned to the Church, took an MA from the Franciscan University of Steubenville in 1999, and began his very influential career as a Catholic biblical scholar, apologist, and evangelist. Together with his wife, Emily, he has lead over fifty pilgrimages to the Holy Land. He is often seen on EWTN and was the founding host of EWTN's "Life On the Rock." Cavin's many books and videos have had a wide circulation and inestimable influence.

---

222 Jeff Cavins, *When You Suffer: Biblical Keys for Hope and Understanding* (Welland, ON: Servant Books, 2015), loc. 97 of 156, Kindle Edition.

DAY 221

ST. THOMAS AQUINAS (1225–1274)

For Passion Thursday—

"The strongest of human loves is the love with which a man loves himself. Therefore this love must be the measure, by comparison with which we estimate the love by which a man loves others than himself. Now the extent of a man's love for another is shown by the extent of good desired for himself that he forgoes for his friend. As Holy Scripture says, 'He that neglects a loss for the sake of a friend, is just' (Prov. xii, 26). . . . It is then already a sign of love that, for another, a man is willing to suffer loss of things outside himself."[223]

Meditations for Lent

This argument is also found in the *Summa Theologica*, but it's helpful when St. Thomas expresses it in a more straightforward and compact way. Yet, don't let the simplicity mask the profundity of what is expressed: we all know the powerful intensity of self-love, but we must ask ourselves, "Do I love others with an intensity that would lead me to forget my own needs to serve others?" The innate self-regard of natural love, common to all, starkly contrasts with the infusion of divine charity. The

---

223 St. Thomas Aquinas, *Meditations for Lent*, trans. Father Philip Hughes (Fort Collins: Roman Catholic Books), 121.

comparison also reinforces a constant theme in Aquinas, the perfecting power of grace upon nature.

DAY 222

ST. JOHN HENRY NEWMAN (1801–1890)

He shows you how to become as gods—

"Far be it from any of us to be of those simple ones who are taken in that snare which is circling around us! Far be it from us to be seduced with the fair promises in which Satan is sure to hide his poison! Do you think he is so unskillful in his craft, as to ask you openly and plainly to join him in his warfare against the Truth? No; he offers you baits to tempt you. He promises you civil liberty; he promises you equality; he promises you trade and wealth; he promises you a remission of taxes; he promises you reform . . . he offers you knowledge, science, philosophy, enlargement of mind. He scoffs at times gone by; he scoffs at every institution which reveres them. He prompts you what to say, and then listens to you, and praises you, and encourages you. He bids you mount aloft. He shows you how to become as gods. Then he laughs and jokes with you, and

gets intimate with you; he takes your hand, and gets his fingers between yours, and grasps them, and then you are his."[224]

Tracts for the Times, no. 83, 1838

St. John Henry Newman describes how Satan's power relies on our believing a long list of false promises that remove all the difficulties everyone faces in life. Satan also promises us the fulfillment of all our desires and dreams—thus, the mythical Faust traded his soul to gain all the knowledge and love which he had been unable to possess. The moral should be drawn that beware of anyone or any group who promises to solve life's problems if you follow them.

DAY 223

ST. BERNARD OF CLAIRVAUX (1090–1153)

Exhausted wickedness—

"The wicked, therefore, walk around in circles, naturally wanting whatever will satisfy their desires, yet foolishly rejecting that which would lead them to their true end, which is not

---

224 Dave Armstrong, ed., *The Quotable Newman: A Definitive Guide to John Henry Newman's Central Thoughts and Ideas* (Manchester: Sophia Institute Press, 2012), loc. 366, Kindle Edition.

in consumption but in consummation. Hence they exhaust themselves in vain instead of perfecting their lives by a blessed end. They take more pleasure in the appearance of things than in their Creator, examining all and wanting to test them one by one before trying to reach the Lord of the universe."[225]

On Loving God, 1129

This comment anticipates the depiction of sinners inhabiting the circles of hell by Dante in the *Inferno* (1320). St. Bernard of Clairvaux imagines the wicked walking in circles for the simple reason that they continue to find fulfillment in the same actions that never satisfied. They are exhausted physically and spiritually by receptive expectation, action, and outcome. These repetitive actions all share the same error—seeking in the temporal what can only be found in the eternal. It's like watching an athlete using the same technique over and over without showing any improvement. In fact, the athlete is only causing the technique to become more ingrained, insuring poor performance.

---

225 St. Bernard of Clairvaux, *On Loving God, Treatises II: The Steps of Humanity and Pride and On Loving God*, trans and intro Robert Watson OSB (Kalamazoo: Cistercian Publications, 1973), 112.

DAY 224

LÉON BLOY (1846–1917)

A heart in bronze—

"Do you know that to be a real Christian, that is to say a *Saint*, one must have a tender heart within a shell of bronze? Saint Luke tells us that in the midst of the most unutterable suffering, Christ had pity on the brutes who were crucifying Him and that he entreated His Father to forgive them. Now remember that a filthy butcher or pigsticker who, not satisfied with slaughtering his poor animals, unworthily and ridiculously mutilates them after their death, carries on—after a fashion—in the most unfathomable darkness, the immolation of the Savior and that they are enfolded in his Prayer. All the more do they need it as they are more abject, more unfeeling, more smug in an appalling ignorance of what they do."[226]

Le mendiant ingrat: (journal de l'auteur, 1892-1895), 1895

Léon Bloy himself was a man with a soft heart but a forbidding exterior. Part of the exterior was what he said as a writer and how he said it. Bloy pulled no punches and respected no norms of social propriety. For him, to be a Christian was to

---

226 Léon Bloy, *Pilgrim of the Absolute*, trans. John Coleman and Harry Lorin Binsse, ed. Raïssa Maritain, introduction by Jacques Maritain (London: Eyre & Spottiswoode, 1947), 283.

pursue sanctity and nothing less. Thus, he conjures the narrative above of Jesus praying for the centurions who crucified
Him, just as he prays for all of humanity who have continued
to crucify him daily as some butchers relentlessly carve on
their animals after killing them.

DAY 225

ALICE THOMAS ELLIS (1932–2004)

On making the Mass more relevant—

"One is tempted to stroll up and ask for a double martini and
enquire who forgot to put the doings on the canapés. I wonder
why they didn't keep the real Mass for me and just bring in
this one for the kiddies and the mentally subnormal . . .? It is
as though one's revered, dignified and darling old mother had
slapped on a mini-skirt and fishnet tights and started ogling
strangers. A kind of menopause madness, a sudden yearning to
be attractive to all. It is tragic and hilarious and awfully embar-
rassing. And of course those who knew her before feel a great
sense of betrayal and can't bring themselves to go and see her
anymore."[227]

The Serpent on the Rock, 1985

---

227 Alice Thomas Ellis, *The Serpent on the Rock: A Personal View of Christianity*

Alice Thomas Ellis was "old school" in the best sense: she didn't merely complain but did so with a unique sense of humor and genuine insight. Ellis knew she was ruffling feathers not just of the ecclesiastics but also those of the laity who enjoyed an informal Mass. The changes in liturgy after Vatican II felt quite abrupt to many life-long Catholics, and studies have shown that some of them never recovered their felt sense of connection to the Church. Ellis calls it "a sudden yearning to be attractive to all," but in so doing the parishioners who have been practicing their faith for decades were left wondering why they practiced at all.

DAY 226

DIETRICH VON HILDEBRAND (1889–1977)

On true feeling—

"The truly affective man is preoccupied with the good which is the source and basis of his affective experience. In loving he looks at the beloved; in happiness he directs his thoughts to the reason for his being happy; in his enthusiasm, he focuses on the value of the good to which the enthusiasm is directed. The true affective experience implies that one is convinced of its objective validity. An affective experience which is not justified

(London: Trafalgar Square, 1985), 25

by reality has no validity for the truly affective man. As soon as such a man realizes that his joy, his happiness, his enthusiasm, or his sorrow is based on an illusion, the experience collapses. Thus what matters primarily is not the question, 'Do we *feel* happiness?' But rather, 'Is the objective situation such that we have reason to be happy?'"[228]

Transformation in Christ, 1919

Dietrich von Hildebrand makes a point that is almost always overlooked: emotions have objects—that is, things that emotions are *about*. As von Hildebrand insists, to be in a state of euphoria is not intrinsically good if the euphoria is the result of taking drugs, torturing animals, or watching pornography. Happiness, he says, might involve feelings—it usually does— but derives from living a life devoted to the right purpose. In our age, positive emotion and states of mind have become ends in themselves, meaning that *any way* of achieving them is considered acceptable. Von Hildebrand, in all his work, constantly addresses this self-deception.

228 Dietrich von Hildebrand, *Transformation in Christ* (Chicago: Franciscan Herald Press, 1949), 47.

DAY 227

BLAISE PASCAL (1623–1662)

Our heart's desire—

"What else does this craving, and this helplessness, proclaim but that there was once in man a true happiness, of which all that now remains is the empty print and trace? This he tries in vain to fill with everything around him, seeking in things that are not there the help he cannot find in those that are, though none can help, since this abyss can be filled only with an infinite and immutable object: in other words by God Himself. God alone is man's true good, and since man abandoned Him it is strange fact that nothing in nature has been found to take His place: stars, sky, earth, elements, plants, cabbages, leeks, animals, insects, calves, serpents, fever, plague, war, famine, vice, adultery, incest. Since losing his true good, man is capable of seeing it in anything, even his own destruction, although it is so contrary at once to God, to reason and to nature."[229]

Pensées, 1662

Blaise Pascal might have been laughing or crying when he wrote the last sentence above, because a man's foolish rush to find ultimacy in wealth, possessions, sex, celebrity, and power

---

229 Blaise Pascal, *Pensées,* trans. and introduction by A. J. Krailsheimer (New York: Penguin Books, 1984), 75.

is comic from the perspective of Eternity. Imagine a comedy sketch about a man looking for happiness in a leek or a cabbage, and you will share in Pascal's irony. Having been influenced by Jansenism, Pascal emphasizes the consequence of the Fall, one being the inclination to misjudge the value of worldly goods. However, that "empty print and trace" of happiness that still exists in the human person is the ground both for our return to Him and, more importantly, our reception of His grace.

DAY 228

FRANÇOIS MAURIAC (1885–1970)

In the novel The Vipers' Tangle, *Monsieur Louis, a wealthy and unhappy lawyer, writes a journal to be read by his wife of forty-five years, his children, and grandchildren. He explains that since their wedding night, when she confessed to an affair with another man, he had been so wounded he began to hate her. He has also realized that she never had any genuine concern for him. His journey becomes a struggle to remove the viper's tangle in his heart. His efforts, however, fail—*

"Even the genuinely good cannot, unaided, learn to love. To penetrate beyond the absurdities, the vices, and, above all, the stupidities of human creatures, one must possess the secret of a love that the world has now forgotten. Until that secret shall

have been rediscovered, all betterment in conditions of life will be in vain. I used to think that it was selfishness that kept me uninterested in questions of sociology and economics, and to some extent that was true, for I have been a monster of solitude and indifference. Still, I had a feeling, an obscure certainty, that it was no use merely to revolutionize the face of the world, that what was needed was the power to reach the world through the medium of the heart. Him whom I seek can alone achieve that victory, and he must needs be the heart of all hearts, the burning center of all love. . . . I had been a man so horrible that he could have no friend. But wasn't that, I asked myself, because I had always been incapable of wearing a disguise? If all men went through life with unmasked faces, as I had done for half a century, one might be surprised to find how little difference there was between them. But, in fact, no one lives with his face uncovered, no one. Most men ape greatness or nobility. Though they do not know it, they conform to certain fixed types, literary or other. This the saints know, and they hate and despise themselves because they see themselves with unclouded eyes. I should not have been so universally condemned had I not been so defenseless, so open, and so naked."[230]

The Viper's Tangle, 1932

---

230 François Mauriac, *The Viper's Tangle*, trans. Pamela Morris, preface by Stephen Mirachi, notes and introduction by Timothy O'Malley (Providence: Cluny Media, 2017), loc. 254-256, Kindle Edition.

François Mauriac believed his vocation as a novelist, like that of Flannery O'Connor, was not to skate the surface of the Christian life providing simplistic depictions of saintly virtue. To know the Christian life, like all human existence, requires an unflinching look at how tangled and poisonous an individual's life can become. Monsieur Louis, in other words, is far more common than we think. It's remarkable that Mauriac's novels are still read given the demanding nature of his spirituality.

DAY 229

JEAN-LUC MARION (1946–)

The will to power (Nietzsche)—

"Our era is characterized by nihilism. . . . If we wanted to provide a serious account of the ecological crisis, the demographic situation, or the ethical situation of our societies, then we would have to consider all these phenomena as symptoms of the same situation, which finds its logic and its setting totally in nihilism. Nihilism is defined as the situation where the highest values are devalued. The highest values are devalued not only because one can destroy them and knock them down but also because one wants to establish other values at will, by the will to power. Whether it is opposed or defended, in fact, value

is always intrinsically a matter of nihilism: To describe a reality with *sinister* qualification of value consists in saying that being, which has been reduced to its representation and its cogitability by triumphant metaphysics, must in the last analysis be reduced to the judgment of value that affirms or denies it, that is to say, to the will to power. One could radicalize Nietzsche's definition by deeming all beings to be values, depending from beginning to end on the power of affirmation or negation of the will to power—which is instituted by its unique guarantee and unique authority. In the end, nihilism lies as much—in some way maybe more—in defending or affirming these values ('Let's fight over our values!' wails the right and the left, without having any clue what they are saying) because in the best of cases it actually amounts to pushing them even further into the servile function of value. Value, as the share of the one who evaluates it, eliminates the thing, is alienated."[231]

The Rigor of Things, 2017

Jean-Luc Marion became prominent in the United States when he published the provocatively titled *God Without Being* (1991). But those who read Marion then realized his was not another attempt of a theologian, as in the 1960s, to announce the "Death of God." *God Without Being*, in fact, is about idolatry which can take the form of rationalist metaphysics. His

---

231 Jean-Luc Marion, *The Rigor of Things: Conversations with Dan Arbib*, trans. Christina M. Gschwandtner (New York: Fordham University Press, 2017), 164–65.

philosophical-theological project has been to build an understanding of Christian living around the reality of "givenness." The idea of love is central to Marion's thought. In his *Prolegomena to Charity* (2002), he warns against trying too hard to define love, to sum it up in a concept, because it can make love only the occasion of loving oneself.

DAY 230

FULTON J. SHEEN (1895–1979)

A lost soul—

"The bald fact the enemies of God must face is that modern civilization has conquered the world, but in doing so has lost its soul. And in losing its soul it will lose the very world it gained. Even our own so-called liberal culture in these United States, which has tried to avoid complete secularization by leaving little zones of individual freedom, is in danger of forgetting that these zones were preserved only because religion was in their soul. And as religion fades so will freedom, for only where the spirit of God is, is there liberty."[232]

Characters of the Passion, 1947

---

232 Fulton J. Sheen, *Characters of the Passion* (Kettering: Angelico Press, 2015), loc. 422 of 947. Kindle Edition.

Fulton J. Sheen says what is no longer obvious to most Americans—that our nation's commitment to individual freedom was spurred by the demand for religious liberty. Before there were the Enlightenment Founders, there were the Puritans who landed at Plymouth Rock having suffered the intolerance of the Anglican establishment. Two decades later in 1634, a group of Catholics found a home in Maryland, only one generation after the end of Elizabeth I's tireless persecution of Catholics. If American freedom is understood in only civil terms, as freedom from monarchical or totalitarian rule, it will lack an understanding of how American liberty was conceived and ignore the Christian principle of human dignity that grounds it.

DAY 231

SHUSAKU ENDO (1923–1966)

Silence *is a celebrated and controversial Catholic novel. Its setting is Japan in the seventeenth century as Catholics are being tortured to recant their faith. The Jesuit priest Sebastião Rodrigues, based upon an actual Jesuit missionary, is captured and imprisoned in a small hut—*

"Since he had no rosary he began to recite the Paters and Aves on the five fingers of his hand; but just as water dribbles back down from the mouth of the man whose lips are locked by

sickness, the prayer remained empty and hollow on his lips. Rather was he drawn by the voices of the guards outside the hut. What was so funny that they should keep raising their voices and laughing heartily? His thoughts turned to the fire-lit garden and the servants; the figures of those men holding back flaming torches and utterly indifferent to the fate of others. This was the feeling that their laughing and talking stirred up in his heart. Sin, he reflected, is not what it is usually thought to be; it is not to steal and tell lies. Sin is for one man to walk brutally over the life of another and to be quite oblivious of the wounds he has left behind. And then for the first time a real prayer rose up in his heart."[233]

Silence, 1966

The climax of *Silence* by Shusaku Endo comes when the Jesuit Rodrigues and a fellow Jesuit are forced to watch other Japanese Catholics tortured until they themselves recant by placing their foot on a carved image of Christ called *fumi-e*. Even those who have already recanted are being tortured. Rodrigues does not know what to do until he hears the voice of Christ, "You may trample. You may trample. I more than anyone know of the pain in your foot. You may trample. It was to be trampled on by men that I was born into this world. It was to share men's pain that I carried my cross."

---

233 Shusaku Endo, *Silence*, trans. William Johnston, foreword Martin Scorsese (New York: Picador Modern Classics, 2016), 91-92

DAY 232

ST. AUGUSTINE (354–430)

How doubt fled—

"So I hurried back to the spot where Alypius[234] was sitting, for I had put there the volume of the apostle when I got up and left him. I snatched it up, opened it, and read in silence the chapter on which my eyes first fell. 'Not in rioting and drunkenness, not in chambering and impurities, not in strife and envying; but put you on the Lord Jesus Christ, and make not provision for the flesh in its concupiscences' (Rom 13:13–14). No further wished I to read, nor was there need to do so. Instantly, in truth, at the end of the sentence, as if before a peaceful light streaming into my heart, all the dark shadows of doubt fled away."[235]

The Confessions, 397

Because of his intellectual gifts, St. Augustine had few peers in the fourth century, or in all the centuries afterward for that matter. After moving from Carthage in North Africa to Rome, he attained the most prestigious academic position in the Roman world, as a rhetoric tutor at the imperial court in

---

234 St. Alypius, a lifelong friend, was the bishop of Tagaste.

235 St. Augustine, *Confessions*, Book 8.12, trans. and introduction by John K. Ryan (Garden City: Doubleday and Company, Inc., 1960), 202.

Milan. None of his worldly pursuits, whether intellectual or sensual, left Augustine satisfied with his life. His own unhappiness leads him to reevaluate his life. His description of his conversion finds him setting his learning aside to deal directly with his sensual sins, the last barrier to his leap of faith. This comports with other comments in this volume about the moral life having a direct impact on the ethics and worldview a person chooses. In other words, a person wedded to sin will likely embrace a set of principles that justify his habits and actions.

DAY 233

ST. JOHN HENRY NEWMAN (1801–1890)

The hope of purgatory—

"Again, consider what a frightful doctrine purgatory is—not the holiest man who lived but must expect to find himself there on dying, since Christ does not remit all punishment of sin. Now, if Christ has promised to wipe away all guilt and all suffering upon death, what a great affront it must be to Him, thus to obscure His mercy, to deprive His people of the full comfort of His work for them! Nor would it be surprising if, in God's gracious providence, the very purpose of their remaining thus for a season at a distance from heaven, were, that they may

have time for growing in all holy things, and perfecting the inward development of the good seed sown in their hearts. . . . Consider how many men are very dark and feeble in their religious state, when they depart hence, though true servants of God as far as they go. Alas! I know that the multitude of men do not think of religion at all;—they are thoughtless in their youth, and secular as life goes on;—they find their interest lie in adopting a decent profession; they deceive themselves, and think themselves religious, and (to all appearance) die with no deeper religion than such a profession implies. Alas! there are many also, who, after careless lives, amend, yet not truly;—think they repent, but do not in a Christian way. There are a number, too, who leave repentance for their death-bed, and die with no fruits of religion at all, except with so much of subdued and serious feeling as pain forces upon them. All these, as far as we are told, die without hope. But, after all these melancholy cases are allowed for, many there are still, who, beginning well, and persevering for years, yet are even to the end but beginners after all, when death comes upon them;—many who have been in circumstances of especial difficulty, who have had fiercer temptations, more perplexing trials than the rest, and in consequence have been impeded in their course. Nay, in one sense, all Christians die with their work unfinished. . . . Who can tell then, but, in God's mercy, the time of waiting between death and Christ's coming, may be profitable to those who have been His true servants here, as a time of maturing that fruit of grace, but partly formed in them in this life,—a

school-time of contemplation, as this world is a discipline of active service?"[236]

Parochial and Plain Sermons, 3.25

This explanation of purgatory by St. John Henry Newman must be close to definitive. He contrasts those of deep faith who enter purgatory with those whose faith is slight. "All Christians die with their work unfinished," but some, it must be said, have more work ahead of them than others.

DAY 234

BOETHIUS (477–524)

God's eternal present—

Lady Philosophy speaks to Boethius:

"If we may aptly compare God's present vision with man's. He sees all things in his eternal present as you see things in your temporal present. Therefore, this divine foreknowledge does not change the nature and properties of things; it simply sees

---

236 Dave Armstrong, ed., *The Quotable Newman: A Definitive Guide to John Henry Newman's Central Thoughts and Ideas* (Manchester: Sophia Institute Press, 2012), loc. 331-321, Kindle Edition.

things present before it as they will later turn out to be in what we regard as the future. His judgment is not confused; with a single intuition of his mind. He knows all things that are to come, whether necessarily or not. Just as, when you happen to see simultaneously a man walking on the street and the sun shining in the sky, even though you see both at once, you can distinguish between them and realize that one action is voluntary, the other necessary; so the divine mind, looking down on all things, does not disturb the nature of things which are present before it but are future in respect to time."[237]

The Consolation of Philosophy, 527

Confined to his prison cell, Boethius addresses the issue of God's omniscience, his knowledge of past, present, and future. To do this, Boethius must distinguish between human vision, which is subject to time and space, and the divine vision that, being outside of the constraints of time, sees all that *is.* Our vision of *is* is confined to the past and the immediate present. God's vision takes in all that is, past, present, and future. Boethius faces the immediate question of how God's foreknowledge doesn't limit or eliminate human freedom. "If God knows what I am going to do, how can I be held responsible for it?" His answer is that God's knowledge is an everlasting present: he sees, but he does not make our decisions for us.

---

237 Boethius, *Consolation of Philosophy,* trans., introduction, and notes by Richard Green (Bloomington: The Bobbs-Merrill Company, Inc., 1962), 117.

DAY 235

HENRI DE LUBAC, SJ (1896–1996)

Wounded not destroyed—

"Still, according to Catholic teaching, which on this point differs from that of Luther and Calvin, our sinful nature is not completely corrupted by sin. Freedom, that prerogative of man created in God's image, was wounded, but not destroyed, so that grace in its triumph will not reign over a helpless enemy; it will not have to displace man, but free him from slavery. Thus, in a second stage and by God's initiative, a new relationship will be established between nature and grace, no longer one of antagonism but of union."[238]

A Brief Catechesis on Nature and Grace, 1980

Even though Catholics rarely talk about it these days, there are fundamental theological differences between Catholicism and Protestantism—one of them is the effect of the Fall on the human condition. The argument centered on the question of the freedom and the will and the reception of grace. Luther regarded the will as in "bondage" so that it was "grace alone" that bestowed salvation. Catholic theologians never denied the primacy of grace, but as de Lubac writes, in spite of the

---

238 Henri de Lubac, S.J., *A Brief Catechesis on Nature and Grace*, trans. Brother Richard Arnandez, F.S.C. (San Francisco: Ignatius Press, 1984), 122.

Fall, human freedom remained, wounded but not destroyed. The logical outcome of Luther's stance is that becoming a Christian is an entirely passive event. With human freedom destroyed, the conclusion must follow that the original image of God in man has also been destroyed. But de Lubac, relying on a theological premise traced back to Aquinas, the Church Fathers, and Scripture, affirms that freedom remains because the highest part of the human intellect survived intact.

DAY 236

MATTHIAS JOSEPH SCHEEBEN (1835–1888)

The fallen angels—

"The sin of the fallen angels is manifestly sin in its worst form. It proceeded from pure malice; not, as in the case of man, from ignorance and weakness. It is a direct insult to God and an open contempt of the order of grace, and hence it has the character of sin against the Holy Ghost. It is an open rebellion against God, carried out, and unrelentingly persisted in with all the energy of which a pure spirit is capable. It is, lastly, an uninterrupted sin, a perpetual act, thanks to the spiritual and ever vigilant nature of the angels. For all these reasons, the pride of the angels was a sin unto death—far more than mortal sin in man, more even than final impenitence in man. The great sin of

the angels was immediately punished with eternal damnation. God granted them neither the time nor the means of repentance. Holy Writ and the formulated teaching of the Church do not directly express this doctrine; they only state the fact that at present the fallen angels are in a state of damnation, and without hope of salvation. . . . The sin of the angels was immediately followed by the complete depravation and corruption of their spiritual life. The demons' depravity consists in the obscuration of their intellect and the hardening of their will, so that mendacity and wickedness become their second nature; they are 'powers of darkness and spirits of wickedness.' Their intellect is darkened by the withdrawal of all supernatural light as principle of supernatural knowledge, albeit they retain the bare knowledge of the truths revealed to them before their fall, or which they may learn by some external revelation. Then the perversity of their will influences their judgment, so as to make evil appear to them as good. The hardening of the will of the evil spirits consists in this, that the hatred of God is the impelling motive of all their actions. As the good spirits do all they do for the love of God, so the evil spirits are moved in all their actions by hatred of Him. This hatred is partly the result of the original perversity of their will, partly an effect of their resenting the punishment inflicted upon them."[239]

A Manual of Catholic Theology, 1906

---

239 Matthias Joseph Scheeben, *A Manual of Catholic Theology* (Lex De Leon Publishing), loc. 8351–19866, Kindle Edition.

Matthias Joseph Scheeben explains why the sin of the angels in rejecting God was "pure malice" and remains "an uninterrupted sin, a perpetual act." When the angels were created, they clearly saw who created them. There was no ambiguity or confusion about their status before God—yet, they rejected him nonetheless!

DAY 237

ALICE MEYNELL (1847–1922)

Meynell's "In Portugal, 1912" describes Jesus as waiting and biding his time amid the contemporary chaos. After the 1910 revolution in Portugal, Catholicism was declared an enemy of national aspirations, and anti-Catholic violence ensued.

Portugal, 1912

> "And will they cast the altars down,
> Scatter the chalice, crush the bread?
> In field, in village, and in town
> He hides an unregarded head;
> Waits in the corn-lands far and near,
> Bright in His sun, dark in His frost,
> Sweet in the vine, ripe in the ear –
> Lonely unconsecrated Host.

In ambush at the merry board
The Victim lurks unsacrificed;
The mill conceals the harvest's Lord,
The wine-press holds the unbidden Christ."[240]

Alice Meynell was born to parents who had been introduced by Charles Dickens. Alice was encouraged to write poetry by another family friend, Alfred Lord Tennyson. She did become a poet. After her mother converted, Alice was received into the Catholic Church. From that point onward, her Catholic faith was central to both her life and her poetry and criticism. Her first books of poems, *Preludes* (1875), was praised by those who mattered at the time, and, shortly after, she married an admirer, Wilfred Meynell, a prominent journalist. They had eight children. She published many volumes of essays and poems before she died in 1922.

240 https://www.bartleby.com/236/264.html.

DAY 238

BENEDICT J. GROESCHEL, CFR (1926–2011)

Hollywood saints—

"The most important experience of the Dark Night, however, is the rescuing by God, which marks the end of the darkness. It is like the resurrection on Easter morning. We arrive like Mary and often at first do not realize what has happened. The light dawns upon us gently and slowly we realize that indeed we have learned something that we really never knew before. The lives of the saints abound with examples which unfortunately are often presented by hagiographers as Hollywood-type happy endings. Of course the actual working of God is very different. The causes of darkness may still remain and tears of sorrow may still flow, but in spite of it all a new soft and gentle light is rising in the inner being of the individual."[241]

Spiritual Passages, 2007

Through his writings, Father Benedict J. Groeschel repeatedly brought up the subject of suffering and the "Dark Night" of the soul. He met Catholics all the time who assumed that their Catholic faith would lead to prosperity and happiness—they were not prepared, he said, for the *way of the Cross* which the

---

241 Benedict J. Groeschel, C.F.R., *Spiritual Passages: The Psychology of Spiritual Development* (New York: The Crossword Publishing Company, 2007), 134.

saints themselves attest to. Films about the saints made until recently made sanctity seem like little more than overcoming an unaccepting family, the town agnostic, and a skeptical church hierarchy. Mel Gibson's *The Passion of the Christ* (2004) changed that, but even before that a quite remarkable film about the Little Flower had been made that did not look away from her tuberculosis: *Thérèse* (1986) directed by Alain Cavalier. Films about St. Joan of Arc have been of higher quality because writers and directors have no choice but to end with her painful death.

DAY 239

ST. TERESA OF CALCUTTA (1920–1997)

I want the child—

"But I feel that the greatest destroyer of peace today is abortion, because Jesus said, 'If you receive a little child, you receive me.' So, every abortion is the denial of receiving Jesus—is the neglect of receiving Jesus. It is really a war against the child, a direct killing of the innocent child, murder by the mother herself. And if we accept that a mother can kill even her own child, how can we tell other people not to kill one another? How do we persuade a woman not to have an abortion? As always, we must persuade her with love and we remind ourselves that

love means to be willing to give until it hurts. Jesus gave even His life to love us. So, the mother who is thinking of abortion should be helped to love—that is, to give until it hurts her plans, her free time, to respect the life of her child. For the child is the greatest gift of God to the family because they have been created to love and be loved.

The father of that child, however, must also give until it hurts. By abortion, the mother does not learn to love, but kills even her own child to solve her problems. And, by abortion, the father is told that he does not have to take any responsibility at all for the child he has brought into the world. So that father is likely to put other women into the same trouble. So, abortion just leads to more abortion. Any country that accepts abortion is not teaching its people to love one another, but to use any violence to get what they want. This is why the greatest destroyer of love and peace is abortion. . . . Please don't kill the child. I want the child."[242]

Speech at National Day of Prayer Breakfast, 1994

This speech of St. Teresa of Calcutta made headlines around the world. In the presence of a pro-abortion president and an even more pro-abortion first lady—Bill and Hilary Clinton—Mother Teresa made no attempt to be diplomatic, no attempt to save the Clintons from embarrassment. She told the truth

---

242 https://www.americanrhetoric.com/speeches/motherteresanationalprayerbreakfast.htm.

that needed to be heard, the same truth so often not heard from other prominent church leaders.

DAY 240

SAMUEL GREGG (1969–)

It all makes sense—

"The West's integration of creation, freedom, justice, and faith is always fragile, and undermining any one of them undercuts the others. Without creation, the intelligibility of the universe is hard to sustain. Without intelligibility, freedom is only a mirage, justice a sophism, and faith nothing more than emotivism or ideology. If freedom is meaningless, people cannot be held responsible for their actions. Without personal responsibility, there is no true justice. Without justice, the existence of an intelligent Creator to whom all must eventually answer is thrown into doubt. . . . Again and again, we see that belief in Logos—or at least an acknowledgement that it is more plausible than assertions that all is flux or that everything begins in nothingness—is crucial for preserving the West's civilizational achievements from the rule and consequences of irrationality. Few have explained the need for this type of enlightenment better than someone who experienced the full force of the

power of senselessness and its implications in a land where unreason triumphed beyond anyone's expectations."[243]

Reason, Faith, and the Struggle for Western Civilization, 2019

Samuel Gregg is the research director at the Acton Institute, a fellow of the Center for the Study of Law and Religion at Emory University, and a fellow of the Royal Historical Society. He directs the Acton Institute's research and international outreach, including budgeting, personnel, and programming development and implementation. He is the author of thirteen books, including *On Ordered Liberty* (2003), *The Commercial Society* (2007), *Becoming Europe* (2013), and, most recently, *Reason, Faith, and the Struggle for Western Civilization* (2019). Gregg has a DPhil in moral philosophy and political economy from Oxford University working under the direction of Prof. John Finnis.

---

243 Samuel Gregg, *Reason, Faith, and the Struggle for Western Civilization* (Washington, DC: Regnery Gateway, 2019), 164-65.

DAY 241

BISHOP FULTON J. SHEEN (1895–1979)

Make a choice—

"If Christ is not all He claimed to be, the Son of the Living God, then he was not a good man! A good man never lies! But He was a liar if He was not God, for He said that He was God. A good man never leads others into false belief. But He asked that men die for belief in His divinity, which they are doing even in this day. If Christ was not God, then He not only was not a good man; He was the most villainous imposter and scoundrel the world has ever seen. If Christ is not God, He is the antichrist."[244]

Lord, Teach Us to Pray, 2019

Bishop Fulton J. Sheen poses a question meant to force the reader to answer the question about the Savior. Sheen regards belief in Jesus Christ as an all-or-nothing proposition, which implies that if the man who claims to be the Son of God is not, then He must be the most wicked man who ever lived, the antichrist in fact. This directness must be one of the reasons that Sheen was such an effective evangelist—he was not shy about asking for a commitment. Sheen was willing to make

---

244 Archbishop Fulton J. Sheen, *Lord, Teach Us to Pray: An Anthology* (Manchester: Sophia Institute Press, 2019), 166.

argument after argument about the truth of the Catholic faith, but he never left it at exposition only, the Catholic version of an altar call always followed—you must decide!

DAY 242

DAVID JONES (1895–1974)

The blacksmith rules—

"Man of his material tends to make objects of beauty. The lack, therefore, of this quality, is the sure sign of an imposed tyranny. Civilizations are always subject to some such subjection in varying degrees. In our day . . . the subjection is complete. Yet even if one took an English village smith of the more typical sort, and locked him in his shop for a week with instructions to make an image of iron of, say, the Mother of God, it is probable that his finished work at the week's end would be (of this I am sure) infinitely more in the universal tradition than anything that the frantic efforts of all the Arts and Crafts centers in England could produce. It is unlikely that the smith himself would approve of his work, because even village smiths are blasted by the conviction that beauty has wedded the camera, and that there can be no beauty without verisimilitude. Nevertheless, what this man produces, in so far as he is free from obnoxious influences, will be in fact a thing of beauty

and beloved of God, and therefore fit for use in the house of God."[245]

"Beauty in Catholic Churches," 1926

David Jones knew he would be an artist at an early age and attended the Camberwell Art School. He enlisted to fight in WWI and served in the trenches of the Western front. In 1921, he converted to Catholicism in the midst of making his name as both a poet and a painter. His epic work, a poem entitled *In Parenthesis* (1937), was an account of a soldier leaving England and fighting in the Battle of the Somme. Jones wrote in detail about every aspect of that excruciating experience. He had spent more time in the midst of the fighting than any other English writer. *The Anathemata* of 1952 compared the Allies' occupation of Europe to the Roman conquest of its empire. His drawings, calligraphy, inscriptions, and paintings remain greatly admired. He considered painting the highest of the art forms, and his biographer relates that Jones regarded all art as sacramental. Jones lived a life of suffering, some of it self-inflicted but much more from the trauma of the war. He is buried in the Poet's Corner in Westminster Abbey.

---

245 David Jones, "Beauty in Catholic Churches," *The Chesterton Review*, Vol. 23, Nos. 1 & 2, February and May, 1997, 86.

DAY 243

ANGELUS SILESIUS (1624–1677)

Love is the password. He to whom it is not given
Must never hope to cross the frontier-line of Heaven.

Did not God love Himself through thee and in thee, Man,
Thy love for Him would ever fail of its full span.

Being Himself so great, greatly God loves to give,
But ah! man's little heart is so small to receive.

When Love is new, it foams like young and heady wine:
When stiller grown, 'tis proof that it is old and fine.

Thou lovest none? 'Tis well. He has the better mind
Who loves not any man, but loves in man Mankind.

He wills and loveth right who wills and loveth naught:
Who loveth what he wills, loveth not what he ought. . . .

Love is the quickest thing and of itself can fly
To topmost Heaven in but the twinkling of an eye.

A Heart which God hath never wounded with Love's wound,
Scatheless though it appear, is never whole and sound.[246]

---

246 St. Angelus Silesius, *The Cherubinic Wanderer*, 244–256, trans. and intro-

Angelius Silesius was a Catholic convert from the Lutheranism received from his father who was a pastor. His conversion was chiefly influenced by the mysticism of Jakob Böhme and a reading of Patristic theologians. He spent six years in Vienna serving as the physician to Ferdinand III, the Holy Roman emperor. Once ordained a priest in 1661, Silesius became a zealous opponent of the Protestantism of his youth. Yet, he is most known for is a poetic work, *The Cherubinic Wanderer*, published in 1657 consisting of rhyming couplets on the mysteries of the Catholic faith.

DAY 244

DANTE ALIGHIERI (1265–1321)

Virgil, leading the poet upward, explains how purgatory is structured by the level of love in our lives—

Not the Creator nor a single creature,
 as you know, ever existed without love,
 the soul's love or the love that comes by nature.
The natural love is just and cannot rove.
 the soul's love strays if it desires what's wrong
 or loves with too much strength, or not enough.

duction by J.E. Crawford Flitch (London, 1932); read at https://www.sa-cred-texts.com/chr/sil/scw/scw10.htm.

When toward its prime good it is led aright
>   and keeps good measure in the second goods,
>   it cannot be the cause of bad delight,
But when it twists to evil, or does not,
>   race for a good with appropriate care,
>   the potter finds rebellion in the pot.
Hence you can understand how love must be
>   the seedbed where all virtuous deeds must grow,
>   with every act that warrants punishment.
Now then, since by its logic love can't turn
>   its glance from the well-being of the one
>   who loves, all things are shielded from self-hate;
And since you can't conceive yourself cut free
>   from your first cause, and standing on your own,
>   you cannot truly hate the Deity.[247]

Purgatory, Canto 17.91–111

Virgil explains to Dante's pilgrim that "you cannot truly hate the Deity." Love is the basis of all existence because it's an act of Creation, not just "once upon a time," but present at every moment. Since God as Creator has shared his being by creating, all that exists possesses love. That love directs the motions of all existing beings towards their perfection, and in the case of

---

247 Dante, *Purgatorio*, trans., ed., and introduction by Anthony Esolen (New York: The Modern Library, 2004), 185.

man becomes refracted through freedom. Every human action is propelled by love but not necessarily towards the true End.

DAY 245

ST. JOHN HENRY NEWMAN (1801–1890)

A rugged laity—

"I want a laity, not arrogant, not rash in speech, not disputatious, but men who know their religion, who enter into it, who know just where they stand, who know what they hold, and what they do not, who know their creed so well, that they can give an account of it, who know so much of history that they can defend it. I want an intelligent, well-instructed laity; I am not denying you are such already: but I mean to be severe, and, as some would say, exorbitant in my demands, I wish you to enlarge your knowledge, to cultivate your reason, to get an insight into the relation of truth to truth, to learn to view things as they are, to understand how faith and reason stand to each other, what are the bases and principles of Catholicism, and where lie the main inconsistencies and absurdities of the Protestant theory. . . . You ought to be able to bring out what you feel and what you mean, as well as to feel and mean it; to expose to the comprehension of others the fictions and fallacies of your opponents; and to explain the charges brought

against the Church, to the satisfaction, not, indeed, of bigots, but of men of sense, of whatever cast of opinion."[248]

Lectures on the Present Position of Catholics
in England, Lecture 9, 1851

St. John Henry Newman sets a high bar for the laity. He wants a laity that can know and defend the Church in all respects, from its creed and history to its quarrel with Protestantism and modernity. "I mean to be severe," he says, and no doubt if he were to inspect the troops of today's lay Catholics, there would be some serious dressing down.

DAY 246

G. K. CHESTERTON (1874–1936)

The illusion of evolution—

"Most modern histories of mankind begin with the word evolution. . . . There is something slow and soothing and gradual about the word and even about the idea. As a matter of fact, it is not, touching these primary things, a very practical word

---

248 Dave Armstrong, ed., *The Quotable Newman: A Definitive Guide to John Henry Newman's Central Thoughts and Ideas* (Manchester: Sophia Institute Press, 2012), loc. 30, Kindle Edition.

or a very profitable idea. Nobody can imagine how nothing could turn into something. Nobody can get an inch nearer to it by explaining how something could turn into something else. It is really far more logical to start by saying, 'In the beginning God created heaven and earth,' even if you only mean, 'In the beginning some unthinkable power began some unthinkable process.' For God is by its nature a name of mystery, and nobody ever supposed that man could imagine how a world was created any more than he could create one. But evolution really is mistaken for explanation. It has the fatal quality of leaving on many minds the impression that they do understand it and everything else; just as many of them live under a sort of illusion that they have read the *Origin of Species*."[249]

Everlasting Man, 1923

G. K. Chesterton precisely locates the fatal flaw of evolutionary theory—"how nothing could turn into something." No matter how sophisticated the theory of existing things coming-into-being, there will always be the question of where the "primal matter," so to speak, came from in the first place. Chesterton then turns specifically to Darwin: "Nobody can get an inch nearer to it by explaining how something could turn into something else." By that he means how one species can become another species, a problem the evolutionists have

---

249 G.K. Chesterton, *Everlasting Man* (Angelico Press, 2013), loc. 29 of 549, Kindle Edition.

yet to solve. They can account for the change within species
but have no evidence, only assumptions, about one species
evolving into another.

DAY 247

HANS URS VON BALTHASAR (1905–1988)

An omnipresent fragrance—

"The world as it concretely exists is one that is always already
related either positively or negatively to the God of grace and
supernatural revelation. There are no neutral points or sur-
faces in this relationship. The world, considered as an object
of knowledge, is always already embedded in this supernatural
sphere, and, in the same way, man's cognitive powers operate
under the positive sign of faith or under the negative sign of
unbelief. Of course, insofar as it works in a relative abstract-
ness that prescinds from creaturely nature's embedding in the
supernatural, philosophy can indeed highlight certain fundamental structures of the world and knowledge, because this
embedding does not do away with, or even alter the essential
core, of such structures. Nevertheless, the closer philosophy
comes to the concrete object and the more fully it makes use
of the concrete knowing powers, the more theological data it
also incorporates, either implicitly or explicitly. After all, the

supernatural takes root in the deepest structures of being, leavens them through and through, and permeates them like a breath or an omnipresent fragrance. It is not only impossible, it would be sheer folly to attempt at all costs to banish and uproot this fragrance of supernatural truth from philosophical inquiry; the supernatural has impregnated nature so deeply that there is simply no way to reconstruct it in its pure state (*natura pura*) [pure nature.]"[250]

Theo-Logic, Volume I, 1985

For Han Urs von Balthasar, the idea of pure nature is a philosophical construct which does not exist in reality. We speak of the natural but forget there is no nature that is not embedded in the "supernatural sphere." As the philosopher moves beyond the false notion of nature, he will make use, knowingly or not, of theology. Von Balthasar creates a marvelous image, or should it be said "scent," of the supernatural as an "omnipresent fragrance." Could he have had in mind Gerard Manley Hopkins, who wrote, "And for all this, nature is never spent; / There lives the dearest freshness deep down things."

---

250 Hans Urs von Balthasar, *Theo-Logic, Volume 1; The Truth of the World: Theological Logical Theory: The Spirit of Truth*, trans. Adrian J. Walker (San Francisco: Ignatius Press, 2000), 11–12.

DAY 248

MSGR. RONALD KNOX (1888–1957)

The vice of pantheism—

"We must not conceal from ourselves the fact that in so defining the Nature of God as transcendent, omnipotent, and personal, we have parted company with a great number of the more religiously affected of mankind. We have said nothing, so far, which could not be echoed by a Jew or by a Mohammedan. But we have quarreled, already, with that pantheistic conception of the Divine Being which has had such a profound influence on other religions of the East. The vice of Pantheism is that its theology takes Life, not Spirit, as its point of departure. Dichotomising the world (wrongly) into matter and life, the Pantheist assumes that the animal organism is the mirror of the universe. As, in the animal, matter finds a principle of life to organize it, so the whole sum of matter in existence must have a Life to organize it, a Life which is the summing up of all the life (vegetable or animal) which exists. This Life is God; God is to the world what the soul (in the widest sense) is to the body. Thus, on the one hand, the Pantheist theology contrives to give an explanation of existence which is no explanation at all; for the totality of our experience plus a World-Soul does not, by reason of the addition, provide any account of how or why it came into existence. And on the other hand it encumbers our thought with the concept of a God who is no God;

who is, indeed, but an abstraction, as animal life divorced from matter is an abstraction; who can neither affect our destinies, nor prescribe our conduct, nor claim our worship; impotent, unmoral, and only demanding by courtesy the typographical compliment of a capital G."[251]

The Belief of Catholics, 1927

Msgr. Ronald Knox takes apart the claim of pantheism that God and the world are the same. Some pantheists take this literally, others nuance their pantheism with the notion that God inhabits the world. In either case, Knox argues pantheism is one more abstraction that offers the presence of religiosity without making any demands on our lives. A pantheist does not worship, unless in the most contrived sense. A pantheist does not possess moral rules or commandments by which the quality of one's life may be measured. Self-proclaimed pantheists who achieve actual spirituality, such as the poet Walt Whitman, must burst the pantheist's boundaries.

---

251 Ronald Knox, *The Belief of Catholics* (Victoria, BC: Reading Essentials), loc. 790 of 2920, Kindle Edition.

DAY 249

MORLEY CALLAGHAN (1903–1990)

In the novel Such Is My Beloved, *a young priest, Father Dowling, is sent to a parish in a rundown part of the city during the Great Depression. When he meets two prostitutes on the street, Midge and Olsen, his first instinct is to try to help them find other jobs. They explain that prostitution became the only option when they couldn't secure other jobs in a depressed economy. Father Dowling suddenly realizes—*

"Somehow, he himself had always thought of vice as yielding to the delights of the flesh, as warmth and good soft living and laziness, but as he looked around this room and at these angry girls he felt close to a dreadful poverty that was without any dignity." Father goes to various members of the parish to find them work—none want former prostitutes working them. Then he goes to the wealthiest family in the parish, the Robinsons, and he takes both ladies. "I must say, Father, I don't thank you for bringing street walkers into my house," she [Mrs. Robinson] informs him. "And I can hardly compliment you, Madam, on the charitable way you received them." She finds his effrontery "too scandalous to be believed." The young cleric counters, "And I've been more scandalized in this house to-night than I've ever been in my life." Mrs. Robinson tells Father he should realize "all prostitutes are feeble-minded," to

which Father Dowling replies, "That's a sociological point of view. It's not a Christian point of view."[252]

Such Is My Beloved, 1974

Morley Callaghan was a major Catholic writer of the twentieth century, but because he was Canadian, his work receives far less attention than it deserves. Born in Toronto in 1903, he graduated from the University of Toronto and Osgood Hall Law School. He never practiced law but became known as a master stylist in short stories and novels. *Strange Fugitive* (1929) was his first novel of thirteen, and *A Wild Man On the Road* (1988), his last. A great friend of Hemingway, Callaghan wrote a delightful memoir, *That Summer in Paris: Memories of Tangled Friendships with Hemingway, Fitzgerald and Some Others* (1963), featuring a famous boxing match between himself and Hemingway. Callaghan, an experienced fighter, put the braggadocious Hemingway on his back and won the fight. His several volumes of short stories rival Hemingway but do not surpass him. All Callaghan's work bears the mark of the author's faith that contributed, no doubt, to his psychological and penetrating portrayal of his characters.

---

252 Morley Callaghan, *Such Is My Beloved* (Toronto: The New Canadian Library, 1989), 185–86.

DAY 250

JOHN EMERICH EDWARD DALBERG-ACTON, 1ST BARON ACTON (1834–1902)

Christian liberty—

Acton considers the temporal power of the Roman pontiff in the context of modern revolutions.

"There is a wide divergence, an irreconcilable disagreement, between the political notions of the modern world and that which is essentially the system of the Catholic Church. It manifests itself particularly in their contradictory views of liberty, and of the functions of the civil power. *The Catholic notion, defining liberty not as the power of doing what we like, but the right of being able to do what we ought, denies that general interests can supersede individual rights.* It condemns, therefore, the theory of the ancient as well as of the modern state. It is founded on the divine origin and nature of authority. According to the prevailing doctrine, which derives power from the people, and deposits it ultimately in their hands, the state is omnipotent over the individual, whose only remnant of freedom is then the participation in the exercise of supreme power; while the general will is binding on him. Christian liberty is lost where this system prevails: whether in the form of the utmost diffusion of power, as in America, or of the utmost concentration of power, as in France; whether, that is to say, it is exercised by

the majority, or by the delegate of the majority, — it is always a delusive freedom, founded on a servitude more or less disguised."[253] (Emphasis added.)

"The Roman Question," 1860

Lord Acton was a monarchist who distrusted democracy, government based on the "will of the people." His view is that Catholicism is always on the side of a free person conforming himself to God's will. In other words, both the rule of the ancient tyrants and modern democracy claims authority over an individual's exercise of freedom. Christianity seeks to preserve human dignity, the foundation of freedom and human rights. We live in an era in which Catholics and their beliefs are being marginalized by the media, the academy, and the courts. Lord Action has a point, to be sure. Both tyrants and elected legislators can exert themselves to quash religious practice and belief. The Church must oppose this.

---

253 John Dalberg-Acton, "The Roman Questions," *The Rambler* (January 1860).

DAY 251

SIGRID UNDSET (1882–1949)

Love and hate—

"All this talk about love being stronger than hate, and about good always triumphing over evil in the end and so on, is sheer nonsense—when it is a question of natural love and purely human goodness; although natural human love is a mighty power, and mere pagan goodness has shown itself to be a great and glorious and beautiful thing, an infinite number of times. Nevertheless it has been forced over and over to yield to evil— fear and hatred and revolt against our earthly lot are the things which impel the natural man to his greatest displays of energy."[254]

"The Strongest Power," 1939

Sigrid Undset, the author of *Kristin Lavransdatter* (1922), will have nothing to do with the old adage "love conquers all." Human love is fallible, she says, and subject to the temptations of the world. Undset experienced that herself in her marriage, but she does not talk with bitterness but with a realism that can forewarn and protect the innocent. Love is often glorious, the most treasured of human experiences, but when it breaks

---

254 Sigrid Undset, "The Strongest Power," trans. Arthur G. Chater (New York: Alfred E. Knopf, 1939), 163.

down either among friends or family, the pain is enormous. Only the love of God can be counted upon.

DAY 252

GUSTAV HERLING (1919–2000)

A writer at prayer—

"Every authentic piece of writing ultimately takes the form of prayer, I am convinced of that. A prayer in the broadest sense, let us say, is the equivalent of submitting questions to the Creator. However, an authentic writer—believer or not, on his knees with his head humbly bowed or on his feet with the glint of challenge in his eyes—should not be conscious of the fact that prayer is flowing through his voice like an underground stream, sometimes clearly audible and sometimes muffled or totally soundless. When he is aware of it, prayer becomes a form of literature, generally bad literature. A few days ago, to prepare for a trip to Assisi that was proposed for various reasons, I read Julien Green's book about St. Francis [*God's Fool*, 1985]. It is, indeed, prayer in the form of literature."[255]

Diary entry, January 14, 1985

255 Gustav Herling, *Volcano and Miracle: A Selection of Fiction and Nonfiction From The journal Written at Night*, trans. and selected by Ronald Strom (New York: Viking Penguin, 1996), 166.

Gustav Herling, who spent two years in a Soviet prison camp, experienced writing as a kind of prayer. Good writing, he says, shouldn't be so much a conscious act as it flows "like an underground stream" from within the writer. If a writer becomes self-conscious, prayer stops "flowing through his voice" and mere literature is the result. As readers, we can be aware of the difference between writers who seem to be speaking from somewhere outside of themselves and those who, however brilliant, say only what they already know. (In a personal letter to me, Julien Green admitted that he had the feeling of "being helped" as he wrote about St. Francis.) Born in Southern Poland, Gustav Herling-Grudzinski studied neo-Thomism and Polish literature at the University of Warsaw, and after witnessing the German invasion, he helped to form an anti-Nazi resistance in Warsaw. After the Soviets moved in to take over Eastern Poland, Herling was arrested by the Soviet secret police, accused of being a German spy, and imprisoned. After being tortured, he was sent to a forced-labor camp in Kargopol. Once released in 1942, he fought with the Polish army in the famous battle of Monte Cassino and received Poland's highest military honor. But it was his 1951 memoir, *A World Apart*, an account of his prison experience, that made Herling known throughout the world. One reviewer said its intensity surpassed Dostoevsky; another called it a masterpiece that should be read for its humanity.

DAY 253

JULIEN GREEN (1900–1988)

Be without care—

> "The contemplative life is almost impossible to summarize in a few sentences. Without risking any confused explanations, one might propose this minimal statement: Contemplation asks the individual to leave himself behind, to give way to God and be united with him. As far as I can see, it's not simply a matter of giving up habits that pose an obstacle to the inner life, but of breaking away from the cares of the world in solitude and silence, of driving away what the seventeenth century called diversion, in all its forms, whatever the eyes can see, the ears hear, and the senses experience."[256]

God's Fool, 1985

The novelist Julien Green, in his biography of St. Francis, characterizes contemplation as a state completely free from diversion and the press of daily chores. Life in a digitalized world has put diversion in our pockets, and hands, in the form of portable phones which double as carry-around computers. How much of the time we spend looking at a screen is mere diversion? Contemplation, thus, requires being untethered

---

256 Julian Green, *God's Fool: The Life and Times of Francis of Assisi*, trans. Peter Heinegg (New York: Harper & Row, Publishers, 1985), 142.

from the virtual world, allowing the mind to quiet down and "give way to God."

DAY 254

ADRIENNE VON SPEYR (1902–1967)

A familial unity—

"Man, woman, and child according to God's plan; and even the concrete instance of a particular family, they are a unity of thought and willed by God. The woman is intended by God for this particular man, and this particular child is reserved to them. And so in God's plan the child is the unity of the parents, even though, in the physical world of time, he merely slumbers potentially within them, who bear him within them separately. Potentially the *one* child is already present in both of them. He forms their potential unity. In begetting and birth, they bring forth the child as a real unity by surrendering what made them one in God and realizing that unity in the form of the child given them by God, thus taking back their unity unto the grace of marriage. This unity was sent forth that it might be realized; it was surrendered to God, and that is why it is the parent's duty to allow their unity to become fruitful in God, giving fruit to God. That means that they must give their

child to the Church and to the community of those belonging to God."[257]

The Word Made Flesh, 1949

For Adrienne von Speyr, marriages and families are not accidental. The spouses of each individual woman and man are known to God in advance. Their offspring is also known to God because the in unity of husband and wife, the potentiality of a child is present. That child completes the unity pronounced with the sacrament of marriage. The child is the gift of God bringing wholeness to their union. It is, therefore, appropriate that the parents offer the fruit of their union to the Church, "to the community of those belonging to God."

DAY 255

JOSEF PIEPER (1904–1997)

Faceless sex—

"What makes this consumer sex without *eros* so ugly and so inhuman is essentially this: it empties the love encounter of

---

257 Adrienne Von Speyr, *Water and Spirit: Meditations on Saint John's Gospel 1:9 —5:47*, trans. Sr. Lucia Wiedenhover, O.C.D. (San Francisco: Ignatius Press, 2019), 100.

its inner significance without the larger framework of human existence, its essence of stepping out from self-centered limitation by opening up to—and becoming one with—another person. A mere partner in *sex*, however, the other is not looked upon as a person, a living human being with an individual human face. An American author has described this reality with the tongue-in-cheek yet accurate observation that from a playboy's point of view the fig leaf has simply been transferred—it more conceals the human face. . . . The man who merely lusts after a woman does not, indeed, really desire 'a woman,' in spite of the words."[258]

Uber die Liebe, 1972

Josef Pieper describes sex without love as two persons objectifying the other—they become faceless in an act God designed to be the most intimate form of human union. The word *eros* is used as the root of the word *erotic*, which has become synonymous with self-gratifying desire. Pieper uses *eros* in its ancient and biblical sense as the natural desire for that which is good. In faceless sex, a man, for example, doesn't want a true woman in all her complexity and beauty as created by God and has no interest in her desire or well-being. *Degrading* is exactly the right word!

---

258 Josef Pieper, *Josef Pieper: An Anthology*, foreword by Hans Urs von Balthasar (San Franciso: Ignatius Press, 1989), 40-41.

DAY 256

PAUL CLAUDEL (1868–1955)

The vocation of the artist—

"Visible things must not be sundered from things invisible. Both together make up the Universe of God and have mutual relationships clear or mysterious; indeed, the Apostle tells us that by the one we are guided to a knowledge of the others. Science is concerned only with 'things visible.' Her business is to go from the effect to the cause, from one material thing to another material thing; from the fact to the measurement. Her concern is with what things are, not what they signify. Of human faculties it utilizes principally the reason—reason fed by memory, and stimulated by the imagination. It is a power of ascertaining, not a power of creation. Science endeavors to classify, to systematize, and to utilize what is round about us, and thus she has no need to bring into play all the faculties of the human mind, soul, and body, intelligence and heart. It is quite a different matter to see a thing and to do it. And the proper domain of Art and Poetry is, as its name connotes, to *make*. Out of a thing perceived by sense, man makes something which reading can understand and feeling can enjoy; of a material thing he makes a spiritual entity. To give the word its full meaning for our mind for our senses, Poetry is, as you say in English, the power which fully realizes beings—which transmutes them into realities. In order to know a thing you

have only to understand what it is, but to make a thing you have to understand how it is made, and to understand how it is made, you must understand the end for which it has been made, its relationship with other beings, and the Idea of Him Who in the beginning made all."[259]

"Religion and Poetry," 1927

Paul Claudel is considered by many literary scholars as the most important Catholic poet of modernity. Claudel excelled as a poet, playwright, literary critic, essayist, and the writer of memoirs. Critic George Steiner called him one of three "masters of drama" in the twentieth century. His plays, like his poetry, are clearly Catholic but always challenging even to the pious readers—one is about Our Lady, *The Tidings Brought to Mary* (1910), another is about Satan, the seven-hour long *The Satin Slipper* (1930). His play on Joan of Arc was first performed with Ingrid Bergman in the title role and then set to music as an oratorio by Arthur Honegger. Among his poetry, the "Five Great Odes" are the most celebrated. During much of his writing career, Claudel also served as an outstanding diplomat to Brazil, China, Japan, New York, and Boston. Paul Claudel deserves to be better known by Catholics in the English-speaking world.

---

259 Paul Claudel, *Ways and Crossways*, trans. Rev. John O'Connor (Port Washington: Kennikat Press, 1968), 4–5.

DAY 257

ROMANO GUARDINI (1885–1968)

Man the creator—

"The Middle Ages had wrought a world of beauty, a social order of magnificence; they had fashioned a culture of the highest reach. But everything that medieval man achieved was understood by him in light of the service he owed to God and to God's creation. With the Renaissance new meaning came both to the work of man and to the worker himself; meaning and value for both artist and artifact were found solely within themselves. Prior to the Renaissance only the Work of God had an absolute meaning; after the Renaissance the world ceased to be the Creation of God. It had become the work of Nature. Similarly the work of man ceased to be an act of obedience to God's ordained service; it became a 'creation' in itself. Previously a worshipper and a servant, man now took to himself the prerogatives of a 'creator.'"[260]

The End of the Modern World, 1950

The Renaissance is usually praised as the era in Western civilization when men and women began discovering the richness of their humanity and began exerting their own desires

---

260 Romano Guardini, *The End of the Modern World*, trans. Joseph Theman and Herbert Burke (Chicago: Henry Regnery Company, 1961), 59.

beyond the limits imposed upon them by the rule of kings and popes. This cannot be denied, but with this shift of human self-understanding, Guardini sees a fundamental loss of faith in God as Creator and God as the source of meaning for human existence. Guardini speaks, of course, in generalizations; he knows as well as any the exceptions to this first step in secularization. But the exceptions were too few to keep civilization from declaring itself "creator."

DAY 258

EVELYN WAUGH (1903–1966)

The power to survive—

"Today we can see it on all sides as the active negation of all that Western culture has stood for. Civilization—and by this I do not mean talking cinemas and tinned food, nor even surgery and hygienic houses, but the whole moral and artistic organization of Europe—has not in itself the power of survival. It came into being through Christianity, and without it has no significance or power to command allegiance. The loss of faith in Christianity and the consequential lack of confidence in moral and social standards have become embodied in the ideal of a materialistic, mechanized state. . . . It is no longer possible

. . . to accept the benefits of civilization and at the same time deny the supernatural basis upon which it rests."[261]

"Why It Happened to Me," October, 20, 1930

The conversion of the writer Evelyn Waugh, who was a "Jazz Age" celebrity in the United Kingdom, required him to write a front page column about "why." It had been on his mind for years since he gave up on Anglicanism and frolicked through his years at Oxford and as a young journalist and novelist in London. His first novel, *Decline and Fall* (1928), had been a great success, and the same year, he had married Evelyn Gardner. However, the following year, he found out that Evelyn had taken a lover, and he filed for divorce. His second novel, *Vile Bodies* (1930), was a pointed satire on the same group of people, the "Bright Young Things," with whom he had identified. Waugh was disappointed and depressed, but a friend who was a Catholic convert, Olivia Plunket-Greene, introduced Waugh to Father Martin D'Arcy. Waugh's conversion was an embrace of the religion that created Europe and which made life endurable and intelligible.

---

261 Evelyn Waugh, "Why It Happened to Me," *Daily Express*, October, 20, 1930; read at https://resurgimientocatolico.files.wordpress.com/2014/05/waugh-daily-express.pdf.

DAY 259

BLAISE PASCAL (1623–1662)

The motive of all—

"All men seek happiness. There are no exceptions. However different the means they may employ, they all strive towards this goal. The reason why some go to war and some do not is the same desire in both, but interpreted in two different ways. The will never takes the least step except to that end. This is the motive of every act of every man, including those who go and who hang themselves. Yet for very many years no one without faith has ever reached the goal at which everyone is continually aiming. All men complain: princes, subjects, nobles, commoners, old, young, strong, weak, learned, ignorant, healthy, sick, in every country, at every time, of all ages, and all conditions. A test which has gone on so long, without pause or change, really ought to convince us that we are incapable of attaining the good by our own efforts. But example teaches us very little. No two examples are so exactly alike that there is not some subtle difference, and that is what makes us expect that our expectations will not be disappointed this time as they were last time. So, while the present never satisfies us, experience deceives us, and leads us on from one misfortune

to another until death comes as the ultimate and eternal climax."[262]

Pensées, 1662

Blaise Pascal is good on the subject of human folly. He asks why we do not learn from our mistakes, and the mistakes we observe in others, in seeking happiness. He answers: the human mind, always seeking to protect our self-deceptions, finds in the examples of failure "some subtle difference" that keeps us from drawing a general lesson. It's useful to keep in mind that those who want the most to appear seeking the good are often the most susceptible to self-deception, the refusal to recognize what failure has to teach. Such people are so concerned about their appearance to others they will allow themselves to rot on the inside.

---

262 Blaise Pascal, *Pensées*, trans. and introduction by A. J. Krailsheimer (New York: Penguin Books, 1984), 74-75.

DAY 260

HILAIRE BELLOC (1870–1953)

Grief and immortality—

In a letter to a friend after the death of her fourteen-year-old daughter, Belloc wrote:

> "Human beings can rely permanently on doctrine, much as a man who has fallen into the water can rely upon his foothold when he has put his feet on the ground and knows that the depth is not enough to drown him. Doctrine is much drier than emotion and it is difficult to understand its full value today because the world has come to depend wholly on emotion for its creed and its values. For my part I am convinced that doctrine is meat and drink; I mean by doctrine that the core of Catholic truth which is not to be referred to as experience and not confirmed by experience—*the doctrine of immortality is of this kind.*"[263] (Emphasis added.)

Letter of January 28, 1941

The letter of Hilaire Belloc to a friend grieving from the loss of her child is surprising: it contains nothing personal or

---

263 Hilaire Belloc, *The Essential Belloc: A Prophet for Our Times*, eds. Rev. C. Mc-Closkey, Scott J. Bloch, Brian Robertson (Charlotte: Saint Benedict Press, 2010), 222.

emotional; the usual sentimentality of such notes is completely missing. Belloc's form of consolation is doctrinal—he reminds the mother about the doctrine of immortality. The message is straightforward: your daughter has left earthly life, but she lives in eternity so stop your sniffling! He knows that doctrine is "much drier than emotion," but he also claims that "the world has come to depend wholly on emotion for its creed and its values." Thus, the lack of emotion in his letter is deliberate. Belloc wants the doctrine of immortality to quell, at least in part, his friend's suffering.

DAY 261

ALLEN TATE (1899–1979)

One lost truth—

"The man of letters has, then, in our time a small but critical service to render to man: a service that will be in the future more effective than it is now, when the cult of the literary man shall have ceased to be an idolatry. Men of letters and their followers, like the parvenu gods and their votaries of decaying Rome, compete in the dissemination of distraction and novelty. But the true province of the man of letters is nothing less (as it is nothing more) than culture itself. The state is the mere operation of society, but culture is the way society

lives, the material medium through which *men receive the one lost truth which must be perpetually recovered*: the truth of what Jacques Maritain calls the 'supra-temporal destiny' of man."[264] (Emphasis added.)

"The Man of Letters in the Modern World," 1952

Allen Tate has the right words to explain the importance of culture: "culture is the way society lives" and a "material medium." We live and breathe our culture every day without being aware of it. Customs, manners, values, attitudes, and affections, all are to a great extent scripted in us by our culture. Tate views "the Men of Letters" as those whose mission it is to use culture to deliver "the lone lost truth which must be perpetually recovered . . . the "supra-temporal destiny of man." Don't let the elitist sound of "Men of Letters" put you off: it was an accepted way of talking about writers in his day.

---

264 Allan Tate, *Essays of Four Decades*, (New York: William Morrow and Company, Inc., 1970), 22.

DAY 262

FLANNERY O'CONNOR (1925–1964)

The realist of distances—

"The fiction writer should be characterized by his kind of vision. His kind of vision is prophetic vision. Prophecy, which is dependent on the imaginative and not the moral faculty, need not be a matter of predicting the future. *The prophet is a realist of distances*, and it is this kind of realism that goes into great novels. It is the realism which does not hesitate to distort appearances in order to show the hidden truth. In the Catholic novelist, the prophetic vision is not simply a matter of his personal imaginative gift: it is also a matter of the Church's gift, which, unlike his own, is safeguarded and deals with greater matters. It is one of the functions of the Church to transmit the prophetic vision that is good for all time, and when the novelist has this as a part of his own vision, he has a powerful extension of thought."[265] (Emphasis added.)

"Catholic Novelists and Their Readers," 1963

Flannery O'Connor is sometimes referred to as an author of the "grotesque." Many of her characters say and do things that

---

265 Flannery O'Connor, *Mystery and Manners: Occasional Prose*, ed., and selected by Sally and Robert Fitzgerald (New York: Farrar, Straus and Giroux, 1975), 179-180.

are disgusting, unsettling, and completely unpredictable—their character is morally vacuous, lopsided, or turned upside down. In her short story "Good Country People" (1955), a Bible-salesman, Manley Pointer, has dinner with Mrs. Hopewell and her atheist daughter Joy, who has a doctorate in philosophy. He invites the daughter, who has changed her name to "Hulga," on a date the following evening. That evening, he takes Hulga into a loft in the barn where he talks her into removing her prosthetic leg. Manley then tries to seduce her. She refuses his advances. At this point, he stands up and starts to leave with her leg, explaining that he collects prostheses and doesn't believe in God at all. One grotesque meets another, and the point is made that Joy's academic knowledge did not protect her from a predator who successfully treated her as an object, carrying away her leg because of her refusal to have sex.

DAY 263

ALICE THOMAS ELLIS (1932–2004)

Precious quality of being "me"—

"It has infiltrated most areas of everyday life, but its most damaging effect is perhaps its insistence, derived in part from psychoanalysis, on the precious quality of ME. You must love and trust yourself, prescribe the practitioners, and then everyone

will proceed to love and trust you. This is demonstrably untrue and a cruel distortion and simplification of the case. The advice is not that you should strive to be a better person but that you are already implicitly godlike. The Christian position is that we are made in His image and are members of the Body of Christ. . . . Thinking that I should familiarize myself to some extent with more tenets of the New Age, I went out and spent good money on a few books dealing with these matters. I wished I hadn't. Reading them, incredulity gave way to mirth, and mirth to depression. In their blind subjectivity they are like a sort of pornography of the mind: exaggerated, bizarre and ultimately inhuman, dealing as they do with unreal and unanswerable desires—horrid fantasies of darkness represented as the path to fulness and enlightenment."[266]

The Serpent on the Rock, 1985

The takeaway from this Alice Thomas Ellis excerpt is her description of New Age books as "as a sort of pornography of the mind: exaggerated, bizarre and ultimately in human." For Ellis, the tenets of New Age echo the promise of the snake in the Garden of Eden, "you shall be as gods" (see Gn 3:5). The opposite, in fact, happened, but the New Agers haven't noticed that, still repeating the promise that convinced Eve to eat fruit from the forbidden tree and offer it to Adam.

---

266 Alice Thomas Ellis, *The Serpent on the Rock: A Personal View of Christianity* (London: Trafalgar Square, 1985), 191.

DAY 264

CHARLES PÉGUY (1873–1914)

Holy war is everywhere—

"Our faiths are citadels.—The least among us is a soldier. The least among us is literally a crusader. Our fathers like a flood of people, like a flood of armies, invaded the infidel continents. Nowadays, on the contrary, it is a flood of infidelity that holds the seas, the high seas, and that continuously assails us from all sides. All our houses are fortresses, *in periculo Maris*, in peril of the sea. The holy war is everywhere. It is ever being waged.— All of us stand on the breach today. We are all stationed at the frontier. The frontier is everywhere."[267]

Basic Verities, c. 1912

Charles Péguy lost his life in a WWI trench serving for France. Here he describes every Christian as a soldier standing "in the breach" against the armies of unbelief. He is not speaking hyperbolically; he intended his reader to view this war as a spiritual reality. Christians stand guard at the frontier, and "The frontier is everywhere." A half-century before, the poet Matthew Arnold had issued a similar warning in his poem "Dover Beach":

---

267 Charles Péguy, *Basic Veritites: Prose and Poetry*, trans. Ann and Julian Green (New York: Pantheon Books, Inc., 1943), 177.

The Sea of Faith
Was once, too, at the full, and round earth's shore
Lay like the folds of a bright girdle furled.
But now I only hear
Its melancholy, long, withdrawing roar,
Retreating, to the breath
Of the night-wind, down the vast edges drear
And naked shingles of the world.

DAY 265

THOMAS MERTON (1915–1968)

At peace with loneliness—

"The man who fears to be alone will never be anything but lonely, no matter how much he may surround himself with people. But the man who learns, in solitude and recollection, to be at peace with his own loneliness, and to prefer its reality to the illusion of merely natural companionship, comes to know the invisible companionship of God. Such a one is alone with God in all places, and he alone truly enjoys the companionship of other men, because he loves them in God in Whom

their presence is not tiresome, and because of Whom his own love for them can never know satiety."[268]

No Man Is an Island, 1955

In the seventeenth century, Blaise Pascal wrote, "All of man's misfortune comes from one thing, which is not knowing how to sit quietly in a room." The monk Thomas Merton knows solitude even more intimately. In solitude, Merton explains, we learn not simply how to be alone and at peace but to transform the relationships we have with others. To be at peace in solitude means to "know the invisible companionship of God." Our love for others is directed towards God rather than to our own needs and desires. This is the answer to those who wonder what good it does for a monk to spend so much time alone.

DAY 266

JOSEF PIEPER (1904–1997)

How good it is that you exist—

"What matters to us, beyond mere existence, is the explicit confirmation: it is *good* that you exist: how wonderful that you

---

268 Thomas Merton. *No Man Is an Island* (HMH Books, 1955), loc. 228-229, Kindle Edition.

are! In other words, what we need over and above sheer existence is: to be loved by another person. That is an astonishing
fact when we consider it closely. Being created by God actually does not suffice, it would seem, the fact of creation needs
continuation. . . . We say a person 'blossoms' when undergoing
the experience of being loved; that he becomes wholly himself
for the first time; that a 'new life' is beginning for him—and
so forth. For a child, and to all appearances even for the still
unborn child, being loved by the mother is literally the pre-
condition for its own thriving. This maternal love need not
necessarily be 'materialized' in specific acts of benevolence.
What is at any rate more decisive is that concern and approval
which are given from the very core existence—we need not
hesitate to say, which comes from the heart, of the child. Only
such concern and approval do we call real 'love.'"[269]

Uber die Liebe, 1972

Josef Pieper probes deeply into the gift which is true love. The
lover is saying, "I consider it marvelous that you exist." This
marvel experienced by the lover does not remain subjective
but activates a wishing and willing the good of the beloved. In
this way, the love of another can spur the "blossoming" because
the beloved has concrete evidence of his or her worth. It's part
of the human condition to be plagued by doubts about our

---

269 Josef Pieper, *Josef Pieper: An Anthology*, foreword by Hans Urs von Balthasar
(San Francisco: Ignatius Press, 1989), 30-31.

worth, especially how we are regarded by others. But when love is declared by one of those "others," it injects confidence and hope that good lies in the future.

DAY 267

PAUL CLAUDEL (1868–1955)

Saint Joseph

> When the tools are put in their places and the day's
>   work is done,
> When between Carmel and the Jordan, Israel falls
>   asleep in the wheat fields and the night,
> As when he was once a young boy and it began to get
>   too dark for reading,
> Joseph enters with a deep sigh into conversation with
>   God.
> He preferred Wisdom and she had been brought to him
>   for marriage.
> He is as silent as the earth when the dew rises,
> He feels the fullness of night, and he is at ease with
>   joy and with truth.
> Mary is in his possession and he surrounds her on all
>   sides.

It is not in a single day that he learned how not to be
    alone any more.
A woman won over each part of his heart which is now
    prudent and fatherly.
Again he is in Paradise with Eve!
The face which all men need turns with love and sub-
    mission toward Joseph.
It is no longer the same prayer and no longer the
    ancient waiting since he has felt
Like an arm suddenly without hate the pressure of this
    profound and innocent being.
It is no longer bare Faith in the night, it is love ex-
    plaining and working.
Joseph is with Mary and Mary is with the Father.
And for us too, so that God at last may be allowed,
    whose works surpass our reason,
So that this light may not be extinguishable by our lamp
    and His word by the noise we make,
So that man cease, and Your Kingdom come and Your
    Will be done,
So that we may find again the beginning with bound-
    less delight,
So that the sea may quiet down and Mary begin,
She who has the better part and who consummates
    the struggle of ancient Israel,

Inner Patriarch, Joseph, obtain silence for us![270]

Translated by Wallace Fowlie

Paul Claudel pays tribute to the often-neglected St. Joseph. For Claudel, it is Joseph's silence that evinces his sanctity: "He is as silent as the earth when the dew rises," an image suggesting a silence of awakening, new birth, and healing. Joseph is not troubled by his wife's condition, having received the angel's assurances, "he is at ease with joy and with truth." Joseph's silence overcomes "the noise we make. . . . So that we may find again the beginning with boundless delight." It's no wonder the poet Claudel concludes with a prayer to St. Joseph that he "obtain silence for us!" Claudel was the most important Catholic poet of the first half of the twentieth century, but his achievement not only in poetry but also in theatre, apologetics, and biblical commentary is known to very few in the English-speaking Catholic world.

---

270 https://www.poetryfoundation.org/poetrymagazine/browse?volume=87&issue=3&page=11.

DAY 268

ROY CAMPBELL (1901–1962)

Purveyors of hate—

"The artist as romantic 'rebel' is the tamest mule imaginable. He dates from the industrial era and has been politicized to play into the hands of the great syndicates and cartels first by dogmatizing immorality, breaking up the 'Family', that one defensive unit that has withstood the whole effort of centuries to enslave, dehumanize and mechanize the individual, there cheapening and multiplying labour. . . . The last century has seen more class wars, and wars between generations, than any other period. They had been deliberately misled by capitalism, of which bolshevism is merely an anonymous form. 'Divide and rule,' said Cato: 'encourage your slaves to quarrel and your authority will be supreme. A thousand artists and reformers with the highest ideals have leaped ignorantly and romantically into these rackets, and by means of carrying hate between man and woman, father and son, class and class, white and black, almost irretrievably embroiled the human individual in profit-less, exhausting struggles which leave him at the mercy of the unscrupulous few."[271]

"Uys Krige: A Portrait," 1935

---

271 Joseph Pearce, *Bloomsbury and Beyond: The Friends and Enemies of Roy Campbell* (London, HarperCollinsPublishers, 2001), 173–74.

Roy Campbell was a poet whose translations of St. John of the Cross remain unsurpassed. No wonder a man of his Catholic sensibility would find nothing of value in the self-ordained rebel artist. Campbell takes his critique in a surprising direction, arguing those rebels who attack traditional morality, marriage, and the family are creating a mindless, rootless working class that will serve the captains of industry with a minimum of complaint. Why stand up for your dignity and rights if you don't really believe they exist anymore?

DAY 269

MALCOLM MUGGERIDGE (1903–1990)

In this interview, Muggeridge was asked about his claim that civilization itself is coming to an end. He answers—

"Yes, and the Dark Age is likely to intervene anyway. It is very unusual for one moral order to slide into another with no intervening chaos. There are many other symptoms. The excessive interest in eroticism is characteristic of the end of a civilization, because it really means a growing impotence, and a fear of impotence. Then the obsessive need for excitement, vicarious excitement, which of course the games provided for the Romans, and which television provides for our population. Even the enormously complicated structure of taxation

and administration is, funnily enough, a symptom of the end of a civilization; these things become so elaborate that in the end they become insupportable because of their very elaboration. Above all, there is this truly terrible thing which afflicts materialist societies—boredom; an obsessive boredom, which I note on every hand. Mine is, admittedly, a minority view; a lot of people think that we are just on the verge of a new marvelous way of life. I see no signs of it at all myself. I notice that where our way of life is most successful materially it is most disastrous morally and spiritually; that the psychiatric wards are the largest and most crowded, and the suicides most numerous, precisely where material prosperity is greatest, where most money is spent on education. I don't regard this at all as a gloomy point of view. . . . Consider our actual circumstances at this moment: We have made ourselves so strong that we can destroy ourselves. . . . Our corner of the world is getting richer, to the point that its main preoccupation is to stimulate consumption by all sorts of asinine means, while the rest of the world is getting poorer and hungrier. And the only answer we can produce is that there are too many of the others. Our ultimate offering to our less fortunate brethren is what? A contraceptive! I don't think any civilization has ever produced such a contemptible product as its major offering to the world."[272]

Interview with Roy Trevivian, 1968

---

272 Malcolm Muggeridge, *Seeing Through the Eye: Malcolm Muggeridge on Faith* (San Francisco: Ignatius Press 2005), loc. 4216-4242 of 4484, Kindle Edition; Reprinted from Malcolm Muggeridge, *Jesus Rediscovered* (Garden City, Doubleday, 1969), 181-235.

Malcolm Muggeridge predicts a new Dark Age, the original version of which was actually a time in Western history when religious belief, morality, and culture were stored by the monks in their monasteries. His comment on contraceptives is worth pondering and sharing with others.

DAY 270

PAUL JOHNSON (1928–)

Modern paganism—

"So it has been in the twentieth century. Its horrors were instrumental in turning men and women towards God rather than against him. Most people saw the wars as themselves the products of Godlessness, materialism and sin, and their perpetrators as those who had banished God from their hearts. And it is undeniable that the two greatest institutional tyrannies of the century—indeed of all time—the Nazi Reich and the Soviet Union, were Godless constructs: modern paganism in the first case and openly proclaimed atheistic materialism in the second. The death-camps and the slave-camps were products not of God but of anti-God. Hitler was born and brought up Roman Catholic and Stalin was once a Russian Orthodox apprentice-monk, but it is hard to imagine any two men in history who were more bereft of basic Christian instincts or

more systematically committed to the destruction of Christian values."[273]

The Quest for God, 2009

Paul Johnson presents a paradox. On the one hand, he argues the death camps of Stalin and Hitler turned many back to belief in God. On the other, Johnson reminds us that both Hitler and Stalin were raised in religious homes, Catholic and Russian Orthodox. In the case of Stalin, he spent years being educated in a seminary considering a vocation to the priesthood. Yet each of them sought to eradicate Christianity from their empires. It's true, as Johnson claims, they were not successful, not only because of conversions, but even more so because of those who clung to their faiths more tightly as a result of persecution. However, it should be said that the innate religiosity of the Russian and German peoples was crushed; in the case of the Germans, it seems rather definitively so at present, while in Russia, the embers of Orthodoxy that remained show promise to enkindle the flame of faith once more.

273 Paul Johnson, *The Quest for God: A Personal Pilgrimage* (New York: Harper-Collins ebooks, 2009), loc. 297 of 3917, Kindle Edition.

DAY 271

SIGRID UNDSET (1882–1949)

Undset is asked by a priest why in some of the essays she wrote before her conversion, marriage is referred to as a sacrament—

"There is however one side of the matter to which no very great attention appears to have been devoted to the discussion on 'birth control.' It is natural enough that young people, the first time they feel disappointed with the world and their fellow-creatures, should turn around to their parents and yelp: 'I didn't ask for life' — 'why did you bring me into the world?' Formerly, parents could decline to answer — could leave their children to find out for themselves. But now? When it is preached far and wide that only those who are 'fitted for it' should bring children into the world; nay more, only these who in their own opinion 'are qualified to give their children a good bringing-up.' God have mercy on them when they have to face the criticism of their offspring."[274]

"Reply to a Parish Priest," 1934

Sigrid Undset remarks that with the coming of contraception, the dynamics between querulous children and parents has been changed. Children can rightly say they did not ask

---

274 Sigrid Undset, *Stages on the Road*, trans. Arthur G. Chater (New York: Alfred A. Knopf, 1934), 258.

to be born, but prior to contraception, and widespread abortion, a parent didn't need to get entangled in trying to explain why they were born. Now the birth of a child has a question mark hanging over it—*why did the parents allow this to happen?* Parents could have contracepted or could have aborted, but they didn't. Now the question needs to answered, and that is a good thing: it gives parents the opportunity to express in words why they wanted their child to come fully into being, to say, "We loved you from the moment you were conceived, and once you existed our love wanted nothing else than to see you live, flourish, and realize the kind of love that led to your existing."

DAY 272

VENERABLE BEDE (673–735)

Bede recounts a miraculous episode in which "a heavenly light indicates where the bodies of the nuns of Barking should be buried"—

"In this convent many proofs of holiness were effected, which many people have recorded from the testimony of eyewitnesses in order that the memory of them might edify future generations; I have therefore been careful to include some of this history of the Church. When the plague that I have often mentioned was at its height, it attacked the men's part of the

monastery, and daily carried off some to meet their God. The watchful Mother of the Community therefore began to ask the sisters of the convent where they wished their bodies to be buried, and where the cemetery should be made when the plague should enter the enclosure where these handmaids of God lived separately from the men, and snatch them out of this world by the same deadly stroke. But when her frequent enquiries of the sisters had elicited no definite reply, both she and the whole Community received a very clear indication of the wishes of heaven. For one night when they had finished singing the morning psalms of praise to God, these servants of Christ left the oratory to visit the graves of the brothers who had departed this life before them. And as they were singing their customary praises to our Lord, a light from heaven like a great sheet suddenly appeared and shone over them all, so alarming them that they even broke off their singing in consternation. After a short while, this brilliant light, compared to which the noonday sun would appear dark, rose and travelled to the south side of the convent westward of the oratory and, having remained over that area for a time, withdrew heavenwards in the sight of them all. This occurrence left no doubt in their minds that the light, which was to guide or receive the souls of Christ's servants into heaven, had also indicated the spot where their bodies were to rest and await the day of resurrection. So brilliant was this light that one of the older brothers, who was in the oratory at the time with another younger brother, reported next morning that the rays of light

penetrating the chinks of doors and windows seemed brighter than the brightest daylight."[275]

Ecclesiastical History of the English People, Bk. 4, Ch. 7

Venerable Bede is the only English Doctor of the Church. *Ecclesiastical History of the English People* (731) is indispensable to understanding the early medieval Church. He wrote over forty books on theology and history and is considered the greatest scholar of the Anglo-Saxon period.

DAY 273

ST. THOMAS MORE (1478–1535)

Silly little pleasures—

"Those who lie in hell for the wretched way they lived in this world do not perceive their foolishness in having taken here the greater pain for the lesser pleasure. They now admit their foolishness. . . . Yet, while they were journeying along those paths and through those deserts, they would not rest themselves. In their weariness they kept running on, and kept

---

275 Venerable Bede, *The Ecclesiastical History of the English People*, Bk. 4, Ch. 7, trans. Leo Sherley-Price, rev. R.E. Lantham (London: Penguin Publishing), loc. 217-218, Kindle Edition.

putting themselves in more and more pain, for silly little pleasures. . . . So help me God, I truly cannot help but think that
many people buy Hell with so much earthly pain, they could
have bought Heaven with less than half that pain."[276]

Dialogue of Comfort Against Tribulation, 1553

The abrupt simplicity of these words from St. Thomas More
is startling. He takes a look at heaven and hell from a utilitarian point of view—the comparison of pleasure and pain:
whether a person ending up in hell experiences more pleasure
and less pain than one who lives well and ends in heaven. More
finds those who experience the of pain of hell have earned it,
ironically enough, by experiencing a great deal of pain in this
world through their own sinfulness. The question becomes:
why would anyone want to do that for "silly little pleasures?"
Good question!

---

276 St. Thomas More, *Dialogue of Comfort Against Tribulation,* rendered into
modern English by Mary Gottschalk (Princeton: Scepter Publishing, 1998),
168-69

DAY 274

ARNOLD LUNN (1888–1974)

A poor investment—

"Happiness is the test, but the world is not divided into fanatics who prefer unhappiness to happiness, average Christians who don't mind one way or the other, and sensible Snooters who very definitely prefer happiness to misery. It is not as simple as all that. It would be more plausible to divide people into those who feverishly pursue pleasure without achieving happiness, and saints who have discovered that suffering is a triumph which purchases a happiness unobtainable by self-indulgence. Plausible, but misleading, for no true saint is capable of such cold-blooded calculation. The saint is not a prudent investor but an ardent lover, and the extravagances of his devotion cannot be measured in terms of profit and loss."[277]

A Saint in the Slave Trade: Peter Claver (1581-1654), 1935

Arnold Lunn makes an important point here about distinguishing between those who pursue pleasure without knowing it leads to unhappiness and the saints who "have discovered suffering is a triumph which purchases a happiness unobtainable by self-indulgence." But he calls this distinction "misleading"

---

277 Arnold Lunn, *A Saint in the Slave Trade: Peter Claver (1581-1654)* (New York, Sheed & Ward, 1936), 191-92.

on the basis that saints do not calculate how to reach happiness; saints love, they do not make their choices based upon what they will gain or lose. Lunn need not worry: no sensible person could look up the sufferings of a typical saint and conclude that it's part of a plan or scheme to obtain a spiritual goal. When saints give themselves up to Mystery, they receive no roadmap.

DAY 275

CHARLES DE KONINCK (1906–1965)

The seat of Wisdom—

"Order is implied by wisdom. Wisdom is at once one and manifold, steadfast and mobile. Wisdom may be predicated of the principle of the sapiential order insofar as this principle is the root, and pre-contains the order, of which it is the principle. Together with her Son at the very origin of the universe, she [Mary] is in a way the root of the universal order: *Ego sum radix*—I am the root. That which God principally desires in the universe is the good of order. This order is better in proportion as its principle, which is interior to the universe, is the more profoundly rooted in God. But Mary is the purely created principle of this order, the purely created principle which is nearest to God and the most perfect that can be conceived.

As a principle of the sapiential order, she participates in the unity and the unicity of this principle, she is at once an emanation and an indwelling, her power extends to all things which take from her their constant renewal. We conceive vital emanation as a constant renewing from within, and in their relation to the first principle things receive being in an ever-new procession."[278]

"The Wisdom That Is Mary," 1943

Charles de Koninck was an important Belgian-Canadian Thomistic philosopher who wrote in French. He was the founder of the Laval School of Philosophy which produced a number of distinguished philosophers, including Ralph McInerny. Born in Belgium, de Koninck and his family immigrated to Detroit in 1914 as WWI broke out. After the war, he returned to Belgium to study at Louvain where he embraced the philosophy of St. Thomas Aquinas. After his doctorate, de Koninck was hired by the University of Laval in Quebec where he taught philosophy for the rest of his life. Two volumes of de Koninck's philosophical work were translated and published by his former student Ralph McInerny just before the latter's death in 2010 and published by Notre Dame Press in 2016.

---

278 Charles de Koninck, *The Writings of Charles de Koninck: Volume 2*, ed. and trans. Ralph McInerny (Notre Dame: University of Notre Dame Press, 2009), loc. 268-299 of 8273, Kindle Edition.

DAY 276

MSGR. RONALD KNOX (1888–1957)

The mystery that lies behind—

"Of all the features in the Catholic system which appeal powerfully to men's minds at the present moment, the least, assuredly, is the mere beauty of her external adornment—the merely aesthetic effect of vestments made in art stuffs, of blazing candles, of gold and silver altar furniture, of lace and flowers. Chloe and Clorinda did feel, I think, a sneaking attraction towards these Romish bedizenments [mode of dressing] tempered, of course, by a strong moral reprobation. In our day, their appeal is of the slightest. If for no other reason, because these characteristics of our own system are easily imitable and have been freely imitated. It is, perhaps fortunately, no longer necessary to betake yourself to Catholic churches in order to glut your senses with artistic appreciation of ceremonial. Our High Church friends do it as well or better—their churches provide, as it were, a mimic Riviera on the soil of home to suit these sickly temperaments. Mere beauty, mere pageantry, is no speciality of ours, and no appreciable boast. But there is something else underlying the pomp of our ceremonial which

makes, I think, a more powerful impression, though one far more difficult to analyse. I mean the sense of mystery."[279]

The Belief of Catholics, 1927

Msgr. Ronald Knox admits that the Anglican liturgy of his time made greater use of the beauty to be found in the Catholic liturgy than Catholic parishes themselves. However, he also senses something missing from the Anglican Mass, the underlying "mystery" of the Catholic liturgy. Knox rather interestingly offers an advance critique of *Mere Christianity* (1952) by C. S. Lewis. Knox asserts the Church did not specialize in "Mere beauty, mere pageantry." Lewis, the reader may recall, used "mere" to describe the Christian faith stripped of its unnecessary accouterments. For Knox, the mystery represents the "sacred deposit" that has remained intact and unbroken since the Church was instituted.

---

279 Ronald Knox. *The Belief of Catholics*, (Victoria: Reading Essentials), loc. 260–285 of 2920, Kindle Edition.

DAY 277

AUREL KOLNAI (1900–1973)

A descent into barbarism—

"A completely or an originally irreligious civilization has in all likelihood never existed, but it is not, in itself, unimaginable; what is more important, the modern civilization of Western mankind, originally (and still, in part, actually) Christian, has revealed a trend of evolution towards a society in which, practically speaking, religion as a determining factor of private and public life is to yield its place to a nonreligious, immanentistic, secular moral orientation which may best be described as 'humanitarian.' While such a prospect cannot but appall the believer, it has also evoked misgivings and apprehension in a good many nonreligious or not emphatically religious students of human civilization; nay, terrified some of them, perhaps, to an extent to which it could never terrify the believer himself. For it is precisely the nobler and more perspicacious kind of mundane thinker who is apt to be worried primarily about the fate of human civilization as such, than which he knows no higher thing. Yet it is a grave problem, and one that poses itself on a purely worldly level of thinking, how far an irreligious civilization can subsist at all, or how soon it is bound to degenerate into a state of barbarism; in other words, whether humanitarianism is essentially capable of maintaining itself in actual reality or is fated to defeat its own end, thus marking

but a brief transition toward disintegration and anarchy—coupled, of necessity, with new phenomena of tyranny and new forms of gross and superstitious creeds widely dissimilar to its own mental world. It goes without saying that the rise of Communism and of Fascism—most characteristically, however, of Nazism—is entirely calculated to impress the observer as premonitory signs (if not more) of just such a turn of evolution."[280]

"The Humanitarian versus the Religious Attitude," 1944

Aurel Kolnai was born in Budapest to a Jewish family but became a Catholic in 1926 after reading Chesterton. As a journalist, Kolnai publicly opposed the rise of the Nazis and contributed to the anti-Nazi magazine edited by Dietrich von Hildebrand. As a result, he left Austria in 1937, moved to France, then England and Canada. He taught briefly at Laval but, regarding its teaching of Thomism too restricted, moved back to England. Kolnai ended his career teaching at Marquette University having published in five languages.

---

280 Daniel J. Mahoney, *The Idol of Our Age: How the Religion of Humanity Subverts Christianity* (New York: Encounter Books, 2018), 129-30.

DAY 278

FRANÇOIS MAURIAC (1885–1970)

Not a matter of calculation—

"Nothing is less congenial than this love [exhibited in the foot-washing ceremony] to the nature of man. Since Holy Thursday, the charity of Christ has been making its way painfully against human cruelty. Men used it for selfish purposes, even when they pretended to adopt it. Love for the lowly served as a pretext for atrocious slaughters, for unbending tyranny. Love flourishes only in Christ. The world accuses the faithful of not doing anything except out of self-interest and with the hope of future rewards; it is because the world is blind to the nature of that love which is the source of the superhuman devotion of which the Catholic Church presents innumerable examples. To love Christ, particularly in the Eucharist, and to love one's neighbor, are one and the same thing; the two commandments are blended with one another. 'Amen, I say to you, as long as you did it for one of these, the least of my brethren, you did it for me.' It is not a question of calculating, or anticipating the reward in advance—it is a question of love."[281]

Holy Thursday, 1931

---

281 François Mauriac, *Holy Thursday: An Intimate Remembrance* (Manchester: Sophia Institute Press, 2019), 44.

When new converts, or non-Catholics, witness the foot-washing ceremony, they might well agree with Mauriac's interpretation. It's one thing to *say* "love your neighbor" or "welcome the stranger" and quite another to go down on a hard floor with your bended knee and wash someone's foot fresh out of their shoes. We can easily forget "the least of my brethren" codicil contained in Christ's teaching. The spectacle of a priest in full cassock on his knees before men and women he may not even know reminds us that "a picture is worth a thousand words."

DAY 279

GREGORY OF NYSSA (335–394)

Satan was deceived—

"We must remember that man was necessarily created subject to change (to better or to worse). Moral beauty was to be the direction in which his free will was to move; but then he was deceived, to his ruin, by an illusion of that beauty. After we had thus freely sold ourselves to the deceiver, He who of His goodness sought to restore us to liberty could not, because He was just too, for this end have recourse to measures of arbitrary violence. *It was necessary therefore that a ransom should be paid, which should exceed in value that which was to be ransomed; and*

hence it was necessary that the Son of God should surrender Himself to the power of death. God's justice then impelled Him to choose a method of exchange, as His wisdom was seen in executing it. But how about the power? That was more conspicuously displayed in Deity descending to lowliness, than in all the natural wonders of the universe. It was like flame being made to stream downwards. Then, after such a birth, Christ conquered death. A certain deception was indeed practiced upon the Evil one, by concealing the Divine nature within the human; but for the latter, as himself a deceiver, it was only a just recompense that he should be deceived himself: the great adversary must himself at last find that what has been done is just and salutary, when he also shall experience the benefit of the Incarnation. He, as well as humanity, will be purged."[282] (Emphasis added.)

The Great Catechism, 385

The opening line of St. Gregory of Nyssa's instruction here is an attention-grabber: man was created "subject to change." Our mind moves to the scene in the Garden of Eden when Adam and Eve were faced with the choice of obeying or disobeying the only thing in the Garden forbidden to them by God. So human nature changed for the "worse." The "illusion of beauty" which was presented to them by the snake—"you shall be as gods"—resulting in the loss of the Beauty that

---

282 Gregory of Nyssa, *The Great Catechism*, 26, newadvent.org/fathers/2908. htm.

would have been the guide for their free will. Because God is Just, as well as Loving, a price must be paid, a punishment applied, but no one in the human community can pay the debt. God Himself pays the debt through His Incarnate Son Who undergoes an undeserved death.

DAY 280

REGINALD GARRIGOU-LAGRANGE, OP (1877–1964)

On knowing the real—

"The limited moderate realism of Aristotle and Aquinas is in harmony with that natural, spontaneous knowledge which we call common sense. This harmony appears most clearly in the doctrine's insistence on the objective validity and scope of first principles, the object of our first intellectual apprehension. These principles are laws. . . . Yet even in these primary laws we find a hierarchy. One of them, rising immediately from the idea of being, is simply the first principle, the principle of contradiction; it is the declaration of opposition between being and nothing. It may be formulated in two ways, one negative, the other positive. The first may be given either thus: 'Being is not nothing,' or thus: 'One and the same thing, remaining such, cannot simultaneously both be and not be.' Positively

considered, it becomes the principle of identity, which may
be formulated thus: 'If a thing is, it is: if it is not, it is not.' This
is equivalent to say: 'Being is not nonbeing." . . . According to
this principle, that which is absurd, say a squared circle, is not
merely unimaginable, not mere inconceivable, but absolutely
irrealisable. . . . And here already we have afforded the validity
of our intelligence in knowing the laws of extramental reality."[283]

Reality, 1921

When Father Reginald Garrigou-Lagrange published this
work in 1921, it was entitled "Common Sense" (*Le sense com-
mun* in French), a title which gives a better idea of what is
found in a book whose English title is *Reality*. In this brief
passage, he explains why the mind's commonsense knowledge
can be trusted. Within the mind are laws which govern mental assent to knowledge set forth in propositions: "The tree is
green." Starting with the principle of non-contradiction—a
thing cannot be itself and its opposite—and the principle of
identity—a thing is what it is, not something else. So when
we say, "the tree is green," we can distinguish its identity from
other trees of different sizes and shapes bearing different colors.
"That is x and not y." Unlike the famous scene in Jean-Paul

---

283 Rev. Reginald Garrigou-LaGrange, *Reality: A Synthesis of Thomistic Thought,*
trans. Rev. Patrick Cummins, O.S.B. (St. Louis: B. Herder Book CO., 1950),
33.

Sartre's novel *Nausea* (1938), chestnut trees do not dissolve before our senses into nothingness.

DAY 281

BISHOP FULTON J. SHEEN (1895–1979)

Too grown up for the truth—

"Holiness had been evidenced by the insignia on the sacerdotal forehead, now it was to be in the heart through the Spirit Who sanctifies. It was not enough that they be holy; they must be 'holy in truth.' As the light of the sun purifies the body from diseases, so His truth, He said, sanctified the soul and preserved it from evil. Holiness must have a philosophical and theological foundation, namely, Divine truth; otherwise it is sentimentality and emotionalism. Many would say later on, 'We want religion, but no creeds.' This is like saying we want healing, but no science of medicine; music, but no rules of music; history, but no documents. Religion is indeed a life, but it grows out of truth, not away from it. It has been said it makes no difference what you believe; it all depends on how you act. This is psychological nonsense, for a man acts out of his beliefs. Our Lord placed truth or belief in Him first; then came sanctification and good deeds. But here truth was not a vague ideal, but a Person. Truth was now lovable, because only a Person

is lovable. Sanctity becomes the response the heart makes to Divine truth and its unlimited mercy to humanity. Then Our Lord added that as He had been sent on His Father's business, so they, sanctified by the Spirit of holiness, were to go through the earth as His ambassadors."[284]

Life of Christ, 1958

Bishop Fulton J. Sheen's surgical dissection of "religion without dogma" is needed as much today as it was in the 1950s. If anything, such mottos are heard more often now than they were then. After all, Bishop Sheen had not yet experienced the '60s which must have given him serious heartburn. There is one line that should finish the argument with any intellectually honest person: "This is like saying we want healing, but no science of medicine." *Truth* is perhaps the most highly scorned term of the twenty-first century. Instead, we have "my truth" and "your truth," neither of which make any sense at all if it's really truth they are talking about: Truth is the same for everyone whether they see it or not. Christianity has its basis in Truth not in joy, raptures, singing, or hugs. It's a Truth which became, as Sheen explains, "lovable, because only a Person is lovable." So that which measures us, Truth, has declared itself to be on our side, reaching down to offer us forgiveness and entry into His heaven.

---

284 Fulton J. Sheen, *Life of Christ* (General Press), loc. 452-453, Kindle Edition.

DAY 282

FRANK SHEED (1897–1981)

A dark kind of light—

"In studying God we begin with darkness, knowing nothing, we progress into light and revel in it, and at last we find ourselves face to face with darkness again, but a very different darkness from the first, a darkness richer than our light. It is the experience of all who have set themselves to a real study of divine revelation, that as the mind begins to take hold of the great realities proposed to it, they seem to be all light; and it is only as they come to live in the light that they are aware of the mightier darkness, which must be because God is infinite and we are not. . . . It was one of the greatest of theologians who created the phrase *caligo quaedam lux*—the darkness is a kind of light. It is a kind of light in two ways, a lesser and a greater; the lesser because it involves seeing why the mind can see no further: it is not merely baffled by mystery, but to that extent enlightened by it; the greater because of the very richness of the felt darkness—if the light that they can see be such, what must the darkness be which is light too bright for human eyes? Mystery presents itself to us not only as something we cannot see because the light is too strong for our eyes; but also, and sometimes worryingly, as the appearance of contradiction in the things we do see. As we come to grasp what God has taught us through His Church, we find certain elements at

which our intellects cry a challenge, certain others which stir our feelings to something very much like revolt. We find the notion of eternal suffering so painful that we cannot reconcile it with a loving God; or we find the doctrine of human freedom impossible to reconcile with God's omniscience. *The answer, of course, is that all these elements are reconciled in the whole, and we do not see the whole.*"[285] (Emphasis added.)

Theology for Beginners, 1957

Frank Sheed corrects a common misunderstanding about mystery. Mystery is not what is unknowable, it's what is unknowable *to us*. What the mystery is about remains intelligible in itself because it bears the stamp of the *Logos* through which God made the world. What is mysterious to us can change, just as one period of darkness can be followed by another one even more disorienting. The mystery and the darkness can change not because we know more but because we realize how much less we know than we previously thought.

---

285 Frank Sheed, *Theology for Beginners* (Aeterna Press, 2019). loc. 549-574 of 2759 Kindle Edition.

DAY 283

JULIEN GREEN (1900–1988)

He could walk with the animals—

"The wolf of Gubbio is so well-known that he needs no introduction. This was the least miraculous of Francis's miracles. The real miracle would have been if the wolf had eaten Francis, since there is no record of any animal ever harming him. The entire animal kingdom respected him for reasons that are still a secret. The simple fact is that beasts loved him. Did they see in him an aura of love that our eyes can't discern—perhaps in the form of a halo we see only in portraits of saints, something that worked on them and made them happy?"[286]

God's Fool, 1985

There are some animals—horses, dogs, and cats, certainly—that have a way of sizing people up. They will allow some to approach, even to touch, while backing away, or growling, at others. It could be said they sense kind hearts. What Julien Green depicts in the life of St. Francis is his incomparable rapport with animals and, particularly, with the fierce wolf of Gubbio. The wolf held the town of Gubbio under siege, having started with eating the livestock before moving onto

---

286 Julien Green, *God's Fool: The Life and Times of Francis of Assisi*, trans. Peter Heinegg (New York: Harper & Row, Publishers, 1985), 218.

human flesh exclusively. St. Francis, though advised against it, went to confront the wolf in his lair. When the wolf rushed at him open-mouthed, the saint made the sign of the cross and told him to stop his attacks: the wolf, it is told, was immediately tamed and put his head in the hands of St. Francis. Green turns the miracle around: "The real miracle would have been if the wolf had eaten Francis, since there is no record of any animal ever harming him."

DAY 284

JACQUES MARITAIN (1882–1973)

Seeking to please—

"If I truly love my neighbor, it will of course . . . be painful to me to see him deprived of the truth I happen to know. For all things considered, it is truth I must love above everything, while at the same time loving my neighbor as myself. If my neighbor is in error, it is a pity for him, and for truth, too. How to escape suffering from this? That is part of the inherent delight of fraternal dialogue. On the other hand, the latter would completely degenerate if the fear of displeasing my brother got the better of my duty to declare the truth. . . . Let us beware of those brotherly dialogues in which everyone raptures while listening to heresies, blasphemies, stuff and

nonsense of the other. They are not brotherly at all. It has never been recommended to confuse 'loving' with 'seeking to please.' . . . Salome pleased Herod's guests; I can hardly believe she was burning with love for them. As for poor John the Baptist (who did his dialogue in prison, except with his Master), she certainly did not envelop him in her love."[287]

The Peasant of the Garonne, 1966

Jacques Maritain shocked much of the leadership in the Catholic world with his critique of the direction the Church had taken after the Second Vatican Council (1962–1965) where Paul VI, who had translated two of Maritain's books into Italian, honored Maritain by presenting him with the Council's message to the intellectuals of the world. When asked if in *The Peasant of the Garonne* he had repudiated himself, Maritain answered, "There is a difference between changing dogma and changing a perspective on it. Even though dogma may evolve, it is always the same dogma."

---

287 Jacques Maritain, *The Peasant of the Garonne: An Old Layman Questions Himself about the Present Time,* trans. Michael Cuddihy and Elizabeth Hughes (New York: Holt, Rinehart and Winston, 1968), 91.

DAY 285

OSCAR WILDE (1854–1900)

E Tenebris

> Come down, O Christ, and help me! reach thy hand,
>   For I am drowning in a stormier sea
>   Than Simon on thy lake of Galilee:
> The wine of life is spilt upon the sand,
> My heart is as some famine-murdered land
>   Whence all good things have perished utterly
>   And well I know my soul in Hell must lie
> If I this night before God's throne should stand.
> 'He sleeps perchance, or rideth to the chase,
>   Like Baal, when his prophets howled that name
>   From morn to noon on Carmel's smitten height.'
> Nay, peace, I shall behold, before the night,
>   The feet of brass, the robe more white than flame,
> The wounded hands, the weary human face.[288]

As the scholar, Joseph Pearce comments, "Wilde is only remembered for the tragedy of his life and not for its happy ending." Wilde became a Catholic on his deathbed, the consequence of a period of extreme suffering beginning with his two-year

---

288 Joseph Pearce, compiler, *Poems Every Catholic Should Know* (Charlotte: TAN Books, 2016), 224.

sentence for "gross indecency" to hard labor in the Reading goal. We already read an extract from his long letter, *De Profundis* (Day 134), which clearly attests to his self-examination and repentance. But his concern for spiritual matters was life-long as seen in "E Tenebris" ("Out of Darkness") first published in 1881 many years before his public scandal and incarceration. Wilde was just entering London society after glittering years at Oxford where his brilliance, wit, and outrageous dandyism prefigured the slippery surface of the success and fame to come.

DAY 286

WALKER PERCY (1916–1990)

A boon for novelists—

"I have the strongest feeling that, whatever else the benefits of the Catholic faith, it is of a particularly felicitous use for novelists. I can think of no better. What distinguishes Judeo-Christianity in general from other world religions is its emphasis on the value of the individual person, its view of man as a creature in trouble, seeking to get out of it accordingly on the move. Add to this anthropology the special marks of the Catholic Church: the sacraments, especially the Eucharist, which, whatever else they do, confer the highest significance upon the ordinary

things of this world, bread, wine, water, touch, breath, words, talking, listening—and what do you have? You have a man in a predicament and on the move in a real world of real things, a world which is a sacrament and a mystery; a pilgrim whose life is a searching and a finding."[289]

"The Holiness of the Ordinary," 1989

Walker Percy gives the reasons why the novel was primarily the invention of the West—Christianity places men and women within an epic struggle between good and evil, heaven and hell, God and Satan. A human life ends up either in eternal pain or unceasing bliss; these are big stakes. Catholicism, as Percy says, is a particular advantage for the novelist because Catholics experience the religious significance of human gestures and postures, the movement of the hands, the tilt of the head, and the water becoming wine and the bread flesh. The novelist's job is to create characters that seem real to the reader, whose story is recognizably human, and the Church's realism does not shy away from any part of that story.

---

289 Walker Percy, *Signposts In a Strange Land*, ed. and introduction by Patrick Samway S.J. (New York: Farrar, Straus and Giroux, 1991), 369.

DAY 287

JACQUES MARITAIN (1882–1973)

Attention teachers—

"Beauty is the mental atmosphere and the inspiring power fitted to a child's education, and should be, so to speak, the continuous quickening and spiritualizing contrapuntal base of that education. Beauty makes intelligibility pass unawares through sense-awareness. It is by virtue of the allure of beautiful things and deeds and ideas that the child is to be led and awakened to intellectual and moral life. On the other hand the vitality and intuitiveness of the spirit are quick in the young child and sometimes pierce the world with his imaginative thought, with the purest and most surprising flashes, as if his spirit, being not yet both strengthened and organized by the exercise of reason, enjoyed a kind of bounding, temperamental, and lucid freedom. . . . This vitality of spirit should be relied upon as an invaluable factor in the first stages of education."[290]

Education at the Crossroads, 1957

Jacques Maritain knew that teaching involved the intuitive guidance of an artistic temperament in addition to a firm grounding in the subjects being taught. A successful teacher

---

290 Jacques Maritain, *Education at the Crossroads* (New Haven: Yale University Press, 1957), 61.

instantly notices what makes a student's mind come alive, his or her body sit up straighter, and the eyes more focused. A teacher who employs imagination and beauty is touching the open nerves of a child's life—they will begin learning but their sheer enjoyment will make them unaware of the effort they are taking. As Maritain writes, "Beauty makes intelligibility pass unawares through sense-awareness." Heroic is the teacher who in these days of standardized testing can find uses for the imagination to connect with a child's instinctual hunger for beauty.

DAY 288

MALCOLM MUGGERIDGE (1903–1990)

No place for granny—

"Another method of, as it were, keeping death under the carpet is to stow away the debilitated old in state institutions, where they live in a kind of limbo between life and death, heavily sedated and inert. Private institutions for the affluent old are naturally better equipped and staffed, but can be very desolating, too. Those under Christian auspices, especially when they are run by nuns, usually have long waiting lists, not so much because the prospective inmates are particularly pious, as because they want to be sure that some zealot for

mercy killing will not finish them off arbitrarily by administering excessive sedation; or, if they happen to need to be in an iron lung or attached to a kidney's machine, by pulling the plug, as it is put in today's jargon. In any case, disposing of people who live inconveniently long, and of defectives of one sort and another, has, from the point of view of governments, the great advantage of saving money and personnel without raising a pubic hullabaloo—something governments are always on the lookout for. It is, of course, inevitable that in a materialist society like ours death should seem terrible, and even inadmissible. If Man is the very apex of creation, with nothing greater than himself in the universe; if his earthly life exhausts the whole content of his existences, then, clearly, his definitive end, his death, is too outrageous to be contemplated, and so is better ignored."[291]

Seeing Through the Eye, 2005

Malcolm Muggeridge observes what we rarely discuss: how the elderly are often treated as if their lives were less valuable than those who are younger. When they are put in the hands of the government, their plight becomes far worse because they may threaten the "bottom line" and become expendable. It's legal now in some US states not only to "pull the plug" but

---

291 Malcolm Muggeridge, *Seeing Through the Eye: Malcolm Muggeridge On Faith*, ed. Cecil Kuhne, introduction by Williams F. Buckley, Jr. (San Francisco: Ignatius Press, 2005), loc. 1429-1448 of 4483, Kindle Edition.

also to inject death directly into the veins of those wanting to die.

DAY 289

ST. TERESA BENEDICTA OF THE CROSS (1891–1942)

Holy Father!

"As a child of the Jewish people who, by the grace of God, for the past eleven years has also been a child of the Catholic Church, I dare to speak to the Father of Christianity about that which oppresses millions of Germans. For weeks we have seen deeds perpetrated in Germany which mock any sense of justice and humanity, not to mention love of neighbor. For years the leaders of National Socialism have been preaching hatred of the Jews.... Everything that happened and continues to happen on a daily basis originates with a government that calls itself 'Christian.' For weeks not only Jews but also thousands of faithful Catholics in Germany, and, I believe, all over the world, have been waiting and hoping for the Church of Christ to raise its voice to put a stop to this abuse of Christ's name. Is not this idolization of race and governmental power which is being pounded into the public consciousness by the radio open heresy? Isn't the effort to destroy Jewish blood an

abuse of the holiest humanity of our Savior, of the most blessed Virgin and the apostles? Is not all this diametrically opposed to the conduct of our Lord and Savior, who, even on the cross, still prayed for his persecutors? And isn't this a black mark on the record of this Holy Year which was intended to be a year of peace and reconciliation? We all, who are faithful children of the Church and who see the conditions in Germany with open eyes, fear the worst for the prestige of the Church, if the silence continues any longer. We are convinced that this silence will not be able in the long run to purchase peace with the present German government. For the time being, the fight against Catholicism will be conducted quietly and less brutally than against Jewry, but no less systematically. It won't take long before no Catholic will be able to hold office in Germany unless he dedicates himself unconditionally to the new course of action."[292]

Letter to Pope Pius XI, 1933

On August 2, 1942, St. Teresa Benedicta of the Cross and her sister Rosa were arrested by the SS. A Dutch official who was impressed with her offered an escape plan. She refused. On August 9, she was deported with 968 other Jews to Auschwitz where she and his sister were murdered in the gas chamber.

---

292 https://web.archive.org/web/20150521042416/http://www.baltimore-carmel.org/saints/Stein/letter%20to%20pope.htm.

Historians are still debating the response of the Church and the popes to Nazi anti-Semitism and anti-Catholicism.

DAY 290

BENEDICT GROESCHEL, CFR (1933–2014)

An untimely element—

"As someone more interested in spiritual development than in abstract moral theology, I hope that the theologians never completely solve the puzzle of the sinning and struggling believer. What would Peter and Paul amount to without their sins? How artificial they would look. Even late in life with martyrdom not far off, they showed signs of inconstancy and aggression. Certainly, their tendencies were not mortal sins, but if they had surrendered to the tendencies—Peter to his life-long vacillation and Paul to his Olympian wrath—we might have been deprived of two outstanding models of the spiritual life. The sins and failings of the apostles, especially early on, like the sins of all others on the spiritual journey, are an untidy element in the spiritual life."[293]

Spiritual Passages, 2007

---

293 Benedict Groeschel, C.F.R., *Spiritual Passages: The Psychology of Spiritual Development* (New York: The Crossword Publishing Company, 2007), 110-11.

Benedict Groeschel, CFR, was the founder of the Office for Spiritual Development for the Roman Catholic Archdiocese of New York, associate director of the Trinity Retreat House, professor of pastoral psychology at St. Joseph's Seminary in New York, and an adjunct professor at the Institute for Psychological Sciences in Arlington, Virginia. His TV show, *Sunday Night Live with Father Benedict Groeschel*, was seen on EWTN for many years. His many books include *Healing the Original Wound* (1993), *The Virtue Driven Life* (2006), and *Tears of God* (2009).

DAY 291

BERNARD NATHANSON, MD (1926–2011)

An inevitable explosion—

The former abortionist Dr. Bernard Nathanson wrote in response to the violence of anti-abortion protestors—

"Think of it this way: The cultural war is a vessel filled with water and put on a high flame. Normally there are outlets of political action and peaceful protest from which the steam may escape, but someone has blocked the escape valves while neglecting to turn off the flame. The vessel will inevitably explode like a grenade, spewing shards of metal and glass all

over the vicinity—and someone will be hurt. This is precisely what led up to the climatic events of the Civil War—and we appear to be on that identical path now."[294]

The Hand of God, 1996

After becoming pro-life and Catholic, Dr. Bernard Nathanson found himself being asked to justify or condemn the violence of a few pro-lifers. Nathanson wisely responded by drawing a large picture of a culture where pro-life voices were being ignored, dismissed, and publicly scorned. For how many consecutive years did the Annual March for Life in Washington, DC fail to be mentioned in the mainstream news? It was the handful of pro-abortion protesters who were featured on the evening news. The pro-life advocates who do make it into the major media are usually treated shabbily and dismissively. Peaceful pro-life demonstrators near abortion clinics are harassed and demonized. Since the 1990s, we have witnessed in our nation an unexpected rise in opposition to abortion due to the advances in science and the unceasing commitment and ingenuity of pro-life leaders. The progress has been quite remarkable and has succeeded in removing some of the built-up tension Dr. Nathanson describes.

---

294 Bernard Nathanson, M.D., *The Hand of God: A journey from death to life by an abortion doctor who changed his mind* (Washington, DC: Regnery Publishing, 1996), 180.

DAY 292

MSGR. RONALD KNOX (1888–1957)

Hitler struck quickly—

"'Six days after the signing of the Concordat, the State duly promulgated the Sterilisation Law, which gave powers for sterilization, by force, even of the blind.' Suddenness is a recognized part of the Nazi technique: the moving of a piece on some quite different part of the board, to make your opponent wonder how this move is connected with the one before, or whether it is connected at all. In this case, it can hardly have been an accident that the new rulers of the Reich proceeded so quickly from an instrument of peace with the Catholic authorities to a legislative act so repulsive to Catholic principles. There is no need to consider here the ethical implications of the measure. We are concerned with it, not as an act of persecution, but as an act of provocation. This, surely, was its immediate purpose. It was the thick end of the wedge, this time, thrust in to open the door for that crusade of race and force which has been the chief characteristic of the Nazi philosophy. Catholics were to realize, without loss of time, that the regime which had gained respectability by the signing of the Concordat intended to flout the convictions, not only of all Catholics, but of all Christians in Europe. It was clear

provocation; why was it important that the provocation should come so soon?"[295]

Nazi and Nazarene, 1940

Msgr. Ronald Knox notes how quickly Hitler's Reich moved to pass its sterilization laws after signing its 1933 Concordat with the Holy See. Knox asks why the provocation came so soon. Perhaps Hitler thought the Concordat gave him a "green light" and had concluded that the Vatican was not going to interfere publicly with his eugenics, anti-Semitism, and, ultimately, the Final Solution itself. The history surrounding the Concordat, negotiated by Cardinal Pacelli, the future Pope Pius XII, is complicated and has been explored in detail since the wildly exaggerated attack on Pius XII by John Cromwell in his 1999 book *Hitler's Pope: The Secret History of Pope Pius XII*. Knox rightly points out that Hitler was usually in *Blitzkrieg* mode and took full advantage of the cover unintentionally provided by the Concordat signed by Pope Pius XI. In contrast, probably no human institution moves more slowly than the Vatican. But it's not clear if Catholics recognized the horror, "without loss of time," as Knox says, but the Church's outcry was initially muted.

---

295 Ronald Knox, *Nazi and Nazarene* (CrossReach Publications, 2017) loc. 11-13, Kindle Edition.

DAY 293

THEODORE HAECKER (1879–1945)

How faith laughs—

"Humor is a finite spiritual sphere in which faith is the infinite. That may be seen from the nature of despair, and its dialectic. A man deeply in despair, a man that is, who has not got faith, or has lost it, can perfectly well have a high degree of humor, even to the point of genius. Shakespeare is full of examples. The humorous rejoinders of a man in despair are flung back, as it were, from the walls of the infinite spiritual sphere, which to him are impenetrable, and they have a particular, unmistakable and sinister ring. The humorous rejoinders of Thomas More at the moment when his faith looked into heaven strike a very different note; the tone is of this world like the tone of all humor, but it is not the tone of a solitary, 'lost,' man, as in the case of the man in despair; he strikes a chord in which sounds the heavenly harmony of the seen and the unseen world. At times the believer may see himself in this world bereft of every finite possibility, he may be deprived of humor altogether, even the humor of despair, and yet with the eye of faith he will see the quintessence of every possibility, and of what is for man the impossible possibility; God himself."[296]

Journal In the Night, 1940

---

296 Theodor Haecker, *Journal In the Night,* trans. Alexander Dru (New York: Pantheon Books, 1950), 97.

Theodore Haecker contrasts the humor of despair with the humor of hope. St. Thomas More knew he would be convicted and executed, but his last words to his jury were these: "I verily trust and shall therefore right heartily pray, that though your lordships have now in earth been judges to my condemnation, we may yet hereafter in heaven merrily all meet together to our everlasting salvation." Merrily, indeed! Here's a man whose eye is fixed on heaven even though very great suffering lies in the way. Shakespeare's Hamlet has lost all hope after hearing from his father's ghost that he was killed by his brother, Hamlet's uncle, and married his queen, Hamlet's mother. His best friend Horatio arrives and asks, "My lord, I came to see your father's funeral. Hamlet replies, "I pray thee, do not mock me, fellow-student; I think it was to see my mother's wedding." We smile at both St. Thomas More and Hamlet, but in the case of the latter, it fades quickly.

DAY 294

ST. TERESA OF AVILA (1515–1582)

Becoming our own enemy—

"May it please His Majesty that we fear Him whom we ought to fear, and understand that one venial sin can do us more harm than all hell together; for that is the truth. The evil spirits

keep us in terror, because we expose ourselves to the assaults of terror by our attachments to honours, possessions, and pleasures. For then the evil spirits, uniting themselves with us,—*we become our own enemies when we love and seek what we ought to hate,—do us great harm.* We ourselves put weapons into their hands, that they may assail us; those very weapons with which we should defend ourselves. It is a great pity. But if, for the love of God, we hated all this, and embraced the cross, and set about His service in earnest, Satan would fly away before such realities, as from the plague. He is the friend of lies, and a lie himself. He will have nothing to do with those who walk in the truth. When he sees the understanding of any one obscured, he simply helps to pluck out his eyes; if he sees any one already blind, seeking peace in vanities,—for all the things of this world are so utterly vanity, that they seem to be but the playthings of a child,—he sees at once that such a one is a child; he treats him as a child, and ventures to wrestle with him—not once, but often. May it please our Lord that I be not one of these; and may His Majesty give me grace to take that for peace which is really peace, that for honour which is really honour, and that for delight which is really a delight. Let me never mistake one thing for another—and then I snap my fingers at all the devils, for they shall be afraid of me. I do not understand those terrors which make us cry out, Satan, Satan! when we may say, God, God! and make Satan tremble. Do we not know that he cannot stir without the permission of God? What does it mean? . . . I am really much more afraid of those

people who have so great a fear of the devil, than I am of the devil himself."[297] (Emphasis added.)

The Life of St. Teresa by Herself, 1567

St. Teresa of Avila describes how those who seek "peace in vanities" become like "playthings" for Satan. She is more afraid of "those people who have so great a fear of the devil," than the Evil One himself. Imagine a woman such as St. Teresa who can make the devils jump by snapping her fingers at them and make Satan "tremble" when she speaks the name of God.

DAY 295

ST. AUGUSTINE (354–430)

He owes you nothing—

"But God owes nothing to anyone, for he freely maintains the universe. But if someone should say that God owes him something for his merits, surely God is under no obligation for having given the man existence; it is not to the man that something is owing. Besides, what is the merit in turning to God, from whom you have your existence, since you do so to

---

297 Santa Teresa de Jesús, *The Life of Saint Teresa of Ávila by Herself*, 25. 26–27; https://www.gutenberg.org/files/8120/8120-h/8120-h.htm.

better yourself through Him who gave you your existence? What then do you ask—as if you were demanding payment of a debt? If you do not turn to Him, what loss is it to God? It is your loss, for you would be nothing without him who made you something. Unless you turn to Him and repay the existence He gave you, you won't be 'nothing;' you will be wretched. All things owe to God, first of all, what they are insofar as they are natures."[298]

On the Free Choice of the Will, 388

On the Free Choice of the Will was written shortly after St. Augustine was ordained a priest in 391. It reflects his expertise in persuasive rhetoric. Augustine addresses one of the main theological controversies at this time: whether it's a matter of merit if a man turns towards God. St. Augustine's answer is both furious and keenly analytic, a dialectical style he used to demolish Manichaeism and Pelagianism among other heresies. The power of his argument here is found in the contrast between the utter majesty of God in His gift of existence itself and an individual who is prideful about accepting the divine words, "I AM WHO I AM" (Ex 3:14). It makes one think of a man drowning in the ocean but, once rescued, congratulated himself for paddling long enough to be picked up.

---

298 *St. Augustine, On the Free Choice of the Will*, trans. Anna S. Benjamin and L.H. Hackstaff, introduction by L. H. Hackstaff (Indianapolis: The Bobbs-Merrill Company, Inc., 1964), 123–24.

DAY 296

PAUL JOHNSON (1928–)

The trouble with smart people—

"One of the principal lessons of our tragic century, which has seen so many millions of innocent lives sacrificed in schemes to improve the lot of humanity, is—beware intellectuals. Not merely should they be kept well away from the levers of power, they should also be objects of particular suspicion when they seek to offer collective advice. Beware committees, conferences and leagues of intellectuals. Distrust public statements issued from their serried ranks. Discount their verdicts on political leaders and important events. For intellectuals, far from being highly individualistic and non-conformist people, follow certain regular patterns of behavior. Taken as a group, they are often ultra-conformist within the circles formed by those whose approval they seek and value. This is what makes them, *en masse*, so dangerous, for it enables them to create climates of opinion and prevailing orthodoxies, which themselves often generate irrational and destructive courses of action. Above all, we must at all times remember what intellectuals habitually forget: that people matter more than concepts and must come

first. The worst of all despotisms is the heartless tyranny of ideas."[299]

Intellectuals, 1988

Paul Johnson is one of the most admired intellectuals of the past century—it's hard to imagine anyone as knowledgeable of Western history as he was when you look at the array of books he published in his lifetime. Yet, Johnson wrote a book called *Intellectuals* which pulls no punches; one-by-one he exposes the harm and suffering caused by the plans and schemes of these very smart people who had one thing in common: they thought it was possible to ignore or change human nature. Their vast plans to improve humanity have ended in a "heartless tyranny of ideas" and millions of deaths.

DAY 297

THOMAS MERTON (1915–1968)

Revolutions change nothing—

"A revolution is supposed to be a change that turns everything completely around. But the ideology of political revolution

---

299 Paul Johnson, *Intellectuals* (New York: Harper & Row, Publishers, 1988), 342.

will never change anything except appearances. There will be violence, and power will pass from one party to another, but when the smoke clears and the bodies of all the dead men are underground, the situation will be essentially the same as it was before: there will be a minority of strong men in power exploiting all the others for their own ends. There will be the same greed and cruelty and lust and ambition and avarice and hypocrisy as before. For the revolutions of men change nothing. The only influence that can really upset the injustice and iniquity of men is the power that breathes in Christian tradition, renewing our participation in the Life that is the Light of men. . . . Each individual and each new age of the Church has to make this rediscovery, this return to the sources of Christian life."[300]

New Seeds of Contemplation, 1949

Thomas Merton writes a few years after the end of WWII. He has witnessed the Nazi death camps, the Soviet rape and pillage of Berlin, and the dropping of two nuclear bombs. "For the revolutions of men change nothing," he writes. One could argue with Merton that some revolutions, especially the American, did bring about important changes but that would be to miss his point. He's talking about the impact of revolutions and revolutionaries on human nature and the way our fallen nature

---

300 Thomas Merton, *New Seeds of Contemplation* (New York, New Directions Publishing Corporation, 1949), 14–15.

inevitably impels us to fight our way to the top of the heap. After the dust of any revolution settles, Merton writes, "there will be a minority of strong men in power exploiting all the others for their own ends." History continues to bear that out.

DAY 298

FLANNERY O'CONNOR (1925–1964)

Writing for unbelievers—

"The problem of the novelist who wishes to write about a man's encounter with this God is how he shall make the experience—which is both natural and supernatural—understandable, and credible, to his reader. In any age this would be a problem, but in our own, it is a well-nigh insurmountable one. Today's audience is one in which religious feeling has become, if not atrophied, at least vaporous and sentimental. When Emerson decided, in 1832, that he could no longer celebrate the Lord's Supper unless the bread and wine were removed, an important step in the vaporization of religion in America was taken, and the spirit of that step has continued apace. When the

physical fact is separated from the spiritual reality, the dissolution of belief is eventually inevitable."[301]

"Novelist and Believer," 1963

For Flannery O'Connor, the loss of sacramental vision, as
evidenced in Emerson's declaration, complicates the task of
the novelist, or any artist, who seeks to portray the reality of
God's presence—the supernatural—in all our lives. Although
O'Connor does not say it, Ralph Waldo Emerson's famous
address to the Harvard Divinity School in 1838 was considered
too radical, then at least, for the unitarian community in and
around Boston. It was thirty years before Emerson received
another invitation to speak at Harvard. That makes Emerson
the prophet of the secularized society to come when only
Catholics believe in the supernatural character of Communion.
O'Connor may have called the problem "insurmountable," but
her legacy attests to the fact that she, herself, did overcome it.

---

301 Flannery O'Connor, *Mystery and Manners: Occasional Prose*, ed., and selected by Sally and Robert Fitzgerald (New York: Farrar, Straus and Giroux,
1975), 161-62.

DAY 299

ST. BERNADINE OF SIENA (1380–1444)

The backbiter is a dung beetle—

"The one who keeps busy uncovering the sins of others is like the dung beetle. Such is the nature of this beetle that as soon as dung falls to the ground, it's as if the beetle has messengers to tell him where the pile is to be found. The very instant he knows about it, he's right on it. Within only a minute, he's made a little ball of the dung, and he occupies himself with it. I tell you, that's exactly what the backbiter does. He makes little balls of dung and makes sport with them. Somehow he gets pleasure out of hearing and reporting what's dishonest and shameful. See what the dung beetle does? He never uses any matter other than dung. He makes his ball; he positions himself with head down and legs in air; and then backwards he goes with it, walking along in this way until he arrives at a ditch. Then he and the ball of dung both fall into the ditch, and the dung beetle eats it. Again, I tell you, that's what the backbiter does: He delights in this rotten, stinking stuff, and acts like the beetle, making the ball and walking backwards with it until finally both he and the dung fall into the ditch. And this is because he doesn't seem to know how to act any other way, and he never occupies himself with any but the foulest kinds

of matter. So listen, children! When you hear somebody saying bad things about somebody else, just call him a dung beetle!"[302]

Sermons

St. Bernadine of Siena could certainly make his congregation smile. Imagine being compared to a "dung beetle"! And then hearing him graphically describe how the beetle shapes "dung" into playthings with which to darken the reputations of other people, to literally make them repel people by their smell. This is preaching at its best, arresting, memorable, and compellingly honest.

DAY 300

ÉTIENNE GILSON (1884–1978)

False, deadly gods—

"A world which has lost the Christian God cannot but resemble a world which has not yet found him. Just like the world of Thales and of Plato, our own modern world is 'full of gods.' There are blind Evolution, clear-sighted Orthogenesis, benevolent Progress, and others which it is more advisable not to

---

302 Paul Thigpen, *A Year With the Saints: Daily Meditations With the Holy Ones of God* (Charlotte: Saint Benedict Press, 2013), 247.

mention by name. Why unnecessarily hurt the feelings of men who, today, render them a cult? It is important for us to realize that mankind is doomed to live more and more under the spell of new scientific, social, and political mythology, unless we resolutely exorcise these befuddling notions whose influence on modern life is becoming appalling. Millions of men are starving and bleeding to death because two or three of these pseudo-scientific or pseudosocial deified abstractions are now at war. For when gods fight among themselves, men have to die."[303]

God and Philosophy, 1941

Étienne Gilson compares our secular society to the ancient world and finds that polytheism has returned. The new gods are the "-isms" that have directed masses of people since the beginning of the twentieth century. Gilson gave these lectures during the second year of WWII when Hitler's military was at its zenith. In the previous year, the Blitzkrieg had conquered France and occupied Paris with minimal resistance. Gilson had been born in Paris where he was educated and eventually taught at the Sorbonne. He talks about the "deified abstractions" that caused the war, the carnage, and the loss of life. Societies go to war over what they regard as an absolute,

---

303 Étienne Gilson, *God and Philosophy* (New Haven: Yale University Press, 1941), 136-37.

inviolable principle, what Gilson here calls the "gods [who]
fight among themselves."

DAY 301

DANA GIOIA (1950–)

PENTECOST

After the death of our son

Neither the sorrows of afternoon, waiting in the silent house,
Nor the night no sleep relieves, when memory
Repeats its prosecution.

Nor the morning's ache for dream's illusion, nor any prayers
Improvised to an unknowable god
Can extinguish the flame.

We are not as we were. Death has been our pentecost,
And our innocence consumed by these implacable
Tongues of fire.

Comfort me with stones. Quench my thirst with sand.
I offer you this scarred and guilty hand

Until others mix our ashes.[304]

The poet Dana Gioia writes during Pentecost about the loss of his son and defiantly declares, "Death has been our / pentecost." As a grieving father, he is not ready for a liturgical celebration, but using the imagery of Acts 2:4, he describes the experience of his son's death: "our innocence consumed by these / implacable / Tongues of fire." He finds no comfort in remembering the early Church united by the gift of tongues, but he does raise his "scarred and guilty hand" in recognition of the Church's remembrance.

DAY 302

JEAN DANIÉLOU, SJ (1905–1974)

Allied to the angels—

"What allies the soul to the angels is its detachment from the life of sense. Scripture admonishes our souls to contemplate the stable nature of the angels, so that our stability in virtue will be fortified by their example. For since it has been promised us that the life after the resurrection will resemble the condition

---

304 Dana Gioia, *99 Poems: New and Selected* (Minneapolis: Graywolf Press, 2016), 63.

of the angels — and He who made that promise does not lie — it follows that already our life in this world should be in conformity with that which will follow, so that living in the flesh and finding ourselves upon the battlefield of this world, we ought not to live according to the flesh and join forces with this world, but we should already begin to conform with the life we hope for after this world. That is why the Bride exhorts the soul to turn toward the powers of heaven, in imitation of their detachment, to attain to the purity of the angels."[305]

Angels and Their Mission, 1952

Jean Daniélou, SJ, earned his doctorate at the Sorbonne in Paris after becoming a Jesuit and being ordained a priest. He served in the French Air Force, and after the German occupation, he focused on patristics with a particular interest in Origen and wrote a biography of him. In 1944 he taught at the Institute Catholique as professor of Early Christian History, where he wrote several of his celebrated books—*The Bible and the Liturgy* (1951), *The Lord of History* (1953), and *God and the Ways of Knowing* (1956). Daniélou was appointed a cardinal in 1969 and was elected to the Académie Française in 1972. He was a consultant to the Second Vatican Council but became a critic of how its documents had been implemented. When Daniélou died in 1974 in the home of a woman who was

---

305 Jean Daniélou, *Angels and Their Mission* (Manchester: Sophia Press, 2009), loc. 849-855, Kindle Edition.

alleged to be a prostitute, his liberal critics did all they could to ruin his legacy. The Jesuits, after an investigation, determined that Daniélou was in the apartment, delivering money to pay for the bail of the woman's husband.

DAY 303

MATTHIAS JOSEPH SCHEEBEN (1835–1888)

Necessity of revelation—

"The purpose of positive revelation is first and immediately to bring the truths contained in it to man's attention, and as needed to perfect and broaden the imperfect knowledge that man may already have of these truths; mediately, however, to help man through this knowledge to strive for the goal that God has set for him, and as needed to support him in attaining this goal. The goal set by God for man determines the necessary measure of knowledge needed for the pursuit and attainment thereof; considering his actual inability to fulfill that goal, however, this measure determines the necessity of positive revelation. The necessity of revelation will therefore be different, depending on the different aspects of the goal that man is supposed to reach, and on his inability to reach this goal. Above all and principally the actual revelation is intended to help man to strive for and reach his supernatural end, i.e.,

the vision of God. But because the religious-moral demands
entailed in man's natural calling are not abolished by his calling
to a supernatural end, but rather are reiterated, and moreover
because man in the present [fallen] state of his nature is not
completely up to those demands: therefore the revelation can
and should at the same time contribute to the realization of
them, and to that extent also to the attainment of man's natural
end. Only through a careful distinction between the two ends
can one thus arrive also at a clear and correct understanding of
the real necessity of revelation, and of its supernatural character
as well."[306]

Handbook of Catholic Dogmatics, 1.1, 1906

Without revelation, Matthias Joseph Scheeben proclaims, we
cannot know what life is about. Life is given its meaning by
having a final end, one that contains virtually the morality and
spirituality required for us to reach it. But in this case, the final
end is not an "it" but a person, in fact, the three Persons of the
Holy Trinity. Reason alone, as seen in the Greek and Roman
philosophers, can conclude there is a Good that all men and
women should seek. However, this is the Good in the abstract
and can easily be misconstrued by those using reason to exert
power over others. The Final Good not only fills into what

---

306 Matthias Joseph Scheeben, *Handbook of Catholic Dogmatics* 1.1, trans. Mi-
    chael J. Miller (Steubenville: Emmaus Academic, 2019), loc. 636-662 of
    10036, Kindle Edition.

belongs to the abstract Good but also makes the Good available to all, not just the intellectually gifted.

DAY 304

JAMES HITCHCOCK (1938–)

How doctrine develops—

"Quite early, Christians realized that the Gospel did not provide a detailed explanation of every aspect of their faith. Rather, it was an embryo or seed, containing the whole of divine revelation but awaiting a gradual unfolding. Thus fidelity to Tradition is a paradox that has been at the heart of virtually all theological issues over the centuries—the faith must be handed on intact, but the Church's understanding of that faith develops in ways that could not have been anticipated in earlier times. The development of doctrine is a progressive widening and deepening of the meaning of the original truth, and heresy can be either false innovation or a rigid adherence to [non-dogmatic] older teachings. . . . Dogma is seldom officially defined unless it has first been questioned, and heresy perhaps serves the divine purpose of forming the Church to

reflect more deeply on her beliefs, to understanding them in ever more comprehensive and precise ways."[307]

History of the Catholic Church, 2012

James Hitchcock applies a common-sense answer about the dogmas that were defined centuries past the life of Christ. In other words, what is it about *tradition* that can be trusted in the same manner we trust the Scriptures? Hitchcock's explanation is so simple, readers may wonder why it had not occurred to them before: "Quite early, Christians realized that the Gospel *did not provide a detailed explanation* of every aspect of their faith" (emphasis added). Scripture contained the Word of God, but it was going to reveal its truth over time, in what Hitchcock calls an "unfolding." Dogma does not instantly appear: it gets drawn out of Scripture, Tradition, and liturgical practice over time. The Scriptural canon, the divine-human nature of the Son of God, and the Trinity are each examples. And, yes, as Hitchcock points out, it was the determination of what is heretical that led to these dogmatic developments.

---

307 James Hitchcock, *History of the Catholic Church: From the Apostolic Age to the Third Millennium* (San Francisco: Ignatius Press, 2012), 13-14.

DAY 305

MAX PICARD (1888–1965)

Silence came first—

"Silence is a basic phenomena. That is to say, it is a primary, objective reality, which cannot be traced to anything else. It cannot be replaced by anything else; it cannot be exchanged with anything else. There is nothing behind it to which it can be related except the Creator Himself. Silence is original and self-evident like the other basic phenomena; like love and loyalty and death and life itself. But it existed before all these and is in all of them. Silence is the firstborn of basic phenomena. It envelops the other basic phenomena—love, loyalty, and death; and there is more silence than speech in them, more of the invisible than the visible. There is also more silence in one person than can be used in a single human life. That is why every human utterance is surrounded by a mystery. The silence in a man stretches out beyond the single human life. In this silence, man is connected with past and future generations."[308]

The World of Silence, 1948

Max Picard reminds us that before time was created God existed. Silence belongs to that moment, to speak metaphorically,

---

308 Max Picard, *The World of Silence*, trans. Stanley Godwin (Chicago: Henry Regnery Company, 1952), 21.

between God and the creation. "Silence is the firstborn of basic phenomena," and silence infuses all that God made including man. Picard views silence as more fundamental to speech and all human habits and actions. He claims there is more silence and invisibility—mystery—in the human person than that which is heard or knowable. That same silence connects the present with the past and the future as the mysterious graciousness of God's Word to all humanity.

DAY 306

XAVIER ZUBIRI (1897–1983)

Making it mine—

"God happens in me, whether I know it or not, whether I wish it or not. In order for this to be my business something more is needed: it is necessary that I make it mine. And this *making it my business* is the acceptance, the surrender. . . . The surrender consists in my incorporating formally and deeply into my happening, as something brought about by me, the happening through which God happens in me. That God occurs in me is a *function of God in life*. But the surrender to God is to make *life into a function of God*. . . . We can very well know by

demonstrating the existence of God and his grounding characteristics, and yet have an attitude other than surrender."[309]

Man and God, 1948

Xavier Zubiri reflects on his surrender to the God who "happens in me, whether I know it or not." This surrender involves reversing his attitude from God as a "function" in life to his life being a "function of God." As a philosopher who was one of the leading metaphysicians of his time, Zubiri adds that demonstrating the existence of God falls far short of "surrendering" to Him. His book *On Essence* (1963) was a critical rethinking of the concept of essence across the entire history of philosophy. Between 1980 and 1983, Zubiri published his major three-volume systematic work, *Sentient Intelligence*. Zubiri died on September 21, 1983, while editing *Man and God* for publication.

---

309 Xavier Zubiri, *Man and God*, trans. Joaquin Redondo, translation critically revised by Thomas Fowler and Nelson Orringer (Lanham: University Press of America, 2009), 173.

DAY 307

FRANK SHEED (1897–1981)

Loss of foundations—

"A society can accept a moral code without any conscious awareness of its foundation, provided the code is of long standing and not questioned. But in a generation like ours where everything is questioned the foundation must be clearly seen; and apart from God, the foundation cannot be clearly seen. The practical result for the average man of our generation is that when he is faced with what his grandparents would have called a temptation, he has nothing to judge it by. His first reaction is, 'Why shouldn't I?' he passes with an uneasiness too slight to affect his decision to 'I don't see why I shouldn't.' As we have already seen, this last statement is precise almost to the point of pedantry. He does not see why he shouldn't: he does not see anything, because he has turned out the lights, or had them turned out for him: he is simply conscious of a lot of urges and appetites in the dark and there is no mistaking their direction."[310]

Theology and Sanity, 1946

---

310 F. J. Sheed, *Theology and Sanity* (Aeterna Press, 2019), loc. 279 of 332, Kindle Edition.

There was a time in Western culture, as Frank Sheed points out, when morality was learned by living in a society whose individuals generally agreed about fundamental values. Every level of those societies—family, community, state, and church—reinforced shared moral norms along with their rewards and punishments. When those foundations were removed, during the period from approximately 1500 to 1900, individuals, families, and institutions no longer knew the reason why the past moral norms were obligatory. Moral questions came to predominate over moral answers. Some philosophers and theologians tried to put Humpty-Dumpty back together again. Sheen remarks, "there is no mistaking" the directions human "urges and appetites" will take where the moral foundation is missing: he naturally leans toward self-gratification and little else.

DAY 308

MALCOLM MUGGERIDGE (1903–1990)

The fate of truth—

"Truth is very beautiful, more so, as I consider than justice — today's pursuit — which easily puts on a false face. In the nearly seven decades I have lived through, the world has overflowed with bloodshed and explosions whose dust has never had time to settle before others have erupted; all in purportedly just

causes. The quest for justice continues, and the weapons and hatred pile up; but truth was an early casualty. The lies on behalf of which our wars have been fought and our peace treatises concluded! The lies of revolution and of counter-revolution! The lies of advertising, of news, of salesmanship, of politics! . . . Ignazio Silone told me once how, when he was a member of the old Comintern, some strategy was under discussion, and a delegate, a newcomer who had never attended before, made the extraordinary observation that if such and such a statement were to be put out, it wouldn't be true. There was a moment of dazed silence, and then everyone began to laugh. They laughed and laughed until tears ran down their cheeks, and the Kremlin walls seemed to shake. The same laughter echoes in every council chamber and cabinet room, whether two or more are gathered together to exercise authority. It is truth that has died, not God."[311]

Chronicles of Wasted Time, Chronicle 1, 1973

Muggeridge is lamenting the fate of truth. Truth has been manipulated to serve the goals of the advertiser, the media, the salesperson, and the politicians. Most egregious is the manipulation of truth to justify unnecessary violence and wars. He relates an incident when he was at a conference with the KGB discussing plans, and he pointed out that the proposal was not

---

311 Malcolm Muggeridge, *Chronicles of Wasted Time—Chronicle I: The Green Stick* (New York: William Morrow & Company, Inc., 1973), 19-20.

true. Instead of being angry, the KGB uproariously laughed—Muggeridge had said aloud what all of them had been thinking for years. He had burst momentarily the balloon of deception, but "the same laughter echoes in every council chamber and cabinet room, whether two or more are gathered together to exercise authority. It is truth that has died, not God."

DAY 309

MARSHAL MCLUHAN (1911–1980)

Facing the question—

"I was reading Chesterton and Dawson and Maritain and those people. That's how I came in. I had no instruction from clergy at any time but there was a friend of mine who said, 'Well, since you don't believe in Christianity' — I was an agnostic — he said 'you could pray to God the Father. So you pray to God the Father and simply ask to be shown.' And so I did. And I didn't know what I was going to be shown, all I said was, 'Show me,' and I didn't ask to be relieved of any problems. I had no problems. I had no belief and no problems. Well, I was shown in a quite an amazing way and quite unexpected: I was arguing about religion with a whole group of grad students one night at Wisconsin, and one of them said to me suddenly, 'Why aren't you a Catholic?' And I shut up because I didn't

know. Up to that moment, it had never occurred to me that I would ever become a Catholic. But I was suddenly caught. I became a Catholic at once within a few days."[312]

Marshall McLuhan relates how he became Catholic. His journey to conversion was not at all dramatic, at least on the surface. It appears he asked a friend about Christianity after remarking that the books by Maritain and Chesterton had impressed him. "Where do I go from here?" he might have asked. Some friend casually suggests McLuhan ask God to show him the way. McLuhan did pray, not knowing what to expect, or how he would be receiving the answer to his question. Then one day, after a lecture to graduate students, one of the students asked him, "Well, Professor McLuhan, why aren't you a Catholic?" The student had surmised from McLuhan's lecture that he must be. We don't know the tone of the question, whether it was meant in kindness or in jest. "But I was suddenly caught," McLuhan admits.

---

312 https://mcluhangalaxy.wordpress.com/2012/08/29/marshall-mcluhans-catholic-faith/.

DAY 310

CORNELIO FABRO (1911–1995)

God in nature equals immanence—

"That the situation has become dramatic or tragic is hardly worth saying and almost without meaning. It was outlined, with unequivocal clarity, by philosophy more than three centuries ago with the advent of the principle of immanence and more than a century ago with the elevation, especially by idealism and pragmatism, of consciousness of the will to be as the will to power. What a wonder then if today freedom is at the mercy of ambiguous and angry confrontations between the greatest nuclear powers and if the borders of nations are not so much those of earthly geography as those that are being contested in the race to conquer cosmic space! And this, it seems to me, is a sign that with the advent of modern thought, the inner axis of the spirit has been changed, and with it the relationship of man to nature. The criterion of truth has been turned upside down precisely from its orientation in Being itself to being the activity of mind, from the time when Parmenides stated that "without being there is no thought," and from transcendence to immanence."[313]

"Theology in the Context of a Philosophy of Nothingness," 1968

---

313 Cornelio Fabro, *Selected Works of Cornelio Fabro,* Volume 3, trans. Nathaniel Dreyer (Chillum: IVE Press, 2020), loc. 1646 of 2733, Kindle Edition.

Cornelio Fabro thought the idea of "immanence" was essential to understanding what happened to the idea of God in modern philosophy. Philosophers like Spinoza, Fichte, and Hegel wrote about a God who does not exist above or behind the temporal world but is somehow identical—immanent—with it, in other words. As Fabro points out, this puts man in the awkward situation of no longer being able to look above for help: as he says elsewhere, "only man can save man." With an immanent God, nature no longer is regarded as subordinate to human beings. God becomes god. One consequence, according to Fabro, is that the human will has become "the will to power" as Nietzsche proclaimed it. Human actions have no external or supernatural end to seek. Nothing preexists, or transcends, the individual that he or she needs to discover for wisdom and well-being. Man is now the creator of all values.

DAY 311

EVELYN WAUGH (1903–1996)

Empress Helena (248–330) asks Pope Sylvester a surprising question—

And then Helena said something which seemed to have no relevance: "Where is the cross, anyway?"

"What cross, my dear?"

"The only one. The real one."

"I don't know. I don't think anyone knows. I don't think anyone has ever asked before."

"It must be somewhere. Wood doesn't just melt like snow. It's not three hundred years old. The temples here are full of beams and paneling twice that age. It stands to reason God would take more care of the cross than of them."

"Nothing 'stands to reason' with God. If He had wanted us to have it, no doubt He would have given it to us. But He hasn't chosen to. He gives us enough."

"But how do you know He doesn't want us to have it— the cross, I mean? I bet He's just waiting for one of us to go find it—just at this moment when it's most needed. Just at this moment everyone is forgetting it and chattering about the hypostatic union, there's a solid chunk of wood waiting for them to have their silly heads knocked against it," said Helena.

The Empress Dowager was an old woman, almost of an age with Pope Sylvester, but he regarded her fondly as though she were a child, an impetuous young princess who went well to

the hounds, and he said with the gentlest irony: "You'll tell me, won't you?—if you're successful"

"I'll tell the world," said Helena.[314]

Helena: A Novel, 1950

St. Helena, Constantine's mother, traveled to the Holy Land in search of the cross. As Waugh relates, she is convinced that the cross still exists because Jesus would have made certain that it wasn't totally destroyed or disintegrated. He would have left it for our reassurance in the reality of his crucifixion. She obtains permission from Pope Sylvester and goes. St. Helena found many sacred sites in the Holy Land and built magnificent churches on sacred sites, all of which are preserved today, along with the pieces of what were believed to be the "True Cross."

---

314 Evelyn Waugh, *Helena: A Novel* (Boston: Little, Brown and Company, 1950), 195-96.

DAY 312

MAX PICARD (1888–1965)

Facing the Image—

> "Man's face is the image of God. And the image of God is like a call to the spectator: the whole being of the spectator is called together and held together. It is as if the image of God were being shown that man is still the whole creature that he was when God placed him upon the earth. Therein lies the joy that the sight of a face can give: the onlooker feels once more that he is a complete being and to that is added the greater joy of feeling this before God's image. Not until he looked upon God's image did he feel that he had become whole again."[315]

The Human Face, 1930

Max Picard's *The Human Face* is an unusual book. The book jacket itself contains images of eight faces, all recognizable figures from history, and eight faces on the back. We see Pascal, Flaubert, Leo XIII, Darwin, Machiavelli, Handel, the actress Eleonora Duse, along with Buddha, Nietzsche, Spinoza, and Caesar. Picard claims the image of God is found in a person's face, but an individual can ruin that image by immorality and unbelief. Faces can also record spiritual and moral growth.

---

315 Max Picard, *The Human Face*, trans. Guy Endore (New York: Farrar and Rinehart Incorporated, 1930), 3.

Picard compares Dostoevsky's image as a young man to his image as an older man: "The face of the young man is turned completely toward the outside . . . it is driven toward the outside." In the face of the older Dostoevsky, this face "is so full that it pushes out. The tension is turned toward the interior, toward the depths." It's as if, according to Picard, the "earlier face had been buried,—and then had arisen, and this arisen face was the later face. The burial, however, was in the earth beyond." It's often said by psychologists and sociologists that when we meet a new person, our unconscious sizes them up quickly: surely part of that process is our reaction to what we *read* in their human face. The writer George Orwell put it this way, "At 50, everyone has the face he deserves."

DAY 313

ALFRED DÖBLIN (1878–1957)

A dose of sadness—

"When, at the beginning of my own journey of destiny, I attended a Christian service in France—as an outsider, then—I was surprised by its somber and sad nature. Christianity, after all, bears glad tidings. I saw that sadness was not really the message. Those who are believers, absentminded and playful as they are—like children, really—must be led to the true reality, to

seriousness, to great and then greater things. Solemnity, respect, and humility are required. I was almost a cipher in the face of the inscrutable prime mover that I was led out of my everyday existence in order to become one of God's creatures, a child. In the face of our not very appropriate, not very innocent existence, we need a dose of sadness, of dejection and remorse, they need even to dominate. And when that best of all possible examples of true and pure existence, the Passion, occurred and we experienced how we received that original love, and when a terrible life illuminated our pitiful life—then basically there was room only for a grievous, bitter, if not totally despairing solemnity."[316]

Destiny's Journey, 1968

Alfred Döblin didn't expect to find sad faces when he first attended Mass in France: "Christianity, after all, bears glad tiding." He's probably not alone in having noticed and remarked on this. But then he begins to see the reason behind the serious, even grave, faces. We may become children of God, Döblin remarks, but we don't possess the innocence of children. A "dose of sadness" is appropriate in one who recognizes the sins which have been taken away by God's forgiveness, and these are sins that, some of which, will be repeated as the years pass.

---

316 Alfred Döblin, *Destiny's Journey*, ed. Edgar Passler, trans. Edna McCown, introduction by Peter Demetz (New York: Paragon House, 1992), 322.

DAY 314

CHRISTOPHER DAWSON (1889–1970)

Our common view of life—

"Throughout the greater part of history, the art gallery, the critic, and the collector have been unknown, though artistic production has been continuous and universal. It is in fact one of the most fundamental of human activities. It is common to the savage and the civilized man. It goes back to Paleolithic times, and it is from the artistic record of the human race that almost all that we know regarding the cultures of prehistoric times has been derived. It is indeed difficult to separate the beginnings of Art from the beginnings of human culture, for as I have said, *social activity is of its very nature artistic; it is the shaping of the rough material of man's environment by human skill and creativeness.* . . . In reality, a great art is always the expression of a great culture, whether it be manifested through the work of an individual genius or embodied in a great impersonal tradition. For society rests not only on the community of place, the community of work, and the community of race, it is also and before all a community of thought. We see this in the case of language, which is fundamental to any kind of social life. Here ages of thinking and acting in common have produced a terminology, a system of classification and even a scale of values which in turn impose themselves on the minds of all who come under its influence, so as to justify the old saying that a

new language is a new soul. There is also a common conception of reality, a view of life, which even in the most primitive societies expresses itself through magical practices and religious beliefs, and which in the higher cultures appears in a fuller and more conscious form in religion, science and philosophy. And this common view of life will also tend to embody itself in external forms and symbols, no less than do the more material and utilitarian activities of the society."[317] (Emphasis added.)

Dynamics of World History, 1956

Great cultures, according to Christopher Dawson, will produce art that expresses those things considered of greatest importance, whether it be love, sex, war, power, gods, or heroes. The ruins of Pompeii disclosed an unusual preoccupation with sexual pleasure. The statues of classical Greece glorify an idealized male form. Medieval art depicts the story of Christianity and its Church. With the Renaissance, human individuals appear in all their motley variety.

---

317 Christopher Dawson, *Dynamics of World History*, ed. John J. Mulloy, new introduction by Dermot Quinn (Wilmington: ISI Books), loc.1702-1727 of 9150, Kindle Edition.

DAY 315

YVES R. SIMON (1903–1961)

Duty beyond reason—

"A moral system erected without knowledge of what only revelation can tell us would suppose that human nature is in fact endowed with all the powers a man should have for a perfectly healthy nature. But we know that human nature was not only despoiled by original sin of the supernatural gifts that God had gratuitously conferred upon it in the state of innocence, but also *wounded*. A man was traveling from Jerusalem to Jericho and was set upon by robbers who not only took his money and clothes but also injured him in such a way that they left him incapable of helping himself. The man the Good Samaritan gratuitously cared for is sinful humanity. Let us speak of our capacities as if original sin had not left us in a ditch from which only divine grace can rescue us. . . . But revelation makes known to us that man is in fact destined to a supernatural end. This supernatural ultimate end, and the means God has fashioned for its attainment, not only create absolutely new obligations, such as the frequent reception of the sacraments, but also change, at least in some cases, the rule of obligations already formulated by natural reason. Thus it is, according to the classic example, that purely natural wisdom, though it prescribes sobriety, disapproves of all extreme forms of asceticism. We think that no philosophy could by means of

simple philosophical principles, justify the mortifications of a St. Catherine of Siena."[318]

A Critique of Moral Knowledge, 2002

For Yves R. Simon, the classical account of the virtues, those taught by philosophy alone, do not comport with the Christian virtues as exemplified by the saints or the story of the Good Samaritan. Philosophies of virtue, beginning with Aristotle, viewed virtuous action as belonging to the mean, the measure of moderation. The man of courage then is neither foolhardy or timid. A temperate man is neither a teetotaler or a drunk. But having faith in a supernatural end, a Christian is not called to live in the mean but called to the extreme of faith, hope, and love. Simon uses St. Catherine of Siena as an example— no philosophy can morally justify why she inflicted suffering upon herself for the love of God.

---

318 *A Critique of Moral Knowledge,* trans. with introduction by Ralph McInerny (New York: Fordham University Press, 2002), 59-60.

DAY 316

JORIS-KARL HUYSMANS (1848–1907)

The character Durtal is returning to the Church after a long odyssey—

"The moment of Communion was at hand. The little boy had gently thrown the white napkin back on the table; the nuns and poor women and peasants went forward, all with clasped hands and bowed heads, and the child took a taper and passed in front of the priest, his eyes almost shut for fear of seeing the Host. There was in this little creature such a glow of love and reverence that Durtal gazed with admiration and trembled with awe. Without in the least knowing why, in the midst of the darkness that fell on his soul, of the impotent and wavering feeling that thrilled it without there being any word to describe them, he felt a tide bearing him to the Saviour, and then a recoil. The comparison was inevitably forced upon him between that child's soul and his own. 'Why, it is he, not I, who should take the Sacrament!' cried he to himself; and he crouched there inert, his hands folded, not knowing how to decide, in a frame at once beseeching and terrified, when he felt himself gently drawn to the table and received the Sacrament. . . . Never, not even at Chartres, had he been able to hinder the torpor that overpowered him at the moment of receiving the Sacrament. His powers were benumbed, his faculties arrested. . . . At Chartres, this state of collapse was still present, but some indulgent tenderness presently enwrapped

and warmed the spirit. The soul as it recovered was no longer alone; it was encouraged and perceptibly helped by the Virgin, who revived it. And this impression, peculiar to this crypt, permeated the body too; it was no longer a feeling of suffocation for lack of air; on the contrary, it was the oppression of inflation, of over-fulness, which would be mitigated by degrees, allowing of easy breathing at last."[319]

The Cathedral, 1898

The French writer J. K. Huysmans died at fifty-nine as a devout Catholic after living much of his life as a Parisian dandy and a leading figure in what is called the "decadent movement." His last three novels portray in fictional terms his own conversion to the Church: *En route* (1895), *The Cathedral* (1898), and *The Oblate* (1903). This trilogy had a wide influence on fellow writers and intellectuals who followed his example. From 1899 to 1901, Huysmans lived as a lay monk, a period which he portrayed in *The Oblate*.

---

319 J.K. Huysmans, *The Cathedral*, trans. by Clara Bell, 1898, loc. 65 of 338, Kindle Edition; read more about Huysmans at http://humanityfaithho-pecharity.com/category/j-k-huysmans/.

DAY 317

ST. FRANCIS DE SALES (1567–1622)

Overcoming natural inclinations—

"We have certain natural inclinations that aren't strictly speaking either mortal or venial sins, but rather weaknesses. The acts in which they take shape are faults and deficiencies. St. Jerome, for example, reported that St. Paula had so strong a tendency to excessive sorrow that when she lost her husband and children she nearly died of grief. That wasn't a sin, but an imperfection, since it was against her desire and will. Some people are naturally easygoing, while some are contentious. Some are disposed to be critical of others' opinions. Some are naturally disposed to be angry, while some are inclined to be affectionate. In short, there's hardly anyone in whom we don't find some such weaknesses. Even though these weaknesses may be natural and instinctive in each person, they may be restrained and corrected, and at last eradicated, by cultivating the opposite inclination. And this must be done. Gardeners have found how to make the bitter almond tree bear sweet fruit by cutting the foot of the tree and letting the sap escape. So why shouldn't we, in a similar way, purge out our perverse inclinations and acquire better ones? No disposition is so good by nature that it can't acquire bad habits. Nor is any natural disposition so

perverse that it can't be conquered and overcome by God's grace, joined to our earnest and diligent endeavor."[320]

Introduction to the Devout Life

A sense of grace and acceptance pervades these words of St. Francis de Sales. He's a wise observer of human frailty and behavior and acknowledges that every individual starts from a different place in their journey towards God. Some are naturally full of glee, others tend toward sadness, and, he insists, there is no sin in possessing these "inclinations." The sin arises from actions that can arise from them: The gleeful man who fails to notice those whose sadness need his care and concern, or the sad woman who cannot join in the celebration of her friend's achievements are examples. Notice, in particular, the last paragraph beginning with "No disposition is so good by nature that it can't acquire bad habits." Put a strong accent on the word "so" and its meaning will become more clear. In other words, even those naturally blessed with charm, intelligence, and confidence can turns these inclinations into weapons that hurt others.

---

320 Paul Thigpen, *A Year With the Saints: Daily Meditations With the Holy Ones of God* (Charlotte: Saint Benedict Press, 2013), 260.

DAY 318

RENÉ GIRARD (1923–2015)

Wolves in sheep's clothing—

"The most powerful anti-Christian movement is the one that takes over and 'radicalizes' the concern for victims in order to paganize it. The powers and principalities want to be 'revolutionary' now, and they reproach Christianity for not defending victims with enough ardor. In Christian history, they see nothing but persecutions, acts of oppression, inquisitions. This other totalitarianism presents itself as the liberator of humanity. In trying to usurp the place of Christ, the powers imitate him in the way a mimetic rival imitates his model in order to defeat him. They denounce the Christian concern for victims as hypocritical and a pale imitation of the authentic crusade against oppression and persecution for which they would carry the banner themselves. In the symbolic language of the New Testament, we would say that in our world Satan, trying to make a new start and gain new triumphs, borrows the language of victims."[321]

I See Satan Fall Like Lightning, 1999

321 Girard, René, *I See Satan Fall Like Lightning*, trans. and foreword by James G. Williams (Maryknoll: Orbis Books, 1999), loc. 180-181, Kindle Edition.

René Girard uses his understanding of scapegoating to explain how totalitarian regimes make scapegoats of the nations and institutions they overthrow. His example of Satan borrowing "the language of the victims" makes explicit the evil being perpetrated by those political leaders who flip the common sense of the world on its head. Those who have previously been recognized as men of charity and good will are seen as false and fake. They are exiled, arrested, jailed, or killed and the true liberators are put in their place. They promise happiness to the people and deliver enslavement. The liberators claim to have eliminated the so-called victimizers only to create an all-powerful State. Think, for example, of how Athens treated Socrates, condemning to death a citizen who had been widely admired for his wisdom.

DAY 319

G. K. CHESTERTON (1874–1936)

The world upside down—

"If a man saw the world upside down, with all the trees and towers hanging head downwards as in a pool, one effect would be to emphasize the idea of dependence. There is a Latin and literal connection; for the very word dependence only means hanging. It would make vivid the Scriptural text which says

that God has hung the world upon nothing. If St. Francis had seen, in one of his strange dreams, the town of Assisi upside down, it need not have differed in a single detail from itself except in being entirely the other way round. But the point is this: that whereas to the normal eye the large masonry of its walls or the massive foundations of its watchtowers and its high citadel would make it seem safer and more permanent, the moment it was turned over the very same weight would make it seem more helpless and more in peril. It is but a symbol; but it happens to fit the psychological fact. St. Francis might love his little town as much as before, or more than before; but the nature of the love would be altered even in being increased. He might see and love every tile on the steep roofs or every bird on the battlements; but he would see them all in a new and divine light of eternal danger and dependence. Instead of being merely proud of his strong city because it could not be moved, he would be thankful to God Almighty that it had not been dropped; he would be thankful to God for not dropping the whole cosmos like a vast crystal to be shattered into falling stars. Perhaps St. Peter saw the world so, when he was crucified head-downwards.[322]

St. Francis of Assisi, 1923

---

322 G.K. Chesterton, *St. Francis of Assisi* (New York: George H. Doran Company, 1924), 108-9.

Chesterton's biographies of St. Francis and St. Thomas are masterpieces of concision and insight set down in perfect prose. Take the excerpt above: Chesterton explains the impact of St. Francis on the tradition of Christian spirituality by comparing his vision to looking at the world upside down. With the land hovering over the sky, all the earth looks like it should collapse to the bottom, but it does not. Why? Because some power is holding the earth in place and we are grateful to God "for not dropping the whole cosmos like a vast crystal to be shattered into falling stars."

DAY 320

MAURICE BARING (1874–1945)

Candlemas

The town is half awe; the nave, the choir,
Are dark, and all is dim, within, without;
But every chapel fringed with the devout,
Is bright with February flowers of fire.

At Mass, a thousand years ago in Rome,
Thus Priest, thus Server at the altar bowed;
Thus knelt, thus blessed itself the kneeling crowd,
At Dawn, with the secret catacomb.

Thus shall they meet for Mass, until the day
The glory of the world shall pass away.
And beauty far away from human reach,

And power, and wealth beyond all mortal price,
And glory that outsoars all thought, all speech,
Speak in the whispered words of sacrifice.[323]

Collected Poems, 1925

Maurice Baring's poetry is often overlooked because of the sheer bulk of his other publications and literary accomplishments. Baring was a successful playwright, novelist, essayist, memoirist, and expert in Russian literature and language. He also knew Latin, Greek, French, German, Italian, and Danish. He was the quintessential European intellectual of his age but a devout Catholic as well. As biographer Joseph Pearce points out, Baring's range of knowledge was so extensive that the writer/actor Robert Speaight described his last book, *Have You Anything to Declare?* as "the best bedside book in the English language."

---

323 Maurice Baring, *Collected Poems* (London, William Heinemann LTD., 1925), 65.

DAY 321

JOSEF PIEPER (1904–1997)

A reason for joy—

"Joy is by its nature something secondary and subsidiary. It is, of course, foolish to ask anyone 'why' he wants to rejoice; and so it might be thought that joy is something sought for its own sake, and consequently *not* secondary. But if we look into the matter more closely it becomes apparent that man, if all works out as it should, does not want to plunge absolutely and unconditionally into the psychological state of rejoicing but that he wants to have a reason for rejoicing. . . . For sometimes things do not work out as they should—for example, when in the absence of a 'reason' a 'cause' is brought to bear by a kind of manipulation, a predeceptive, unfounded feeling of joy. Such a cause may be a drug or it may be the electric stimulation of certain brain centers. Julian Huxley has argued that 'after all, electric happiness is still happiness'; but for the time being I remained convinced that St. Augustine correctly defines the true state of affairs—as well, incidentally, as expressing the viewpoint of the average man—when he says, 'There is no one who would not prefer to endure pain with a sound mind than to rejoice in madness.' Man can (and wants to) rejoice

only when there is a reason for joy. And this reason, therefore, is primary, the joy is secondary."[324]

Uber die Liebe, 1972

Josef Pieper clarifies a common misunderstanding about emotions like joy. As did Dietrich von Hildebrand, Pieper evaluates joy in regard to the thing prompting the joy, what's called the object of joy. Everyone wants to dance for joy, but what about those whose dancing is fueled only by alcohol or some other drug? Is that a joy to be celebrated or remembered with fondness? Or is it somehow fake? Those who seek joy directly are the most likely to take shortcuts. But what about those who find joy in gardens, grandchildren, or books? Joy arrives as a *by-product* of gardening, reading, and playing with the grandchildren, and it's a joy that can be fully celebrated.

324 Josef Pieper, *Josef Pieper: An Anthology*, foreword by Hans Urs von Balthasar (San Francisco: Ignatius Press, 1989), 32-33.

DAY 322

JACQUES MARITAIN (1882–1973)

The voices she hears—

The novelist Caroline Gordon writes to Jacques Maritain to tell him that she used a sentence from his Frontiers of Poetry *as the epigraph to her novel* The Malefactors *(1950).*

"It is for Adam to interpret the voices Eve hears."[325]

Frontiers of Poetry, 1927

Jacques and Raïssa Maritain had a unique spiritual friendship and marriage which had a transforming power not only on their lives but also on the vast array of friends and associates in Europe, England, Canada, and the United States. Just as Hans Urs von Balthasar found in Adrienne von Speyr a spiritual *muse*, Jacques Maritain regarded Raïssa in the same way. These kinds of relationships are not that rare among notable writers and artists as Dante (Beatrice), Petrarch (Laura), Baudelaire (Jeanne Duval), Gustav Mahler (Alma Mahler), James Joyce (Nora Barnacle), W. B. Yeats (Maud Gonne), F. Scott Fitzgerald

---

325 Jacques Maritain, *Art and Scholasticism and The Frontiers of Poetry*, trans. Joseph W. Evans (Notre Dame: University of Notre Dame Press, 1974), 144; see also, *John Dunaway, Exiles and Fugitives: The Letters of Jacques and Raïssa Maritain, Allen Tate, and Caroline Gordon*, (Baton Rouge: Louisiana University Press, 1992), 56.

(Zelda Fitzgerald), and Charles Dodgson (Alice Liddell), among many others. Maritain scholar John Dunaway cites a literary critic who, reviewing *The Malefactors*, again from Gordon's letter, describes Maritain's cryptic remark as "the relationship between practical or critical intelligence and poetic intuition. ...The poet is nourished by his intuitions, but it is the critical intelligence (Adam) which must decide on the authenticity of what the soul (Eve) experiences." Maritain also had carved these words on the tombstone of his wife, Raïssa, who died thirteen years before his own death.

DAY 323

ST. BASIL THE GREAT (329–379)

St. Basil answers those who argue the Holy Spirit should not be considered equal to the Father and the Son in the Holy Trinity—

"For if our Lord, when enjoining the baptism of salvation, charged His disciples to baptize all nations in the name 'of the Father and of the Son and of the Holy Ghost,' not disdaining fellowship with Him, and these men allege that we must not rank Him with the Father and the Son, is it not clear that they openly withstand the commandment of God? If they deny that coordination of this kind is declaratory of any fellowship and conjunction, let them tell us why it behooves us to hold this

opinion, and what more intimate mode of conjunction they have. If the Lord did not indeed conjoin the Spirit with the Father and Himself in baptism, do not let them lay the blame of conjunction upon us, for we neither hold nor say anything different. . . . The one aim of the whole band of opponents and enemies of 'sound doctrine' is to shake down the foundation of the faith of Christ by leveling apostolic tradition with the ground, and utterly destroying it. . . . Whence is it that we are Christians? Through our faith, would be the universal answer. And in what way are we saved? Plainly because we were regenerate through the grace given in our baptism. How else could we be? And after recognizing that this salvation is established through the Father and the Son and the Holy Ghost, shall we fling away "that form of doctrine" which we received? . . . For if to me my baptism was the beginning of life, and that day of regeneration the first of days, it is plain that the utterance uttered in the grace of adoption was the most honorable of all. Can I then, perverted by these men's seductive words, abandon the tradition which guided me to the light, which bestowed on me the boon of the knowledge of God, whereby I, so long a foe by reason of sin, was made a child of God? But, for myself, I pray that with this confession I may depart hence to the Lord, and them I charge to preserve the faith secure until the day of Christ, and to keep the Spirit undivided from the Father and

the Son, preserving, both in the confession of faith and in the doxology, the doctrine taught them at their baptism."[326]

On the Holy Spirit, c. 364

It has been said that St. Basil is to the monks of the East what St. Benedict is to the West. St. Basil lived at a time when Christianity had been legal for only a generation. In addition to the Trinity, he effectively defended, both through oratory and writing, the unity of the human and divine natures in Jesus Christ against the Arian heresy.

DAY 324

JOHN FINNIS (1940–)

Absolutes are Absolutes—

"In short: To deny the truth of moral absolutes by arguing they block the reasonable and responsible pursuit of greater amounts of premoral human good is incoherent with faith in divine providence. It results, necessarily, in reducing morality to a pseudotechnical reasoning in pursuit of goals defined not by reason (or morality) but by feelings which shrink the horizon

---

326 St. Basil, *St. Basil Collection* (Aeterna Press, 2016), loc. 139-140, Kindle Reader.

of deliberation in order to create the illusion of commensuration what is in reality rationally incommensurable. By contrast, to respect the moral absolutes which are made known to us by God through reason and faith is to cooperate with God, who has practical knowledge of everything without limit. And to cooperate thus with God is *to take into account everything* (the principal demand of proportionalists), *in the only way we can.*"[327]

Moral Absolutes, 1991

John Finnis is describing a version of moral reasoning called proportionalism that asserts that one can determine the right course of action by weighing the good against the evil caused by the action. This is how some Jesuit ethicists justify abortion, by including the impact on the mother, etc. In this book, Finnis shows that proportionalism violates both moral absolutes, such as the Ten Commandments, and the Pauline principle that one may never do evil for the sake of good. A native of Australia, he began his schooling at Adelaide University before receiving a doctorate in philosophy from Oxford in 1945 as a Rhodes Scholar. Finnis taught at Oxford for over forty years before taking teaching posts abroad. He specialized in the legal and ethical theory of St. Thomas Aquinas and became a member of the Pontifical Council of Justice and Peace (1990–1995) and the Pontifical Academy Pro Vita (2001–2016). His books

---

327 John Finnis, *Moral Absolutes: Tradition, Revision, and Truth* (Washington DC: The Catholic University of America Press, 1991), 20.

include *Judicial Power and the Balance of Our Constitution* (2018), *Natural Law and Natural Rights* (2011), and *Collected Essays of John Finnis* (2011).

DAY 325

BILL DONOHUE (1947–)

Remember the nuns—

"By the middle part of the nineteenth century, there were over 130 Catholic schools in the United States, all the work of nuns. Hospitals and orphanages were being built at a record pace. Then years later, on the brink of the Civil War, the Irish-Catholic presence was profound: of the 2.2 million Catholics in the United States, 1.6 million were Irish. The Irish foothold was especially visible among the nuns. . . . Like so many other orders, the Sisters of St. Joseph were service-oriented, working in education, nursing, and social agencies. The order drew from a wide array of women, recruiting from cities and the countryside, and from rich and poor families. . . . It is hard to imagine what Catholic life would have been like without the effort of these nuns. They ran everything: schools, hospitals, orphanages, shelters, social services of every kind. And in

the best of the Catholic tradition, they never turned away the dispossessed because of their religion or any other social consideration."[328]

Why Catholicism Matters, 2012

In our generation, Bill Donohue has done more than any other American layman to defend the Church against public slanders and insults, and to insist upon the rights of Catholics, and the proper role of the Catholic Church in the public square. Donohue has been president of the Catholic League for Religious and Civil Rights since 1993. He began his career as a scholar and academic, receiving his doctorate in sociology from New York University, teaching at the college level for over decade, before publishing a devastating critique, *The Politics of the American Civil Liberties Union*, in 1985. More books would follow, but Donohue's national reputation was created by his usually successful attacks on anti-Catholicism in politics, the arts, academic institutions, and the lawyers who ignored the facts to cash in on the sexual scandals of many priests. Donohue has constantly said aloud that the scandal is not about pedophilia but about homosexuality since 81 percent of the victims were male and 78 percent were post-pubescent according to the bishop's official report. Given his intelligence, education, and doggedness, Bill Donohue has succeeded in

---

328 Bill Donohue, *Why Catholicism Matters* (New York: Crown Publishing, 2012), 130-31.

defending the Church where others have failed. He's one of the leading Catholic laymen of the late twentieth and early twenty-first centuries.

DAY 326

LOUIS BOUYER, CONG, ORAT. (1913–2004)

Grace alone—

"For St. Thomas Aquinas, when grace moves the heart of man to surrender himself to God for the accomplishment of his will, if this grace is efficacious, if man believes, is regenerated, and lives accordingly in the love of God, it is by no means the free consent of man that made grace effective. On the contrary, his consent was due solely to the will of God that his grace should be efficacious in that man at that moment. The great mystery lies in the fact that this consent should remain free; but the reason is that God, the Lord and Creator of all, is Lord and Creator of our very freedom. He is not just the master of freedom in a general way, as a faculty given to us once for all, which we can use, subsequently, in complete independence. For St. Thomas, God is the absolute master not only of the faculty but of its entire range of employment, and of its least acts. As such, he moves us, albeit freely, to assent to grace when we actually do so. It is this divine impulse that makes grace efficacious in

us; it is not we who make it so. . . . Is anything more needed to convince Catholics that the *sola gratia*, as generally understood among Protestants, in the sense we have seen that they give it, is perfectly in accord with Catholic tradition?"[329]

The Spirit and Forms of Protestantism, 1954

Louis Bouyer answers Luther's charge that Catholics do not believe that God's grace is necessary to salvation. Bouyer's point is this: the Catholic understanding of *sola gratia* (grace alone) recognizes that a person's freedom of choice is not annihilated by the reception of grace. Another way of understanding this distinction is to ask: How would it be just for a person to be eternally damned or blessed if he or she had no part in choosing to receive or reject God's love? Bouyer writes, "The great mystery lies in the fact this consent should remain free" while receiving efficacious grace. The mystery points back to God's creation of human freedom itself, which explains why it's not necessary to create an either/or choice between human freedom and God's saving grace.

---

329 Louis Bouyer, *The Spirit and Forms of Protestantism*, trans. A.V. Littledale (New York: The World Publishing Company 1964), 73-74.

DAY 327

MATTHAIS JOSEPH SCHEEBEN (1835–1888)

He suffered completely—

"Christ suffered something from all external causes which can inflict pain upon man; but from organic disease He was free: on account of His supernatural perfection. Heathens and Jews, princes and their servants, and His own Apostles, contributed their share to His sufferings. He suffered in all that is dear to man: in His friends, who deserted Him; in His honour and good name through insults and blasphemy; in His possessions, when even His garments were taken from Him; in His soul through sadness and sorrow; in His body through blows and wounds nay, in all the members of His body, and in all His senses. The pains He suffered exceeded all those which man can suffer in this life: not only because of their bitterness and their number, but also because of the supernatural perfection of the Sufferer's constitution, and of His voluntary assuming an amount of suffering proportionate to the end for which He suffered, namely, the liberation of man from sin."[330]

A Manual of Catholic Theology, 1906

---

330 Matthias Joseph Scheeben, *A Manual of Catholic Theology* (Lex De Leon Publishing), loc. 33479-16886, Kindle Edition.

Matthias Joseph Scheeben's description of the sufferings of Jesus Christ resembles the experience of Job who loses all he owns and holds dear. However, that comparison falls far short when Scheeben reminds us that Jesus suffered everything that a human being can suffer but as the Christ of "supernatural perfection." His pain, thus, is multiplied by his awareness that nothing of it is deserved, that He is taking all the sins of the world upon Himself. Scheeben adds that this extremity of Christ's suffering was necessary to be proportionate to man's need for redemption.

DAY 328

LÉON BLOY (1843–1917)

Answering the question: why animals suffer in zoos?

"Ah Mademoiselle! We should first have to inquire where man's *limit* lies. The sociologists writing out their little labels two steps from where we stand would tell you exactly the natural peculiarities that distinguish the human animal from all the lower species. They would inform you that it is altogether essential to have only two feet or hands and to be covered—at birth—with neither feathers nor scales. But that would not explain why this unfortunate tiger is a prisoner. We should have to know what God has revealed to no one—namely, what

is this feline's place in the universal apportionment of our joint burden since the Fall. You must have been taught, if you were in catechism class, that in creating man, God gave him dominion over the beasts. Do you know that in his turn Adam gave a name to each animal, and that in this way the animals were created in the image of his reason, even as he himself was shaped in the image of God? For the name of a being is that being itself. Our first ancestor, in naming the animals, made them his, after an inexpressible fashion. He did not merely subject them to himself like an emperor. His essence penetrated them. He fastened them, sewed them to himself forever—joining them to his equilibrium and enmeshing them in his own destiny. Why should you wish the animals about us not to be captive when the human race is seven times captive? It was needful, after all, that everything falls into the same place where man fell."[331]

The Woman Who Was Poor, 1937

Léon Bloy was not a man to avoid taking an unpopular position, in this case, the dominance of humans over animals. If the book of Genesis is believed, then Bloy is perfectly right. Of course, Bloy exacerbates the argument rather than shrugging it off. Bloy reminds the Mademoiselle of the created order where man was explicitly given dominion over the beasts to such an

---

331 Léon Bloy, *Pilgrim of the Absolute,* trans. John Coleman and Harry Lorin Binsse, ed. Raïssa Maritain, introduction by Jacques Maritain (London: Eyre & Spottiswoode, 1947), 308–9.

extent that he was called upon by God to name them. Bloy makes his point but cannot resist a final irony: "Why should you wish the animals about us not be captive when the human race is seven times captive?"

DAY 329

JOHN HALDANE (1954–)

Hell is reasonable—

"A common objection to the idea of Hell is that a good God could not inflict or allow eternal suffering. This, however, rests on, at best, a partial conception of the situation. The active verb 'to damn' encourages us to think about the agency of God in the matter, but I believe that this is the wrong place to look. If there are damned, then they are such not because of what God has chosen to do to them, *but because of what they have made of themselves.* The kind of evil that is beyond purification is that which has so transformed the soul that it does not seek salvation and resists the measures provided to mankind for its perfection. Someone might respond that surely God can change a soul as to fit it for Heaven. This is doubly flawed: first, because I am envisaging a state of being so profoundly corrupt that there is nothing left to purify; and second, because justice

baulks at the idea that nothing one does can deny one a place in Heaven."[332] (Emphasis added.)

An Intelligent Person's Guide to Religion, 2003

John Haldane explains why God does not *place* persons in hell; they are there because they preferred living without Him up until the moment they die. These persons may have had, and probably did have, opportunities to make a fundamental change in their lives when experiencing a painful loss or disappointment. These moments of extreme suffering could have prompted self-correction or conversion. Those who proudly and stubbornly refuse to take an honest accounting of themselves make themselves, as Haldane puts it, "so profoundly corrupt that there is nothing left to purify."

DAY 330

SHUSAKU ENDO (1923–1966)

Loving the stranger—

"What draws our hearts in the consolation stories is the way they picture Jesus spending his time on these sorrows with the

332 John Haldane, *An Intelligent Person's Guide to Religion* (London: Gerald Duckworth and Co. Ltd., 2003), 205-6.

sort of men and women to whom others paid no attention. In the towns of Galilee, Jesus would sit so as to be at the level of the lepers and the cripples who came crawling to him from the dismal hovels; nor did he hide his sympathies for people like the harlots and the tax collectors who were openly despised by others. The towns around the lake were small and wretched, but they were the world of Jesus. He felt that one by one the griefs of all the people in the world were coming to rest on his shoulders. The sorrows began to weigh on his back with an onerous crunch, like the heavy cross that he himself would have to carry some time in the future."[333]

The Life of Jesus, 1973

Read the passage above by Shusako Endo and ask yourself how often you think of people like those Jesus called around the Sea of Galilee? Endo calls them "the sort of men and women to whom others paid no attention." It's only human to want attention and praise, but it's a far deeper and humane need to want care and love. Jesus cared for those whom no one else cared for and, perhaps, even noticed. For Endo, this form of caring was the beginning of his experience of the cross—"the griefs of all the people in the world were coming to rest on his shoulders."

---

333 Shusaku Endo, *The Life of Jesus*, trans. Richard A. Schuchert, S.J. (Mahwah: Paulist Press, 1978), 51–52.

DAY 331

HENRI DE LUBAC, SJ (1896–1996)

The fullness of faith—

"Today, as in the past, everything in the faith of the Church summons us to the most personal life. Everything in her liturgy speaks of it to us and furnishes its realization in us in the most concrete union. Today, as yesterday and since the beginning, she resists all attempts—which are so consistent with one of the inclinations of our intelligence, but so destructive for our personal existence itself—to transform the faith addressed to the person of Jesus Christ into a clever *gnosis* [knowledge], an impersonal *gnosis*. It is indeed supremely desirable that the consciousness of this personalizing force which was given to her forever not be blunted by contact with the depersonalizing forces which are at work everywhere around her.... More insidiously, perhaps, and without our even being on guard against it, something similar is insinuating itself into our lives today: 'The abstraction which is rife everywhere,' observes Pierre Emmanuel, 'has conquered Christian thought, whose faith is weakening in its symbols, in religious sensibility, in visionary power' (*Le bonheur*, 57). The very ones who suppose they can reach a more personal faith by excluding from Christian life all that they disdainfully term 'religion' tend, without traditional

roots, to a secularized faith which would soon lose, to say nothing more, its power to unify and liberate."[334]

The Motherhood of the Church, 1971

When Henri de Lubac, SJ, talks about *gnosis*, he is not simply talking about "knowledge" in the straightforward sense but a kind of knowledge proclaimed by heretical sects of early Christianity. These heretics, some of whom were called Gnostics, bragged of knowing the essence of Christianity, an essence they claimed was denied to the common believer. Note how de Lubac describes *gnosis* as "clever," meaning a knowledge that not only twists the meaning of the faith but also makes the faith into an abstraction. De Lubac contrasts a life lead by *gnosis* with "the most personal life" of belonging to the Body of Christ.

---

334 Henri de Lubac, S.J., *The Motherhood of the Church*, trans. Sr. Sergia Englund, OCD. (San Francisco: Ignatius Press, 1982), 159-60.

DAY 332

ST. THOMAS AQUINAS (1225–1274)

Aquinas asks whether we ought to love those who are better more than those who are more closely united with us—

"The intensity of love is measured with regard to the man who loves, and accordingly man loves those who are more closely united to him, with more intense affection as to the good he wishes for them, than he loves those who are better as to the greater good he wishes for them. Again a further difference must be observed here: for some neighbors are connected with us by their natural origin, a connection which cannot be severed, since that origin makes them to be what they are. But the goodness of virtue, wherein some are close to God, can come and go, increase and decrease. . . . Hence it is possible for one, out of charity, to wish this man who is more closely united to one, to be better than another, and so reach a higher degree of happiness. Moreover there is yet another reason for which, out of charity, we love more those who are more nearly connected with us, since we love them in more ways. For, towards those who are not connected with us we have no other friendship than charity, whereas for those who are connected with us, we have certain other friendships, according to the way in which they are connected. Now since the good on which every other friendship of the virtuous is based, is directed, as to its end, to the good on which charity is based, it follows

that charity commands each act of another friendship, even as the art which is about the end commands the art which is about the means. Consequently this very act of loving someone because he is akin or connected with us, or because he is a fellow-countryman or for any like reason that is referable to the end of charity, can be commanded by charity, so that, out of charity both eliciting and commanding, we love in more ways those who are more nearly connected with us."[335]

'Treatise on Charity,' *Summa Theologica*, Pt. II-II, Q. 26, Art. 7

In reading the *Summa* of St. Thomas Aquinas, one is often struck by his practicality. Much of the *Summa* consists of pastoral theology relating basic principles of dogma and morality to questions of ordinary life. For example, here Aquinas assures his reader that the natural desire to love a family member, in spite of his or her moral failings, does not contradict the order of love.

---

335 St. Thomas Aquinas, *Summa Theologica*, trans. Dominican Fathers, loc. 50596–50621 of 117511, Kindle Edition.

DAY 333

JOSEPH PEARCE (1961–)

The ongoing rupture—

"Another truer label for the Protestant and English Reformations could be the Rupture, since they have led not merely to religious division but to the fragmentation of the Protestant denominations into a plethora of subdividing particles. Looking at the history of the past five hundred years, it can be seen that Protestantism is an explosion of faith, not in the positive sense of the fruits of 'reform,' but in the negative sense of a violent disintegration of one body of Reformers under Luther into thousands of individual denominations. As with any explosion, the individual pieces do not simply fragment, they move further and further away from the center. So it is that the 'churches' of the 'Reformation' are becoming more eccentric, or, in the language of the Catholic Reformation, more heretical. Only the Rupture could have spawned the Rapture! As we witness the disintegration of the misnamed Protestant and English 'Reformations,' dare we see some mystical significance in the past five hundred years of religious conflict? Might we not see the Reformation as a catastrophe through which God had worked His mystical will? Tolkien invented a word, *eucatastrophe,* to describe the good that God brings out of evil; it is the good which could not have happened without the evil that preceded it. A eucatastrophe is the *felix culpa,* the

blessed fault or fortunate fall, from which God brings forth unexpected blessings. Thus, the catastrophe of the Fall brought forth the eucatastrophe of the Redemption, and the catastrophe of the Crucifixion brought forth the eucatastrophe of the Resurrection. Might it not be equally true that the catastrophe of Protestantism brought forth the eucatastrophe [a positive turn of events] of the Catholic Reformation?"[336]

Heroes of the Catholic Reformation, 2017

It's not fashionable in Catholic circles today to make much of the differences between Protestant and Catholic. But to ignore those differences is to be ignorant of four hundred years of Church history, everything that happened in the Church since the sixteenth century. Joseph Pearce is not shy about addressing the calamity—the Rupture, he calls it—which separated half of Europe and millions of Christians then living and yet to be born from full communion with the Church Christ founded. Books have been written about the impact of the Reformation on the early modern period and the gradual secularization that followed. Pearce, however, points out how God brought good out of evil in the form of the blessing that came to the Church as a result, specifically the Catholic Reformation.

---

336 Joseph Pearce, *Heroes of the Catholic Reformation: Saints Who Renewed the Church* (Huntington: Our Sunday Visitor, 2017), loc. 20, Kindle Edition.

DAY 334

MARTIN D'ARCY, SJ (1888–1976)

Not the best of all possible worlds—

"The charge then that a world with evil in it cannot come from God is based on misunderstanding and false sentiment. The misunderstanding lies in thinking that only one form of creation is possible to Him; the creation, that is, of the best of all possible worlds. On this supposition any universe with various levels of beauty and goodness would be forbidden; there must be no flowers because an animal is more perfect; there must be no animal, no human being, not even, perhaps, an angel, because they are all inferior to the best God might do. Nor let it be said that the argument fails because a flower can do no wrong, but a man can and does. It is of a man's essence that he should grow and struggle by his own efforts to his end. He cannot enjoy and appreciate his special form of goodness which constitutes his perfection without the risk of failure. One might as well invite the athlete to enjoy a certain peculiar glow of bodily health without the preceding exercise, or expect the pedestrian on Ludgate Hill to have the sensations of a climber in the Himalayas. *The only retort possible to this is that the gift of freedom is not worth the pain; to which the whole world makes answer that it is freedom and adventure which make life worth living.* Only the tactics of the ostrich can prevent us from drawing the obvious moral from the facts that men

have braved revolutions and given their lives for freedom."[337] (Emphasis added.)

The Problem of Evil, 1935

It was Voltaire who first lampooned "the best of all possible worlds" in his satire, *Candide* (1759). But Father D'Arcy finds that skeptics continue to ask that question while *blaming* God for the existence of evil. He counters that claim with the argument that the variety of Creation demands the passage of time, of birth and death, and *a gradation of beings*. When the skeptic asks whether or not God could have created human creatures incapable of doing moral evil, D'Arcy replies that for humans freedom itself is a form of perfection and was not given to any other being, sentient or not. With this perfection of freedom comes the moral evil, and the reply to the skeptic is this: would you rather be an animal like a cat or a dog than the unique animal you are?

---

337 Martin C. D'Arcy, S.J., *The Problem of Evil* (Ebook Edition, 2017), loc. 29-30 of 48, Kindle Edition.

DAY 335

SHUSAKU ENDO (1923–1966)

He loved Judas—

"Judas Iscariot. His motives likely were not quite as simplistic as what is written in the Gospel of John. Were he the owner of a simple mentality, he would have quit the master long before, near the Lake of Galilee, or during the days of those painful wanderings in the north. His failure to break with Jesus would seem to indicate that he shared the other disciples' dream that Jesus would stage a comeback and would then restore the ancient glory of Israel in accord with their hopes. Those scholars who interpret Judas as a rabid patriot with a bent for politics are not necessarily wrong. Judas, however, had felt his dream crumble when Jesus spoke at Caesarea Philippi. . . . But if so, why did he string along with Jesus as far as Jerusalem? Probably not even Judas himself was able to sort out the intricate forces at work in his own hurt psyche. This Jesus with the sunken eyes, looking older than his years: the more wretched Jesus appeared to be, the more he exerted some indescribable fascination for Judas. . . . Did he continue to think that Jesus yet might change his mind? There were still two days remaining until Passover. Maybe Judas hoped that in these two days Jesus could still change his mind. He loved Jesus as he loved himself. This ambivalent attitude, this brew of love and hatred,

made him keep his eyes glued to Jesus from close up after they arrived in Jerusalem."[338]

The Life of Jesus, 1973

The novelist Shusaku Endo explores the character of Judas from the inside. Endo remarks that Judas loved Jesus but also harbored an ambivalence towards him. One wonders what finally pushed Judas over the edge to betray Jesus for a bag of coins? Was it a revolutionary's disappointment or some imagined wound of rejection by the man he called "Master." Or, is it because "he loved Jesus as he loved himself." The pride of Judas masked a self-hatred which led to his betrayal.

DAY 336

CORNELIO FABRO (1911–1995)

A struggle with the invisible—

"The saints are given to us in order to console and incite us. Though, for a while, they appear to walk in stride with us, at a certain point, the impetus of divine attraction seems to set them at such a distance that it is impossible to see them as still

---

338 Shusaku Endo, *The Life of Jesus*, trans. Richard A. Schuchert, S.J. (Mahwah: Paulist Press, 1978), 111-12.

being within the same sphere as our own temporal existence. Henceforth, we are left without any gauge by which to judge a life whose principle of movement is drawn from somewhere else, from the very depths of Providence. Moreover, if each saint fulfills a particular function in building up the Mystical Body of the Church, often, he does so in the manner of one who walks in darkness. God wills that nature be broken in the life of reason, which is the core of autonomy, and the saints often walk in the darkness of the purifying tension of faith, making a total sacrifice of the ego and of all those offshoots which modern culture has conceived of under the sumptuous term of personality. Feeling new and ineffable impressions, it would seem to the soul that the entire array of virtues found in the *Nicomachean Ethics* had been placed under ban; it is beset by such awful doubts regarding its path and regarding the very truths of faith that it asks itself how this can be reconciled with the presence of grace. To suffer simultaneously both the greatest attraction toward and the strongest revulsion for the Infinite Good, and to be pulled by parallel but opposing motivations is surely the most disconcerting experience that a creature can have of the divine. In the case of those saints who have left us direct testimony of this struggle with the invisible, the essential reference points of which are in the Agony in the Garden of Gethsemane and the abandonment of Christ on

the Cross, these contradictions assume features that shake and trouble us."[339]

"Poor Gemma," 1953

Cornelio Fabro brings a philosopher's eye to the life of a saint. In his essay on St. Gemma Galgani (1878–1903), Fabro remarks that saints "often walk in the darkness of the purifying tension of faith" which distances them from the preoccupations of their culture and gradually frees them from the ego's demands. The spiritual virtues of the saints disregard Aristotle's principle of moderation in the *Nicomachean Ethics*. The willingness of saints to participate fully in Christ's agony and crucifixion is what arrests our attention and shakes our foundations.

DAY 337

ST. AUGUSTINE (354–430)

The trinitarian image of God in man's mind—

"The trinity, then, which we were presenting was constituted in this way, that we placed that from which the gaze of thought was formed in the *memory*; next, the conformation

---

339 Cornelio Fabro, *Profiles of Saints*, trans. Giulio Silano, ed. Nathaniel Dreyer (Chillum: IVEPress, 2019), loc. 1023 of 2133, Kindle Edition.

[*understanding*] itself, which is as it were the image impressed on by it; and finally, that by which both are joined together, namely, *love or will*. When the mind, therefore, sees itself through thought, it understands itself and recognizes itself; consequently, it begets this, its own understanding and its own knowledge. For an incorporeal thing is understood when it is seen and is known when it is understood. Yet the mind does not indeed so beget its own knowledge when it beholds itself as understood by thought, as though it had been previously unknown to itself. But it was known to itself as things are known which are contained in the memory, even though they are not thought, since we say a man knows letters, even when he is thinking of other things and not of letters. But these two, the begetter and the begotten, are bound together by love as a third, and this is nothing else than the will seeking for or holding on to the enjoyment of something. And, therefore, we thought that a trinity was insinuated by these three names, memory, understanding, and will."[340] (Emphasis added.)

On the Trinity, Bk XIV, Ch. 6, 417

St. Augustine locates an inner trinity in the human person made up of memory, understanding, and will or love. In his *On the Trinity,* St. Augustine locates reflections of the Divine Trinity in everything that exists which testifies to the fact that

---

340 St. Augustine, *On the Trinity*, trans. Stephen McKenna, C.SS.R. (Washington, D.C.: The Catholic University of America Press, 1970), 421-22.

the world is God's creation. Since God exists as a Trinity of three Persons, so His Creation reflects that Trinity at every level. The trinity he discovers in the human person—memory, understanding, and will—is nothing less than the image of God in man (Gn 1:27).

DAY 338

ST. PETER DAMIAN, OSB (1007–1072)

St. Peter Damian exhorts the sinful to rise again—

"Arise, arise, I implore you! Wake up O man who sinks in the sleep of wretched pleasure! Revive at last, you who have fallen by the lethal sword before the face of your enemies! . . . If Life the vivifier wishes to raise you up, why do you bear to continue lying in your death? Beware then, beware, lest the abyss of despair swallow you up. May your soul faithfully trust in divine kindness, lest it become hardened in impenitence by the magnitude of the crime. For it is not sinners who despair, but the impious, nor is it the magnitude of offenses that leads the soul into despair, but rather impiety. For if only the devil was able to submerge you in the depths of this vice, how much more is the strength of Christ able to return you to that pinnacle from which you fell? Shall he that fell rise again no more? . . . That most strong Samson, because he wrongly disclosed

the secret of his heart to a coaxing woman, not only lost seven strands of hair by which his strength was maintained, but also, after being captured by the Philistines, lost his eyes. However, after his hairs had regrown, he humbly requested the help of the Lord God, leveled the temple of Dagon, and annihilated a much greater number of the enemy than he had before. Therefore, if your unchaste flesh has deceived you by enticing you to pleasures, if it has taken away the seven gifts of the Holy Spirit, if it has extinguished the light not of the countenance, but of the heart, do not falter in your courage, do not despair utterly; continue to gather your strength, strive manfully, dare to attempt the courageous, and you will be able to triumph, by the mercy of God, over your enemies. The Philistines certainly were able to shave the hair of Samson, but not to uproot it, and so although evil spirits have excluded the charisms of the Holy Spirit from you for a while, by no means are they able to irrecoverably deny the remedy of divine reconciliation."[341]

The Book of Gomorrah, 1051

St. Peter Damian, made bishop of Ostia in 1057, served frequently as a papal envoy and aggressively sought reforms within the Church against simony, sodomy among the clergy, and an over-reliance on philosophy. He was made a doctor of the Church by Leo XII in 1828.

---

341 St. Peter Damian, *The Book of Gomorrah*, trans. annotations and introduction by Matthew Cullinan Hoffman (New Braunfels: ITE AD THOMAN BOOKS AND MEDIA, 2015), loc. 146-148, Kindle Edition.

DAY 339

CHARLES E. RICE (1931–2015)

No better than the Nazis—

"To kill defective children in the womb, of course, is no different in principle from the Nazi 'final solution to the Jewish problem.' But this does not seem to bother the liberal proponents of the scheme. The logical extension of abortion for this purpose is infanticide, the killing of unwanted children after they are born. Indeed, infanticide is more merciful, for it at least has the virtue of certainty and involves no danger to the life of the mother. When you abort a child who is likely to be born defective, you run a risk that you will abort a child who in fact would have turned out to be physically sound. It would be more scientific to wait until after the birth to see whether the child in fact is defective. The notion that a newborn but unwanted infant should be slain at birth does not sit well with modern sensibilities."[342]

The Vanishing Right to Life, 1969

Charles E. Rice practiced law in New York and taught at New York University School of Law and Fordham Law School before joining the Notre Dame Law School faculty in 1969.

---

342 Charles E. Rice, *The Vanishing Right to Live: An Appeal for a Renewed Reverence for Life* (Garden City: Doubleday & Company, Inc., 1969), 8.

During the war years, he served in the US Marine Corps and was a lieutenant colonel in the Marine Corps Reserve. Rice was one of the first Catholic intellectuals to engage fully the pro-life movement in the years before *Roe v. Wade* (1973). His thirteen-part series "The Good Code: The Natural Law" was broadcast on EWTN. He met his wife, Mary, in law school—they had ten children together and also adopted a son born in South Vietnam. As a teacher in the Notre Dame Law School, Rice was greatly loved and admired. Far from being a detached intellectual, he helped coach the Notre Dame boxing club for thirty years. Sadly, in the fifty years since he wrote the above passage, things have changed and not for the better. Many people no longer draw the line at outright infanticide.

DAY 340

ST. FRANCIS DE SALES (1567–1622)

Speaking ill of others unjustly—

"Speaking ill of others unjustly is a pest of society. Whoever could purge the world of it would cleanse it from a great part of its sinfulness! Whoever unjustly takes away his neighbor's good name is guilty of sin and is obliged to make reparation, according to the nature of what he has said unjustly. For no one can enter heaven loaded with stolen goods, and of all

worldly possessions the most precious is a good name. Slander is a kind of murder. We all have three lives: a spiritual life, which depends upon the grace of God; a bodily life, which is in the soul; and a civil life, which consists of a good reputation. Sin deprives us of the first, death of the second, and slander of the third. But the slanderer commits a triple murder with his idle tongue. He destroys both his own soul and the soul of the one who listens to him through a kind of spiritual homicide. In addition, he deprives the one he has slandered of civil life. As St. Bernard says, the Devil has possession both of the slanderer and of those who listen to him: of the tongue of the one, and the ear of the other. I urge you, then, never to speak evil of anyone, either directly or indirectly. Beware of ever unjustly imputing crimes and sins to your neighbor (which is slander); of needlessly disclosing his true faults (which is detraction); of exaggerating those that are overt; of attributing wrong motives to good actions; of denying the good that you know to dwell in someone; of maliciously concealing that good or minimizing it in conversation. In all these ways you grievously offend God. But the worst is false accusation, or denying the truth in a way that injures your neighbor."[343]

Introduction to the Devout Life

---

343 Paul Thigpen, *A Year With the Saints: Daily Meditations With the Holy Ones of God* (Charlotte: Saint Benedict Press, 2013), 246.

The importance of this exhortation can hardly be over-emphasized. The sin of slander has infected the culture to such a degree that its destructive power is rarely acknowledged. Aristotle, too, discussed the importance of reputation in living a happy life, and here St. Francis de Sales adds the spiritual consequences of those who commit slander and those whose reputations are ruined. It's sometimes said, "If you don't have something good to say about someone, don't say anything," but how often is this good advice heeded. Rather, slander has become a kind of public game, played in the arena of politics as broadcast on the nightly news. All sides of the political spectrum are willing participants in this game of soul-destroying 'I-got-you.'

DAY 341

ST. THOMAS AQUINAS (1224–1274)

Grace does not destroy nature—

Aquinas asks whether sacred doctrine is a matter of argument—

"But sacred doctrine makes use even of human reason, not, indeed, to prove faith (for thereby the merit of faith would come to an end), but to make clear other things that are put forward in this doctrine. *Since therefore grace does not destroy nature but perfects it, natural reason should minister to faith as the*

natural bent of the will ministers to charity. Hence the Apostle says: "Bringing into captivity every understanding unto the obedience of Christ" (2 Cor. 10:5). Hence sacred doctrine makes use also of the authority of philosophers in those questions in which they were able to know the truth by natural reason, as Paul quotes a saying of Aratus: "As some also of your own poets said: For we are also His offspring" (Acts 17:28). Nevertheless, sacred doctrine makes use of these authorities as extrinsic and probable arguments; but properly uses the authority of the canonical Scriptures as an incontrovertible proof, and the authority of the doctors of the Church as one that may properly be used, yet merely as probable."[344] (Emphasis added.)

Summa Theologica, I.1. Q. 1, Art. 8, Reply 2

Here St. Thomas Aquinas explains how human reason can and should be used to read and interpret Holy Scripture. This anticipates the claims of some radical Reformers that the proper interpretation of Scripture comes by direct illumination of the Holy Spirit. It's important to notice, however, that St. Thomas distinguishes between the "probable" arguments made with the help of the philosophers and "incontrovertible proof" based on the Scriptures themselves and the authority of the Doctors of the Church. This is a distinction, by the way,

---

344 St. Thomas Aquinas, *Summa Theologica* (e-artnow), loc. 554 of 117511, Kindle Edition.

that's crucial in understanding how Catholic and Protestant paths diverged.

DAY 342

ROBERT SPAEMANN (1927–2018)

Lovers who hide—

"I am arriving now at a final paradox of the concept of love, the paradox of human sexuality. It is a *topos* of morality that it is one of the tasks of a human being to integrate his sexuality into personal love, and that this is often difficult to achieve. . . . In brothels, the animal drive, which leads to sexual relations, is satisfied with total strangers. It is a submersion in the anonymous stream of life as it perpetuates itself. It is here that man takes off the *persona* in the ancient sense of a social role. This is why he typically hides from the sight of third persons; and often wants to erect a barrier between this sphere and the bourgeois world. What he says, swears, and promises in this sphere must not be taken seriously. It does not count in the social world. Often men and women who have 'been intimate' with each other no longer want to be seen together outside."[345]

Love and the Dignity of Human Life, 1939

---

345 Robert Spaemann, *Love and the Dignity of Human Life, On Nature and Nat-*

Robert Spaemann explains love's paradox with the precision of a fine novelist. That paradox is the human person's natural sexual desire towards self-satisfaction existing in a necessary tension with the call of Christian love which begins with the love of neighbor. Spaemann might seem too pessimistic in his description of hiding "from the sight of third persons," but he's accurately describing how many, sadly, have lived their lives. What makes Spaemann provocative is how he explains that promiscuity is *a sin against society*, a breakdown in the mutual expectations that keep orderly relations between persons and communities. We can see how far from the Christian ideal our own society has fallen by noting that people who, to use an old-fashioned term, fornicate now do so openly and matter-of-factly. No more hiding "from the sight of third persons." They shout their flouting of God's laws from the rooftops and dare anyone, parent, priest or politician, to challenge them.

ural Law, foreword by David L. Schindler (Grand Rapids: W.B. Eerdmans Publishing Company, 2012), 22-23.

DAY 343

ST. JOHN HENRY NEWMAN (1801–1890)

A living religion—

"When we consider the succession of ages during which the Catholic system has endured, the severity of the trials it has undergone, the sudden and wonderful changes without and within which have befallen it, the incessant mental activity and the intellectual gifts of its maintainers, the enthusiasm which it has kindled, the fury of the controversies which have been carried on among its professors, the impetuosity of the assaults made upon it, the ever-increasing responsibilities to which it has been committed by the continuous development of its dogmas, it is quite inconceivable that it should not have been broken up and lost, were it a corruption of Christianity. Yet it is still living, if there be a living religion or philosophy in the world; vigorous, energetic, persuasive, progressive; *vires acquirit eundo*; it grows and is not overgrown; it spreads out, yet is not enfeebled; it is ever germinating, yet ever consistent with itself. Corruptions indeed are to be found which sleep and are suspended; and these are usually called 'decays:' such is not the case with Catholicity; it does not sleep, it is not stationary even now; and that its long series of developments should be corruptions would be an instance of sustained error, so novel, so unaccountable, so preternatural, as to be little short of a miracle, and to rival those manifestations of Divine Power which

constitute the evidence of Christianity. We sometimes view with surprise and awe the degree of pain and disarrangement which the human frame can undergo without succumbing; yet at length there comes an end. Fevers have their crisis, fatal or favourable; but this corruption of a thousand years, if corruption it be, has ever been growing nearer death, yet never reaching it, and has been strengthened, not debilitated, by its excesses."[346]

An Essay on the Development of Doctrine, 1845

This essay by St. John Henry Newman is a key document in the history of Catholic theology. From the beginning of the Reformation, Protestant theologians accused the Catholic Church of disregarding the Holy Scriptures or, to put it more crassly, of "not being biblical." What Newman shows masterfully is how Catholic teaching organically grew out of the revealed Word of God and the life of the Church. For example, in the first centuries of Christianity, decisions had to be made about the doctrine of the Trinity, the dual nature of Christ, and the canonical books of Scripture.

---

346 St. John Henry Newman, *An Essay on the Development of Christian Doctrine* (Aeterna Press), loc. 296-297, Kindle Edition.

DAY 344

ST. AUGUSTINE (354–430)

The good is everywhere—

"And therefore there is a nature in which evil does not or even cannot exist; but there cannot be a nature in which there is no good. Hence not even the nature of the devil himself is evil, insofar as it is nature, but was made evil by being perverted. Thus, he did not abide in the truth, but could not escape the judgment of the Truth; he did not abide in the tranquility of order, but did not therefore escape the power of the Ordainer. The good imparted by God to his nature did not screen him from the justice of God by which order was preserved in his punishment; neither did God punish the good which He had created, but the evil which the devil had committed. God did not take back all He had imparted to his nature, but something He took and something He left, that there might remain enough to be sensible of the loss of what was taken. And this very sensibility to pain is evidence of the good which has been taken away and the good which has been left."[347]

The City of God, 426

---

347 St. Augustine, *On The City of God Against the Pagans*, 8.26, trans. Marcus Dodds, introduction by Thomas Merton, New York: The Modern Library, 1993), 691.

Even Satan retains some measure of "good," argues St. Augustine, but only in a very specific way. To call a person or an angel *good* does not necessarily refer to a moral quality: to be called good can refer to the *fact of existence*. "And God saw everything that he had made, and behold, it was very good" (Gn 1:31). The evil of Satan is a moral evil, the consequence of his first and only choice to love or reject his Creator. And St. Augustine describes Satan's eternal suffering as the fallen angel's constant awareness of his loss: For Satan, the good of existence became his platform for suffering eternal pain.

DAY 345

ROMANO GUARDINI (1885–1968)

Freedom in truth—

"But freedom is even more than this. A man is free when he can see the great as great, and the small as small; the worthless as worthless and the valuable as valuable; when he views correctly the distinctions between different objects and different conditions; the relations between objects and their measure. He is free when he recognizes honestly the hierarchy of objects, and their values, placing its base and its apex, and each intermediate point in its right position. He is free when he apprehends the idea in its purity, but contemplates in its

light the complete reality; when he sees everyday life with all its rough and tumble and all its shortcomings, but also what is eternal in it. He is free when his vision of the idea does not blind him to reality, and everyday existence does not make him oblivious to the idea, when he 'can gaze upon the stars, but find his way through the streets.'"[348]

The Church and the Catholic, 1935

Romano Guardini describes the misunderstanding of freedom that pervades modern culture—freedom has come to mean *the ability to do whatever I want*. In other words, freedom disregards constraint whether by law, custom, creed, or fear of ostracism. Guardini stresses that to be free requires being oriented to what is true. Freedom, thus, embraces the constraints that guide a person towards true happiness both in this world and the next. This is what is sometimes called "ordered liberty," one that does not chafe at the restraints of law or tradition but takes its final cues from the highest measure of all.

---

348 Romano Guardini, *The Church and the Catholic*, trans. Ada Lane (Veritatis Splendor Publications, 2012), loc. 37-38, Kindle Edition.

DAY 346

ST. EDMUND CAMPION (1540–1581)

Plain talk from an unassuming man—

St. Edmund Campion was a modest man with a large reservoir of self-control, both of which aided him during the years of avoiding arrest while ministering to Catholics in England. While at Oxford, Campion's rhetorical skill had been admired by Elizabeth I. She is now aggressively hunting him down along with his fellow Jesuits. Historian Claire Asquith reports:

"Noticing an inscription on the wall at Christchurch attributing to Henry [VIII] the dazzling building actually erected by Wolsey, he suddenly explodes, The King, he says was 'a man who has destroyed all honesty, completely confused the human and divine, and destroyed root and branch both the religion and the Commonwealth of England.' This is the single recorded instance of intemperate language from the normally equitable Campion."[349]

Even the mild-mannered St. Edmund Campion could lose his temper! This moment recorded by historian Claire Asquith

---

349 St. Edmund Campion, quoted in Claire Asquith, *Shakespeare and the Resistance: The Earl of Southampton, the Essex Rebellion, and the Poems that Challenged Tudor Tyranny* (New York: Public Affairs, 2018), 47.

is, on the one hand, charming, and, on the other, tragic. In his outburst, Campion puts his finger on the sea-change in Western culture brought on by Henry VIII's desire to divorce his wife, Catherine of Aragon. The king who once wrote credible theological essays is now employing Catholic theology and Scripture to justify an act which is simply lust. Anne Boleyn will not give herself to him unless he divorces Catherine and makes her queen. Campion is describing the kind of man who will use the Church to lie and defame in order to get one woman in his bed. He is also describing a man who will go even farther, Henry VIII will destroy the unity of Church, embrace the Protestant beliefs he once scorned, and declare England out of communion with the Church of Rome in order to have his way with Anne Boleyn.

DAY 347

THEODORE HAECKER (1879–1945)

Better to be losers than apostates—

"He is alone! Everything that he feels, thinks and does has a question mark to it, questioning whether it is right. The leadership of Germany today, and there is not the faintest doubt, and it cannot be evaded, is consciously anti-Christian—it hates Christ whom it does not name. . . . And one cannot therefore

avoid recognizing the fact, that over and above being a war of power—it is a war of religion. And we Germans are fighting on the wrong side! We are, as to the majority, making war as willing slaves without honor. . . . Today is Whitsunday, but my spirit is healing, and the shadow of affliction is upon it. For I must live, whether the apostate is victorious or defeated, and with him—no, that is not true: the German people will be beaten, but struck down and wiped out. The one ray of light in my mind is this: is it better for a people to be defeated and to suffer, than to win and apostatize. But if it were to be victorious? I should not then give up my faith. I can always pray: Lord, help thou my unbelief!"[350]

"On the German Christian," May 12, 1940

Theodore Haecker, writing in secret, had officially been under house arrest by the Nazis since 1935. Germany before the rise of Hitler was populated mostly by Lutherans and Catholics— there were different political parties representing the entire spectrum of Christian belief and practice. In the Weimar Republic, which Hitler took control of in 1933, there were forty political parties represented in the Reichstag, many of which represented Christian denominations. Haecker viewed Germany as a predominately Christian nation struggling internally against a regime openly opposed to Christianity,

---

350 Theodore Haecker, *Journal In the Night*, trans. Alexander Dru (New York: Pantheon Books, 1950), 53–54.

while with regards to the World War, he noted, "We Germans are fighting on the wrong side!" Haecker predicts defeat but readies himself for what is worse, victory. Haecker vows to keep his faith even in the face of a Nazi victory. The book to read side-by-side with *Journal In the Night* is Victor Klemperer's three-volume war diary, *I Will Bear Witness* (1995).

DAY 348

ÉTIENNE GILSON (1884–1978)

Gilson points out a fascinating distinction between Dante and St. Thomas Aquinas on the concept of happiness. Aquinas specified two final ends, earthly happiness and heavenly happiness. Dante argues the quest for either happiness needs help of the law—

"This is the exact point at which Dante will epitomize his whole doctrine in a wonderfully compact sentence. . . . 'Although these conclusions and means have been shown to us, some by human reason, which has been explained to us in its entirety by the philosophers, others thanks to the Holy Spirit which has revealed to us the supernatural truth essential to man through the Prophets, the sacred writers, the co-eternal Son of God, Jesus Christ, and his disciples, human greed would none the less turn its back on them if men, like horses which in their brutishness run wild, were not curbed by bridle and

bit.'[351] Nothing could be clearer than the distinction between these three authorities: philosophy, which teaches us the *whole* truth about the natural goal of man; theology, which alone leads us to our supernatural goal; finally, political power, which holding human greed in check, contains men, by the force of the law, to respect the natural truth of the philosophers and the supernatural truth of the theologians."[352]

Dante and Philosophy, 1985

Étienne Gilson's comment on Dante's *De Monarchia* catches the spirit of the early Renaissance with its effort to overcome old hierarchies and attend to the necessities and pleasures of this life rather than preparing for the next. Dante was the citizen of the sophisticated and politically-charged city of Florence. He entered politics and rose nearly to the top before the takeover of the city by Charles de Valois (1301). A year later, Dante was banished for allegedly selling political offices and ordered to pay a fine. Dante refused to pay and was sentenced to death. He spent the remainder of life in exile from the city he loved. While living in Verona in 1314, Dante published the first part of the *Divine Comedy*, the *Inferno*.

---

351 Gilson is quoting from Dante's book *On the Monarchy* (1313) about secular and religious power.

352 Étienne Gilson, *Dante and Philosophy*, trans. David Moore (Gloucester: Peter Smith, 1968), 195–95.

DAY 349

CHARLES E. RICE (1931–2015)

Homosexual acts—

"This book is an appeal for a renewed reverence for life. Legalization of homosexual acts, in any manner and to any degree, can only have the opposite effect. For respect for life entails a regard for all its aspects, including its source. One evil effect of contraception is that it willfully separates the generative from the pleasurable. The act in which life is begun is deliberately turned aside, by artificial means, from any possibility of achieving this end. The possible generation of life is thus regarded as a nuisance and responsibility is evaded. If this is true of contraception, how much more it would be true of homosexuality. What a parody of civilized society it would be were it a matter of legal indifference whether sexual intercourse occurred between man and woman or between two of the same sex. It has been seriously proposed by homosexual groups that homosexual marriages be legitimized and raised to parity with heterosexual unions. In fact the proposed elimination of the penalty on private homosexual acts between consenting adults would permit such 'marriages' to flourish on a *de facto* basis, avowedly and undisturbed."[353]

The Vanishing Right to Life, 1969

---

353 Charles E. Rice, *The Vanishing Right to Live: An Appeal for a Renewed Reverence for Life* (Garden City: Doubleday & Company, Inc., 1969), 166.

Charles E. Rice wrote prophetically about the impact of homosexual marriage. As early as 1969, and even earlier, at a time when few public intellectuals thought it possible, Rice saw what was coming on the horizon—the rise of the homosexual, or "gay," lobby. He links what was beginning to be called the "contraception mentality" to the proposed legalization of homosexual acts: "What a parody of civilized society it would be were it a matter of legal indifference whether sexual intercourse occurred between man and woman or between two of the same sex," which is precisely what has happened. Rice wrote this book fifty years ago, and much of what he foresaw has come to pass, but the principles that inform his critique remain the teaching of the Church regardless of what gay activists and theologians have to say about it.

DAY 350

JAMES MCAULEY (1917–1976)

On the danger of utopias—

"Progress in fact had its own mythology. But the poets found that the new myths were barren of poetic nutriment. As the nineteenth century wore on this became more painfully obvious. The secular mythologies of Democracy, Socialism, Imperialism and so on were celebrated by a sub-standard verse.

... As the disillusionment set in, the poets turned back, partly
to what they could appropriate of Christianity, but mainly
towards a more archaic form of cosmic mysticism. The reason
for their retreat was that the radical secularization of gnosis
[knowledge] undertaken by the Enlightenment made a difference that was crucial for poetry. It meant the loss of over-
tones, symbolic resonance, of those transcendental dimensions
of experience in which wisdom and mystery are felt to lie.
Marxism, for instance, might itself recognize its kinship with
the revolutionary millenarianism of the medieval heresies, but
the coming of the Classless Society is a barren thing to the
imagination in comparison with the apocalyptic splendors of
millennialism enthusiasm. . . . Rulers like Hitler or Stalin have
hardly the cosmic grandeur of the Divine Kings of archaic
states. All is flattened down to one naturalistic level, and the
sense of correspondences linking ascending levels of being in a
magical-religious cosmos disappears."[354]

"Journey Into Egypt," 1975

James McAuley sounds Chestertonian with his eloquent and
colorful account of the rise of the totalitarian state, which has
proven itself deadly to the arts. McAuley notes the decline in
poetry during this period when poets felt the authorities looking over their shoulders, which was literally the case in Stalin's

---

354 James McAuley, *Selected Prose 1959-1974* (Melbourne: Oxford University
Press, 1975), 178-79.

Russia. Stalin kept close tabs on all Russian writers—some were silenced, others sent to the Gulag, and some, such as Boris Pasternack, strangely favored. The kitsch produced by the official artists of the Third Reich, as McAuley describes them, "flattened down to one naturalistic level." Kitsch, art made to flatter the taste of the public, was put to work by Hitler to confirm German nationalism and Germanic superiority. In doing so, some poets employed what McAuley calls "cosmic mysticism," a harmless, toothless style of pseudo-religious poetry.

DAY 351

HILAIRE BELLOC (1870–1953)

Courtesy

> Of Courtesy, it is much less
> Than Courage of Heart or Holiness,
> Yet in my Walks it seems to me
> That the Grace of God is in Courtesy.
> On Monks I did in Storrington fall,
> They took me straight into their Hall;
> I saw Three Pictures on a wall,
> And Courtesy was in them all.
> The first Annunciation;
> The second the Visitation;

The third the Consolation,
Of God that was Our Lady's Son.
The first was of Saint Gabriel;
On Wings a-flame from Heaven he fell;
And as he went upon one knee
He shone with Heavenly Courtesy.
Our Lady out of Nazareth rode –
It was her month of heavy load;
Yet was Her face both great and kind,
For Courtesy was in Her Mind.
The third it was our Little Lord,
Whom all the Kings in arms adored;
He was so small you could not see
His large intent of Courtesy.
Our Lord, that was Our Lady's Son,
Go bless you, People, one by one;
My Rhyme is written, my work is done.[355]

Hilaire Belloc's poem "Courtesy" is about kindness, graciousness, and consideration, all of which are infused by the descent
of Divine charity, *Agape.*

---

355 *Dreams and Images: An Anthology of Catholic Poets*, ed. Joyce Kilmer, 1917,
   loc. 6 of 286, Kindle Edition.

DAY 352

JOSEPH PEARCE (1961–)

Stages of civilization—

"Viewing the panoramic vista of the history of the West, we can see three broad ages of man: The first of these is the pre-Christian or pagan age; the second age is the age of Christendom; and the third age may be called the age of Disenchantment.... In the age of Christendom we see, subsumed within the very fibre of the individual's conscience and in the very fabric of society, the affirmation of *homo viator* [journeying man] and the condemnation of *homo superbus* [proud man]. Christendom's chief characteristic is its overarching unity in the realms of philosophy and theology, a unity in which *homo viator* is not only admired but enshrined.... In the age of Disenchantment, the wholeness and oneness of Christendom is lost in a progressive fragmentation of thought that continues to this day. From its earliest manifestation in the decay of the Christian humanism and Neo-classicism of the Renaissance and its coming age in the pride of the superciliously self-named Enlightenment, to its self-defeating victory in the nihilistic nonsense of deconstructionism, the age of Disenchantment represents the triumph of *homo superbus* over *homo viator* and, therefore, the triumph of barbarism over civilization."[356]

Literature: What Every Catholic Should Know, 2019

---

356 Joseph Pearce, *Literature: What Every Catholic Should Know* (San Francisco: Ignatius Press, 2019), 2-3.

Joseph Pearce puts the reading of classic texts, such as the Great
Books, into a historical perspective of three distinct epochs.
Such periodization is very helpful for readers who are not
aware of how the dominant values of a particular age impact its
books, poems, and plays. Pearce distinguishes the pre-Christian
era from the period of Christendom that followed and, most
importantly, the age of Disenchantment resulting from the rise
of skepticism, disbelief, and materialism. This is not to say there
are no Great Books that buck the trend of the age in which
they were written, but rather to underscore the courage and
vision of the authors who wrote them.

DAY 353

CHRISTOPHER DAWSON (1889–1970)

Not right or left—

"With regard to my political position, I do not think it is any
longer permissible to divide Catholic opinion by Right and
Left. There was some justification for the distinction when the
Left stood for the freedom of the individual and the Right for
the authority of the State. But today when the totalitarians
of the Left deny freedom and the totalitarians of the Right
reject Law, the old distinctions have become meaningless and
Catholics are obliged to unite in order to defend principles far

more vital than the issue of the Left-Right party dog-fight. . . . The fact is that the problem transcends politics; and the old political attitudes and party alignments are as inappropriate as the old military tactics are in regard to the atom bomb."[357]

Letter in response to A. Cardinal Hinsley, September 30, 1945

Christopher Dawson weighs in on a question that often arises when Catholics start talking about politics. Bear in mind, the political Left and Right of Dawson's day were not the same as today, though there is a definite analogy. For Dawson, the Left represents individual freedom and the Right state authority, and if we simply switch the meanings by Dawson ascribed to Left and Right our contemporary political situation comes into view. Today's political Right defends individual freedom against the centralization of power preferred by the Left. But Dawson's point is this: the Catholic faith does not belong to one or the other, however the sides are construed, and Catholics should not be pressured to choose between one or the other.

---

357 Christina Scott, *A Historian and His World: A Life of Christopher Dawson 1889-1970* (London: Sheed and Ward, 1984), 138-39.

DAY 354

HANS URS VON BALTHASAR (1905–1988)

Into the theatre—

"If God is to deal with man in an effective way and in a way intelligible to him, must not God himself tread the stage of the world and thus become implicated in the dubious nature of the world theatre? And however he comes into contact with this theatre—whether he is to take responsibility for the whole meaning of the play or is to appear as one of the cast. . . . The analogy between God's action and the world drama is no mere metaphor but has an ontological ground: the two dramas are not utterly unconnected; there is an inner link between them. . . . Thus, by entering into contact with the world theatre, the good which takes place in God's action really is affected by the world's ambiguity and remains a hidden good. This good is something *done*: it cannot be contemplated in pure 'aesthetics' nor proved and demonstrated in pure 'logic.' It takes place nowhere but on the world stage—which is every living person's present moment—and its destiny is seen in the drama of a world history that is continually unfolding."[358]

Theo-Drama, Volume 1, 1973–83

---

358 Hans Urs von Balthasar, *Theo-Drama: Theological Dramatic Theory, Volume 1, Prolegomena*, trans. Graham Harrison (San Francisco: Ignatius Press, 1988), 19.

Hans Urs von Balthasar explains the context of the last third of his theological trilogy, the *Theo-Drama*. In spite of its association with a specific art form, von Balthasar uses theatre to represent the drama of world history, the stage where Jesus Christ was incarnated and lived before being crucified and resurrected. The point is this: how else could God redeem man if He Himself did not enter into human history and take the stage where He could be seen and heard, where His story could be told, and His Church created and sustained. By taking the stage of human history, Christ became fully human, making his death efficacious as the One who paid the price of sin for all.

DAY 355

GEORGES BERNANOS (1888–1948)

Man and machine—

"The tragedy of our new Europe is precisely the lack of adaptation between man and a rhythm of life that no longer follows the beat of his heart but rather the dizzying rotations of turbines, a rhythm under continual acceleration. . . . I'll go farther and say that such adaptation appears to be less and less possible. . . . A machine can do good or evil, indifferently. A more perfect machine—that is, one that is more efficient—should correspond to a more reasonable, a more human humanity.

But has the civilization of machines improved man? Have they made man more human? . . . In all probability, machines have changed nothing in man's basic wickedness—up until now, in any event; but they have exercised this wickedness, making it grow strong, and they have revealed to man the power of his wickedness, the fact that the exercise of this power in a certain sense has no boundaries."[359]

Bernanos: An Ecclesial Existence, 1988

George Bernanos believed that Western civilization had gotten so far from its Christian roots that the possibility of recovery was highly unlikely. Using the image of the heartbeat to represent the natural law, Bernanos describes how technology came to dominate human consciousness and aspiration. At the same time, he asks aloud whether any of the modern technology has substantially improved the lives of men. The answer being in the negative, Bernanos presses on and asks whether or not those same machines made it possible for human evil to become far more destructive than before. Bernanos is a Catholic writer who focused on the moral darkness that men and women must overcome if they are to find God's forgiveness. Like his friend Jacques Maritain, Bernanos saw the good and the evil in history as it moves forward.

---

359 Hans Urs von Balthasar, *Bernanos: An Ecclesial Existence*, trans. Erasmo Leiva-Merikakis (San Francisco: Ignatius Press, 1996), 30.

DAY 356

ST. CYRIL OF JERUSALEM (376–444)

Faith moves mountains—

"For the name of Faith is in the form of speech one [word], but has two distinct senses. For there is one kind of faith, the dogmatic, involving an ascent of the soul on some particular point: and it is profitable to the soul, as the Lord saith: 'He that heareth My words, and believeth Him that sent Me, hath everlasting life, and cometh not into judgment': and again, 'He that believeth in the Son is not judged, but hath passed from death unto life': Oh the great loving-kindness of God! For the righteous were many years in pleasing Him: but what they succeeded in gaining by many years of well-pleasing, this Jesus now bestows on thee in a single hour. For if thou shalt believe that Jesus Christ is Lord, and that God raised Him from the dead, thou shalt be saved, and shalt be transported into Paradise by Him who brought in thither the robber. And doubt not whether it is possible; for He who on this sacred Golgotha saved the robber after one single hour of belief, the same shall save thee also on thy believing. But there is a second kind of faith, which is bestowed by Christ as a gift of grace. For to one is given through the Spirit the word of wisdom, and to another the word of knowledge according to the same Spirit: to another faith, by the same Spirit, and to another gifts of healing. *This faith then which is given of grace from the Spirit is*

not merely doctrinal, but also worketh things above man's power. For whosoever hath this faith, shall say to this mountain, Remove hence to yonder place, and it shall remove. For whenever anyone shall say this in faith, believing that it cometh to pass, and shall not doubt in his heart, then receiveth he the grace."[360] (Emphasis added.)

The Catechetical Lectures, 350

St. Cyril of Jerusalem became bishop just as the heresy of Arianism was beginning to take hold around the Mediterranean. His *Catechetical Lectures* were decisive in promoting Church unity and highlighting God's forgiving love rather than God's wrathful justice often emphasized by some of the other Church Fathers. Cyril was present at the First Council of Constantinople (381), where the credal language of *homoousios*—Christ as one in being with the Father—was approved.

---

360 St. Cyril of Jerusalem, *The Catechetical Lectures* (Veritatis Splendor Publications, 2014), loc. 256–257, Kindle Edition.

DAY 357

POPE ST. LEO THE GREAT (395–461)

He changed everything—

"The Incarnation has changed all the possibilities of man's existence. The bodily Nativity therefore of the Son of God took nothing from and added nothing to His Majesty because His unchangeable substance could be neither diminished nor increased. For that, the Word became flesh does not signify that the nature of God was changed into flesh, but that the Word took the flesh into the unity of His Person: and therein undoubtedly the whole man was received, with which within the Virgin's womb fecundated by the Holy Spirit, whose virginity was destined never to be lost, the Son of God was so inseparably united that He who was born without time of the Father's essence was Himself in time born of the Virgin's womb. For we could not otherwise be released from the chains of eternal death but by Him becoming humble in our nature, Who remained Almighty in His own. And so our Lord Jesus Christ, being at birth true man though *He never ceased to be true God, made in Himself the beginning of a new creation, and in the form of His birth started the spiritual life of mankind afresh*, that to abolish the taint of our birth according to the flesh there might be a possibility of regeneration without our sinful seed for those of whom it is said, 'Who were born not of blood, nor of the will of the flesh, nor of the will of man, but of God'

[John 1:13]. What mind can grasp this mystery, what tongue can express this gracious act? Sinfulness returns to guiltlessness and the old nature becomes new; strangers receive adoption and outsiders enter upon an inheritance. The ungodly begin to be righteous, the miserly benevolent, the incontinent chaste, the earthly heavenly. And whence comes this change, save by the right hand of the Most High? For the Son of God came to destroy the works of the devil [1 John 3:8], and has so united Himself with us and us with Him that the descent of God to man's estate became the exaltation of man to God's."[361] (Emphasis added.)

Homily on the Feast of the Nativity, VII, c. 450

The papacy of St. Leo the Great was called by Benedict XVI, "undoubtedly one of the most important in the Church's history." Also, a Roman aristocrat, Pope Leo met with Attila the Hun in 452 and convinced him to retreat from his destructive swath through Italy. His letter on Christology, the *Tome of Leo*, had a direct influence on the Church's definition of the hypostatic union of the two natures in the person of Jesus Christ.

---

361 St. Leo the Great, *The Complete Works of the Church Fathers* (Toronto, 2016), loc. 481028-481042, Kindle Edition.

DAY 358

YVES CONGAR, OP (1904–1994)

Disembodied heresies—

"Heresy comes, in large part, from a purely intellectual grasp of a single aspect [of doctrine]: a grasp which easily becomes an impatient one, freeing itself from the delays of life and from lengthy schooling of living perception. The mind easily grasps a one-dimensional truth, but an idea, in the process of life is being held and sustained by the life of a man or woman, in finding itself in contact with the questions and conditions of life develops with time other aspects, which a dialectical spirit could not have grasped on its own. Accordingly, there is an immense difference between a truth perceived solely by the mind, dialectically, and a truth matured in solitude or in faithful service, a truth that one has long carried within oneself and nourished with one's life. A too-rapid formulation—the fruit of a purely dialectical intelligence—yields a dried-out product of little inner substance."[362]

Power and Poverty in the Church, 1963

Yves Congar, OP, identifies the tendency of heretics to over-simplify a Church doctrine. For example, if you rely too

---

362 Yves Congar, *Yves Congar: Essential Writings*, selected and introduction by Paul Lakeland, (Maryknoll: Orbis Books, 2010), 73.

heavily on only one nature in the divine and human person of Jesus Christ, you create an aberration in doctrine. The Pelagians so highly regarded Jesus Christ as a moral example of his human nature that they taught that merely following his example was sufficient for salvation. Docetists, on the other hand, do just the opposite—deny the human nature of Christ, arguing his body was only apparent, not real. Congar argues that in both cases, human intelligence is at work without a lived connection to a life lived as a servant of God. Considering Christ as just another moral exemplar equates him with any other guru who develops a following by his good works and charisma. A merely apparent or "seeming" Jesus Christ, on the other hand, means he did not share our human condition and that his suffering, too, was only apparent.

DAY 359

ST. AUGUSTINE (354–430)

And it made all the difference—

"Thus you obtained for me . . . certain books by Platonists translated from Greek into Latin, and there I read—not in exact words, but it was the same thesis entirely, put forward with many arguments of many kinds. [Here Augustine quotes John 1:1–4.] And I read that the soul of a human being, though

it gives testimony to the light, is nevertheless not itself with the light; instead, the Word was God, 'the true light which lights every person who comes into the world.' And I read that 'he was in this world, and the world was made through him, but the world did not know him' [John 1:7–10]. But that 'he came into what was his own, yet his own people did not accept him; but to however many accepted him and believed in his name, he gave the power to become sons of God' [John 1:12]—this part I didn't read in the books given me. Likewise, I read there that the Word, God, was born not from the body, not from blood, not by the will of a man or the body's will, but from God; yet that the Word became a body and lived among us [John 1:13–14]—this part I didn't read in the books given to me."[363]

Confessions, 397

St. Augustine thanks God for having read, as a young man, in some Platonic philosophers' ideas about the "Word" and "God" that prepared him to read the prologue to the Gospel of John. But the "Word" [*Logos*] he read in the philosophers could not compare to the *Logos* of the Gospels because the philosophers "Word" never became flesh. St. Augustine is not the first example of how philosophical reading of the classics can lead a person to the threshold of Christianity, but he is, by

---

363 St. Augustine, *Confessions: A New Translation by Sarah Ruden*, 7.13–14, trans. Sarah Ruden (New York: The Modern Library, 2017), 184–85.

far, the most famous. The use of the term *logos* in the Gospel of John, the latest of the Gospels to be written, made that Gospel a bridge between the world of Greek philosophy and the beginning and growth of the Church. These lines from the *Confessions* have been the starting point for countless conversions ever since.

DAY 360

ST. CATHERINE OF SIENA (1347–1380)

What you cannot give ME—

"How an imperfect lover of GOD loves his neighbor also imperfectly, and of the signs of this imperfect love. 'And I would have you know that just as every imperfection and perfection is acquired from Me, so is it manifested by means of the neighbor. And simple souls, who often love creatures with spiritual love, know this well, for, if they have received My love sincerely without any self-regarding considerations, they satisfy the thirst of their love for their neighbor equally sincerely. If a man carry away the vessel which he has filled at the fountain and then drink of it, the vessel becomes empty, *but if he keeps his vessel standing in the fountain, while he drinks, it always remains full.* So the love of the neighbor, whether spiritual or temporal, should be drunk in Me, without any self-regarding

considerations. I require that you should love Me with the same love with which I love you. This indeed you cannot do, because I loved you without being loved. All the love which you have for Me you owe to Me, so that it is not of grace that you love Me, but because you ought to do so. While I love you of grace, and not because I owe you, My love. Therefore to Me, in person, you cannot repay the love which I require of you, and I have placed you in the midst of your fellows, that you may do to them that which you cannot do to Me, that is to say, that you may love your neighbor of free grace, without expecting any return from him, and what you do to him, I count as done to Me.'"[364] (Emphasis added.)

The Dialogue of St. Catherine of Siena, 1370

St. Catherine of Siena entered the Dominican Third Order at eighteen. Once she developed a popular following, Catherine was investigated by her order, who found her innocent of any wrongdoing. As her influence and following grew, Catherine became influential in papal affairs, playing an instrumental role in bringing the pope back to Rome from Avignon, and later, during the Great Schism of 1378, when Christendom began to take sides, Catherine spent all her energies in Rome defending Pope Urban VI and the cause of Church unity. She died in

---

364 St. Catherine of Siena, *The Dialogue of St. Catherine of Siena* (1907 translation), loc. 78–79 of 168, Kindle Edition.

1380, having offered herself as a victim for the Church's tra-
vails, and was canonized in 1461.

DAY 361

DANTE ALIGHIERI (1265–1321)

"Thus from my Lady; then she said, 'Take what
    I'll tell you now, if you'd be satisfied,
    and hone your understanding over it.
These corporeal rings are narrow or wide
    as there is less or greater power diffuse
    through all their parts. Their influence for Good
Is greater, as the power is bounteous;
    greater the good, greater the body's size,
    if all its parts are equally complete.
And so this heaven that seizes, as it flies,
    all of the other heavens, corresponds
    to the ring that loves most fully and most knows;
So if you gird your measure to the bounds
    of actual power, and not the mere appearance
    of substances that look like rings of flame,

You'll see the just and wondrous consequence:
more power, more speed and size; less power, less;
fitting for every sphere's intelligence.'"[365]

Paradiso, Canto 28, 61--8

In Dante's *Paradiso*, the poet is near the end of his journey towards the vision of God. He's told by "my Lady," Beatrice, that the multitude of various rings he sees forming correspond to the measure of love that certain groups have for their Creator. Given this recognition of merit, the role of Divine Justice has not been surpassed; it has a hand, as it were, in the organization of Paradise itself: "more power, more speed and size; less power, less." At a moment when Dante might be swept away by the approach of Love Itself, he remains aware that the measure of Love is also what created both the levels of hell and purgatory.

---

365 Dante, *Purgatorio*, trans., ed., and introduction by Anthony Esolen (New York: The Modern Library, 2007), 301.

DAY 362

WILLIAM SHAKESPEARE (1564–1616)

On the Rialto in Venice, Lorenzo romances Jessica—

"How sweet the moonlight sleeps upon this bank!
Here will we sit and let the sounds of music
Creep in our ears: soft stillness and the night
Become the touches of sweet harmony.
Sit, Jessica. Look how the floor of heaven
Is thick inlaid with patines of bright gold:
There's not the smallest orb which thou behold'st
But in his motion like an angel sings,
Still quiring to the young-eyed cherubins;
Such harmony is in immortal souls;
But whilst this muddy vesture of decay
Doth grossly close it in, we cannot hear it."[366]

The Merchant of Venice, Act 5.1.61–72

William Shakespeare lived in a period of Western history when religious skepticism was being generated by the arguments of the early modern philosophers and the findings of Renaissance scientists. Yet, here the classical and medieval "harmony of the spheres" has not been put aside. This cosmic harmony is both melodious and representative of the way to heaven. There's a

366 http://www.shakespeare-online.com/plays/merchant_4_1.html.

bit of the lover's special pleading in this speech, but this is offset by his confession that "we cannot hear" the heavenly harmony while living in bodies of flesh. But, one can say, the poetic language of Shakespeare seems to be grounded in that unheard harmony of the spheres.

DAY 363

ÉTIENNE GILSON (1884–1978)

The gift of the Church to the Church—

"Let us realize, however, that this temporal embodiment of the Church is the one that she herself has given to herself as Church, and that it is therefore wholly spiritualized. This hierarchy that proceeds from the Pope down to the humblest believers; these churches, missions, and parishes, with all their Christian members; these convents without number with their religious men and women; finally, all those institutions, whether of corporal mercy or instruction, that form as it were the flowing and growth of the Christian life of grace in the temporal order—all these manifestations are nothing other than the soul of the Church herself in her sensible incarnation and thereby rendered visible before all eyes. Created by the Church and her ends, the temporal body of the Church is consequently an integral part of the Church herself; and this is precisely why

it is not exactly the temporal body of Christendom. As subject to the State, we Christians are all members of a society of
which the State is seeking the common spiritual end, and the
very temporal part of the Church is integrally directed to this
end; as members of Christendom, we are part of a third social
group, one that is neither the state nor quite the Church, but
one that is formed by the various members of various states in
so far as they are aware of belonging to the same Church and
of being all disciples of Christ."[367]

"Where Is Christendom?" 1956

Étienne Gilson acknowledges the distinction between the
temporal and supernatural Church but points out that the former is not completely separate from the latter. The historical
Church with all its fallibilities is "an integral part of the Church
herself." There are two more overlapping communal ends that
make up the historical Church: the state's obligation to seek
the common good of its citizens and the community created
by the variety of vocations—lay or religious—embraced by
the Church's members.

---

367 Étienne Gilson, *A Gilson Reader: Selected Writings of Étienne Gilson*, ed. and
introduction by Anton C. Pegis (Garden City: Image Books, 1957), 346.

DAY 364

ST. JOHN OF THE CROSS (1542–1591)

Taking a new road—

"The reason, again, why the soul not only travels securely, when it travels thus in the darkness, but also achieves even greater gain and progress, is that usually, when the soul is receiving fresh advantage and profit, this comes by a way that it least understands—indeed, it quite commonly believes that it is losing ground. For, as it has never experienced that new feeling which drives it forth and dazzles it and makes it depart recklessly from its former way of life, it thinks itself to be losing ground rather than gaining and progressing, since it sees that it is losing with respect to that which it knew and enjoyed, and is going by a way which it knows not and wherein it finds no enjoyment. It is like the traveller, who, in order to go to new and unknown lands, takes new roads, unknown and untried, and journeys unguided by his past experience, but doubtingly and according to what others say. It is clear that such a man could not reach new countries, or add to his past experience, if he went not along new and unknown roads and abandoned those which were known to him. Exactly so, one who is learning fresh details concerning any office or art always proceeds in darkness, and receives no guidance from his original knowledge, for if he left not that behind he would get no farther nor make any progress; and in the same way, when the soul is

making the most progress, it is traveling in darkness, knowing naught. Wherefore, since God, as we have said, is the Master and Guide of this blind soul, it may well and truly rejoice, once it has learned to understand this, and say: 'In darkness and secure.'"[368]

Dark Night of the Soul (1578–1585)

At age twenty-five, St. John of the Cross was ordained a Carmelite priest in 1567. St. Teresa of Ávila asked his help in reforming the Carmelites, and in a year, St. John created the first Discalced Carmelite monastery. He was put in prison twice due to conflicts within the monastery. He escaped and became the provincial vicar of Andalusia. More trouble at his own monastery caused him to live the rest of his life in solitude. He died in the Franciscan monastery at Úbeda at the age of forty-nine. His writings, collected under the title *Dark Night of the Soul*, portray the soul's progress toward a mystical union with God.

---

368 St. John of the Cross, *Dark Night of the Soul*, trans. E. Allison Peters, ed. P. Silverio de Santa Teresa, C.D. (Minecla: Dover Publications, Inc., 2003), loc. 147-149, Kindle Edition.

DAY 365

ANTHONY ESOLEN (1959–)

The fire of love—

"The Evangelists tell us that the earth shook on the day when Christ died upon the cross. But that was the great after-tremor of Jesus' first act of love, when in the silence of Mary's house he became flesh and dwelt among us, and then, on the night of the Nativity, first showed to Mary and Joseph, then to the humble animals, and only then to mere shepherds, his sacred face. The earth shook with the fire of love, and from that day unto this, wherever men and women still remember the name of Jesus and how he was born in a lowly stable, they will feel that tremor, and know, somehow, even if they have forgotten the words, that the meek shall inherit the earth, that the first shall be last and the last shall be first, and that all the pomp and glamour of the world will pass away, all its capitols and senates and universities and towering dynamos of business leave not one scorched stone upon a stone, but the Child born in the manger will remain, and he alone can tell us the secret of who we are and where we must go."[369]

How the Church Has Changed the World, 2019

---

369 Anthony Esolen, *How the Church Has Changed the World,* Volume 1 (Yonkers: Magnificat, 2019), loc. 112 of 1935, Kindle Edition.

Anthony Esolen eloquently describes the fundamental fact of the Catholic faith: the Incarnation, an act of God given to a humble family far from the centers of power and commerce. The coming of Jesus Christ did not fit into the expectation at the time of a savior arriving in power and glory. The Son of God came into the world in a manger, and as Esolen puts it, "he alone can tell us the secret of who we are and where we must go." Amen.

ABOUT THE AUTHOR

Deal W. Hudson taught philosophy for fifteen years at three major universities; published, edited, and managed print and digital magazines for over twenty years; founded, led, and managed a Catholic advocacy organization for seven years; created the strategy to lead Catholic outreach in four national elections (three winning); and created and managed three Catholic websites.

In February 2014, Dr. Hudson launched a radio show, *Church and Culture*, on the Ave Maria Radio Network which airs twice a week, Saturday and Sunday, in all the major media markets in the country. And in January 2015, Dr. Hudson launched "The Christian Review" (www.thechristianreview.com). He most recently published *How to Keep from Losing Your Mind: Educating Yourself Classically to Resist Cultural Indoctrination* with TAN Books.